BENJAMIN SCHLESINGER teaches in the Faculty of Social Work at the University of Toronto. He is the author of *Family Planning in Canada: a source book.*

This collection of papers, written by some thirty doctors, psychiatrists, educators, lawyers, social workers, sociologists, and natural scientists, is the first Canadian book devoted to the study of sexual behaviour. It provides an important resource for teachers and students in medicine, nursing, social work, family life studies, sociology, psychology, and psychiatry. It will also be useful to those who conduct in-service courses for the helping professions, and to any teachers or schools planning to introduce the topic. An extensive section on resources includes a glossary, a ┗   brary on sexuality, a list of Canadian references, a bibliography, an i   ¬nd a list of organizations in Canada and the United States acti

EDITED BY
BENJAMIN SCHLESINGER

Sexual Behaviour in Canada: Patterns and Problems

UNIVERSITY OF TORONTO PRESS
Toronto and Buffalo

© University of Toronto Press 1977
Toronto and Buffalo
Printed in Canada

Canadian Cataloguing in Publication Data

Main entry under title:
Sexual behaviour in Canada

Bibliography: p.
ISBN 0-8020-2262-6 bd. ISBN 0-8020-6314-4 pa.

1. Sex customs – Canada – Addresses, essays,
lectures. 2. Sex – Addresses, essays, lectures.
I. Schlesinger, Benjamin, 1928–

HQ18.C2S49   301.41'7971   C77-001183-7

This book has been published during the
Sesquicentennial year of the University of Toronto

Preface

For this first Canadian collection of articles on human sexuality I have selected papers written by doctors, psychiatrists, educators, lawyers, social workers, sociologists, and natural scientists. This selection contains a variety of views about sex, not all of which, of course, are mine. Nine of the twenty-seven papers selected have never been previously published. It is interesting to note that of thirty-one authors sixteen are female and fifteen male; for as a rule, readings on human sexuality tend to be written by men.

The articles have been arranged in five sections and are followed by a resource section.

Part I AN OVERVIEW examines attitudes, sexual identity, and current sex research in Canada.

Part II SEXUALITY AND THE LIFE CYCLE discusses the baby bust in Canada, female teenagers, and contraceptives; family life and sexuality; sexuality and the aged; and family planning and the poor. This section also includes papers on sexual counselling. Sexuality for the physically handicapped and the mentally retarded is reviewed.

Part III SEXUAL BEHAVIOUR AMONG SELECTED GROUPS highlights female and male homosexuality, transsexualism, and drugs and sexuality.

Part IV SEXUALITY AND THE LAW reports on such important issues as incest, rape, child molesting, prostitution and obscenity.

Part V EDUCATION FOR SEXUALITY looks at sex education in the primary and secondary schools and at the university level. Examples of programs are described. A paper on the future of human sexuality is also included in this section.

Part VI RESOURCES contains a glossary, a basic library on sexuality, Canadian references dealing with human sexuality (1966-76), bibliographic sources, films, and organizations in Canada and the United States which are active in this area.

This book is intended as a companion volume to *Family Planning in Canada: A Source Book* (University of Toronto Press, 1974) which I edited. It is hoped that this collection of articles will serve as a resource for teachers and students in medicine, nursing, social work, family life studies, sociology, psychology, and psychiatry, who offer or take courses dealing with human sexuality. It will also be useful to those who conduct in-service courses for the helping professions, and to teachers in the varied educational settings of Canada's professions who plan to introduce this topic in their curricula.

I realize that I have not included all the topics relevant to human sexuality in Canada, but I had to put a limit to the number of articles and topics in this first publication. The reader can continue his or her own exploration of varied issues by using the resource section in this volume.

I am grateful to Health and Welfare Canada, Family Planning Division, for their Family Planning Grant #4490-5-9, which enabled me to produce this book. Special thanks go to Mr. C.N. Knight, the Grants Officer, Cenovia Addy, Social Work Consultant, and Ms. Suzanne Brazeau, Director of the Family Planning Division for their encouragement of this project and for their valuable suggestions.

In polishing the content and style of presentation, I had the help of Sadie Gerridzen and Diana Swift as editors, and R.I.K. Davidson of the University of Toronto Press as general editor. The typing, at various stages of preparation was done by Dorothy Jenkins and Esther Bogo. The final copy was prepared by Helen Romanick. I am also grateful to the authors and publishers for allowing me to reproduce their material in this volume; the original source is credited at the foot of the opening page of each article.

I received continued support and encouragement from Dean Albert Rose of the Faculty of Social Work, University of Toronto, who allowed me to proceed with this effort. Last, but not least, I want to thank my wife Rachel and children Ari, Leo, Esther, and Michael for discussing with me my ideas as I developed the outline and content of this project.

B.S.
Toronto, 1977

Contents

BENJAMIN SCHLESINGER

Introduction

What is human sexuality? A constantly evolving and changing constellation of gender identities, attitudes, patterns of behaviour, emotions, perceptions, and beliefs – the list is almost endless. For individual Canadians the unique experience of human sexuality in its physical and psychological aspects is influenced by present and past environment, and by real and vicarious life experiences. To every reader of this book human sexuality will have a very personal meaning.

The so-called 'Sexuality Revolution' of the past twenty years has had a tremendous impact upon individuals and families in Canadian society. Sexuality plays an important part in the life cycle of every Canadian from birth to old age, and everyone has some claim on having a good and healthy sex life, including people who have physical and mental disabilities. It is up to each person to determine and to assume responsibility for her or his own sexuality.

In order to experience a healthy and fulfilling sex life, we need to learn about and appreciate our own bodies, know our feelings and our own sexual responses, become sensitive to the physical and emotional needs of others, and develop meaningful intimacy in our sexual relationships. The morals of sex are changing in the light of increased knowledge and the new waves of liberation in our society. There is no point or virtue in holding to past views based on ignorance and repression; but equally there is no reason to forget that good and healthy sex depends on good and healthy personal relationships and mutual – at least – understanding.

In 1970 I decided to introduce the first course on human sexuality at a Canadian school of social work, and was pleased to find that by 1976 quite a few universities had included this topic in their varied professional schools (medicine, nursing, social work, etc.). My contacts enabled me to gather material relevant to our Canadian scene, and from this sprang the idea for this volume.

I was not surprised to find very little research and only a handful of published articles dealing with human sexuality in Canada. We had relied almost completely on the American output of books, booklets, and research (see Resource section). It seems that sex research and sex discussion have been introduced more openly into our lives only during the past five years. The media have helped by reporting various sexual issues which arise from day to day. I also believe that Women's International Year has given impetus to discussion and review of areas of sexuality of special concern to Canadian women. But Canada is still conservative in the open discussion of many of the critical issues dealing with sexuality. This may not be a negative aspect but rather a cautious positive aspect of our country.

Underlying the topic of human sexuality is the debate about the teaching of this subject. There is a popular misconception that sex education is concerned exclusively with the human reproductive system and its functions. But though human beings are sexual creatures, male and female, this fact encompasses vastly more than genitalia. Sex education at its best focuses on human relationships and is concerned with *all* the ways men and women relate to each other.

A narrow erotic view of sex permeates much of our literature and is particularly exploited by the mass media: a view which is limiting, distorting, and unhealthy. Many people tend to think only of the physical aspects of sex, erotic behaviour and intercourse, and fail to comprehend the psycho-social character of sexuality. It is this narrow, inadequate frame of reference which education about family life and human sexuality seeks to change.

Sex can be defined so broadly as to encompass much of what we are, not just an act or the genital organs. Sex is what it means to be and live effectively as men or women and to enjoy being what we are. The human being as a sexual creature begins when sperm and ovum unite. At that moment the person's physical sex is determined genetically and certain genetic capacities are effected. Sex becomes a growing and developing process implying a total range of behaviour patterns, in which males and females interact as whole organisms and bring into play not only physical but social, emotional, spiritual, esthetic, intellectual, and economic factors.

As the human being moves through his life cycle, the ways he expresses his sex is called his sexuality. This term recognizes that sexual expression as a male or female is a deep pervasive aspect of the whole personality, including the sum total of a person's feelings and modes of behaviour not only as a sexual being, but totally as man or woman. Sexuality involves human relationships and interrelationships between and among the two sexes. It includes the development of self-respect and self-esteem and respect and responsibility toward others. It involves an examination of men's and women's roles in society; their relations with and reactions to each other; the responsibility of each toward the other in all relationships in life; and the responsible use of sexual powers as a creative force.

The human being's sexuality, largely psychological and sociological, is learned throughout life, as the result of exposures to emotional, physiological, social, and cultural forces. What sexuality becomes is the sum total of all the experiences encountered and transacted through unplanned learning, directed instruction, indoctrination, and guidance. Learning sexuality is much like learning one's native language. As Anna Freud said more than thirty years ago, 'The sexual instincts of man do not suddenly awaken between the 13th and 15th year, i.e. at puberty, but operate from one form to another, progress from one state to another, until at last adult sexual life is achieved as the final result from this long series of developments.'

The terms 'family life education' and 'sex education' have posed problems of definition for most people, as well as fostered the erroneous opinion that they are separate areas of instruction.

In fact, it is impossible to discuss family relationships and functions without including the sexuality and sexual behaviour patterns involved, and equally so to discuss sexuality outside the context of the family and its relationships.

Education in family living and human sexuality has areas of instructional emphasis. As such, it would include the study of the behaviour of people as family members and the biological and learned sexual needs of those family members, as they can be fulfilled within a stable family environment. A number of specialized areas are also included, among which are interpersonal relationships, human growth and development, preparation for marriage and parenthood, human physiology, sexuality as part of total personality, sexual behaviour patterns of men and women in developing self-understanding, value priorities, child-rearing, socialization of young people for adult roles, decision-making, management of human and material family resources, personal, family, and community health care, family-community interaction, and the effects of change on cultural patterns affecting family and individual roles. Effort is made to provide the student with an understanding of the choices he has in functioning as an individual and family member in a changing society which places new responsibilities on roles as husband or wife, parents, children, siblings, and grandparents. The knowledge for such instruction derives from social work, psychology, sociology, economics, biology, physiology, anthropology, medicine, and home economics. Ideally, education about family living and human sexuality focuses on human relationships and is concerned about all the ways men and women relate to each other.

TEACHING THE SUBJECT

Ideas or points of emphasis for teaching have been derived from the many and varied questions asked by thousands of children and youths in actual programs, as well as from the teaching experiences of educators working with young people. They suggest directions for those developing curricula and family life programmes at various educational levels.

Preschool

By age two children are aware of differences between male and female, and by age four have intellectual and emotional responses and feelings about being a male or female, such as being glad about being a boy or girl, or easily accepting differences. These are examples of developmental tasks which parents and other influencing adults must help the child work through.

Kindergarten–Grade 3

The possibilities here involve such topics as how the child has changed since babyhood; telling about the mother's or father's work; what the child does in the family and his contributions; family responsibilities and accepting responsibility; friends; self-worth, sharing; manners; responsibility toward others and their feelings; the wonder of new life; how all living things come from living things; how baby grows; the home; changing roles; mother's and father's roles; family stories; family fun; role-playing; pets; correct terminology; the child as an individual; one's feelings about different situations and looking at one's self; animal babies and their care at birth compared to human babies as members of the family unit; different growth rates and individual differences; telling about one's self; body care and body growth; how mother and father help the family; different kinds of families; shelter; creation of life as a great miracle; feeling of belonging; family rights such as privacy and respect for family members; safety in going to and from school; how people grow in many ways; how everyone has a mother and father in the beginning; showing love to each other.

Grades 4–6

Heavy emphasis on anatomy and physiology; how the body works; growth patterns; physical changes and individual differences; inherited characteristics; basic genetics; values in family living; family responsibilities; coming changes of puberty; facts about reproduction, including menstruation; the story of birth; functions of various glands relating to growth and development; function of reproductive organs; masturbation and nocturnal emission; family activities; effects of hormones on growth and development in boys and girls; assuming greater personal responsibilities for self; creation of a new life as one of most beautiful acts of nature; responsibilities of parenthood; how life begins; individual differences in growth; useful habits and those that interfere with well-being; specialized functions of different kinds of cells; effects of emotions on behaviour; self-control as a task of maturity; maleness and femaleness; masculinity and femininity as patterns of behaviour and part of one's self.

Grades 7-9
Family roles; personal relationships inside and outside the family; who and what we are as individuals; meanings of love, affection, infatuation, and attraction; basic sex drive as one of many human needs; meaning and characteristics of adolescence; feelings and attitudes; genetic effects in families; dating behaviour and responsibilities; standards of human behaviour as responsibilities; choosing a husband or wife; responsibilities in sexual behaviour and problems arising therefrom; family as basic unit in society; understanding one's self; family changes, pregnancy and problems of pregnancy; masturbation and nocturnal emission; various value systems; emotional maturity; self-control; factors of personality; understanding the sex drive in males and females; creative use of sexuality and personal responsibilities connected with it.

Grades 10-12
Emotional and physical development of sexuality; masculinity and femininity; feelings and behaviour arising from masculinity and femininity; creative and positive use of sexuality and sexual behaviour; kinds of love; engagement and its responsibilities; readiness for marriage; family and interpersonal communications; sex as a life force; sexual standards and responsibilities; social and sexual attitudes; sex roles in society; the role of family; families in different cultures; family finances; buying; child care; health care in the family; genetics; problems of family disorganization; social problems such as abortion, divorce, early marriage, premarital sex, exploitation of others; unwed mothers and fathers, homosexuality, contraception; humane behaviour, human relationships; development of values in a pluralistic society; values and value systems; examination of values, standards, and modes of behaviour.

A number of studies have pointed out that married couples place education in family life and sex high on the list of the ten areas that most need understanding for good marriage relationships. Studies have also shown that children who were openly and frankly presented with the facts of sex by their parents were more adequate in marriage; when this information is supplemented by school, church, and other agency efforts, young people are better able to maintain socially acceptable standards of behaviour. David Mace, Dean of the American Marriage Counselors, feels that the real need of young people is to come to terms with emotional attitudes toward sex.

Strengthening families to meet the influential challenges of fast-moving, ever-changing social, scientific, and technical advances is of utmost concern at all levels of government. An age of automation, space exploration, cybernetics, mobility, speed, and complex human interactions is producing profound effects upon family structure and function. Certainly, building strength in individuals and families is an underlying goal of much of education and the social services.

Historically, mankind has found that the family is the best and basic unit in which to provide growth, support, and security. But throughout time, from culture to culture, the role and responsibilities of the family have changed. Today's family as a voluntary institution is vulnerable as never before to complex and varied pressures of social conditions, social groups, and sources of information. In turn, the family influences the social institutions of education, politics, economics, and religion. A complex and ever-changing environment results in new opportunities for enriched human experiences, communication, and relationships. But problems for children, youth, and adults, in living with themselves, each other, and society also appear, and create both additional responsibilities and expectations.

Although the study of family life and human sexuality is not new, it has recently grown in importance in the public mind. Through the mass media and other sources, irresponsible, sensationalized impressions about sex now impinge upon the lives of all young people. In addition, the misinformation they receive from their peers and other ill-informed segments of society leads us to believe that the problem is not a matter of whether there will be education about the family and human sexuality, but rather whether responsible and caring Canadians will be interested and involved in the quality of education taking place.

I hope that this volume will aid in discussing human sexuality in Canada, and will enable many Canadians to share their viewpoints in this important area of life.

PART ONE

AN OVERVIEW

F. MICHAEL BARRETT

Attitudes and sexuality*

When Alex Comfort tells us in *The Joy of Sex* that 'the sense of play ... is essential to a full, enterprising and healthily immature view of sex between committed people,' he is at one and the same time inviting us to indulge our 'playfulness' and conveying an attitude towards one aspect of our sexuality. The following quote, with similar conviction but somewhat less invitation, presents another attitude: 'Today's society is filled with all manner of sexual sin. Fornication (unmarried sex) probably heads the list. But it is followed closely by adultery (extramarital sex), homosexuality (male-with-male sex), lesbianism (female-with-female sex), and even so vile a sin as beastiality (mankind-with-beast sex). Pornography floods the newsstands and mens' minds are focussed on sexual fantasies. Society has clearly lost its way in a sexual wilderness. Permissiveness dominates much of modern society.'[1]

Our reactions to these quotations are tempered by our own attitudes toward sexuality and by our assumptions and beliefs about the role of sex in human life. The diversity of such attitudes in Canadian society, their origins, and the various sexual 'philosophies' they foster, are the subject of this paper. Anyone presuming to write about sexual attitudes would do well at the outset to admit the bias that his own attitudes will inevitably introduce. This admission, while implying an attempt at objectivity, produces no special capacity to recognize when the attempt has failed. Only the conviction that, by definition, it must! If attitude is defined as 'manner, disposition, feeling or position with regard to a person or thing; tendency or orientation especially of the mind,' the scope of the definition

*Reprinted from *The School Guidance Worker* 29 (May-June 1974), 45-50.

reminds us of the pervasive influence of attitudes on all aspects of human life. Attitudes toward sexuality are but one part of this influence, although it seems likely that the peculiar 'erotophobia' that has characterized much of North America's recent past has left many of us particularly sensitive to the effect of such attitudes. We recognize today in Canada, as in ourselves, a host of conflicting attitudes. They influence the formal sex education we give, the important but largely unconscious messages we convey to our children about their bodies and themselves, the legal sanctions we place on certain sexual activities, the social customs inculcated as if they were law, and ultimately even our individual enjoyment of sexuality. As Allen Fromme observes, 'Our sexual behaviour is essentially the result of our attitudes towards sex; and these attitudes, in turn, are a product of how we have been brought up.'[2]

Since North Americans have traditionally viewed sexuality as a threat to social stability and therefore something to be controlled, it is not surprising that many of us were reared in a cultural setting that fostered sex-negative attitudes. Social historians trace the origins of such attitudes to a variety of sources including: the loss of the Naturalistic Hebrew philosophy which allowed men (although not women) an unrepressed sex life; the development of dualistic philosophies that viewed mind and body as separate; the impact of the early Christians who used denial of bodily pleasure as a sign of spiritual commitment; the nearly universal subjugation of women in Western society; the development of body taboos against nudity; the 'Puritan' work ethic; and a variety of other factors.[3] However, one needs only to look to the recent past in Canada to see the instilling of sexual fears encouraged as enlightened social doctrine. Historian Michael Bliss[4] points out that less than fifty years ago Canadians were reading the 'Self and Sex Series,' eight books that purported to give all ages the best available information on sexuality. For instance, young boys were told that: 'If persisted in, masturbation will not only undermine, but completely overthrow the health. If the body is naturally strong, the mind may give way first, and in extreme cases imbecility and insanity may, and often do, come as the inevitable result.'

Mothers were encouraged to watch their children closely and to teach them that handling their genitals 'will hurt them and make them sick ... and many times idiotic and insane, or develop epileptic fits.' Husbands were warned to avoid the dire physical and mental losses associated with sexual 'excess' but were given the reassurance that God had made their wives 'generally indifferent; often absolutely averse' to protect them from such consequences. Older men were advised that ejaculation would entail 'use of a secretion which can now ill be spared.' This belief in the physically and mentally debilitating effect of any form of sexual activity, prompted by assumptions about a 'vital force' in seminal fluid, gave rise to what Michael Bliss calls the 'doctrine of creative sexual repression.'

This doctrine is eloquently summarized in the lectures of Arthur W. Beall, who from 1905 until the 1930s, gave 'advanced purity lectures' in Ontario schools. In a published account of his lectures he describes the function of seminal fluid: 'If the *life fluid* feeds the muscles, and brain, and nervous system – and if you want clean, strong, healthy muscles – and clean, strong, healthy brains, what must you do with those two beautiful, wonderful *life glands*? There can be but one answer: "Keep them clean and leave them alone."'[5]

Although the goals of genetic purity and maximized individual health were noble ones, it would be a unique individual, raised under the influence of such attitudes, who managed to avoid feelings of guilt, shame, or anxiety about his or her sexual desires and interests. Needless to say, such feelings have persisted long after the belief in a 'vitalist physiology.' To what extent have social changes and scientific discoveries in the ensuing years had a modifying influence on attitudes? Admitting that our pluralistic society houses a wide spectrum of belief about sexual propriety, I nevertheless find the temptation irresistible to make some general comments about current attitudes and trends.

PREMARITAL INTERCOURSE

Attitudes towards premarital intercourse are seen as sufficiently potent indicators of general sexual philosophy that they provide us with oft-quoted definitions of the four predominant North American sexual standards,[6] namely:

1 Abstinence – premarital intercourse is wrong for both men and women regardless of circumstances.

2 Permissiveness with affection – premarital intercourse is right for both men and women under certain conditions when a stable relationship with engagement, love, or strong affection is present.

3 Permissiveness without affection – premarital intercourse is right for both men and women regardless of the amount of affection or stability present, providing there is physical attraction.

4 Double standard – premarital intercourse is acceptable for men but it is wrong and unacceptable for women.

While the sexual 'double standard' is far from dead, its inherent unfairness to women and an increased sense of egalitarianism among the young appear to be signalling its ultimate demise. Recent US studies (a disappointingly small amount of Canadian data is available) indicate that a somewhat higher percentage of today's women have had intercourse before marriage than was the case at the time of Kinsey's landmark investigation. Interestingly, from the 1920s through the 60s nearly 50 per cent of all women married in each decade had experienced intercourse prior to marriage (this figure was above 80 per cent for males). Thus, even when 'abstinence' was widely and publicly espoused as the only socially acceptable standard of behaviour, it was contravened regularly, although probably not without the occasional overlay of fear or guilt. Today proponents of this standard represent a diminishing, but still noticeably vocal segment of society.

While the young today are generally more permissive about the behaviour of others than they are about their own, it seems likely that premarital 'abstinence' will be rare in practice and even less frequently held as an acceptable sexual philosophy. This does not, however, support the widespread attitude that the alternative is 'promiscuity.'

Recent trends suggest an expanding acceptance of 'permissiveness with affection' in which approval of premarital sexual involvement increases as the presumed level of emotional commitment between the partners goes up. Perhaps, as a result, most sex education literature for adolescents invests considerable energy in defining and analysing appropriate conditions for premarital intercourse. One commonly used ethical approach developed by Lester Kirkendall states that: 'premarital sex is all right if it increases the capacity to trust, brings greater integrity to personal relationships, dissolves barriers separating people, enhances self-respect, engenders attitudes of faith and confidence in other people, fulfils individual potentials, and fosters a zest for living.'[7] Attitudes concerning the likelihood that premarital relationships will meet these high standards include: (1) Never ('young people are not sufficiently mature or responsible to deal with such intense experiences, and, besides, sex is for marriage, and people who are not ready for the responsibility of marriage should not be permitted the right to sexual intercourse'). (2) Seldom ('in general younger adolescents will be less able to cope with the intense feelings and demands of sexual involvement and should therefore be encouraged to refrain since the potential for mutual harm is so great'). (3) Often ('young people are becoming more egalitarian in their premarital relationships and are increasingly aware of mutual needs and will be most likely to develop caring attitudes toward each other in a society that does not have rigid "rules" about premarital sex').

My own opinion is that idealized demands around the conditions that make premarital intercourse acceptable are more frequently used by parents and teachers to encourage conformity to a traditional standard than as an aid in the development of ethical relationships and responsible decision-making. While resistance to change is not an uncommon human characteristic, at least two other attitudes (not arising directly from religious convictions) appear to encourage a traditional stance. The first of these is a feeling of responsibility for the behaviour of others (particularly dependants) and a concern about their well-being. This attitude attempts to protect the young from exploitation or sadness, both of which are seen as likely consequences of premature sexual intercourse. For instance, Ira Reiss[8] reports that acceptance of premarital intercourse decreases within the same age group (45-year-olds) from the single person, to the married, to the married with young children, and finally to the married person with adolescent children.

The second attitude fostering misgivings about the acceptability of premarital intercourse is the adult perception that adolescent sexuality is predominantly a pursuit of physical pleasure devoid of concern for relationship. Perhaps this explains the almost universal absence of pleasure-valuing descriptions or pleasure-enhancing suggestions in sex education literature for younger people, while adult literature, by contrast, contains an abundance of such detail. Perhaps adults need reminding? Adolescents recognize this attitude towards their sexuality but see their own values somewhat differently. In a recent major study of thirteen- to nineteen-year-olds in the US, Sorensen[9] wrote: 'A majority of adolescents oppose having sex for physical pleasure alone. At the same time many feel that adults assume physical pleasure is the main or only reason adolescents engage in sexual intercourse before marriage.'

PETTING, PLEASURE, AND SEX ROLES

To me, one of Sorensen's most intriguing observations concerns adolescents who have begun sexual activities (petting, mutual masturbation, experimentation, etc.) but have not yet had intercourse for the first time. He argues that they are likely to move rapidly, and he believes, prematurely, into the next phase of actually having intercourse. If, as he states, 'momentum, thrust, and male orgasm seem to be the dominant elements' of early adolescent intercourse, then the couple may have had insufficient time to reap the benefits of a longer period of beginning activities (i.e., enhanced communication about sexual matters; awareness of personal potential to give and be given pleasure; discussion of contraception and venereal disease; de-emphasis of sexual performance according to arbitrarily defined sexual roles). A number of attitudes toward sexuality might contribute to this rapid arrival at first intercourse.

1 Our society has encouraged the attitude that sexual intercourse is the only valid expression of sexual love. Petting is an 'adolescent' precursor of 'adult' behaviour, and 'technical virgins' are denigrated. Many marriage manuals introduce foreplay as a prelude to intercourse with emphasis on the 'fore' rather than the 'play.'

2 The emphasis on stereotyped male and female roles in sexual activity encourages 'role-appropriate behaviour' even when it may inhibit recognition of common needs and desires.

3 Masturbation has received a 'bad press' for many years, and it is not surprising that the increasing acceptance of its naturalness and desirability has only begun to penetrate the psyche of a population numbed by earlier misinformation and taboo.

Sorensen argues that a valuing of 'beginning sexual activities,' rather than an over-emphasis on sexual intercourse, might encourage 'sexual love and mutuality rather than early sexual intercourse in accordance with arbitrarily defined sexual roles.' He does not decry the breaking of a traditional code (premarital abstinence), simply the failure to develop full sexual potential, which may occur if intercourse takes place prematurely. Given the durability of attitudes, it will not be surprising if some misread his argument to be: 'The young shouldn't be allowed to have sexual intercourse until they have practised enough to deserve it.' Goal-orientation and striving for achievement influence our sexual attitudes, as well.

CHANGES OF ATTITUDES

Attitude towards one aspect of sexual behaviour may influence opinions on other behaviour about which doctrinal beliefs are less intense. For example, strong disapproval of abortion might temper attitudes toward 'premarital' or 're-creational' aspects of sexuality, not primarily because of the acts themselves but because of the possibility of an unwanted pregnancy. As attitudes about a single activity are altered others may follow. It can be argued that the 'sexual revolution' of the 1960s was predominantly a revolution of attitudes evidenced most dramatically by an increased openness to public discussion of sexuality. Sex educators will agree that simply providing access to information and the opportunity for discussion about sexuality can encourage attitudinal change, usually as a result of reduced fear and anxiety about something previously misunderstood or simply never discussed. On the other hand, many argue that the flood of sexually oriented materials has introduced misinformation, increased preoccupation with genital performance, and generally made it more difficult for the uninitiated to distinguish between fact and fallacy, between liberty and licence.

In the face of this concern and given the likelihood of a continued wide disparity of sexual attitudes in society, we should perhaps heed the advice of the late Isadore Rubin[10] who argued that: 'We must seek our core values for sex education in the core values of a democratic society.' These have been described as:
1 Faith in the free play of critical intelligence and respect for truth as a definable moral value.
2 Respect for the basic worth, equality, and dignity of each individual.
3 The right of self-determination of each human being.
4 The recognition of the need for co-operative effort for common good.

In the past the widely held attitude that sexuality was a socially disruptive force led us to the belief that, in the interest of the common good, it should be controlled through wholesale restriction on individual freedom.

Perhaps the often confusing value-conflicts in today's society, particularly around sexual behaviour, represent the beginnings of a transition to the view that sexuality is a pro-social force to be valued and therefore also to be liberated from unreasonable constraints.

Throughout this transition, young people may find their sexual behaviour increasingly analysed by adults rethinking their own values. This places a considerable burden on individuals who are themselves undergoing the natural sorting out of values and attitudes that occurs during adolescence. Guidance counsellors face a formidable task in dealing with such students from disparate ethnic and religious backgrounds, many of whom will have accepted their parents' attitudes and values, but now find them in conflict with the behaviour of their peers or difficult to reconcile with their own sexual development. Counsellors recognizing their ability to influence sexual attitudes through honesty, openness, free discussion, and adequate information (or the reverse of these) will also recognize the ongoing nature of the challenge this ability presents.

NOTES

1 *Is Sex Sin?* A publication of Ambassador College Department of Theology, 1973. Available in Canada from PO Box 44, Station A, Vancouver, 1, BC.

2 Allen Fromme, *Sex and Marriage* (New York: Barnes & Noble, 1955).

3 Robert Whitehurst, 'American Sexophobia,' in *The New Sexual Revolution*, ed. Kirkendall and Whitehead (New York: David White Company, 1971).

4 Michael Bliss, *Pure Books on Avoided Subjects: Pre-Freudian Sexual Ideas in Canada.* The Canadian Historical Association, Historical Papers, 1970.

5 Arthur W. Beall, *The Living Temple: A Manual on Eugenics for Parents and Teachers* (Whitby, 1933).

6 Ira Reiss, 'The Four Sexual Standards,' in *Sex in America* (New York: Bantam Books Inc., 1964).

7 Lester Kirkendall, *Premarital Intercourse and Interpersonal Relationships* (New York: Julian Press, 1961).

8 Ira Reiss, 'Premarital Sex Codes: The Old and the New,' in *Sexuality: A Search for Perspective*, ed. Grummon and Barclay (New York: Van Nostrand Reinhold, 1971).

9 Robert C. Sorensen, *Adolescent Sexuality in Contemporary America* (New York: World Publishing, 1973).

10 Isadore Rubin, 'Transition in Sex Values: Implications for the Education of Adolescents,' *Journal of Marriage and the Family* 27 (1965):185.

CONNIE YOUNG

Sexual identity and sexual roles*

THE ORIGIN OF OUR PRESENT-DAY SEXUAL ROLES

The history of human beings on this earth is hundreds and thousands of years old. But long before the great civilizations of China and Egypt existed and long before human-like creatures resembled modern man, it was understood by these primitive people that little human creatures emerged alive from the half of the population who exhibited certain physical characteristics such as protruding breasts. The other half of the creatures who never produced little ones were understood to have other characteristics, like a penis. Also, the half of the population which produced the little ones, or 'babies' as they came to be called in our language, also produced milk from their breasts to nourish these babies until they could accommodate themselves to chewing foodstuff and to feeding themselves.

With these given circumstances it naturally evolved that the half of the population that produced babies were useless on hunting trips, especially during pregnancy, when they were liable to be tired and unable to climb or march strenuously, or could hold up the hunting party by giving birth at any time. Also, once they produced their young, the women were virtually tied to their babies through breastfeeding – at the conclusion of which period they usually produced another baby. It naturally evolved that women stayed close to the caves, taking care of the young, making clothing, and preparing food for the men. They also scrounged close to the caves for growing carrots and berries, and, in some cultures, cultivated small gardens.

*Reprinted from *The School Guidance Worker* 29 (May-June 1974), 23-28.

It equally naturally evolved that the other half of the population who did not reproduce took part in hunting trips and warfare with neighbouring tribes. To be successful hunters men had to broaden their knowledge. They had to learn how to read the weather expertly so they could plan their hunting trips. They had to use their creative ability to develop weapons. They also became experts in the habits of the animals they were tracking. They had to develop sophisticated methods of tracking and overcoming these animals, and to provide for their own safety they became shrewd and cunning. With their primitive self-made weapons they had to become skilled in killing and transporting these animals. Young men were not born with this broader knowledge. It was passed down from father to son – and the greatest hunters and warriors became the people of the tribe considered to be the wisest, and, therefore, best suited to be the leaders. (There are some primitive tribes in which women are considered superior and in these instances we see a different cultural message being passed down through the generations.)

WHY SEXUAL ROLES HAVE CONTINUED UNCHANGED

Men and women today, for the most part, are living out their roles as they were handed down to them as part of a social conditioning that is centuries old. And these people very often mistake this social conditioning as being part of the biological order of things.

The traditional stereotype that exists today continues to equate masculinity with physical strength, independence, courage, imagination, leadership, bravery, and, ambition – all the personality qualities a man had to possess in order to be a 'success' in primitive tribes. It equates feminity with personality characteristics such as softness, nurturing mannerisms, gentleness, kindness, passivity, dependence, and chastity – again, the personality qualities needed by women to be 'successful' tribal members many centuries ago.

This has happened without our conscious awareness. Experts tell us that by the age of eight, boys and girls are socialized into stereotyped sex roles. Even if parents make a planned effort to give each of their children the feeling that he or she can develop into his or her fullest potential – that is, to use all of their intelligence and special talents – children are also greatly influenced by what they absorb through the culture. School books and TV are often cited as two of the most powerful media for transmitting these traditional sexually stereotyped roles. The message about their sexual roles that school books and school personnel give to young children has an especially great impact and credibility because it is presented within the schoolroom.

The question to answer is 'Are these centuries-old sexual stereotypes really out-of-date?' If they are not, it is not necessary to consider new ones. But if they are irrelevant to the final decades of twentieth-century reality, then new definitions of 'feminine' and 'masculine' will have to be found. And young people living today will have that difficult task to perform for themselves and will have to lead the way for future generations.

CHANGES IN MODERN SOCIETY AFFECTING SEXUAL ROLES

Cultures resist change the same as people do. Our culture would like to continue evolving slowly by making minor changes. But four historical realities have emerged within the last twenty years that will not allow such complacency. These realities are: (1) realization of our planet's ecological needs; (2) automation; (3) human liberation movements; and (4) effective birth control. These are irreversible realities, and in the process of reacting to these realities our society as a whole and all the individuals in it will emerge drastically changed.

Our planet's ecological needs
Ecologists tell us that our planet is running out of air, water, and energy and that to survive we must learn to use our resources with more care and creativity and to curtail drastically the rate of human reproduction. So we are living in the first generation of mankind where it is not considered abnormal if couples choose not to have children. It is actually unfashionable to have large families, and many young couples are not having any children at all.

This is quite a turnabout. Throughout recorded history women have been told that motherhood was their mission on earth. This message was strengthened by the support of most organized religions and reinforced by the laws of most governments. The same women who were taught that producing a child expressed their unique creativity are being asked not to be so creative. How will some of these young women fulfil themselves, and, especially, how will they fulfil their need to be creative? What is the essence of 'woman'? Young women of today and the young men with whom they share this planet are being forced to reassess women as individuals and as a group, as well as the relationship between men and women.

Automation
The development of automation in our world affects the basis of sexual attitudes in several ways. Automation eliminates jobs! Automation also often eliminates the need for physical strength to be used on jobs, and this, in turn, increases the opportunity for women to compete with men for the same jobs.

Automation has lessened the opportunity for many men to fulfil their traditional masculine role as 'provider.' It also lessens the opportunity for some men to feel that they are using the traditional masculine qualities of physical strength to provide sustenance for their families. Unless men learn to define themselves as male sexual beings divorced from the role of provider and possessor of brute strength, they will perhaps not be able to function in a sexually satisfying way in the years to come. For today, young men will have to deal with the situation where women compete with them for jobs or earn more than they earn. Many young men will have to deal with working under the direction of a woman – a new situation for both the young men and the young women.

And how will the young women handle these new situations? They are the product of our culture. Their pre-eight-year-old socialization has taught them that the woman's role is to 'keep the home fires burning' and to thrive in the sheltering protection of their men. If a young woman chooses to follow a vocation, and to learn a skill and compete equally, will she be able to redefine herself as a female with the qualities of assertiveness, ambition, and competitiveness that she will need to succeed vocationally? And how will she handle being 'boss' to male workers? Unless women learn to define themselves as female sexual beings divorced from the role of compliance and helplessness, they will perhaps not be able to meet some of the demands the twentieth century will place upon them in a way that they will find personally satisfying.

Human liberation movements
In the 1960s we saw students in many countries organizing themselves, taking stands, and demanding recognition. The blacks in the United States also organized themselves and began fighting for their rights as human beings while identifying with their uniqueness as blacks. Around the same time, women began to band together to share feelings and concerns and to take stands and make demands. This has resulted in the enactment of much legislation against sex discrimination in employment practices, and laws have been liberalized in areas such as abortion and adoption of children by single people. Communities are responding to demands for day-care centres for working parents.

Success such as this has nurtured other political and social pressure movements. Indians in Canada are organizing themselves to fight for their rights as human beings and for their uniqueness as Indians. Communities have organized to stop or to start expressways. Movements affecting traditional sexual mores are also active. Homosexual organizations are openly demanding understanding and acceptance for their members. Even clergymen are challenging the traditional vows of chastity.

Men are starting to form groups to look more closely at themselves. Some men are beginning to question the demanding role of 'provider' that society insists on laying upon them. Men are demanding 'paternal leave' at the birth of their children. Men are demanding the right to feel frightened about the responsibilities of life, the right to cry, the right to express their tenderness and softness and gentleness openly. Why is it acceptable for female children to be tomboys for many years and to be allowed to become familiar with these qualities within themselves, while male children until now have been denied the same right to express their gentler qualities?

A seventeen-year-old young man who is an excellent flautist recently told me that, when he originally picked the flute as his instrument to study, his male high school music teacher advised him against it, 'Because,' said the teacher, 'the flute is a feminine instrument.' Men are beginning to realize that they have human rights that they must fight for.

The women's liberation organization has been emerging for three hundred years and is well organized and vocal, but men and women are really saying the same thing: 'I am unique and important and I demand to be accepted without being judged by out-of-date, stereotyped criteria of what I should be and how I should act.'

Effective birth control

Even with the immense forces towards social change such as automation, social reform movements and ecological demands, it might not have been possible for human beings to change their sexual stereotyping without the invention of such effective means of birth control as the Pill and the IUD. Some people have ranked the invention of effective birth control with that of the wheel in terms of its far-reaching results for the human race. When reproduction is 100 per cent controllable (as it is when the Pill is used correctly), women are physiologically as free as men to set goals and to fulfil them without an unexpected interruption of pregnancy. Couples can plan and control their lifestyles to be most fulfilling to themselves and to their children.

The reality of effective birth control and its easy availability for young women places an unprecedented pressure on young people to make decisions about their sexual activities based on new criteria. When the fear of pregnancy is removed, young women have to take the full responsibility of saying 'yes' or 'no' to sexual intercourse, based on their own ethical code and their own assessment of their ability to handle such intimacy. And many young women are saying 'yes' when they would like to say 'no.' Some young women who fear that they are not emotionally ready for sexual encounters force themselves to become involved sexually to prove to themselves that they are grown up. There is also an element of having to prove that they are 'normal,' i.e., that they can enjoy sex the way advertising and movies model that it should be enjoyed – constantly and with natural abandon!

Many young men are equally confused about how they fit into this new sexual picture and what their sexual responsibilities are towards young women and the adult society. Remember, this is the first generation in history where men have to relate to sexual partners who consider themselves equal. Young men are also concerned with proving that they are 'normal.' Recently in Toronto a well-known doctor met with a high school class to discuss sexuality. He asked the young women for their definition of 'virility.' Some of the answers given were 'being a responsible person,' 'caring about my feelings,' 'listening to my point-of-view,' 'being affectionate,' and 'being reliable.' Most of the young men were astounded! They were still at the 'stud' level of development and many of them admitted to thinking that females equated virility with such things as physical strength, physical build, sexual equipment, or sexual ability. Today, anyone who can read can learn to make love very adequately. Women want more than studs in their men.

At the same time, society continues to identify virility with brute strength. Our professional sportsmen are the most highly paid people in our society and almost worshipped by many of its citizens. In this atmosphere young men have to come to their personal definition of virility.

Effective birth control is certainly a powerful catalyst for change in our society, but it is placing new demands on young people to solve completely new problems. It is tragically ironical that effective birth control has created an acceptable climate for sexual equality for women – but many young women are responding to the climate of sexual freedom without using the protection of the birth control which, in the beginning, made that climate possible. Some young women equate the birth control pill with 'drug taking' and refuse to take it on that basis. Other young women try to retain a picture of themselves as responding to a male in a spontaneous, unplanned, romantic fashion to overcome their guilt about taking part in premarital sex. Taking birth control involves a commitment to personal responsibility for which they are not ready.

It is a giant step for women to take from being helpless and clinging to becoming responsible and assertive. It is a giant step for women to change from being sexually dependent to being sexually independent – that is, to prepare themselves and to protect themselves. The male cannot reproduce and is therefore biologically free to have sex without worrying about reproduction. And if a female wants this same freedom it is available to her today, but at the cost of using effective conception controls. Unless a woman is psychologically able to accept sexual freedom she will not be able to exhibit the types of responsible behaviour that will make that sexual freedom an enjoyable experience and not a nightmare of guilts, doubts, and put-downs.

THE CHALLENGE TO THE ADOLESCENT

In past generations there were reliable cultural guidelines to help adolescents get through their 'identity crisis' and reach some comfortable level of adulthood. Today, the guidelines are fuzzy at times and non-existent at other times. Living today as a sexual being – whether male or female – means living in uncharted territory. It is almost like being the first humans on a new planet. Young men and women today are being forced to disentangle themselves from the traditional beliefs about men's and women's roles and personalities and to create a new concept of the relationship between the sexes. Young men and women have to make decisions never made before because they are based on entirely new historical developments. People living decades from now will see the resolution of this process. But for today, adolescents have to come to a definition of 'masculine' and 'feminine' that is satisfactory for themselves for their own lifetime.

THE CHALLENGE TO THE COUNSELLOR

Young people today need extra help in order to meet these historically unique and sometimes overwhelming challenges. I believe that one of the main reasons that young people have not been able to handle their 'new world' more positively and creatively has been their lack of knowledge and the lack of direction given to them on how to assimilate this new knowledge in a personally meaningful way. Counsellors are in a strategic position to be of real service in this area.

When the counsellor sees and appreciates the student-client as a sexual being struggling to find a fulfilling niche in this world, the counsellor is able to offer informed empathy to help that youngster to make some of his/her decisions – personally, vocationally, academically – and to encourage each student to pursue his/her own fulfilment. It goes without saying that counsellors should re-examine their own expectations of sexual roles, and, if they are out-of-date, they must be careful not to impose them upon the young. But, since we adults are also being influenced by the same historical realities and since many of us are having to re-assess our sexual identities, a sharing of our feelings and anxieties in this area with students can establish important bridges of communication. Such openness makes the counsellor the kind of person with whom students feel they can share their fears and feelings and allows the counsellor the opportunity to be truly effective.

DOLORES L. SHYMKO

Current sex research in Canada

Although Canadian sex research has not, thus far, received the recognition or acclaim of such sex research notables as Masters and Johnson (1966, 1970) and Kinsey (1948, 1953), there are a number of Canadian studies that have provided a valuable beginning in understanding the specific characteristics of Canadian sexual mores. The majority of this research has examined aspects of the sexual attitudes and behaviour of Canadian university students by comparing intranational and international samples. The authors of these studies have provided empirical and hypothetical interpretations of their findings with reference to how recent changes in the sexual attitudes and behaviour of university students have implications for appraising what might be called the sexual renaissance in Canada. Some of their major observations are summarized below.

Mann (1968) initially planned a Canada-wide research study to investigate the sexual attitudes and activities of youth, but owing to administrative and financial difficulties reduced the size and representation of his sample. The completed study involved samples of university students from Alberta and Ontario, with the majority from the latter. Mann qualified the representativeness of his sample as being strongly Anglo-Saxon, mostly lower middle class, and more 'religiously' inclined than most student groups. He reported that a follow-up telephone survey of the students sampled indicated a readiness to answer questions relating to their present personal sexual attitudes and behaviour.

Mann made some general observations about male-female differences in sexual attitudes and behaviour. Only 29 per cent of the males stated they discussed personal matters about sex or dating with one or more of their parents, as compared to 44 per cent of the females. Although it seemed that parents provided sex education more often for their daughters, 25 per cent of the females sampled had received no sexual information from their parents. Dissatisfaction with the sex education received (or not received) at home was reported by the majority of the male sample. Half of the males and a fifth of the females had experienced guilt feelings about masturbation, and one quarter of the females related guilt to petting. Approximately 10 per cent in both groups denied experiencing any guilt feelings with regard to sexual activities. A small number of males and females reported that they were not familiar with the essential facts about contraception. The females expressed considerably more anxiety about dating and male-female activities. They voiced more particular concerns than the males about their ability to attract members of the opposite sex and about their knowledge of appropriate social behaviour. Regular dating for females began at about age fourteen, intimate kissing at sixteen, and going steady at seventeen years; the males began dating at sixteen, kissing at sixteen, and going steady at seventeen.

Hobart (1970) attempted to evaluate the impact of change in North American sexual mores during the sixties, specifically with regard to orientations to courtship and premarital sexuality among Canadian university students. His sample included university and trade school students from Edmonton, Montreal, and Waterloo. He specifically compared English and French student samples describing both similarities and differences in their reported sexual attitudes and behaviour. When asked about premarital sexuality, an overwhelming majority in both the English and French samples approved of premarital petting for males. Premarital intercourse for males was acceptable to 59 per cent of the English sample and 54 per cent of the French. In the English group, 89 per cent accepted petting for the females as compared to 79 per cent of the French group; and 56 per cent and 51 per cent respectively accepted premarital sexual intercourse for females. Generally, the males sampled were more permissive than the females with regard to all measures of sexual attitudes and experience. The university women were more permissive than the sample of women attending trade schools. More females than males expressed some guilt related to sexual activities. However, within the total sample, a fairly small amount of guilt was expressed in relation to personal sexual behaviour.

Regional differences were noted within the sample groups. The Alberta university students reported more sexual experience than the comparable Ontario sample. Less than the majority, in both the English and French samples, were dissatisfied with the prevalent sexual codes in society. More of the English students than the French students were critical of the teachings of the church about sexuality. A somewhat sizeable minority in the English and French samples expressed personal confusion in deciding ethical questions about premarital sex. About two thirds of the English sample reported increasing permissiveness in their personal dating practices, as compared to 39 per cent in the French group.

Using a factor-analytic technique, Hobart identified sixteen predictive factors in the English data and fourteen in the French. The eight factors that were common to both groups were labelled: religiosity, courtship advancement, sex identity, peer-parent-ego consistency, socio-economic status, family solidarity, alienation, and geographical consistency. Those factors unique to the French data were: age (they were younger), family devoutness, fast involvement with the opposite sex, mother's work involvement, and perceived similarity with peers. The major difference between the French and English samples was attributed to the greater influence of religiosity and the lesser influence of conventionality in the French group, in predicting non-permissiveness. Neither group indicated strong support for trial marriage. Hobart found that the English students were generally more emancipated than the French and the males in both groups were also more emancipated than the females. The principal regulator of sexual morality in the French Canadian sample was the influence of the church, while in the English Canadian sample it was the affect of conventional morality. The females were more concerned with courtship interaction leading to marriage; the males were more inclined to increasing sexual permissiveness.

The major conclusions of this comparative study were that there are notable cultural and sex-related differences amongst English and French Canadian university students. The most powerful correlates of sexual permissiveness relating to attitudes and behaviour were non-conventionality, courtship involvement, irreligiosity, male sex identity, and university enrolment. Hobart concluded that the findings of this study provided support for the emergence of a new morality among Canadian university students. He noted an acceptance in both the English and French samples of premarital sexuality when couples are engaged or in love. A relatively high incidence of intercourse experience was reported particularly in the English Canadian group. Hobart hypothesized that this increased permissiveness in personal sexual attitudes is resulting in more intimate sexual behaviour between persons involved in committed relationships, but is not necessarily leading to increased promiscuity. These findings are very similar to those reported by Reiss (1960), based on American data, that indicated the emergence of a sexual ethic that rejects intimate behaviour in the absence of affection, but accepts premarital sexuality within an established relationship. This change was interpreted by Hobart as a possible indication of the emergence of a more realistic approach hopefully lessening superficiality in dating.

Perlman (1973) questioned several different samples of students attending the University of Manitoba about various aspects of their sexual behaviour and their personal lives. The unmarried students enrolled in a personality course in psychology ($N = 112$) indicated that the determining factor in the degree of acceptable sexual permissiveness was the extent of the emotional closeness in the relationship. The prerequisite of 'being in love' greatly increased the acceptable range and the amount of premarital sexual permissiveness. The males accepted more sexual permissiveness than the females. The students with continuous personal sexual experience also expressed fewer reactions of guilt about premarital sexuality. More frequent use of drugs and liberal views about drug laws appeared to be related to the acceptance of sexual permissiveness in the male but not the female sample.

In a smaller pilot sample, personality characteristics measured by the Tennessee Self-Concept Scale were correlated with the measure of sexual permissiveness used by Reiss (1967). These preliminary findings indicated that sexual permissiveness was associated with 'positive personal adjustment' for females, but not for males. In another sample of 266 social psychology students, the correlates of sexual permissiveness were compared with personal and demographic characteristics. Among the females, sexual permissiveness was related to: being a senior student, less religiosity, and frequency of church attendance; among the males to: coming from a high-income family, having a working mother, and coming from a large community. In the combined sample, the determinants of sexual permissiveness were: religion (the Jews were the highest and the Catholics the lowest), father's ethnicity (English and Scottish were highest and French and Polish lowest), and university faculty (arts and science highest and education lowest). The religious and ethnic variables were found to be interrelated, as French students were usually Catholic. In a further sample of 128 females taking introductory psychology, the degree of sexual permissiveness was found to be related to various personal characteristics such as 'fashionable provocativeness' as indicated by clothing worn, interest in fashion magazines; as well as active dating patterns, earlier dating, going steady, and the intensity and frequency of personal relationships.

Perlman compared his findings with some contemporary studies that were completed in the United States and Canada. He found that the degree of sexual permissiveness reported in his samples was similar to the findings submitted by Hobart (1970) and Luckey and Nass (1969), but was lower than in those reported by Mann (1968). A comparison of the results from Canadian, American, and European samples (although the dissimilarity of the dates of these studies may confuse the comparisons) indicated that the Canadians were more conservative in their sexual attitudes (Luckey and Nass, 1969; Reiss, 1967).

Several research studies have included samples of Canadian university students in cross-cultural comparisons of sexual attitudes and behaviour. Luckey and Nass (1969) conducted an extensive survey of 2,230 male and female college students from five different countries: the United States, Canada, England, Norway, and West Germany. Their results included some interesting observations of differences in attitudes to sex roles. The North American females were less interested in pursuing a professional career than the European females. The males and females in the European sample accepted sexual equality and opportunity more readily in both academic and professional spheres. The Canadian students viewed the female role as primarily oriented to marriage, rather than a career. North American students more strongly adhered to the view that marriage is essential to a satisfying life, and that sexual outlets should be limited to the bounds of marriage. These North American samples were also more supportive of double standard morality. The English and Norwegian subjects supported a single standard, with the latter group strongly rejecting sexual promiscuity. 'Maturity' was the major criterion advocated for determining acceptable sexual standards of behaviour in all cultural groups. The American and Canadian students sought less independence from parents and welcomed adult guidelines more than the European students; the British students were most in favour of early independence and sought self-responsibility at an earlier age than the other groups.

Throughout the total sample, there was an observable general consistency in sexual attitudes and behaviour. Thus, the groups that were more liberal in their attitudes were also more liberal in their reported behaviour. The English males and females proved to be the most liberal and the most convergent in their views, with both freely participating in and supporting a wide range of sexual practices. The male ranking order for frequency of coital experience according to national groups was: England, Norway, the United States, Canada, and West Germany; for females: England, West Germany, Norway, the United States, and Canada. Luckey and Nass generally concluded that North American sexual attitudes and behaviour patterns were comparatively more conservative than the European. Although these authors provided extensive statistical information comparing the sexual mores of European and North American youth, they did not attempt to interpret the associated meanings or motivations that would account for these differences. They strongly suggested that a vast amount of further research is needed to explain the complexity of these social factors.

Whitehurst and Plant (1971) compared attitudes towards marriage and degree of measured alienation scores in samples of university students from the midwestern United States and the province of Ontario in Canada. They found that the Canadian students tended to be more critical of the institution of marriage, appeared more discontent with conventional institutions, and expressed more readiness to consider alternatives to standard marriage practices. The Canadian sample also scored higher on the Middleton Alienation Scale, used to measure alienation factors, although they did not score at the extremes, as did the comparable American sample. These results were interpreted by the authors as suggesting that the more pluralistic approach of the Canadian society may provide a model for social change. They also hypothesized that alienation may be a necessary prerequisite for subsequent social change.

The present author conducted a study of sexual attitudes using a somewhat younger experimental group (Shymko, 1974), where 121 high school students in grade eleven (aged sixteen to nineteen) from a suburban Toronto high school were asked their viewpoints on a cross-section of personal and social issues about sex. They were also asked to identify the present situations associated with their current life role that they considered to be particularly stressful or beneficial. They also predicted the way they perceived their parents would behave, and the motivation for this behaviour, in trust-control situations that frequently occur in the home. Some of these situations had sexual overtones.

The data from a sexual attitudes questionnaire were factor-analysed, and eleven factors were selected as defining the attitude structure within this adolescent sample. These factors were labelled: sexual permissiveness, attitudes to raising children, sex education programs in school, sexual responsibility, sexual responsibility of males, prevalent sexual attitudes, marriage-sex roles, sexual freedom, movie censorship, sexual restrictiveness, sex education and personal issues. An examination of the individual factors indicated that these adolescents had opinions that reflected both the influence of their peers as well as of their society. Like their university seniors described above, they were generally accepting of premarital sex that occurred within a committed personal relationship. The results suggested the presence of a generation gap; the members of adult society were viewed as hypocritical and exploitative in their sexual morality. Peers were seen as competent in making responsible decisions about their sexual behaviour. With regard to controversial public issues pertaining to sex, these adolescents expressed many of the uncertainties and confusions that dominate adult viewpoints. The complexities of the emotional and social implications of pornography, homosexuality, illegitimacy, and changing male-female roles elicited no clear consensus on what practices would be most effective for the good for the individual and society. These students gave strong support for the appropriateness of discussing a wide variety of topics in sex education.

The students also assessed their satisfaction with life experiences pertaining to the home, the school, vocational choice, interpersonal relationships, and psychosexual growth; as well as perceptions of their parents in trust-control situations. The adolescents expressed relatively positive appraisals of their present lives. They were generally satisfied with their social relationships with members of the opposite sex and somewhat satisfied with their family relationships. However, some degree of dissatisfaction was expressed in relation to social attitudes surrounding sex, the amount and type of sex education provided in their homes, the social practices associated with sexual behaviour, their abilities to deal with the more intimate aspects of interpersonal relationships, and the availability of an understanding adult for discussing personal matters. These results suggested that adolescents find the socialization and child-rearing practices associated with aspects of psychosexual growth relatively stressful. The data from the Adolescent Life-Satisfaction Questionnaire were factor-analysed; also incorporated were the data from the Adolescent Perception of Parents Questionnaire. Thirteen of the resulting factors were considered to define the structure of adolescent perception of their life-satisfactions. These factors were termed: social attitudes towards sex, school success, sex education at home, relationships with the opposite sex, self-awareness, extra-curricular activities, vocational choice, family relationships, social relationships, sex education at school, sexual self-acceptance, interpersonal relationships, and parental trust-control.

The analysis of current sex research on Canadian data indicates that most of the available information comes from the sampling of university students' sexual attitudes and behaviour. Apparently, the understanding of the sexual renaissance in Canada has not, as yet, gone much beyond the university campus.

REFERENCES

Canadian Education Association, Research and Information Division. *The Present Status of Sex Education in Canadian Schools*. Toronto, 1964.

Elkin, F. (Director) Report of Family Life Education Survey. Part 1. *Family Life Education in the Media of Mass Communication*. The Vanier Institute of the Family, 1971.

– (Director) Report of Family Life Education Survey. Part 2. *Family Life Education in the Schools*. The Vanier Institute of the Family, 1971.

Hobart, C.W. 'Changing Orientations to Courtship: A Study of Young Canadians.' In W.E. Mann (ed.), *Social and Cultural Change in Canada*. Volume 2, Toronto, 1970.

Kinsey, A.C. *Sexual Behaviour in the Human Male*. Philadelphia, 1948.

– *Sexual Behaviour in the Human Female*. Philadelphia, 1953.

Luckey, E.B. and Nass, G.D. 'A Comparison of Sexual Attitudes and Behaviour in an International Sample.' *Journal of Marriage and the Family*. 1969, 31, 364-79.

Mann, W.E. 'Sex Behaviour on Campus.' In W.E. Mann (ed.), *Canada: A Sociological Profile*. Toronto, 1968.

Masters, W.H. and Johnson, V.E. *Human Sexual Response*. Boston, 1966.

– *Human Sexual Inadequacy*. Boston, 1970.

McCreary-Juhasz, A. 'Sex Knowledge of Prospective Teachers and Graduate Nurses.' *The Canadian Nurse*. 63 (7), 1967.

– 'How Accurate are Student Evaluations of the Extent of their Knowledge of Human Sexuality?' *Journal of School Health*, 1967, 37, 409-12.

Perlman, D. 'The Sexual Standards of Canadian University Students.' In
    D. Koulack and D. Perlman (eds.), *Readings in Social Psychology: Focus on Canada.* Toronto, 1973.
Reiss, I. *Premarital Sexual Standards in America.* Toronto, 1960.
– *The Social Context of Premarital Sexual Permissiveness.* New York, 1967.
Shymko, D.L. 'An Exploratory Investigation of Some Aspects of Psychosexual
    Development in Adolescents.' Unpublished doctoral dissertation, University of Toronto, 1974.
Whitehurst, R.N. and Plant, B. 'Comparison of Canadian and American
    University Students' Reference Groups: Alienation and Attitudes toward Marriage.' In W.E. Mann (ed.), *Canada: A Sociological Profile.* Toronto, 1971.

PART TWO

SEXUALITY AND THE LIFE CYCLE

CARL F. GRINDSTAFF

The baby bust: changes in fertility patterns in Canada

The relatively high population growth rates of the late 1940s and 1950s in Canada and the United States caught most people unawares, and there were many resulting problems in employment positions, schools, teachers, housing, etc. In the middle and late 1960s and continuing into the 1970s, we witnessed a great population decline in terms of growth rates. We must not be negligent during this period in attempting to deal with social changes that are the inevitable results of such demographic swings in fertility patterns. With fertility under control to a large degree, people are opting for having fewer children. We should begin to make plans for this continuing reality.

Certainly, unwanted conception is still a problem for certain population subgroups in Canadian society. In 1972 and 1973, there were approximately 82,000 therapeutic abortions conducted in Canadian hospitals, or about one abortion for every eight births (Tietze and Dawson, 1973, p. 8). Nearly half of these operations were performed on women, usually unmarried, under the age of twenty-one.

A study undertaken in Nova Scotia in 1971 indicated that nearly half of 200 children born in a hospital over a period of one month were unwanted, and a disproportionate number of pregnancies occurred to women from low socio-economic areas (Family Planning Federation of Canada, 1973, p. 4). It would appear that quite often for the young and disadvantaged 'compulsory pregnancy' is still a problem that needs to be solved. However, when examining the Canadian population *in toto* in the 1970s, it appears that fertility is well under control (Table 1).

In 1972 both crude birth rates and total fertility rates fell to their lowest levels in Canadian history (see Table 1). In addition, the actual number of regis-

TABLE 1
Total fertility rates and crude birth rates, for Canada, 1921-1972

Year	Crude birth rates	Total fertility rates
1921	29.3	3.53 (excluding Quebec)
1926	24.7	3.36
1931	23.2	3.20
1936	20.3	2.70
1941	22.4	2.83
1946	27.2	3.37
1951	27.2	3.50
1956	28.0	3.86
1957	28.2	3.93
1958	27.5	3.88
1959	27.4	3.94
1960	26.8	3.90
1961	26.1	3.84
1962	25.3	3.76
1963	24.6	3.67
1964	23.5	3.50
1965	21.3	3.15
1966	19.4	2.81
1967	18.2	2.60
1968	17.6	2.45
1969	17.6	2.41
1970	17.4	2.33
1971	16.8	2.19
1972	15.9	2.02

SOURCE: *Vital Statistics*, Preliminary Annual Report, 1972, Health and Welfare Division, Statistics Canada, Ottawa, February 1974, pp. 8, 12.

tered births in 1972 (347,000) was the lowest since 1946 when Canada's total population was only thirteen million, compared to the current twenty-two million (Statistics Canada, 1973, p. 4). Table 1 shows that the total fertility rate in 1972 was down to 2.02, and that there has been a steady decline in this measure since 1959. This decline over the past decade in Canada has been faster than at any other time recorded previously. Even during the depression years of the 1930s, rates dropped by less than 2 per cent per annum on the average, compared

TABLE 2
Number of live births, children aged 0-4, and women aged 15-34,
for Canada, 1961 and 1971

	1961	1971	Percentage of increase (decrease) 1961 to 1971
Live births	475,700	362,187	(-19.5)
Children 0-4	2,256,401	1,816,155	(-23.9)
Women 15-34	2,522,834	3,415,500	+35.4
15-19	703,524	1,039,915	+47.8
20-24	596,507	947,625	+58.9
25-29	595,400	783,410	+31.6
30-34	627,403	644,550	+ 2.7

SOURCE: *1971 Census of Canada*, Vol. 1, Part 2, Bulletin 4, 'Single years of age'; *1961 Census of Canada*, Vol. 1, Part 2, Bulletin 2, 'Age Groups,' Statistics Canada, Ottawa.

to the more than 4 per cent annual decline in the 1960s (Henripin, 1972, pp. 13, 148). Replacement fertility levels in Canada are calculated to be approximately 2.1, and thus Canadian women are currently reproducing at a rate that would bring about zero population growth within fifty years.

The decline of fertility rates has accelerated in the 1970s, and, paradoxically, the decline in the numbers and the rates of children being born has occurred during a period when the number of women in the childbearing ages has *increased* substantially. Table 2 indicates that the number of children 0-4 years of age decreased by approximately 20 per cent between 1961 and 1971, while the number of women in the prime childbearing ages (15-34) increased by 35 per cent. Women aged 20-24, the most fertile group in Canadian society, increased by nearly 60 per cent between 1961 and 1971 (owing primarily to the entry of baby-boom children into this age group), but actually had fewer children born in 1971 (124, 310) than in 1961 (135, 700). Part of this change is related to age at marriage - the median age of brides in Canada has risen from 21.1 in 1961 to 21.5 in 1971. As a result, there are proportionately fewer women married in the 20-24 prime childbearing age group (see Table 3). While these demographic factors may play a minor role in the recent fertility decline, it seems that the major reasons are not strictly demographic, but rather sociological. Norms and values that have an influence on childbearing seem to have changed dramatically in the past fifteen years, and the 'baby bust' is a reality in the 1970s among married women. In addition, there are indications that this trend will continue into the near future.

TABLE 3
Single and married female population, aged 15–29, for Canada, 1961 and 1971

| Age | 1961 | | | | |
	Single	Married	Widowed	Divorced	Percentage ever married
15–19	642,007	61,197	262	58	8.7
20–24	241,435	353,215	931	926	59.5
25–29	91,940	498,637	2,371	2,452	84.6
Median age of bride: 21.1 years					
	1971				
15–19	962,100	75,715	1,540	565	7.5
20–24	412,190	527,870	2,405	5,165	56.5
25–29	120,695	646,655	3,970	12,085	84.6
Median age of bride: 21.5 years					

SOURCE: *1971 Census of Canada*, Vol. 1, Part 4, Bulletin 2, 'Marital Status by Age Group'; *1961 Census of Canada*, Vol. 1, Part 3, Bulletin 1, 'Marital Status by Age Group'; *Vital Statistics*, No. 84-202, 1971, Statistics Canada, Ottawa.

Some experts in population statistics, for example Philip Hauser, caution against the prediction that low fertility is here to stay. In the past, fertility rates have been volatile, and these experts argue that current low levels may simply be due to recent changes in timing and spacing of children – a postponement of fertility, not a final reduction (*New York Times*, 1974, pp. 1, 14; Greene, 1972, p. 44). It is true that demographers in the 1930s were predicting continuing low and stable fertility, and that in fact from the early 1930s to the late 1950s the crude birth rates increased by some 50 per cent. It is possible that similar increases could occur in the future from the present low levels.

However, in a recent article titled 'Is Low Fertility Here to Stay?' Larry Bumpass (1973) argues that substantial changes have occurred in society relating to fertility that were not present before, and that low fertility rates, with only minor fluctuations, are going to be the norm for the future. Bumpass cites several important developments both in terms of technology and norms of fertility that will, in his view, ensure that current patterns of low fertility are not simply transitional delays in childbearing. Among these changes, the two most important are: (1) more effective means of preventing unwanted conception and widespread distribution of these means – the pill, IUDs, sterilization, and abortion; (such techniques allowing fertility to be a matter of decision rather than accident);

TABLE 4
Percentage of childlessness among women ever married, 15–44 years of age,
for Canada, 1961 and 1971

| | Percentage childless | | Percentage of increase (decrease) |
Age	1961	1971	1961 to 1971
15–44	13.5	18.1	+34.1
15–19	42.3	49.7	+17.5
20–24	26.3	42.0	+59.7
25–29	13.6	20.7	+52.2
30–34	9.7	9.4	(– 3.1)
35–39	9.2	7.4	(–19.6)
40–44	10.3	8.2	(–20.4)

SOURCE: *1971 Census of Canada*, Vol. 1, Part 2, Bulletin 6, 'Women Ever Married by Number of Children Born'; *1961 Census of Canada*, Vol. 4, Part 1, Bulletin 7, 'Women by Age and Number of Children Born,' Statistics Canada, Ottawa.

(2) more alternatives to motherhood for women in the society – employment, education, travel, etc. (Bumpass, 1973, pp. 68-9).

There is some evidence that these changes in society affect not only the number of children any woman might have when her family size is complete, but also whether or not a woman would have any children at all. Increasingly, the question may be not how many children do you want to have, but rather do you want to have children or not. Fertility in terms of number of children per family is decreasing, but also the number of families without any children, especially among younger couples, appears to be increasing at a substantial rate.

Table 4 shows the proportion of ever-married women in Canada who were childless, by five-year age groupings, in 1961 and 1971. The under-30 age categories all show higher rates of childlessness in 1971 than in 1961, and just the opposite is true for the women 30–44. For this latter group, the prime childbearing years began in the late 1940s and continued into the 1960s, the period of the baby boom. Childlessness rates for this group, between 7% and 9%, are probably close to physiological minimums.

The younger married women, especially in the prime childbearing ages of 20 to 30, demonstrate significant increases in the proportion that is childless between 1961 and 1971. Married women 20-24 and 25-29 years of age in 1971 show more than a 50 per cent increase in childless rates in comparison with their counterparts in 1961. These figures may simply illustrate timing changes; a postponement in having children until the couples are ready to make the decision that a child would be welcome in their lives. The relatively high rates may also reflect later age at marriage and thus duration of marriage, but the median age of bride figures cited earlier seem to negate this possibility to a large degree.

In a recent article Jean Veevers (1972, p. 58f) suggests that 'voluntary child-lessness constitutes deviant behaviour in that husbands and wives who decline the opportunity to have children violate norms both of behaviour and motiva-tion.' In the past, couples who were childless for voluntary reasons had been stig-matized as barren, selfish, unfulfilled, abnormal, unnatural, immature and un-happy (Veevers, 1972, pp. 581-82). However, once a few couples decide to remain childless and larger and larger numbers of young married people postpone childbearing, these stigmas may be applied less often, and the norms and motives for having children may well undergo change. A form of social contagion takes place. Research in the United States and Canada on attitudes toward childbear-ing among high school students in the 1970s, however, shows that 70 per cent of the young men and women want to have two or three children, and that about 5 per cent say they will not have any (Gustavus, 1973, p. 337; Nobbe and Okraku).

But let us assume that the high rates of childlessness observed in Table 4 for young married women in 1971 were initially thought of as timing changes, and that a great proportion of these women plan to have children 'when the time is right.' These couples, who are obviously using effective contraception, can delay childbearing to help achieve economic, educational, or professional goals. During this period of delay – perhaps three, four, or five years – a certain lifestyle can develop which the couple views as rewarding and desirable. Thus they may choose to delay having any children a little longer and can easily do so perma-nently. If there are many peer couples in this situation, and the data show that their numbers are growing rapidly, then a cumulative norm can develop between them which makes childlessness not a deviant act, but a perfectly 'normal one.' As more and more couples in the younger ages remain childless, the principle of cumulation works to create a new norm and definition of the situation which makes childlessness an acceptable pattern of behaviour. In general, temporary delay will foster a lifestyle, especially relating to career opportunity and advance-ment for women, that will ultimately result in permanent postponement of child-bearing. We suggest that such a pattern will develop in the 1970s, and this trend will have important effects on many institutions in our society. With the increas-ing participation of women in all aspects of Canadian life, and more opportuni-ties for self-fulfilment outside of motherhood, the number of married women who choose to remain childless as a permanent condition will undoubtedly be higher than in the past decade. We would estimate that in 1981, at least 20 per cent of those women 30-34 years of age who have ever been married will be childless – or approximately double the current rate. This estimation is subjectively based on the changes involving fertility already noted and on the trends from age group to age group in 1961 and 1971.

It is incumbent upon leadership in government, labour, and business to recognize this likely change and to make plans to accommodate fewer children in schools, to make other uses of existing schools, to train fewer educationalists, to explore different recreational needs, to arrange for more and diverse employment opportunities for women, and to create different housing possibilities. The suburban four-bedroom colonial with two and a half bathrooms may not appeal to the potential 20 per cent of the nation's couples who choose to remain childless in the near future. These are but a few of the areas of concern that we will have to deal with in the next decade.

While forecasting future patterns of fertility is risky at best, it is important that we recognize probable demographic changes in our society and make plans for the rippling effects these changes can have on basic educational and economic institutions. The demographic figures are there; it is the responsibility of people in the field of population study to interpret these data and make program recommendations to the men and women who have to make decisions that will affect us all. Family planning, in the sense that most people have a chance to make a rational decision as to the costs and benefits of childbearing, is fast becoming an integral component of life in Canada. For the first time in history, people are gaining control over the consequences of their sexuality, and this is a good thing. However, we must be prepared as a society to recognize that such control has far-reaching implications for social organization and institutional arrangements. For the next decade or more, we must begin to project for total fertility rates at or below the replacement level and for 20 per cent or more of married couples remaining childless. Otherwise, fertility control, which should be a blessing, will simply be another problem.

REFERENCES

Bumpass, L. 1973. 'Is Low Fertility Here to Stay?' *Family Planning Perspectives*, Volume 5, Number 2.

Family Planning Federation of Canada. 1973. *Family Planning and Population*, Volume 1, Number 2.

Greene, W. 1972. 'The Militant Malthusians.' *Saturday Review of Literature*, March 11, 1972.

Gustavus, S. 1973. 'The Family Size Preferences of Young People: A Replication and Longitudinal Follow-up Study.' *Studies in Family Planning*, Volume 4, Number 12.

Henripin, J. 1972. *Trends and Factors of Fertility in Canada*. Statistics Canada, Ottawa.

New York Times. 1974. 'Birth, Fertility Rates at a New Low in U.S.' Tuesday, April 16, 1974.

Nobbe, C. and I. Okraku. Unpublished manuscript. 'An Analysis of Sex Preference Differentials and their Implications for Future Fertility Research.' University of Western Ontario, London, Ontario.

Statistics Canada. 1973. *Statistics Canada Daily*. Ottawa, September, 1973.

Tietze, C. and D. Dawson. 1973. *Induced Abortion: A Factbook*. Reports on Population/Family Planning, Number 14.

Veevers, J. 1972. 'The Violation of Fertility Mores: Voluntary Childlessness as Deviant Behaviour.' In C. Boydell, et al. (eds.) *Deviant Behaviour and Societal Reaction*. Holt, Rinehart and Winston, Toronto.

LIZ ROBERTS

Female teenagers and contraception

I have young friends ages fourteen through seventeen who are mothers. Their education was cut short. Why? Because a girl likes to stay with the crowd, to keep up with fashion and to compete. If she does, she must consider sex ...

Sex is out in the open and it affects every school child – young and old.

Sex is the most 'hip' thing today. If you are not with it you're a square. To be a girl in this day and age means knowing how to cope with sex when it is presented to you. (Kathleen Ross 17)[1]

I wonder whether this is how most teenagers perceive sex. From this excerpt it almost seems that peer pressure has made sex an obligation for young people, just to keep up with the crowd. Irrefutably, today's youth is overwhelmed with exposure to sex. In Toronto one must only walk down Yonge Street, to view the many body-rub parlours and strip joints, watch the baby blue movies, or go to any cinema to be confronted, almost assaulted, by a sex-saturated society. By and large the image created by media, however, is not matched by the reality. As Kathleen Ross most succinctly commented 'you must know how to cope with sex when it is presented to you.' Just how are teenagers coping with and absorbing this bombardment. (For the purposes of this paper coping with, narrowly defined, is equated avoidance of unwanted or unplanned pregnancy.) As the teenage subpopulation obviously includes many for whom fertility regulation is either unnecessary or undesirable, I concern myself primarily with the fraction of the teenage population whose sexual behaviour entails the risk of unwanted pregnancy. Interestingly, available literature deals predominantly with the inevitable results of unprotected intercourse: pregnancy. In discussions of paediatric pregnancies two themes follow almost invariably: abortion and unwed motherhood. Very little has been written from a preventative perspective – that is contraceptive counselling for the nulliparous yet sexually active adolescent. The literature situation has been reflected by a reluctance, until very recently, on the part of services to assume responsibility for contraceptive service to this age group. It is readily noticeable as well that public acknowledgment of adolescent sexuality focuses on unfortunate consequences.

If we are to help this age group avoid the unwanted consequences of uninformed or undisciplined sexual behaviour, we must have a clear understanding of what the situation is, and why. Insight into the present situation may be gained through discussion of four aspects:
(1) the present situation as supported by documented study and personal observation;
(2) why so many adolescents are failing to use contraception;
(3) a worker's assessment of need and the dilemmas that arise during the assessment and in providing the service;
(4) broader implications and conclusions.

PRESENT SITUATION

Abortion represents the ultimate failure of birth control. As there are no available statistics regarding the number of unplanned teenage pregnancies abortion statistics are our prime indicator. In 1971 the Toronto Hospital for Sick Children saw twenty-one pregnant young women. None had practised any form of contraception.[2] In 1973-74 the same clinic saw 182 young pregnant women. The Hospital for Sick Children indicated that over 90 per cent of the patients elected to terminate their pregnancies.[3] Further recent statistics from the Central Abortion Referral and Education Services (CARES) show that in 1974 it counselled 1,300 women. A random study of 844 of these women indicated that 209 or 31.3 per cent of these women were in their teens. Six girls were less than fifteen years of age.[4]

There has been overwhelming concurrence in all sources that although annually more and more teenagers are using birth control services an astounding number of adolescents are engaging in unprotected intercourse. Whereas requests for birth control were an oddity only five years ago they are now an everyday occurrence. The following statistics from the Hospital for Sick Children's Teen Clinic demonstrate the clinic's increasing use:[5]

Reason clinic consulted	67/68	68/69	69/70	70/71	71/72	72/73	73/74
Contraception	–	–	3	24	68	61	64
Pregnancy	2	2	3	7	23	38	182

Youth Clinical Services reports that from May 1 to August 31, 1974, 155 requests were made for birth control.[6] In the last four-month period 250 requests were received. While allowances need to be made for the fact that many adolescents are vacationing during the summer months, the increase is substantial. During the last quarter, only four of the 250 requests were from sexually *inactive* females.[7]

Two other studies, one in process and one just completed, report similar findings. Dr Cowle of Toronto General Hospital is now completing a study that suggests that 80 per cent of the sexually active teens are not using contraception.[8] A study just recently completed by Nicole Le Riche and John Howard of Queen's University indicates that among non-virgins in their teen years at least 70 per cent had intercourse at some time without using contraception.[9] Yvonne Michaelis from the Bay Centre for Birth Control has also reported that most visitors to that clinic came after being sexually active for about three to six months; furthermore, many came when they were afraid they were already pregnant. As often as not, a vague faith in fate to intervene to prevent union of the sperm and ovum had been the method of choice for months. Those utilizing protection intermittently favoured withdrawal or the condom.

Another common and interesting element which became apparent from those interviewed and was further substantiated by Peter Yue's study,[10] was that most referrals were made by friends or self. Word of mouth proved to be the most effective form of advertisement.

WHY ARE SO MANY SEXUALLY ACTIVE ADOLESCENTS NOT USING BIRTH CONTROL?

Presented with the evidence that such a large number of adolescents are sexually active and not consistently protecting themselves against unwanted pregnancy, one must ask why. Is it only our presumption that adolescents are well informed and are aware of ways of avoiding unwanted pregnancy? In reality what have they learned and from where? Interestingly, in a Kingston Study sample 90 per cent claimed to have received some kind of sex education at school.[11] While it is not the purpose of the paper to delve into various aspects of sex education, it is clear that the quality and intensity of sex education within the school is largely contingent upon the school board, the principal, and the individual teacher. Many teachers who feel unqualified or unprepared to teach human sexuality are now contacting planned parenthood or other agencies with qualified and competent staff who are more equipped to deal with the issues.

Often, however, the school board has attempted to relegate the responsibility of sex education to the parents. What a thought! The author visualizes the embarrassed parent mumbling platitudes to the embarrassed teenager. To be considered as well is the notion that many of today's parents are still conveying the same myths as did the previous generation. Some have many 'hang-ups,' and are uncomfortable and uneasy with their own sexuality, let alone the son's or daughter's. While some may be able to discuss the mechanics of sex (i.e. where the baby comes from), they would unlikely be prepared to discuss methods of birth control. Shirley Wheatley at the Hospital for Sick Children suggested that many parents are not prepared to react to their children as sexual beings. She related a case where a sexually active adolescent was given the pill. The mother phoned the next day and wanted to hear only that her daughter was on the pill to regulate her menses; she was unable and unprepared to hear anything else. Generally parents are appalled by the evidence of youthful sexuality yet somehow secure in the knowledge of their own adolescent's innocence of this behaviour. If a parent has difficulty coping with a child's sexuality it is questionable that he/she would be competent in effectively enlightening a son or daughter.

Ultimately, it seems that the sex education of our youth is a hit-and-miss affair. Some teenagers manage to pick up bits of information; some from school, some from parents, and some from friends. Clearly, many receive the information too late. Dr W. Minkowski, who wrote 'Family Planning Services for Adolescents and Young Adults,' made two observations:

(1) Ignorance of basic anatomy and reproductive physiology is striking.

(2) Neither frequency and duration of sexual activity nor education level has any direct relationship with accurate knowledge or understanding of human sexuality, including one's own.[12] This second observation bears particular relevance to a parent's ability to counsel the adolescent on birth control.

Given such a haphazard approach to sex education it is understandable that many have misconceptions and are ignorant of the dangers of engaging in unprotected (or not properly protected) intercourse. It was noted that in the Kingston survey 83 per cent of the non-virgin females (aged 16-19 years) thought it was unlikely they would get pregnant if they practised unprotected intercourse. Of non-virgin males 66 per cent felt the same.[13] There are several reasons for this unfortunate misconception.

Teenagers today, as always, are gullible about myths (i.e. douching with coke or vinegar, using saran wrap, believing withdrawal or sex at the right time of the month is an effective form of birth control). Unfortunately, most lack enough accurate facts to see the ludicrousness of these beliefs. There is, as well, a *predominance* of teenagers who feel they are magically protected, and think that 'It can't happen to me.' As Doris Hopper of the *Toronto Star* commented, 'there is difficulty in getting sexually active adolescents to make the connection between sex and procreating.' What also seems logical as well is that the urgency of the present need prevails over the vague and distant risk of pregnancy. Ms Hopper quoted one person as saying 'Somehow even though they know that intercourse causes pregnancy they just can't relate it to themselves.'[14] In a more concrete vein, even when adolescents are aware of the various contraceptive methods they may feel there are eligibility requirements (marital status and age) and are unsure where and how contraceptives can be obtained. I know a twenty-year-old woman who had had a variety of sexual experiences but was unaware of the various clinics and so felt obliged to tell her physician she was engaged when in reality she had no long-term relationship with a male. Undoubtedly many young adolescents are unaware of the where's and how's of obtaining effective contraception.

The adolescent's perspective of the situation must not be forgotten. If the reader will remember his/her own feelings after his first sexual experience, he will be able to empathize and identify with the adolescent's feelings of anxiety, fear, and embarrassment. An adolescent is, as are most of us, sensitive to the responses of others. Consequently many will avoid using a service for fear of judgmental, moralistic, or preaching attitudes. It was noted in the Kingston Study that one third of the entire sample felt they would be too embarrassed to go to a physician or family planning clinic to ask for help.[15] Further, female readers are asked to remember how they felt the first time they had a pelvic examination. The anxiety created by the knowledge that a pelvic and breast examination will be done before the prescription can be filled deters many and causes many to procrastinate over even the inquiry. It was previously noted that most put off the request for service until they are afraid (period overdue). At this time the level of anxiety regarding the late period overrides the anxiety regarding the medical examination. Some, furthermore, are 'up-tight' about going to the family physician for fear of lack of confidentiality; more specifically, 'the doctor might tell my parents.' Parents and teenagers are notorious for their inability to communicate, but when communication deals with sex it is at an all-time low.

According to the results of the Kingston Survey, the most common reason given for sexually active teenagers' failure to use contraception was 'I did not think I was going to have sex at the time.' All interviewed concurred that today's adolescent now stresses that intercourse should be a spontaneous and unpremeditated event. Sheldine McDonald, Director of Humewood House, says 'They feel you should not plan ahead to be loving and so they don't.'[16] Using birth control clearly means premeditation of sexual intercourse, and many are unwilling to admit that advance preparations have been made. It is easier to say 'Oh well, it just happened; it wasn't my fault,' than to take responsibility and plan.

One writer felt that perhaps one reason why so many young people are not employing sensible contraception was because of today's cult of naturalness. He felt that macrobiotic foods, etc., were followed by natural love which was followed by natural intercourse.[17]

While adolescent pregnancy is just a 'big mistake' for many, in some there may be subconscious motivation toward this desired end. It is important to make the distinction between pregnancy and parenthood; parenthood is rarely considered by the girls as part of the end, and the prospect of their appearance during pregnancy often contributes to a deteriorating situation.[18] Although in the short run becoming pregnant may seem to solve problems and conflicts, it may create them in the long run. When relations with her parents are unstable, a pregnancy may constitute proof that a girl is an adult; it may be a declaration of independence from parental interference or supervision; it may test her parents' love as well. When the home situation is unhappy or strained a pregnancy may allow her to leave home into the promised security of a marriage. The pregnancy may trap the partner into a more committed relationship or it may be used as an ego-booster to prove her femininity. Depending on the degree of fantasy bound up in a young woman's thinking, most of the above 'opportunities' usually backfire and become a heavier burden than the original problems.

Even where there is no lack of knowledge regarding contraceptive methods and there is little fear and embarrassment, some teenagers reject the non-prescription methods (foam and condom) because they are messy or inconvenient in that they interfere with both spontaneity and naturalness of coitus, or because they diminish tactile pleasure for both partners.

Although the author did not attend various clinics as a patient, it would seem that this stage, the assessment of need and delivery of service, varies minimally from clinic to clinic. The atmosphere and physical decor of the clinics, however, was vastly different. Some may be filled with comfortable old furniture that gives a home-like atmosphere, while others contain all the physical trappings of clinics, even to the extent of workers wearing white lab coats. While the importance of physical decor must not be overrated, it would seem to have an effect on a teenager's comfort in the facility. All clinics had pamphlets on contraception available, although Youth Clinical Services was the only facility that routinely gave out written information to those requesting the pill.

The rest of the procedure did not vary much from a clinician's perspective, in that routine questions were asked. Factors which must be considered are: (1) frequency of sexual relations, (2) development of individual, physically and emotionally (i.e. are there medical restrictions preventing her from utilizing oral contraceptives?), (3) her motivation for contraception. In doing contraceptive counselling among a group of abortion-repeaters it was found that motivation for pregnancy was so great that no amount of education or contraceptive availability would be successful.[19]

It is important that these services to adolescents be personal, individual, and not mechanical. This is a more difficult task than would appear, as many who come for service are anxious and withdrawn and not interested in providing more information than is required to get a prescription. A skilled worker in this situation *should* attempt to provide a non-threatening, trusting, accepting, supportive, and non-judgmental environment in order to allay anxieties and fears. A patient *should* be given the opportunity to gain insight into her behaviour, achieve some understanding of her own sexuality, and clarify the meaning of her interpersonal realtionships, including sexual intercourse. Most often clarification of the emotional and physical consequences of sexual behaviour is required as well.

Ultimately the patient and the doctor must select the most appropriate and effective method of contraceptive protection available. Of note, all interviewed commented that 90–95 per cent of those teenagers requesting birth control leave the clinic with a prescription for the pill. This is the most effective method, but are our clinics acting as pill dispensaries? While attempts are doubtless made to keep the service personal and individualized, clinics have the atmosphere of an assembly-line. A girl comes in, waits her turn, gives a brief medical and coital history, disrobes, puts on a gown, and sees the doctor, who, providing there are no medical complications, will most probably prescribe the pill. Someone will see her again for follow-up after the first three months. It is my impression that there is a preoccupation with the facts, methods, and mechanics almost to the exclusion of encouraging adolescents to examine the broader aspects of the situation (i.e., the impact of their changing sexual behaviour on individual lifestyle, relationship with the boyfriend, and relationship with the family). It appears that some practitioners are caught up in the dilemma of 'not wanting to lay something on a kid,' and 'not wanting to over-counsel,' so that the pendulum has in fact swung to the opposite extreme.

Doctors and other clinic workers are confronted by two more dilemmas: (1) By prescribing an effective contraceptive method are they not condoning the behaviour? (2) When working with a teenager less than sixteen years of age how should they handle the issues of parental consent and confidentiality?

Concerning the first issue, many physicians fear that complying with a teenager's request for contraception may make them party to sexual irresponsibility and promiscuity.[20] It seems to me, however, that most would provide the service rather than have a sexually active girl go away without it only to return pregnant. It is my impression that the feeling is 'They'll do it anyway, so they may as well be protected.'

Discussion of the second dilemma is a more complex matter as it affects doctors both legally and ethically. If doctors were obliged to withhold contraceptive

TABLE 1[21]

Provision of contraceptive information and prescriptions by 1,257 physicians
to minor patients with and without parental consent

Patient's age	% with consent		% without consent	
	GP	Gynecologist	GP	Gynecologist
12–14	19	25	4	3
15–17	40	54	11	16
18–19	58	70	42	56

supplies until parental consent was obtained, many young women would hesitate
to seek help. The Society for Adolescent Medicine has unanimously adopted a
statement that 'for a minor, parents' knowledge and consent are always preferable
but if denial of medical treatment due to lack of parental consent would expose
the patient or the community to risk, then self-consent should be allowed.'[22]
Minkler did a study in 1971 of 1,257 gynecologists and general practitioners to
establish what percentages would provide services with and without parental consent. It should be noted that a doctor's willingness varies proportionately with
the increase in age of the patient (Table 1).

IMPLICATIONS AND CONCLUSIONS

Research for this paper has made me acutely aware of several facts:
The high-risk group consists of those girls who date several times a week. A significant number use some form of birth control at some time, indicating some
knowledge of birth control and some desire to use contraception and avoid pregnancy.[23] However, many sexually active youth are not protecting themselves (at
all or effectively) against unwanted pregnancy. Females dominate the picture.
Little effort is made to include the male. We have a hit-and-miss approach to sex
education; in schools, at home, and from friends, and generally start education
too late. Hence many are misinformed and credulous of the common myths.
Some are ignorant of even the basic facts. Many are afraid and embarrassed of
the medical examination and of punitive, moralistic and preaching attitudes.
Teenagers stress the importance of sexual spontaneity. Girls have a subconscious
desire to become pregnant, feeling that the pregnancy will resolve conflict situations.

Our attention in the past has been focused on the consequences of engaging
in unprotected intercourse. We must become more preventative in our orientation. We must reach the sexually active teenagers much earlier. We must not

teach them just the mechanics of sex and methods of contraception but approach the issue from a far broader social perspective. We should establish many more out-reach programs and clinics for teenagers to reduce the stigma of seeking counselling. Males should be encouraged to take a more active role in selecting the contraceptive method. Almost without exception the man has not been discussed in the literature. It is essential that services be extended to parents; to make them sensitive to their adolescents' sexuality and sexual needs. They need to be encouraged to impress upon their children the realities of sex, to help them discern fiction from fact, and to treat sex as a healthy part of everyday life.

With changes as recommended above, time, and consistent efforts from many facets of society the teenage pregnancy rate could drop considerably. It is the author's feeling that the parents need as much help as the adolescents. Interestingly, at the Hospital for Sick Children and Toronto General Hospital the feeling is that 'Although we've never had better contraceptive methods or more information available we've never had less success' in preventing teenage pregnancy.[24]

NOTES

1 Larrick, N. and Merriam, E., *Male and Female under Eighteen*, p. 93. New York: Avon Books, 1973.

2 Wolfish, Dr M., 'Birth Control Counselling in an Adolescent Clinic,' *Canadian Medical Association Journal*, 105 (Oct. 1971), p. 750.

3 Hospital for Sick Children, Division of Adolescent Medicine, Report of Activities May 1, 1973 to April 30, 1974, p. 4.

4 Hopper, D., 'The Sex Gamble Backfires on Teens,' The *Toronto Star*, March 14, 1975, p. D-1.

5 Report, 1973, p. 3 (Note: The 1974 statistic would seem to emphasize the lack of preventative approach.)

6 Youth Clinical Services Activity Report, p. 11.

7 Interview with Pat Tyo, Youth Clinical Services, March 19, 1975.

8 Pistak, T., and Hamilton, D., *The Need for Family Planning Services*, p. 9. Toronto: Dept. of Public Health, Feb. 14, 1975.

9 Hopper, D., 'The Sex Gamble Back-fires on Teens,' p. D-1.

10 Yue, P., *A Comparative Study of Family Planning Services in Hospital Based Clinics and Community Health Clinics in Toronto*, p. 42. Thesis, School of Hygiene, University of Toronto, July 1974, pp. 92.

11 Pistak, T., and Hamilton, D., *The Need for Family Planning Services*, p. 11.

12 Minkowski, W.L. (M.D.) et al., 'Family Planning Services for Adolescents and Young Adults,' *The Western Journal of Medicine*, 120 (February 1974), 120.

13 N.G.H. Le Riche and T.W. Howard. *A Survey of Teen Age Sex Attitudes to Sex and Contraception in Kingston.* Kingston, Ont., 1974, p. 1.
14 Hopper, D., 'The Sex Gamble Back-fires on Teens,' p. D-1.
15 Pistak, T., and Hamilton, D., *The Need for Family Planning Services*, p. 11.
16 Hopper, p. D-1.
17 Katz, S. 'Sex Should Be a Rewarding Experience: Giving Girls Contraceptives without Counselling a Near Crime.' *Toronto Star*, no date.
18 Lowry, P., 'Unwanted Pregnancy – Why?,' p. 7.
19 Marinoff, S.C. 'Contraception in Adolescents,' *Pediatric Clinics of North America*, 19 (August 1972), p. 814.
20 Minkler, D.H., 'Fertility Regulation for Teenagers,' *Clinical Obstetrics and Gynecology*, 14 (June 1971), 424.
21 Minkler, p. 424.
22 Wolfish, M., 'Adolescent Sexuality,' *The Practitioner*, 210 (February 1973), p. 226.
23 Finkelstein, R., 'Program for the Sexually Active Teenager,' *Pediatric Clinics of North America*, 19 (August 1972), 792.
24 Hopper, D., 'The Sex Gamble Back-fires on Teens,' p. D-1.

JULES-H. GOURGUES AND RENÉE CLOUTIER

Sexuality, marital interaction and family planning in the low-income areas of urban Quebec*

This particular survey of low-income urban Quebec was effected principally in the interest of providing these areas with adequate services. In our view, family planning means much more than simply distributing literature and providing access to medical consultation; it also implies and depends upon the psychosocial values of couples and individuals. We therefore felt it essential, before dispensing services in a given area, to become aware of the importance that these groups accord to fertility, the family, and the couple. Approaching the problem in this fashion would, in our opinion, guarantee that these services could both meet the needs of the persons concerned and ensure that the consultations produce positive results.

METHODOLOGY

This research, begun under the auspices of the Centre de Planning Familial du Québec Inc., was continued, after this organization disappeared in 1972, by the Research Laboratory of the Department of Sociology at Laval University in Quebec City. The following is the *principal analytical hypothesis*: success in family planning depends upon the marital interaction of the couples interviewed. However, we deliberately refrained from constructing different typologies for marital interaction. As a first step, we conducted an in-depth study of certain factors pertinent to marital interaction: communication (1), power (2), family roles (3), and sexuality (4). Next (5), we compared these variables with others which have

*Translated by Mary E.B. Ricard. Unpublished.

proved and continue to prove enlightening about fertility. The first (6) of these particular sets of variables deals with the couples' fertility goals and with their concept of the child. A second set (7) summarizes the socio-economic components; a third (8) deals with both the couples' knowledge about family planning and their attitudes towards it (9).

The sample groups comprised 250 couples from low-income areas in six Quebec cities: Montreal (85), Quebec (40), Chicoutimi-Jonquière (38), Sherbrooke (37), Rimouski (25), and Val d'Or (25). The following criteria were used for selecting these couples: (i) one of the spouses had to have completed a maximum of seven years formal education, the other spouse, nine; (ii) the family income could not exceed $3,900.00 for a family with four or fewer children ($250.00 was permitted for each additional child); (iii) the couples had to have at least one child; (iv) they had to be fertile; (v) the couples had to have been married for more than three and less than twenty-two years; (vi) they both had to be French-Canadian.

In each of the six cities, we determined the poverty zones, retaining three couples per zone. Using a semistructured questionnaire, we carried out *individual interviews* lasting on the average two and a half hours. Our questionnaire was an adaptation of the one utilized by Reuben Hill, Kurt W. Back and J. Mayone Stycos in Puerto Rico, both during the exploratory phase and for validating data (10). These interviews took place in 1969-70.

The following is the *robot-portrait* of the couples interviewed: the two partners each have less than eight years formal schooling; they have been married ten years; they have four living children; the woman is thirty-one years old; the man thirty-four; the latter is occasionally or chronically unemployed; the family income is less than $3,900.00. Forty-five per cent of the women were married before age twenty; one out of three was pregnant at the time of the marriage; one out of two women gave birth to her first child before the end of the first year of marriage.

In this article, we shall discuss the work accomplished by two researchers in particular: Jules-H. Gourgues and Renée Cloutier-Cournoyer. The first paper seeks to elucidate the interactions existing between the family planning patterns in low-income areas and the couples' sex life; the second analyses the influence of marital interaction on these same patterns.

SEXUALITY AND FAMILY PLANNING IN LOW-INCOME URBAN AREAS

This study attempted initially to examine all the existing research on the subject, and then to present the main conclusions to be drawn and an interpretation of the most important practical hypotheses.

Some basic questions

In a broad fashion, this first study poses certain very pertinent questions:

1 Does it not seem somewhat incongruous to discuss family *planning* with low-income groups whose lifestyle for the most part is characterized by *a day-to-day* struggle to survive (occupational, marital, and financial instability) and who are guided by a mentality not at all preoccupied with long- or even short-term planning?

2 For individuals who are economically deprived, the child very often represents their sole 'asset,' the one value they have in common with people in other social strata. Should we not then be conscious of the fact that we are attacking something *sacred* when we seek to inform these groups about family planning?

3 If we consider that one of the main characteristics of this milieu is defeatism or a certain feeling of helplessness, that these people are often victims of the 'way things are' (shot gun weddings, limited dating ...), situations they are unable to control, does it not follow that suggesting they curb their fertility by regulating births pose very definite problems?

4 Since the family planning process is usually preceded by distinct stages such as meeting the eventual partner and engaging in sexual activity, does not the fact that many low-income couples manifest their fertility or have their first child without ever having had the time to live through these preparatory stages present very particular problems?

5 Since, in this particular milieu, both fertility and child-bearing are frequently considered as symbols of *virility* or proof of *femininity* or maternal aptitudes, does it not follow that understanding attitudes toward sexuality in general is the key to successful family planning?

6 Since sexuality in low-income areas is reputed to be a taboo subject which couples find difficult to discuss with one another, does it not seem highly doubtful that these people would resort to family planning in the hope of increased sexual fulfilment?

Some hard and fast traditional attitudes

The first section of the empirical research seeks to describe the main characteristics of the attitudes and sexual patterns encountered in this milieu. The following is a brief summary of the conclusions that were drawn:

1 It was observed that views on premarital sexuality seemed to be coloured by sexist attitudes: 71 per cent of the men and 77 per cent of the women feel that the ideal way for a young woman to behave sexually is to refuse 'to give in.' Not a single married man and scarcely any of the married women questioned (0.7%) believe that the young woman should behave in the same way as the young man. Since it is the young woman's responsibility to refuse sexual activity (38 women

as opposed to one man), it follows that the sexual initiative is considered to be male-oriented, thus making the male's refusal unlikely. Moreover, restrictions on premarital sexuality are most often motivated by fear, moral objections, or human respect and not by consideration for the partner or by autonomous choice. Although a large number of couples (3 out of 4) feel that virginity is important because they fear the possible repercussions (40%), those who did not engage in premarital intercourse (52-57%) abstained for the most part because of moral objections (37%).

2 Marital attitudes towards sex remained segregative: 52 per cent of the wives interviewed consider that their husband's role as the breadwinner is most worthy of note, and only 28 per cent his role as an 'excellent lover,' whereas 82 per cent of the men most appreciate their wives as 'good mothers' and only 6 per cent as 'excellent mistresses.' Moreover, such obligations as physically attracting the opposite sex, remaining faithful to one's partner, and refusing to engage in intercourse are incumbent on the woman alone. Finally, when asked to comment upon the equality of the pleasure experienced during intercourse, three wives and two husbands out of ten feel that the man should be privileged in this respect.

A marked lack of sexual knowledge
Couples and particularly wives were shown to be singularly lacking in sexual knowledge. Might not this phenomenon countervail seeking more satisfying sexual relations through the use of efficacious family planning methods?

1 When asked to comment on their knowledge of the opposite sex at the time of marriage, 80 per cent of the wives and 68 per cent of the husbands admitted that they knew 'very little' or 'nothing at all.' Of the wives 65 per cent state that before they married they never once discussed sex with their future husband. In answer to the very basic question 'When you were married, did you know how to have children?,' one man out of ten replied in the negative, as did four women out of ten.

2 Although this study does go back several years, knowledge of birth control methods also seems quite limited: 73 per cent of the wives and 54 per cent of the husbands admit knowing nothing about family planning; 10 per cent and 22 per cent, respectively, affirm knowing 'very little' about the subject.

Patterns consistent with sexual attitudes and knowledge
With respect to both premarital and marital patterns pertinent to sexual satisfaction, certain conclusions seem to follow logically from the attitudes and level of knowledge discussed above.

1 First and foremost, premarital sexual patterns can be observed in a clearly characteristic context and form: 45 per cent of the couples interviewed kept

company less than one year; one woman out of five was married before age eighteen and two to three out of five, before twenty; 33 per cent of the couples had their first child before the ninth month of marriage; 26 per cent of the wives had several relationships with other men before marriage, whereas 45 per cent of the men had other female companions; 51 per cent of the men and only 6 per cent of the women had had premarital sex with a partner other than their present spouse; 30 per cent of the men and 54 per cent of the women reacted negatively the first time they experienced intercourse; the initiative or request rarely came from the woman, (1%) and the atmosphere that reigned seemed somewhat less than relaxed in that 67 per cent of the women and 47 per cent of the men admit that neither partner was naked on this occasion.

2 Moreover, the data on marital sex patterns suggest that the wedding night in no way corresponded to the accepted notion of 'sublime moments of marital love': only 65 per cent of the couples had intercourse on their wedding night, and 13 per cent of the women and 7 per cent of the men admit that they were disappointed; only one couple in five speaks of having had a satisfying experience on this occasion. However, at the time of the survey, 95 per cent of the women and 97 per cent of the men have sexual relations as often as four to eleven times a month for the majority. Of the women 58 per cent and 71 per cent of the men state that they never refuse to engage in intercourse, whereas 39 per cent of the women and 28 per cent of the men refuse occasionally, often, or rarely. Finally, with respect to sexual satisfaction, 77 per cent of the women and 85 per cent of the men say they are happy with their sex life, while 21 per cent and 13 per cent respectively tolerate it at best, and 2 per cent of the couples interviewed find sex loathesome.

Factors conditioning the efficacy of the
family planning practices of low-income couples
The second part of the research goes beyond the range of descriptive data in an effort to relate the diverse variables existing therein, and thus find an answer to this question: which of the following factors most influence efficacious family planning practices: religion, social class, age, or the number of years of marriage?

1 A close look at sexual mores reveals that these are above all a function of masculine socio-economic characteristics (poverty level, religion, and level of formal education), and that these characteristics are manifested from the very start of the relationship even if the man practises his religion in a very detached fashion.

2 However, with respect to sexual knowledge, the woman exercises a greater influence than her partner, and this influence is all the more important if the partners were very young at the time of marriage and if they have been married for several years.

3 Confirming the results of other researchers, the data relative to sexual patterns and the level of satisfaction are linked in a positive way to the husband's job stability. Whether or not the husband practises his religion is also an important factor. A correlation may be traced between a husband's strong religious adherence and the appearance of terms such as 'embarrassment' and 'shame' to describe reactions to the first sexual encounter. Lastly, age at the time of marriage is also an important consideration: for the husbands, the younger the wife the first time the couple had intercourse, the more they experienced guilt feelings. On the other hand, the older the wife at the time of marriage, the less satisfying the couples' present sex life; conversely, if the husband was quite young at the time the couple married, their present sexual relationship is better.

4 Knowledge about family planning is linked in a positive way to both the level of formal education of the two spouses and to the husband's job stability, but negatively to a strong religious adherence on the husband's part.

5 Finally, the husband's job stability and his religious affiliation are significantly related to the efficacy of family planning, the former in positive way, the latter negatively.

The full process of family planning
as an evolutionary factor of personality development

The last part of this research seeks to establish that operational family planning can be considered a complete process with respect to personality development. The following are the seven stages of this process:

1 forming attitudes about sex;
2 acquiring knowledge about sex;
3 engaging in sexual activity and experiencing a level of satisfaction;
4 forming a concept of the child;
5 developing attitudes towards family planning;
6 acquiring knowledge about family planning;
7 utilizing contraceptive methods and establishing the efficacy of these methods.

Very briefly then, this last section establishes the important influence of the first, second, and sixth stages of the process: forming attitudes towards sex and acquiring knowledge about sex and birth control. Furthermore, since the concept of the child and the level of sexual satisfaction has a very limited impact, we have substituted marital satisfaction for these two. variables, as it appears much more important.

Some conclusions

The following are the principal conclusions to be drawn:

1 This study also confirms that among low-income couples living in an urban setting, 'not being parents' is planned much more often than 'being parents.'

2 Here in Quebec totally deprived couples (at physical, social, financial, psychological levels) also seem the least able to plan their families properly and are therefore more likely to have many children.

3 As for the active role of each spouse within the family unit, it appears that although the man, in this particular social setting, has little contact with the child's day-to-day needs, he readily takes the initiative, and with little or no assistance from his wife, makes all the major decisions concerning the family.

4 In this milieu, motives for family planning are developed only over a protracted length of time and after numerous births.

5 Since the family planning process seems to involve much more than 'simple medical or technical acts,' it seems essential to confront the psychosocial aspects, such as the integration of psychosocial consultation within the framework of the services dispensed, if these groups are to control their families efficiently.

6 The nature of the family planning process and the mentality common to low-income couples seem to indicate that these services should be offered to the couple and not just to the wife.

7 The following are seen as necessary conditions for providing effectual services: (a) these services must go further than the 'pre-prescription contraceptive' and must deal also with the 'post-prescription contraceptive stage'; (b) a complete psychomedical record of each couple's fertility should be kept; this record would deal with every aspect of fertility, tracing the evolution of the woman from the menarche on, and that of the couple right to the end of their fertility cycle; (c) if we want to contact the couple before it is too late, that is, when they already have one or two unwanted children, we must be able to intervene preventitively by providing the young people of this particular milieu with all the necessary information about birth control. Ideally, we should attempt to intervene before they have begun an active sex life and while they are still in school, the last structured setting where they can be contacted.

8 Survival before planning: finally, it seems essential that the family planning services dispensed in low-income areas be motivated by and based on the couple's daily psychosocial experiences and not solely on external preoccupations which are often foreign to their everyday life, such as concern for global overpopulation.

MARITAL INTERACTION AND FAMILY PLANNING

Existing structural-functional theories as well as theories on interaction with respect to family sociology helped us to define initially and regard the married couple as an association capable of making decisions and acting upon these. The married couple is considered here as a task group whose main responsibility is to control its fertility as it sees fit. If the married couple is to form an efficient task group, certain conditions must be met; and in our view, these lie mainly at the level of marital interaction. We shall begin by a summary of the most important factors linked to family planning: fertility goals, socio-economic variables, attitudes towards and knowledge of contraceptive methods, and marital interaction. The last part of this research attempts to point out how marital interaction exerts a greater predictive influence on this area than the other variables.

The family planning patterns
The following ten indicators showed the different manifestations of family planning: the period when contraceptive practices were initiated; the degree of non-recourse to contraception before the pregnancies; the efficacy of the methods utilized; the nature of the birth control methods employed since the birth of the last child; the regularity of these methods; their duration; the recognition of the fertility goals of both the men and the women; the couple's success in attaining their fertility goals; and the number of pregnancies. Firstly, we linked these variables to one another and in the succeeding sections we viewed them as dependent variables.

The results show a distinction between the periods before and after 1969-70. Before 1969-70, it is clear that there was very little successful planning:
1 Two-thirds of the pregnancies were not planned, and only one-fourth of the planned pregnancies were successful, if we consider those cases where birth control was discontinued so that the couple could conceive.
2 Only seven per cent of the couples successfully planned the pregnancies *together.*
3 During the period preceding 1969-70, the methods most often utilized before the pregnancies were rhythm (Ogino) method and coïtus interruptus (withdrawal).
4 Only one-fourth of the couples interviewed used contraceptives after marriage or after the first pregnancy.
5 The couples interviewed did not indicate a rise in the Quebec standards in planning for the women who had been interviewed three, four, eight, or nine years earlier (11). These low-income couples are planning births less than ever and are failing in their planning efforts even more than American women interviewed fourteen years earlier (12); and this phenomenon holds true with respect to the American sampling even if we consider only the Catholic population.

However, 1969-70 marked a turning-point:
1 In 1969-70, at the time of the interviews, with an average of four living children, 86 per cent of the couples are using a contraceptive, and among this group 49.5 per cent of the women are taking oral contraceptives; 18.9 per cent of the couples are practising coïtus interruptus and 5.3 per cent of the women have been fitted with intrauterine devices.

2 A greater number (18.9%) of couples in our sample group practise coïtus interruptus, and a lesser number (13.8%), periodic abstinence, than did married Quebec women under sixty-five in 1971 (13) (8.1%–34.4%). The 'male withdrawal method' is apparently still practised in the low-income milieu of Quebec. This is our first indication of the importance of male participation in family planning.

3 Those couples who best succeeded in controlling their fertility in the past and, at the present time utilize 'natural' methods and not oral contraceptives.

4 The duration of contraceptive practices from the birth of the last child on, as well as from the moment when the couple first used a contraceptive appear to be the two most pertinent indicators for predicting the family planning patterns of the population under scrutiny.

5 The earlier the couples began to control and plan their fertility (from the start of their married life or after the first pregnancy), the greater their tendency to continue to control the number of children born. Past experience in family planning is thus linked to the couple's ultimate satisfaction with the size of their family.

Fertility goals
With respect to the importance of the number of children:

1 For these couples, four children represent the ideal family. Nevertheless 30 per cent of the couples interviewed consider that a family of five or more children is the ideal.

2 The number of children is important for the couples. They place great stock in a large family. However, when they consider their economic situation, 39 per cent of the men and 35 per cent of the women feel that they have one or several children too many.

3 In general, the couples interviewed value the large family much more than both the other low-income groups questioned sixteen years earlier (14), and than the married Quebec women in every social stratum (15).

4 At the start of their married life, 62 per cent of the men and 46 per cent of the women had given no thought to the number of children they wanted.

5 Before the birth of their first child, 63 per cent of the couples had not discussed the number of children they wanted to have.

6 At the time of the survey, the majority of the couples are unable to predict exactly the number of children desired by the partner. In general, one of the spouses overestimates the aspirations of the other, whereas the other tends to underestimate these aspirations.

7 The couples' fertility goals are influential factors especially with respect to both the time the couple first used a contraceptive and the realization of their fertility goals and thus the size of their family.

8 Among the thirty-two variables linked to the manifestations of family planning considered here, the most important seems to be the couples' satisfaction with respect to the desired number of children.

Moreover, it appears that the couple frequently perceives the child as a unifying element in their marriage: The majority of the couples see themselves in their children (narcissistic conception) or else they consider them as instruments for guaranteeing familial stability, joy, and harmony. Only one-fourth of the couples consider the child in an altruistic fashion, as a separate entity.

The socio-economic components
1 The woman's age at the time of marriage, whether or not she was pregnant, and the frequency of her religious practice scarcely influence family planning patterns.
2 Among the fifteen variables considered, the two we feel to be the most important are the number of living children, and whether or not the man is gainfully employed.
3 The man's participation in the working population is a determining factor in both active contraceptive practices and a greater probability of efficacious and early family planning; his non-participation in the working force is accompanied by the absence of contraceptive practices or a later recourse to these practices.
4 For the most part, the young couples were unable to plan efficaciously their past pregnancies. However, they differ from their elders in that they utilize contraceptives much earlier in order to hinder their fertility. Considering the predictive importance of the variable of the time the couple first used a contraceptive we can conclude that family planning is an irreversible phenomenon in low-income urban areas.

Knowledge of and attitudes towards contraceptives
1 Knowledge about contraceptives was mainly acquired after marriage: 52 per cent of the women and 20 per cent of the men were ignorant of all methods before marriage.
2 Even at the time of the interviews in 1969-70, knowledge about contraceptives was slight. The only methods sufficiently well known to be used correctly are, by order of importance: (for women) oral contraceptives, coïtus interruptus, and the condom; (for men) the condom, coïtus interruptus, abstinence, and oral contraceptives.
3 The man, as is the case with the woman, does not necessarily share his knowledge with his partner.
4 The majority of the couples and especially those who have less frequently used contraceptives in the past, want to see family planning clinics established and patronized.

5 Only one-third of the couples consider that family planning should concern both the partners. Moreover, half of these couples do not agree with one another on this issue, one partner stating that this responsibility lies with the couple, the other, that only the woman is implicated.

6 Less than one per cent (0.7%) give moral or religious reasons for justifying or forbidding contraception.

7 The extent of the couples' knowledge about contraceptive methods is one of the factors directly influencing the failure or success of family planning during the period before the interviews took place. Other important factors are the regularity and the duration of their use after the birth of the last child.

8 The couples' attitude towards birth control is one of the factors responsible for the type of contraception used at the time of the interviews and also influences the extent to which the partners realize their fertility goals.

9 With respect to family planning, the man's knowledge about contraception wields a greater influence than the woman's.

Marital interaction

1 The two partners do not perceive their union in the same way: 42 per cent of the women and 72 per cent of the men state that they frequently discuss family planning with their spouse. Of the women 45 per cent compared to 28 per cent of the men feel that the woman alone attends to domestic tasks; 42 per cent of the men and 29 per cent of the women hold that, in general, this is also the man's domain.

2 On the whole, the couples are satisfied with their sexual, sentimental, marital, and parental relations, the woman manifesting a greater degree of dissatisfaction than the man at any of these levels.

3 The men and women who are satisfied are not necessarily members of the same couple; for one-third of the couples, one of the partners claims to be satisfied, the other dissatisfied.

4 Among the factors considered, verbal communication within the couple is the variable most often associated with the divers manifestations of family planning. The clarity with which the couple perceive one another with respect to different areas of interest and particularly fertility goals is an equally important variable for predicting the realization of these goals, in addition to the number of pregnancies and the efficacy of family planning.

5 The frequency of sexual activity seems more important than sexual satisfaction with respect to family planning patterns.

6 The thirty-five variables considered as factors of marital interaction appeared much less important than foreseen, at least insofar as they are directly linked to one or other of the ten family planning variables.

However, marital interaction does influence the determination of family planning patterns after the birth of the last child. These different factors of marital interaction are also closely linked to one another.

Marital interaction: the best predictive factor?
Our results reveal that the variables pertinent to marital interaction utilized in this research do not appear to be the sole factors for predicting all of the fertility patterns; other variables must also be considered (socio-economic variables; fertility goals, the knowledge about and the attitudes towards contraception of the women, the men, or the couples).

However, these same results do show that none of the three other sets of variables considered (socio-economic, fertility goals, knowledge of family planning methods, and attitudes towards these) can alone predict all of the following family planning patterns: the time when the couple first practised contraception, the level of non-use of contraceptives, the efficacy of family planning, the type of method in use at the time of the interviews, the regularity and duration of the use of these methods, the realization of masculine and feminine fertility goals, the couples' agreement or conformity with respect to these goals and the number of pregnancies.

The data also show that the marital and familial reality is complex as is the concept of family planning. We have also discovered that the same independent variables do not necessarily affect each of the ten family planning variables. For example, the *subjective* knowledge (attitude) more often determines the type of method(s) employed after the birth of the last child, whereas the *objective* knowledge is usually associated with the regularity and the duration of the use of contraceptives over the same period of time. Moreover, the different sets of independent variables do not affect to the same extent all the family planning variables. As an illustration of this, certain variables at the level of the fertility goals seem more closely linked to the time when the couple first practised contraception, whereas the knowledge about and the attitudes towards contraception are usually associated with the type of method(s) used after the birth of the last child.

Our results underline the importance of considering marital interaction as one of the factors which predict the processes of family planning. We mentioned earlier that the *duration* of the use of a contraceptive method after the birth of the last child was the most reliable variable in terms of predicting the patterns of family planning. Among the four sets of variables, our statistical package selected marital interaction as having the greatest influence on this variable. The same is true for the regularity of the use of contraception during this same period. Marital interaction is second in importance after the knowledge about and attitudes towards contraception, with respect to its impact on the type of method(s) utilized after the birth of the last child.

Were we to retain only the variables most reliable for prediction, that is the duration of use of contraceptives since the birth of the last child, we could verify our theoretical affirmations on the feasibility of considering the married couple as a task group. Thus the conclusions to be drawn from this variable are fairly numerous: it is important not only to have an idea of the number of children desired, but above all to appreciate the full significance of limiting one's fertility because desired goals have been achieved and not because there are exterior pressures such as finances. Acquiring objective rather than subjective knowledge is also important and so is verbal communication about various subjects including family planning. It is also essential that the two partners discuss their fertility goals at the very beginning of their married life. We can also see how important it is that the man participate in the work force. As we have observed in the preceding sections, these different characteristics apply to only a minority within our sampling. Must we therefore conclude that low-income couples are doomed to experience only failure and disillusion in their attempts at family planning?

Finally, our data confirm the man's importance at the level of the active roles (breadwinner, definer of fertility goals, possessor of knowledge about family planning), and that of the woman with respect to the expressive roles (marital interaction).

We would like to conclude by emphasizing the man's dominant influence in family planning. This influence has come to the fore at every stage of our research. This is an important observation in terms of how we will be able to intervene and assist this particular group. It is abundantly clear that the man must play a vital role in our twofold effort: to teach these couples about family planning and to actively help them control their fertility by organizing and furnishing the appropriate services.

NOTES

1 Boivin, Michaeline, *Communication conjugale et planification des naissances en milieu défavorisé urbain québecois*, Laboratoire de Recherches sociologiques, Département de sociologie, Université Laval, Québec, 1973, cahier 1, 372 pp.

2 Angers, Maurice, *Pouvoir dans la famille et planification des naissances en milieu défavorisé urbain québecois*, Laboratoire de Recherches sociologiques, Département de sociologie, Université Laval, Québec, 1973, cahier 4, 509 pp.

3 Paquette, Lucie, *Rôles familiaux et planification des naissances en milieu défavorisé urbain québecois*, Laboratoire de Recherches sociologiques, Université Laval, Québec, 1974, cahier 5, 313 pp.

4 Gourgues, Jules-H., *Sexualité et planification des naissances en milieu défavorisé urbain québecois*, Laboratoire de Recherches sociologiques, Département de sociologie, Université Laval, Québec, 1974, cahier 6, 631 pp.

5 Cloutier-Cournoyer, Renée, *Interaction conjugale et planification des naissances en milieu défavorisé urbain québecois*, Laboratoire de Recherches sociologiques, Département de sociologie, Université Laval, Québec, 1974, cahier 7, 725 pp.

6 21 different indicators providing a total of 42 variables according to whether the same indicator was examined from the feminine, masculine or marital standpoint.

7 16 different indicators for a total of 32 variables.

8 13 different indicators for a total of 15 variables.

9 16 different indicators for a total of 32 variables.

10 Stycos, J. Mayone, *Family and Fertility in Puerto Rico, A Study of the Lower Income Group*, New York: Columbia University Press, 1955.
Hill, Reuben, J. Mayone Stycos, Kurt W. Back, *The Family and Population Control, A Porto Rican Experiment in Social Change*, Chapel Hill, The University of North Carolina Press, 1959.

11 Carisse, Colette, *Planification des naissances en milieu canadien-français*, Montréal, Les Presses de l'Université de Montréal, 1964.
Cloutier-Cournoyer, Renée, *Théorie du développement, aspirations féminines et comportements contraceptifs*, thèse de maîtrise, Département de Sociologie Université de Montréal, 1970.

12 Freedman, Ronald, Pascal K. Whelpton, Arthur A. Campbell, *Family Planning Sterility and Population Growth*, McGraw-Hill Book Company Inc., New York, Toronto, London, 1959.

13 Henripin, Jacques, Evelyne Lapierre-Adamcyk, *La fin de la revanche des berceaux: qu'en pensent les Québécoises?*, Montréal, Les Presses de l'Université de Montréal, 1974.

14 Hill, Back, and Stycos.

15 Henripin and Lapierre-Adamcyk.

KATHLEEN BELANGER

Family planning and 'the poor'*

To continue to believe and perpetuate the myth supported by many writers and family planning 'experts,' that proliferation of family planning clinics will entice 'The Poor' to limit their families so that a salubrious intervention in the poverty cycle will occur, is to minimize and oversimplify seriously the facts of poverty, to misunderstand its causes, results and inevitably related and pervasive life style, and to discredit poor people themselves on the basis of wrong information.

Two of the most glaring pieces of wrong information on which service planning continues to be based are, first, that poor people have more children than other people, and second, that they would rush automatically through the doors of family planning clinics if only the proper public relations and 'outreach' techniques could be devised to encourage them.

The value judgments implicit in this generally accepted piece of misinformation have served to obscure and, in a sense, deny the facts of poverty and its roots and have resulted in the continuation and spread not only of family planning clinics, but other health and social services subliminally wrought to meet the needs of the middle-class patient and the views of the middle-class professional.

The first phase of a medical-social study of women attending Vancouver family planning clinics and a control group not attending revealed that poor people do not go to family planning clinics. The last phase of the study revealed that they do not want to go.

At the time of the study, the population served by the clinics (a trend which has since increased) was mainly upper-middle class. Most of the patients turned

*Reprinted from *The Social Worker* 42 (Summer 1974), 15-20.

out to be unmarried university students. The women attending the clinics were not at risk for unplanned or unwanted pregnancy and their counterparts in the community control who were at risk were few. The risks related to conflict involved in attitudes toward pre-marital sexuality, fear of approaching a known or unknown private physician with a request that might be denied, and minor, probably transient difficulties in self-definition.

While this first phase of the study was enlightening about changes in middle-class sexual mores and the risks arising from them, it threw no light whatever on the possible credibility of the original hypothesis which, viewed retrospectively, was both fatuous and naive – 'Contraception provides the community with an essential and powerful tool to interrupt the vicious cycle of poverty, family disorganization, and ill health.' Almost no evidence of family disorganization, ill health, poverty, or risk for unplanned pregnancy was found among women attending family planning clinics or in the matching community sample. Therefore, if the study was to proceed with any validity, either the hypothesis had to be changed, or the population.

Two further groups of women were studied – women of child-bearing age who were receiving social assistance, or living in publicly subsidized housing, or both; and a group of young women, married to working-class men, who were attending child clinics.

The wives of working-class men, like the university students were found to be an extremely low-risk group for unplanned or unwanted pregnancy. Although less intellectual by far than the university women, they were even more planful, goal-directed, and future-oriented. They were so much in control of their own lives (often to the exclusion of the opinions of the husband) and had such firm ideas about the direction they intended their lives to take, that they could be expected to translate these ideas into rigid practice. Consistently upward-striving, they knew exactly how many children they wanted, when they wanted to have them, and under what conditions. They diverged from the university women mainly when it came to the number of children they wanted – fewer.

The poor women placed no value on their own opinions, perceived themselves as having minimal control over their own lives, were apprehensive about planning for either today or tomorrow ('Nothing ever works out anyway'), saw the formulation of goals as useless because achievement would be impossible, and were, at most times, subjected to the doubtful mercy of the men upon whom they depended or hoped to depend – men who looked upon them as sexual conveniences and who had concomitantly low operating commitments to any women, or to family life. Unused to ordinary decision-making, for themselves or in conjunction with others, pregnancies, like everything else, 'just happened' to them.

While these women were not as high-risk a group at the time of the study as they had been earlier, the contraceptive protection they were now giving themselves, or the birth control procedures they had undergone (over 10 per cent of the women in a group whose mean age was 27.4 years had been sterilized for medical or birth control reasons), had been an after-the-fact phenomenon. Pre-maritally or in the early years of marriage they had been unprotected either by themselves or their partners.

In spite of this lack of protection the number of living children they had brought to term or who had survived after birth was lower (2.68) than the 'ideal' family size projected by the middle-class, clinic-attending women (3.4). Their rate of pregnancy, however, was higher than for the other married women studied. Pre-maritally, this rate was .694 as compared to .228 for women attending the family planning clinics, .185 for the women in the community control group, and .137 for the wives of working-class men. And even though the mean age of the group of poor women was only about three years older than the mean age of the wives of working-class men, their rate of stillbirth or child mortality was five times greater, the number of abortions was triple, and miscarriages were nine times more frequent.

The poor women, then, had been a high-risk group for unwanted, unplanned pregnancy, but more important still, they had been a seriously high-risk group for pregnancies injurious to the health of mother and child. They could not be singled out, however, as 'over-producers' of living children as some of the least perceptive of the 'population' writers continue so carelessly to label them.

What were the factors contributing to the high rate of pregnancy risk found among these women? The characteristics that sharply separated them from most of the other women studied fell naturally into four groupings, with each subdivision as descriptive of the causes of poverty as of risks for unplanned or unwanted pregnancy:

1 Early parental influences
a) Low educational and occupational level attained by both parents.
b) Lack of value placed by parents on educational goals.
c) Lack of understanding by parents of a child's need for emotional support.
d) Poor communication between family members.
e) Low level of commitment to the family by the male partner.
f) High degree of mobility.
g) High incidence of parental death, family disorganization, and breakdown.

2 Influences just prior to or surrounding the beginning of sexual activity
a) Poor scholastic performance.

b) Lack of social comfort in school; feeling of not belonging, of being 'different' from others.
c) Early school leaving.
d) Poor self-image; need to be 'popular.'
e) Lack of self-confidence and self-protectiveness.
f) Poorly paid, low-status occupation, frequent unemployment.
g) Early beginning of sexual activity.
h) Early marriage.
i) Lack of knowledge of ordinary body functions and the physiology of sexuality.
j) Lack of knowledge of contraception.

3 Continuing influences following the start of sexual activity and/or marriage
a) Low occupational level of self and partner, few skills, low income.
b) Poor self-image.
c) Lack of self-confidence and self-protectiveness.
d) Low level of goal-directedness.
e) Low level of verbal skill.
f) High level of distractability.
g) Fear of 'supervisors' and 'superiors.'
h) Difficulty in recall of advice and directions.
i) High level of anxiety, tension, depression, sensitivity, somaticization.
j) Unexpressed hostility, resentment.
k) Distrust of planning.
l) Poor organizational ability.
m) Feelings of hopelessness and despair of achievement, goals, hopes, ambitions rarely perceived, poorly articulated.
n) Lack of hope for children.
o) Frequent illness without definable disease.
p) Lack of knowledge of bodily functioning and the physiology of sexuality.

4 Family supports
a) Few supports from either primary or secondary family.
b) Minimal satisfaction in family life and its tasks.
c) Most decisions made by male partner; joint decision-making rare.
d) Lack of shared interests, little recreation.
e) Depersonalization of the female by the male partner, along with his low investment in family life and minimal interest in living children.
f) Masculine and feminine roles perceived as maintained and strengthened by evidence of virility and pregnancy.
g) Male partner rejecting of, frequently abusive to, the pregnant female.

h) Ambivalence of the female toward the male partner (reliance – lack of trust)

5 Community supports
a) Friendship ties with same sex stronger than other relationships for both male and female.
b) Family physician perceived by the woman as almost the sole community support as well as husband-father surrogate. Physician frequently consulted but communication often poor; woman unable to articulate or have understood her underlying concerns.
c) Public health services not known or viewed as a resource.
d) Public welfare services well known but seen as a resource for financial assistance only – otherwise seen as coercive, suspicious, untrustworthy.
e) Famiy planning clinics rejected as unnecessary (reliance on private physician).

All of this information, which was compiled through the use of two questionnaires (one to collect medical data, the other to obtain social data), and the additional administration of two Scales, led to the conclusion that the life style of the poor is inimical to planned parenthood.

Much more evocative than research results are the words used by the women themselves to describe the maimed nature of their lives, the demands made upon them, their vulnerability, and their lack of practice on defining or defending themselves.

'The last time I got pregnant was when somebody stole my pills. I'm always worrying about getting pregnant. I never enjoyed sex with my husband much except when he wasn't drunk. It's a bit better with the boyfriend I have now. I don't know what he'll do if I get pregnant. We never talk about it. We never talk about anything much. He just sort of comes and goes.'

'I don't have any ideas of my own. I don't talk very well. It's been like that all my life. When I was in school, I felt I didn't have the right clothes or the proper words to explain myself. I felt strange and out of things. My husband and I started having sex when I was in Grade VII. Then I quit school and we were mostly with each other. I don't really like sex much, but it means a lot to him. If he's not working he wants it two or three times a day. What can you do?'

'Maybe if I get pregnant he'll marry me. I'm sick of living this way. I'm not all that crazy about him, but he's a man and you have to have somebody. I don't like using the pill anyway, it causes deformed children. I worry about getting pregnant all the time. What if he doesn't marry me? But I'd never have any boyfriends if I didn't do what they wanted.'

'What's the use of planning anything, nothing ever works out anyway. I can never remember whether I took the pill or not. I try not to forget, but I've got so much on my mind with my husband out of work and everybody sick all the time and not enough money for food. I hate being pregnant. I'm sick the whole time. I'm sorry this place is such a mess. I haven't swept the floor for weeks. Did I tell you I had a miscarriage day before yesterday? I wish I didn't feel so *flat* all the time. The kids are the only decent thing I've got. Maybe they'll have a better chance than I had - but it doesn't look like they're going to, the way things are.'

'He used to say a pregnant women was the most beautiful sight in the world. It was the doctor who made me go on the pill after the last two miscarriages. My husband got suspicious so I told him they were thyroid pills. When I stopped getting pregnant he thought there was something wrong with *him*. Now he's living with somebody else.'

'He keeps trying to persuade me to take out my I.U.D. He thinks if I get pregnant again I won't want a divorce. Maybe he's right. The only time I'm happy is when I'm pregnant. Even if I'm clumsy-looking I feel smug. "Hey!" I feel like shouting, "Look at me! There's life inside me! I count for something!"'

To enlarge the role of the already harried and often untrained public welfare worker to include contraceptive counselling, as suggested in some quarters, would be to legitimize the prevailing community and professional fantasy that women on social assistance would be eager to discuss intimate personal concerns with their financial benefactors, if only caseloads were not so overwhelming, and to confirm for poor people forever what they believe already, that the public welfare worker is intent on equating eligibility for financial assistance with moral worth.

Poor people now see themselves as victimized by the public welfare system; to destroy their last semblance of privacy by adjuring them to limit the size of their families, no matter how carefully couched the admonitions, would be to convince them that control of their own lives is truly lost to them. Emphasis might more suitably and effectively be placed upon inclusion of sequences on the medical and social facts of poverty in the curricula of medical schools.

What the poor women wanted from community agencies unconnected with the public welfare system was for attention to be paid - not to their contraceptive needs, or their medical needs - but *to their social deprivation.* 'Birth control is the *last* thing I'd discuss with that welfare visitor who comes around here. I guess I have a right to *some* privacy. And anyway, only the doctor knows about things like that. If she *really* wanted to help me, she could teach me how to be a better housekeeper and mother to my kids. My mother never taught me anything.'

Although their knowledge of bodily functioning was extremely poor, most of these women, at the time of interview, had adequate knowledge of at least one effective method of contraception. The continuing risks for unplanned, unwanted, or injurious pregnancy arose, not out of lack of knowledge, but out of feelings of hopelessness, of being overwhelmed by the onslaughts of their daily lives, out of loneliness, distractedness, despair, depersonalization. They 'forgot' the pill, or, in order to please the men in their lives, they were afraid to resist any demand made upon them. Some needed, rather than wanted, to become pregnant; for many of these women pregnancy was the only means they had of self-fulfilment and self-definition.

To provide more contraceptive services as they are now constituted and projected would not lure them into family planning, particularly since their needs as they quite properly saw them, had nothing whatever to do with contraceptive services. Moreover, each had a private physician who was often the only repository of her trust. Even when a woman was inarticulate with her physician, or he misunderstood what she tried to tell him, or she neglected out of fear and reticence to tell him about the exigencies of her life style, she was sure he cared more about her than anyone else did, wanted to help her, and eventually would help her even more than he had up to now, if only he were not 'so busy.' 'The Welfare isn't any help to me. My worker is a man about twenty. What does he know about bringing up kids, buying food - things like that? I can't even cook - did I tell you that? None of my foster mothers would let me learn. The training school used hired cooks - they didn't want kids messing around in the kitchen. Don't they have some kind of service to help women like me get along better?'

Once given the opportunity to express their needs, they quite clearly knew what they were, but, with the exception of a very few women who were receiving sustained social services through a family service agency or a mental health clinic, they did not know where to turn for help.

The only poor women who had become effective in their use of contraception were those who had finally entered into stable marriages with kindly men and those enrolled in a particular opportunities program who were now facing the future with some hope. For them, planning had acquired a purpose and credibility, goals were seen as achievable, there was satisfaction in the performance of daily tasks and a growing sense of personal worth and fulfilment.

They did not need, any longer, to become pregnant to survive as human beings; they did not have to acquiesce, submit, deny their sense of self. They saw themselves, most of them for the first time, as having some control over their own lives.

BENJAMIN SCHLESINGER AND RICHARD ALBERT MULLEN

Sexuality and the aged:
taboos and misconceptions must give way to reality*

INTRODUCTION

The 1971 Census of Canada indicated that among our total population of 21,568,310 people, 8 per cent were over the age of 65 years. This constituted 1,744,405 persons (781,865 male and 962,540 female).

We hear today a lot about pensions, senior citizens' power groups, Horizon projects for the aged, but very little about 'sexuality for the aged.'

In this report we do not set out to determine whether or not there is sexual life during later years. Masters and Johnson, David Reuben and others have convincingly established that there is sexuality in the later years. We set out to report their findings against a background of some of society's current myths and misconceptions to give a picture of sex in the later years. For purposes of clarity, the later years are taken to begin with the menopause in the individual male or female.

For generations sex has been linked with reproduction in religious and cultural settings and for economic and political reasons.[1] Thus it followed that involvement in any sexual activity ended with the menopause. Reproductive capacity ends with menopause. The ability to enjoy sexual relations continues well past menopause – for some it continues into their ninth decade of life. But then, sexual enjoyment may be derived through other than actual sexual intercourse.

Old people may treat each other with the dignity and courtesy of a blossoming courtship. At night they go to bed and hold each other throughout the night

*Reprinted from *Medical Aspects of Human Sexuality*, Vol. 3, No. 11 (November 1973), 46-53.

even though they have not exercised their genitalia for years. One elderly gentleman has described their experience as 'having a ten-hour orgasm every night.'[2]

This is a qualitative refinement of sex rarely achieved by the young who must continually prove through performing. Like the young, the elderly also prove themselves by performing the sex act but age brings a balance of sexual quantity and quality. Ironically, the quality and finesse that young swingers and playboys seek as the 'fountain of youth' comes with increased natural ease in old age (when sex is supposed to be dead!).

The task today is to break through myths, taboos and misconceptions to give recognition to the reality, the beauty, the problems, and the pains of sex in the later years so that we can exercise our legitimate rights as sexual beings and help our senior citizens to do the same.

ATTITUDES, MISCONCEPTIONS AND MYTHS

Rueben Baetz, Executive Director, Canadian Welfare Council, has characterized the stereotype of the elderly person.

The majority of the general public has only one model or picture of the aged, which would most likely be that of a person with wrinkled skin, absent teeth, silver grey hair or no hair at all. This person would have a poor memory, especially for recent events; memories of childhood on the other hand are vivid. His health is generally poor; he is without vigor and is sexually dead. His ability to concentrate is poor, and when he talks he rambles. If he insists on driving a car, he is likely to be regarded as a hazard on the highway. On top of all this he has lost his competence, his independence, his job, and much of his income. In other words, it's downhill all the way. And if we happen to meet a retired person who doesn't quite fit into our model of the aged, we offer him the left-handed compliment of saying 'my, but you don't look your age.'[3]

These ideas about the aged have become so real among the younger generation, that a new language is being spawned to explain the phenomenon: psychiatrist Robert Butler calls it ageism, that is, 'just not wanting to have all these ugly old people around';[4] sociologist J.H. Bunzel has coined gerontophobia, the 'unreasonable fear and irrational hatred of the elderly.' Even the elderly suffer from it, through a self-fear and self-hatred of their own advanced age.[5] The advertisers and makers of commercials for TV simultaneously play on this fear and intensify it by pushing youth, beauty and sex at the buying public. For example: Love Cosmetics distributes all of its products for women in phallus-shaped and phallus-sized containers; Loving-Care hair color claims 'You're not getting older, you're getting better!'; Esoterica urges you to use its cream to fade out those horrid age spots, and so on. By contrast, older people in TV commercials need Absorbine Jr. to ease the aching joints of arthritis or Polident Green to bubble away unsightly denture stains. This advertising is having its effect, for current research indicates that the middle years, which once began about forty-five years of age, now with the youth explosion appear to have been pushed down to forty or even thirty-five years.[6]

The misconceptions which follow are many. Society comes to regard the aged as all alike. They are not. Aged people are simply older individuals. Or, broadly stated, most aged people do or should live in institutions when in fact only about five per cent of today's elderly are in institutions. Howard Irving has begun research to examine the misconception that most old people have little or no contact with their family and relatives. The false notion that old people are not able to make decisions is most convincingly disarmed by reading Playboy Magazine wherein panels and symposia are held to discuss current moral issues like drugs and homosexuality – the average age of the contributors is close to 50 years in all cases. Or, there is the misconception that old age is a second childhood during which people must be nursed and babied. Some aged people become infirm and need special care but these are in the minority. Nor is it true that most aged people are in poor health. We are concerned with one other misconception – aged persons have no sex life. This myth is slowly being exploded by researchers like Masters and Johnson and a host of authors who are finding a lucrative market in writing books directly and openly geared to questions of sex and old age. Two authors, Rubin and Newman, have written a 'How to do it' book on sex for the aged, giving positions for intercourse geared to health and physical disabilities frequently encountered in later years. Masters and Johnson[9] consider their research findings in this area to be their single most important piece of research. They have set out two fundamental constants for active enjoyable sex in the later years.

1 The individual must be in a reasonable good state of general health.

2 He or she must have an interested and interesting partner. 'Sexually, the male and female can function effectively into their 80s, if they understand that certain physiological changes will occur and if they don't let these changes frighten them. Once they allow themselves to think they will lose their sexual effectiveness, then, for all practical purposes they will, indeed, lose it – but only because they have become victims of the myth, not because their bodies will have lost the capacity to perform.'[10]

Writing for *Cosmopolitan Magazine*, Dr. David Reuben deals with the myth of sexless old age and sets out his three criteria for active, enjoyable sex in the later years.

The durability of the genitals is unsurpassed. Joints begin to show signs of wear after twenty-five years or so – fifty years of hard use barely puts a wrinkle into the sexual apparatus. The average person can continue enjoyable sexual intercourse until the age of seventy, eighty or beyond provided he or she meets three requirements: adequate hormones, constant practice, and an interested and interesting sexual partner.[11]

The myth that old age equals the end of sex for men and women simply is not true. Through menopause and into their later years people can and do participate in and enjoy sex.

RESEARCH FINDINGS

Arthur Henley[12] has noted that during the middle and later years of life the marriage partners' need for each other increases. This is the empty nest portion of the family life cycle when the children have matured and have gone to live on their own. Spouses are frequently unable to admit or otherwise communicate their needs to each other at this stage. In some cases, the children may have served as buffers for the parents who are suddenly left with only each other and their friction and pain. For these and other reasons, one or both spouses may attempt to reach outside the marriage for love, attention and affection. Here, too, it is not age that interferes with sexual relations but rather years of emotional stress that have no adaptive and healthy outlet in the marriage. Disturbed sex relations may well be a symptom of deeper problem areas. Nevertheless, Henley has found that seven out of ten healthy married couples over sixty years of age lead active sex lives. There is a healthy self-reinforcing spiral that can work here. Sexual energy regenerates itself. The more it is used the more there is available to use next time, coupled with an increased desire to engage in sex. Add in a reduced fear of pregnancy and no children to interrupt love-making episodes and there is greater relaxation and enjoyment. And, as indicated earlier, there is greater emphasis on the joy (quality) of sexual relations as opposed to more achievement (quantity).

All of this provides a receptive base for elderly couples who are faced with Reuben's frank admonition, 'Use it or lose it.' He states this from his findings that past the age of sixty, a period of sexual abstinence of two months or longer effectively means the end of active sex for that individual. There seems to be an innate awareness of this need, for in old age masturbation again occupies the centre of the sexual stage. Often intercourse is not readily available, though sexual urges may continue almost indefinitely. Masturbation is once again the solution. In old people masturbation may even be therapeutic in the sense that it keeps the sexual organs functioning and prolongs sexual activity.[13]

In this regard, Dr. Reuben is a strong advocate of active sex combined with sex hormone replacement therapy – estrogen for women (whose ovaries stop manufacturing at menopause, and testosterone for men (whose testicles stop manufacturing this compound at menopause). Reuben cites positive correlations between estrogen replacement and reduced heart attacks in women (men preferred the heart attacks to the feminizing side effects of estrogen); between more active sex and reduced arthritis and improved heart health in both sexes.

Rubin and Newman[14] give the following rates of sexual activity for various age groups: 21–25 years, 3 per week; 31–35 years, 2 per week; 41–45 years, 2 per week; 55–60 years, 1 per week; 60–70 years, 1 every two weeks; 70–75 years, 1 every two weeks; 75–90 years, 50 per cent of this age group engage in coitus with some degree of regularity.

The decrease in activity is not that substantial. The rate of activity in the later years is certainly much greater than the sexless myth allows. Even at ninety years active sex occurs regularly enough to be tabulated.

Masters and Johnson[15] have found that in old age, as in all ages, ignorance of the facts surrounding sex is the greatest single deterrent to the active enjoyment. They found that the male and female 'slow down' in terms of the physiological activity involved in sexual intercourse but that the four phases of the sexual response cycle are valid at any age. These phases are: 1. Excitement (achieving erection for the male, and vaginal lubrication for the female); 2. Plateau (sustaining sexual excitement during insertion of the penis); 3. Orgasmic (ejaculation in the male and orgasmic vaginal contractions in the female); and 4. Resolution (reduction in sexual excitement and tension after completion of the sex act). Some age, sex and performance comparisons are in order now.

SEXUAL AGING IN MAN

Below is a chart comparing the sexual response cycles of young and old males.

Response cycles of young and old males

Phase	Young male	Old male
1 Excitement	Takes seconds to achieve full erection	Takes minutes to achieve erection
2 Plateau	Fully erect and hard – full sexual tension	May become fully erect and hard only after insertion
3 Orgasmic	4–7 seconds for ejaculation completion (2 stages)	2–4 seconds for ejaculation (single stage)
4 Resolution	Gradual softening over minutes	Softening within seconds of ejaculation

While the sexual response cycle in the older male shortens or weakens – e.g. it takes longer to get an erection, which is not as hard and softens quickly after ejaculation – other beneficial things happen. The older male does not experience the inevitability of ejaculating that the younger male feels. His reduced drive and intensity to ejaculate enables the older man to achieve self-control and thus satisfy his sex partner to a greater degree. Premature ejaculation problems decrease with age and ejaculation control.

Reuben[16] describes male menopause as beginning with the reduced capacity for erection which accompanies the reduced testosterone (male sex hormone) output as cells in the testicles begin to decay. Hormone replacement therapy can help to offset the resultant decline in maleness and thus restore sexual vigor and interest. Problems can become magnified out of all proportion during this period if the male does not understand the natural slowing down processes of his body. Fearing the loss of their manhood, some men will try to compensate for decreasing interest with futile attempts to increase their rate of sexual activity with a variety of women. Failure here becomes even more damaging. Others may turn to alcohol in excessive amounts. This sets up another vicious cycle for, according to Masters and Johnson, alcohol is the primary cause of secondary sexual impotence in men. Then too, the prostate gland which produces semen, may enlarge with age to the point of becoming painful and interfering with urinary functioning. The prostate problem can be relieved easily with medical attention. Problems of reduced sexual functioning can be treated with a program of sexual rehabilitation combining hormone therapy and counselling of the male and his spouse or girl friend.

These hormones affect not only the energy level, but also the sleep patterns, weight, hair growth, coloration and reproductive capacity of an individual.

A person in the throes of the menopause does not even know that something is happening inside his body, a physical change that is affecting his emotions. Yet he is plagued with indecision, restlessness, boredom, a 'what's the use' outlook and a feeling of being fenced in.

While the blue-collar worker may be experiencing similar changes, medical experts agree that he is less likely to have the time or the opportunity to dwell on them than his more affluent, middle-class counterpart.[17]

Just as the male needs an understanding female, so too she needs an understanding man to help her through her sexual difficulties at this stage of life.

SEXUAL AGING IN WOMAN

As in the male, the sexual response cycles in the female shorten and weaken with increased age (as shown in the chart).

Response cycles of young and old females

Phase	Young female	Old female
1 Excitement	15–30 seconds to lubricate vagina	4–5 minutes to lubricate vagina
2 Plateau	Uterus elevates and vaginal· canal increases in size	Reduced vaginal elevation and less increase in canal size
3 Orgasmic	8–12 vaginal contractions per orgasm	4–5 vaginal contractions per orgasm
4 Resolution	Gradual resolution, resume cycle quickly	Rapid resolution, not ready to resume cycle quickly

Masters and Johnson emphasize that menopause in the female does not signify the end of her sexual life. For many women the hot flashes, depression, irritability and nervousness of menopause serve to make them sexually unattractive to their partners. At the same time, physiological changes in the vaginal walls make intercourse painful and unpleasant. The reciprocating effect can well mean the end of sex for the married couple unless they are made aware of the changes that are occurring in the female in her later years – changes that mean an adaptation in sexual activity, not an end. Continued sexual activity is normal and beneficial for the aging female just as it is for her partner. Because her ovaries stop producing estrogen (female sex hormone) her sexual processes slow down. As with men, continued sexual activity plus estrogen replacement therapy plus counselling to understand the life changes can all work to overcome the physical and psychological pain of menopause. Fortunately, a reduced fear of pregnancy frequently leads to an increase in sexual desire in elderly women, so a basic drive is working to spur a search for help with her problems. The problems can be overcome and the process of decreased sexual activity can be reversed.

The sexual compatability of aging males and females is striking and encouraging. The two previous charts served to illustrate the reduced sexual response cycles of the aged male/female cycles. Now we will combine the two to give some perspective to the issue of waning sexuality.

The compatability of the sexes becomes readily apparent. Each sex needs additional time in old age during the excitement phase to prepare for sexual union. In the plateau phase a less elevated, less extended vagina better accommodates a less than erect penis which after insertion becomes fully erect thus causing less pain to a sensitive female organ. Single-stage ejaculation permits more effective orgasm control by the male, thus enabling his partner to achieve orgasm in her own time. Her reduced vaginal contractions roughly match in time his 2-4 second ejaculatory stage, after which both sexes move quickly to the resolution phase together. Physiologically, neither is able immediately to resume sexual activity. Both require a period of rest between coital acts and both necessarily take this rest because both organs move rapidly to a state of non-excitement.

THE ROLE OF THE PROFESSIONALS

One of the most important roles for professionals who become involved with individuals and couples during and after menopause is that of educating them to the realities of sex in their later years. This may mean that counselling services need to be made available to aged people in the area of sex and sexual adjustment. It can include help or initiative in preparing pamphlets or booklets on the subject of sex in the later years. Approaches to the elderly should emphasize the sexual compatibility of the sexes in the later years. Cross-age contrasts should be used carefully and then only to help individuals understand the changes taking place in their own lives. There is some risk here that the elderly person might hear the contrast with his or her youth as evidence of personal sexual failure.

If the aged have to be educated in the realities of their functional sex lives, so too do their helpers, doctors, nurses, attendants, orderlies, social workers, administrators, legislators and the like. Services and facilities for the aged have been designed, built and implemented in keeping with the myth that advancing age means the end of sex for men and women. For example, Homes for the Aged in Ontario either segregate their residents by sex (this is in the process of change), house them four to a room or provide no facilities for married couples to cohabit. Some newer county homes for the aged are including apartment rooms for couples in their design. Part of the problem, too, is that the elderly people of today are at or near the age of our own parents. Helpers will have to be clear how they stand on the question of old age and sex in general, and how they feel about the thought of their parents having sex in particular.

Elderly people must be helped to understand that the process of aging is very much an individual matter, that they and their spouses age at different rates. Understanding this can help to reduce some marital misery in these change-of-life years.

In connection with this, professionals can help elderly couples to re-open channels of communication that are needed when their children leave home. We can help both spouses to accept and face each other realistically without the need to hide or put up false fronts to maintain self-esteem. We can help elderly people find new ways of intimacy and of being together, perhaps through learning to cherish the memories of shared, sexually stimulating experiences.

We must be cautious to learn where our elderly clients stand with regard to sexuality. For many, it is a subject loaded with myths, taboos, secrets and embarrassment. For some, old age and menopause is the long awaited answer to a life full of sexual problems, a time when sex is officially over.

Whatever the situation, we must know clearly where we stand regarding sex and the aged so that we can honestly appreciate their individual needs in this area and leave them to their privacy or help them with their sexuality.

NOTES

1 Collier, James, 'The Procreation Myth,' *Playboy*, vol. 18 (May 1971), pp. 106, 190-194.

2 Lederer, William J. and Don D. Jackson, *The Mirages of Marriage*, New York: W.W. Norton and Co. Inc., 1968, p. 125.

3 Welbourn, Patricia, 'Being Old in a Society that Worships Youth,' *Weekend Magazine*, vol. 20 (Nov. 14, 1970), pp. 4-7.

4 'The Old in the County of the Young,' *Time* (Aug. 3, 1970), pp. 41-46.

5 'Fear of Aging Affects Millions, Gerontological Society is Told,' *Globe and Mail* (Oct. 23, 1970), p. 9.

6 'Beginning of Middle Age May be Coming 5 Years Earlier,' *Globe and Mail* (April 10, 1971), p. 11.

7 Irving, Howard H., 'Relationships Between Married Couples and Their Parents,' *Social Casework*, vol. 52 (Feb. 1971), pp. 91-96.

8 Rubin, Herman H. and Benjamin Newman, *Active Sex after Sixty*. New York: Arco Publishing Co., 1969.

9 Belliveau, Fred and Lin Richter, *Understanding Human Sexual Inadequacy*, New York: Bantam Books, 1970, p. 212.

10 Masters, William H. and Virginia E. Johnson, 'Ten Sex Myths Exploded,' *Playboy*, vol. 17 (Dec. 1970), pp. 124-218, 303.

11 Reuben, David R., '13 Sex Myths Laid to Rest,' *Cosmopolitan*, vol. 170 (April 1971), pp. 136-139, 173.

12 Henley, Arthur, 'Middle Age is a Difficult Time When Many Marriages Go Stale,' *Toronto Daily Star* (Jan. 4, 1971), p. 17.

13 Reuben, David, op. cit., p. 138.

14 Rubin and Newman, op. cit., p. 50-51.

15 Robbins, Jhan and June, *An Analysis of Human Sexual Inadequacy*, New York: New American Library, 1970.

16 Reuben, David, *Everything You Always Wanted to Know About Sex*, New York: Bantam Books, 1969.

17 *Globe and Mail*, op. cit., p. 11.

REFERENCES

Boyd, Rosamonde and Charles Oakes, eds., *Foundations of Practical Gerontology*, Columbia: University of South Carolina Press, 1969.

Branson, Helen K. 'Sex Drive after Forty,' *Sexology*, vol. 37 (March 1971), pp. 67-69.

Carbary, L.J., 'A New Approach to Change-of-life,' *Sexology*, vol. 37 (Jan. 1971), pp. 49-52.

Cohen, Ruth G. 'Casework with Older Persons,' *Differential Diagnosis and Treatment in Social Work*, Francis J. Turner, ed., Toronto: Collier-Macmillan Canada Limited, 1968.

Hurdle, J. Frank, 'You Can Enjoy Sex after Seventy,' *Sexology*, vol. 37 (April 1971), pp. 49-51.

Landau, M.E., *Women of Forty: The Menopausal Syndrome*, London: Faber and Faber Ltd., 1966.

'Over-60's Go Hungry in Search for Romance at Miami Beach,' *Globe and Mail.* Feb. 27, 1971, p. 30.

Pascoe, Jean, 'Sex Hormones: What They Can and Cannot Do for You,' *Woman's Day*, Feb. 1971, pp. 22, 88-90.

'Playboy Interview: Masters and Johnson,' *Playboy*, vol. 15 (May 1968), pp. 67ff.

Rubin, Isadore, *Sexual Life after Sixty*, New York: Basic Books, 1965.

'Sexual Inadequacy,' *Medical World News*, May 1, 1970, pp. 39-49.

Toffler, Alvin, *Future Shock*, New York: Random House, 1970.

Vischer, A.L., *On Growing Old*, London: George Allen and Unwin Limited, 1966.

Vizinczey, Stephen, *In Praise of Older Women*, New York: Ballantine Books Inc., 1965.

Wassersug, Joseph D., *How to be Healthy and Happy after Sixty*, New York: Abelard-Schuman Ltd., 1966.

AVINOAM B. CHERNICK AND BERYL A. CHERNICK

The role of ignorance in sexual dysfunction*

Ignorance is not bliss when it comes to sex. It plays a major role in sexual dysfunction. Occasionally, sexual dysfunction is caused by physical anomalies like imperforate hymen, or by disease such as diabetic impotence.[1] More frequently, it is due to inadequate information about oneself and one's partner, a common finding at the beginning of marriage. Most frequent and most troublesome are cases of sexual dysfunction caused by the inhibitory action of the emergency emotions (fear, anger, and guilt). This inhibition is usually directly related to faulty learning experiences or misinformation.

A burly sailor and his shapely young wife had been married just under two years. She complained of his impotence, while he scored her lack of response. Marriage was becoming intolerable for both of them. Early in the marriage, the husband had prided himself on his ability to complete intercourse with his wife within twenty minutes of landing for shore leave. Now he was bewildered by his inability to attain an erection. His wife complained that not only had she never had an orgasm during intercourse, but now her husband avoided sex altogether and she wanted to have a baby. Ignorance masked as sexual prowess started a cycle in which the angry, frustrated wife, feeling that she was being raped, failed to become sexually excited. She made her husband feel ashamed and guilty until he was unable to perform sexually. This inhibition was directly related to the stereotype that a *real* man is identified by rapid sexual conquest.

*Reprinted from *Medical Aspects of Human Sexuality*, Vol. 1 (Sept. 1971), 22-26 (Canadian edition)

Ignorance is the lack of useful sexual learning due to unavailability of factual information, misinformation such as stereotypes and myths, and distorted information including faulty learning and inability to integrate factual information when it is available.

ETIOLOGY OF IGNORANCE

Unfortunately, we are not endowed with good sexual technique at birth. Sexual learning is acquired in humans.

A married couple, both university graduates, came for treatment of infertility. When asked how often they 'slept together,' they answered 'every night.' When later physical examination of the wife revealed an intact hymen, further questioning revealed that the couple did in fact sleep together, but were not aware that coitus preceded conception.[2]

Cultural taboos have prevented official sanction of sexuality and sexual function as part of health. These taboos have been suppressive and inhibitory of open discussion, enquiry, and the spread of information about sex. The sexual renaissance, which began in the days of Freud, has been considerably prolonged by the prevailing inhibitions. Kinsey's surveys of sexual practices and attitudes and the subsequent anatomical-physiological observations of Masters and Johnson constitute a major breakthrough in terms of scientific inquiry achieved in spite of much adverse opinion.

Even so, the above-mentioned studies have provided us with only a small amount of factual information relative to the large amount of as yet unverified 'information' published in the scientific literature as well as in our folklore. Although Kinsey contributed significantly to expanding our fund of knowledge, when he stepped outside the realm of his particular field of enquiry to describe human sexual anatomy, he perpetuated the misconception that the clitoris lies in the anterior wall of the vagina.[3]

Cultural myths and stereotypes form the majority of the verbal messages transmitted about sex. They are passed on to young people mainly by pornography and by their peer group. Art Buchwald, in *Sex as taught at Sam's*, notes: 'I had no formal sex education when I was a student ... we got all our sex education at the local candy store after 3 o'clock. The information was dispensed by 13-year-olds who seemed to know everything there was to know on the subject, and we 11 and 12-year-olds believed every word they told us ... For example ... the method of kissing a girl on the mouth determined whether she would become pregnant or not. Every time I kissed a girl after that, I sweated for the next nine months ... When I turned 13 I became an instructor myself and passed on my knowledge to 11- and 12-year-olds at the same candy store ... I was amazed with how much authority I was able to pass on the "facts" of sex life as I knew them ... we were all emotional wrecks before we got to high school.'[4]

Myths are also propagated by parents, teachers and even by physicians. In 1961, a survey[5] of the five medical schools in Philadelphia showed that 50 per cent of the medical students believed that masturbation caused mental illness, and that 20 per cent of the medical faculty members had the same impression.

Misinformation is also transmitted nonverbally by the advertising and mass media depictions of idealized, exceptional people and their successes. These images generate unrealistic expectations of what life, love, marriage and sex are like, and provide unfortunate comparisons for us ordinary mortals. One might ask what it is that's so special about the sexuality of an 'Aqua Velva' man?

The suppressiveness of our cultural taboos teaches an attitude to sex which the unproven myths and stereotypes often support. Even today, there are many people who believe that sex is not a 'nice' thing to talk about and that sexual organs and functions are 'dirty.'

Learning that begins earliest and continues longest occurs in the home. As Harry in T.S. Eliot's *The Family Reunion* said: 'I think the things that are taken for granted at home, make a deeper impression upon children than what they are told.'[6] From observing their parents in ordinary day-to-day living, children learn what it is to be male and female and how men and women relate to each other. Faulty learning about sex occurs only occasionally from reactions to specific traumatic episodes, such as an incestuous approach to a girl from her father or seductive behaviour of a mother to her son.

The authoritative nature of information from cultural and especially from parental sources teaches attitudes toward sex, classifying it as good or bad, healthy or unhealthy, moral or immoral, permitted or forbidden. Each message, whether verbal or nonverbal, is invested with a judgmental and consequent emotional accompaniment.

One would hope that the emotions of joy, hope, trust, love, and pride would be prominent. Because of the taboo nature of the cultural influence, however, fear, guilt, anger, or some combination thereof are distressingly common. These emotions are experienced by the person as anxiety, a decidedly inhibiting factor to satisfying sexual function. The person may be quite unaware of the source of this anxiety which, in fact, may have been conditioned in early childhood.

When Johnny was a toddler, his parents slapped his hand every time they observed him exploring or playing with his penis (as all little boys do at that phase of their development). As a teenager, Johnny discovered pleasure and release of tension through masturbation. But this was always accompanied and followed by a distressing feeling of uneasiness which made Johnny promise himself that he would never do it again. He was responding with guilty fear because of the negative conditioning (hand slapping) that he had long forgotten.

A young woman complained that she could not respond to her husband's sexual advances although she claimed to want to do so. History revealed that her father had been verbally abusive to her mother, always running her down. Mother had borne in silence what the patient considered to be degrading treatment. This patient pictured men as brutal. Their brutality evoked fear in her. She saw women as passively submitting to ill-treatment. This made her angry and even more fearful of being submissive. These emotions were aroused whenever her husband made what was perceived by her to be an aggressive advance toward her and overrode her feelings of love and passion for him as an individual.

Anxiety conditioned to things sexual is aroused even when factual information is presented, preventing new learning or the integration of the information unless the anxiety is first dispelled. Paradoxical ignorance sometimes serves the secondary need of avoiding responsibility.

Mrs. R.W. had been married for three years. She was depressed and complained that she had lost all desire for sex in the past few months. She had not had orgasm during intercourse but always pretended that she was ecstatic to avoid further disappointing her husband who ejaculated soon after intromission. Enquiry about sexual technique and response revealed that Mrs. R.W. always lay immobile throughout foreplay, the mechanical quality of which 'turned her off.' She never told her husband how she felt about his lovemaking nor suggested what type of stimulation she would prefer. To tell him would imply that she herself had a role to play in making coitus enjoyable. By not telling, she could comfort herself with the notion that the responsibility for sex was all her husband's and that all the blame for their sexual dysfunction was also his.

Paradoxical ignorance is frequently seen in the woman like Mrs. R.W. who has 'learned' the cultural stereotype of the wife 'serving her husband' as a passive vessel. She, therefore, is prevented from factual learning about herself and her husband, information that could help her to be a responsive and cooperative mate.

Our cultural stereotype of the male as a knowledgeable and expert sexual partner limits his access to factual information. To admit that he does not know is to admit that he is not a man.

Clark Vincent describes the husband who can accept with equanimity numerous instructions from his wife – 'a little higher on the left, no, over a little' – whose back he is scratching. But, let her use the same words to guide him to areas she would like stimulated in the genital regions and his hurt pride may take days to recover.

The physician is in an especially handicapped position, being stereotyped as omniscient about sex. In fact, until recently, medical training not only failed to provide positive sex information, but continued the negative conditioning current in society. The medical profession is now recognizing the management of sexual problems as a significant aspect of practice, as well as acknowledging the physician's relative lack of expertise. Paradoxically, it is estimated that up to one-third of medical students will not attend courses in sex and marriage counselling when they are provided.[7] These students avoid the responsibility of treating patients with sexual problems.

INCIDENCE OF IGNORANCE

The exact incidence of ignorance leading to sexual dysfunction is difficult to determine. Instruments to measure knowledge and attitudes about sex have been difficult to design. The Sex Knowledge and Attitude Test (SKAT)[8] has revealed major ignorance of factual information about sex, along with a substantial investment in invalid cultural myths and stereotypes on the part of college students and medical students. About 20 per cent of medical students are still convinced that 'a woman must have orgasm in order to conceive.' (There must be many surprised fathers around.) A higher level of formal education, therefore, does not ensure a reduction in sexual ignorance.

Both formal testing and clinical observations indicate that it is fair to assume that most patients complaining of sexual dysfunction suffer from ignorance.

For thousands of years, self-defeating behaviour such as alcoholism has been an accepted escape from marital and sexual problems. Symptoms of anxiety or depression soon became appropriate masks for this distress. Hippocrates recognized that somatic complaints such as low back pain or pelvic aching could be related to primary psychic pain. Marital conflict was described in the Old Testament but only recently has a profession devoted to marriage counselling appeared, and only recently has it become acceptable to complain of marital disharmony to one's physician. Presenting the physician with a complaint of sexual dysfunction such as impotence is still fraught with the twin hazards of the patient's fear of revealing his incompetence and his fear of rejection by the physician.

DIAGNOSIS OF IGNORANCE

Diagnosis requires looking beyond these chief complaints to discover the possible underlying ignorance. The physician's task is further complicated because the more remotely related symptoms are still the most presentable. At the same time, sexual dysfunction continues to be a hidden agenda, except for a small proportion of more highly educated women and even fewer men in this social class.

Sexual history and functional enquiry
The medium is as notable as the message to the physician taking a sexual history and functional enquiry. The patient's feelings about each topic as well as about the events of his own life are the significant indicators of areas of ignorance.

It is painful to the patient to have his ignorance uncovered. The following suggestions may facilitate this process:
1 We ask the patient how he feels about talking about sex with us. If he feels uncomfortable, we ask him if he can tell us about the discomfort. This leads gradually into a discussion of attitudes to sex.
2 It is more comfortable to begin history-taking in nonthreatening areas, such as demonstration of affection between his parents or chronology of events, such as age at menarche, first date, etc.
3 We introduce potentially threatening areas with general observations, such as, 'Most people believe that ...'
4 We assume that the patient has experienced most types of sexual expression. For example, when did you first discover masturbation?
5 In taking the functional enquiry, we treat the reproductive system and sexual function as we would any other system. Has there been any change in your weight? Has there been any change in the amount of your menstrual flow? Has there been any change in how often you have sexual intercourse?

These approaches can be applied to specific areas such as those suggested below:
Development Stage childhood
Comfortable Area attitude to nudity in the home
Threatening Area sex play with parents or siblings
Developmental Stage early marriage
Comfortable Area frequency of coitus
Threatening Area masturbation

We are constantly aware that our middle-class norms and stereotypes are different from those of other socioeconomic classes.

For example, some men and women who have less than an eighth-grade education have 'learned' that sexual intercourse is the only acceptable (healthy, good, normal) form of sexual expression. They perceive practices such as masturbation or oral-genital contact as sexual perversions.

Physical examination
A general physical examination should be performed to rule out intercurrent disease and to help differentiate psychosomatic from organic dysfunction.

Pelvic examination in both sexes is a must in ruling out congenital anomalies. The attitude of the patient toward the physical examination may be revealing.

For example, hesitation prior to insertion of a vaginal speculum is usual; vaginismus suggests an up-tight attitude.

Laboratory tests

Laboratory workup includes a complete blood count, blood sugar, renal function tests such as urinalysis and BUN, and a thyroid function test. Diabetes and some blood dyscrasias may be heralded by impotence.

TREATMENT

The main aim of active treatment is the reduction of anxiety followed by education or re-education. A history, if accepted in a nonjudgmental way, conveys not only a feeling of understanding between doctor and patient but it also goes a long way in reducing anxiety. Reassurance that physical and laboratory findings are within normal limits also allays fear, making it possible for the patient to accept information about sexual norms, to integrate this information, and to use it constructively.

Where possible, the history, physical, and lab workup should be done on both spouses. This not only allows the physician to reduce anxiety and educate the marital unit, but makes it possible for the couple to educate each other.

A junior intern and his wife were treated for sexual dysfunction involving the wife's lack of orgasm. He had had successful intercourse with another girl before he met his wife. He had found his wife passionately aroused during premarital petting so their sexual dysfunction after marriage came as a considerable surprise. He consulted a marriage manual for information about effectively stimulating women and followed the recommended techniques to the letter, including vigorous massage of the head of the clitoris. He was amazed to hear from his wife during a review of their sexual techniques that this rubbing was painful and did as much as anything to turn her off.

As part of the treatment in this case, the physician explained our cultural stereotype that men know all about sex, giving the intern permission to admit his ignorance. This reduced the husband's anxiety. The physician then encouraged the wife to educate her husband concerning the kinds of stimulation she did enjoy and in what sequence.

At their next visit, the very pleased young intern reported that his wife could give him more useful information about her sexual response than could the various marriage manuals which he had consulted.

There is a great deal of similarity between the active treatment of sexual dysfuction and the prevention of ignorance. Both involve therapy to relieve anxiety and include re-education. The difference can be seen in the benefit a patient or married couple can get out of a half-hour's counselling by a busy doctor. An ounce of premarital counselling can prevent a pound of marital misery. Surely, a gram of Family Life Education in medical school can reap a kilogram of reward in the health of both doctor and patient.

NOTES

1 Money, J., *Sex Errors of the Body*, Baltimore: Johns Hopkins Press, 1968.
2 Masters, W.H., and Johnson, V.E., personal communication, 1969.
3 Kinsey, A.C., *et al., Sexual Behavior in the Human Female* (Philadelphia: W.B. Saunders Co., 1953).
4 Buchwald, A., *Sex as taught at Sam's*, Philadelphia *Bulletin*, April 22, 1969.
5 Greenbank, R.K., On medical students learning psychiatry, *Penn. Med. J.* 64:989, 1961.
6 Eliot, T.S., *The Family Reunion*, London: Faber and Faber, 1939.
7 Lief, H.I., 'Preparing the physician to become a sex counselor and educator,' *Pediat. Clin. N. Amer.* 16:447, 1969.
8 Lief, H.I., and Reed, D.M., *Sex Knowledge and Attitude Test* (SKAT). (Center for the Study of Sex Education in Medicine, Division of Family Study of Dept. of Psychiatry, University of Pennsylvania School of Medicine, Philadelphia, Pa.)

STEPHEN NEIGER

Short-term treatment methods for delaying ejaculation*

The expression 'premature ejaculation' is generally used to describe a condition of insufficient staying power in men during intercourse or a reduced ability to prolong the act at will. Unfortunately, this label is just as vague as are 'impotence' and 'frigidity,' because it is supposed to cover a great variety of conditions.

Patients who ejaculate even before penetration occurs (*ante portas* ejaculation; *ejaculatio precipitata*), should really not be given the same label as is used in the far more frequent situation where, although able to go on for many minutes, the man still cannot last long enough in intercourse to satisfy his partner. The inexperienced, overanxious groom who spills his semen out of excitement when first seeing his bride in the nude is said to have had a 'premature ejaculation,' and so is the experienced husband who, after a period of absence, has built up so much desire for his wife that he simply cannot contain himself long enough. We even use the same label for a completely different semi-impotent state found in some aging men.

In an attempt to bring at least some order into the confusion, Dr. G. Lombard Kelly,[1] a well-known sexologist, has coined two very useful terms to distinguish between premature ejaculation in sexually sthenic (vigorous) and sexually asthenic (weak) males. The sthenic patient with the complaint of premature ejaculation tends to be young and healthy. His libido, his erection, ejaculation and orgasm are all in perfect order; only the timing of his climax causes him concern. These men – the large majority of those complaining about prematurity – have such an intense sexual desire that they cannot sufficiently prolong the act. This is especially true after a period of abstinence.

*Reprinted from *Canadian Family Physician* (March 1972), 62-66.

The asthenic type, on the other hand, is typically the middle-aged or older man who is trying to maintain his former coital frequency, but finds that he cannot. As a result, premature ejaculation, along with insufficient or no erection, will be characteristic symptoms of exhaustion through conflict between aging and over-exertion in these patients. Unlike prematurity in young men, the condition of the aging asthenic male will often benefit from medical attention to his body. In addition to the simple relief often gained from treating inflammation of the prostate (a condition frequently found to influence potency in this age group), sedation and, in some cases, hormonal treatment are often effective. I will focus mainly on the sthenic type of prematurity, and only on the overwhelming majority of patients in whom the condition is not physically based. I am assuming, too, that neurological and urological conditions of various sorts have been ruled out or cleared up.

SYMPTOM OF MANY CONDITIONS

Most contemporary authorities share Kelly's opinion that 'premature ejaculation' is at best a symptom of many conditions and in the majority of cases not even that. General agreement exists, for example, that every man will experience at least occasional inability to last as long in intercourse as he may wish to. Such sporadic prematurity, of course, hardly deserves a second thought. Even repeated occurrences of sthenic prematurity are rarely caused by physical malfunctioning; they are much more frequently due to strong drive pressure combined with lack of proper sexual learning, inability or unwillingness to exert control, overanxiousness to please, fear of failure and other predominantly psychological factors.

Many sexologists, including Kinsey,[2] consider 'premature ejaculation' in its most frequent, sthenic form not even a psychological but rather a 'social' condition. Kinsey's researchers found that 75 per cent of the men in their sample regularly ejaculated two minutes after entry. In quite a few men ejaculation occurred in less than 20 seconds; hardly any could last five minutes.

Most male mammals tend to ejaculate within a much shorter time: the females, who practically never experience orgasm, do not seem to mind. So the two minutes' lasting power of the average American male represents a considerable feat of civilized self-control already. Of course, these two minutes are still quite insufficient for the human female in this society to reach her orgasm by intercourse, if she was not properly aroused before. Although in self-stimulation she can approximate the speed of the male response,[3] the average Canadian woman may need 15 to 30 minutes of *intercourse* before she can reach orgasm. It is the discrepancy between the speed by which the two sexes can reach orgasm that lies at the bottom of most cases of so-called premature ejaculation.

We recognize then that premature ejaculation, at least in its most frequent manifestation, is hardly an 'illness.' Rather, it is a relative condition caused by woman's need for orgasm, and her comparative slowness in reaching it through intercourse alone. It is certainly far from abnormal and even perfectly natural for a man to want to come to his climax in two minutes or less after entry, just as it is natural for a woman to need 15 minutes or more.

As the Kinsey group puts it: 'This quick performance of the typical male may be most unsatisfactory to a wife who is inhibited or natively low in response, as many wives are; and such disparities in the speed of the male and female response are frequent sources of marital conflict, especially among upper social levels where the female is most restrained in her behaviour ... but it is curious that the term "impotence" should have ever been applied to such rapid response, however inconvenient and unfortunate his qualities may be from the standpoint of the wife in the relationship.'

NON-INTERCOURSE SEX TECHNIQUES

I agree with those authorities (e.g. Ellis[4]) who believe that the focus of therapy in sthenic prematurity is not necessarily to prolong staying power in intercourse. After all, a number of non-intercourse (hand-genital and mouth-genital) sexual techniques are available to a well informed man for bringing his partner to quite satisfactory orgasm – often even more than once on one occasion. Having done this, he can then choose the time for *his* orgasm with a clean conscience and without fear that it will be 'premature.' This method is recommended as a first line of approach, since, if acceptable to both partners, it tends to reduce anxiety and thus vicariously increase resistance to the ejaculation urge.

Unfortunately, many couples are still too inhibited to give this method a try. Some will decide that they still prefer to 'come the normal way.' The husband will envy other men for their staying power if he cannot give his wife this experience with fair regularity. These couples will find little comfort in the information that speedy ejaculation is common and normal, or that ejaculatory control can be a product of civilized lovemaking, rather than something to be cured like some sort of ailment. This is the reason why it may be rewarding for the family physician to review the many methods which can narrow the time gap for reaching orgasm.

At least two main points of attack are available to prolong staying power in 'sthenic men.' The one is to reduce the stimulus acting on the brain and on the ejaculation centre in the spinal cord. The other is to reduce the receptivity of these centres themselves so that they can stand more stimulation without triggering too quick a response.

These two approaches may be compared with the two choices facing a man trying to operate an electric motor with inadequate equipment. Let us imagine that his only available electric power source, while adequate for the motor, is so strong that before reaching its target it keeps burning through the rather fine wire (which is the only one at his disposal to conduct electricity). One thing this man can do is to try and get hold of a weaker source of power. This can be likened to the first approach in premature ejaculation, to lowering the sensory input. If, on the other hand, he will attempt instead to get hold of a stronger wire, he has taken an approach that is similar to the second line of attack on prematurity. There, too, increased storage capacity, increased resistance, and less sensitive paths for conducting can be obtained through a number of practical measures.

Let us review all the practical steps that can be taken in support of both these lines of attack on 'premature ejaculation':

Reducing inner stimulation

The best way to take some strength away from any drive pressure is to satisfy that drive more frequently. Clearly, then, the sthenic man who has intercourse more frequently will run less danger of too quick a response on each subsequent occasion.

Men who are capable of full orgasm and ejaculation two or three times on the same occasion are especially fortunate because it will take them longer to ejaculate each time. Moreover, there is no reason why, in most cases, the repeated act – with effective foreplay resumed in the pauses – would not result in the same or even better female response than the often much envied single act that lasts longer. If the patient can only have one orgasm on any one occasion, he will still find his problem of 'prematurity' much reduced by attempting intercourse as soon again as his capacity will permit, instead of waiting for a strong drive build up.

Since inner sexual stimulation acting on the brain is transmitted in a chemical manner through the bloodstream, it should also be possible to reduce, counteract, or intercept this stimulation by modern pharmacology. At least in theory this is so: estrogens were found to have a libido reducing effect on the male. However, few physicians and even fewer patients would accept the many feminizing side effects of estrogens to gain a few minutes of lasting power in the bargain.

Reducing outer stimulation

Here again, a number of common sense remedies can be employed. To start with the simplest, the average man is very much stimulated by sight. He may be helped, therefore, to respond less quickly if his wife will avoid putting on her most enticing nightie for the occasion. Better still, the couple should try having intercourse with dimmed lights or in full darkness. Touch, of course, is another major stimulus. Again, his wife can help by refraining from actively caressing his body altogether, or at least by not stimulating the most sensitive areas.

The strongest stimuli for ejaculation, of course, come from intercourse itself through coital thrusting and the resulting friction on the penis. Slow pace, minimum thrust and – the woman permitting – maximum depth are the key words to put this knowledge to work towards prolonging intercourse. Several coital positions provide an opportunity for all these conditions to be fulfilled. For example, the female above and astride, face to face position will permit the female to do most of the moving and will help the male to cut down on his own motions. Deeply buried in the vagina and helped by pelvic movements of his partner, he will be able to maintain his erection with short thrusts (one half to one inch at the most) without precipitating ejaculation. (In many cases it will be necessary to prescribe dimmed light or complete darkness, because this position is visually quite stimulating to the male.) The value of this 'non-demanding' position for delaying ejaculation has been well known to sexologists for a long time. The point was reaffirmed and documented recently, however, by Masters and Johnson.[5]

It is also helpful to know that the frenulum (a small fold of skin located on the underside of the rim where the head meets the shaft) is the most sensitive spot on the penis. Thrusts directed upwards rather than downwards in the vagina will greatly reduce friction on this trigger of ejaculation. If ejaculation is imminent (but not yet desired) all motion should be interrupted; if necessary, the male should withdraw completely and resume foreplay.

Reducing inner receptivity

One of the best ways to reduce the receptivity of the mind to sexual stimulation is concentration on a (preferably absorbing) non-sexual image. The advice of delaying male orgasm by arithmetic problem solving, or by mentally reviewing humdrum office duties or stock market reports, or even by distracting actions such as making a fist or squeezing the eyelids tightly shut during intercourse is contained in many modern marriage manuals. Actually this method is very old; its equivalent can be found in many ancient Oriental love books. It is not a method I would recommend as a first choice, and not at all if the boundary between quick ejaculation and loss of erection is a thin one for the patient. However, there is no doubt that it works for many men.

Indian sexologist Dr. A.P. Pillay[6] proposed another useful variation of the same idea. He recommends concentration on breathing. This simple method requires the man, at the point of approaching orgasm, to take a deep breath and hold it for a moment before exhaling slowly.

Dr. Albert Ellis[4] suggests a still more practical diverting action: the 'cooling off period' may as well be spent with further arousing the female partner by petting. Ellis suggests that such an approach will 'kill two birds with one stone' – while delaying the man's orgasm by diverting his attention from himself, it will also help speed up the woman's orgasm. Ellis also warns that unless the male has a detached, task-oriented attitude while stimulating his partner, this method can easily boomerang since most men are easily aroused by the touch of the female body.

Of course, the central nervous system can also be made less receptive to sexual arousal by sedatives and tranquilizers whose main impact, after all, is to reduce receptivity to stimulation of all sorts. Such drugs may include fast-acting barbituates such as nembutal or seconal taken 30 minutes before intercourse, and diazepam. Thioradizine (Mellaril) is also known to delay ejaculation apparently acting without interfering with erection; possibly by direct blocking of the ejaculation response.

Reducing outer receptivity
These methods focus on the penis itself, either by causing it to receive fewer of the sensations to which it is exposed during intercourse, or by desensitizing it, i.e. heightening its resistance so that fewer sensations will be transmitted. The oldest of these methods still in use is the condom, and some men use two or three as so many layers of insulation to reduce sensitivity. Unfortunately, this method also interferes with the female sexual response. Some couples prefer to begin intercourse without a condom; the male puts it on later in a 'pause' prompted by his feeling of approaching orgasm.

It was also known for quite some time that most lubricants reduce the speed of ejaculation by cutting down on penile friction. Early in this century successful experiments with novocaine-based ointments have added an anesthetic component to this friction reducing effect. Kelly,[1] who has done perhaps most systematic experimentation with such ointments on this continent, recommends dibucaine hydrochloride, a preparation that is sold without prescription as *Nupercaine*. Kelly reports that most patients with sthenic problems of prematurity will be effectively helped by thoroughly massaging a quantity about the size of a large pea into the glans penis (and the groove just behind it) some 20-30 minutes before intercourse. The proper dose and strength (one to five per cent) can be determined only by experimentation.

Although the literature is far from unanimous on the value of desensitizing ointments, I have little doubt that a significant number of patients are indeed helped in some manner by Nupercaine. But desensitizing ointments, far from being a remedy for asthenic types of premature ejaculation, will only increase their problem by cutting down on the ability to achieve and maintain erection.

In sthenic men the most efficient dose and strength may vary. Some may need longer massaging with larger quantities.

While the last two methods discussed obviously amount to no more than symptomatic treatment, during the last 15 years quite a few desensitizing techniques have been developed, promising (and in many cases achieving) lasting rather than just momentary results. For this purpose Dr. Hirsch,[7] an experienced urologist, recommends daily massage of about 10 to 15 minutes of the penis and the area under the scrotum, with or without a desensitizing ointment. Unlike the next two methods that will be discussed, however, there is no evidence of how many patients are helped in this way.

A second, better-known method of permanent desensitization, and one of well-documented effectiveness, was developed by Dr. James H. Semans[8] of Duke University School of Medicine some 16 years ago. This approach relies on the woman to stimulate the lubricated penis by hand until the man becomes aware of the feeling that immediately precedes ejaculation. He then signals the woman to stop immediately, but asks her to resume manual stimulation when the sensation has disappeared. Accidental ejaculation is not to be taken as a sign of failure, nor is a disappearance of the erection to be considered a problem; in such cases further efforts are simply postponed for the next occasion. By repeating this procedure as often as necessary (for 5, 10, or even 20 occasions) the man will soon find himself able to tolerate very intense stimulation without ejaculation. In my experience the original Semans method is quite as effective in most cases as the Masters and Johnson variation[5] described below, although the carry-over of the treatment principles into the female astride (and later into the lateral) intercourse positions are additions which patients in the need of somewhat more prolonged and intensive attention may appreciate.

According to Semans, the process of re-education may be aided if the man learns to control the muscles that govern urination. By repeatedly interrupting the flow of urine each time when emptying his bladder, a man can often learn to control his ejaculation in a similar manner during the crucial moment. Just exactly why this is so is not yet fully understood.

Masters and Johnson of the Reproductive Biology Research Foundation at St. Louis have taken over both the Wolpe[9] and the Semans methods. Their major innovation consists of adding the squeeze technique. In this approach, when the man signals imminent ejaculation, his partner applies strong pressure (she has to be persuaded that she can do no damage there) with her thumb on the frenulum and her first two fingers on the opposite side of the corona, three or four seconds. If the pressure is sufficient, the male will lose his urge to ejaculate immediately. He will also lose some of his erection. However, after about 20-30 seconds the procedure can be repeated in a manner very similar to the original

Semans technique. After two or three occasions of non-coital exercises, the couple is encouraged to have intercourse in the female above position with minimum motion. When the male feels his ejaculation approach, he signals, she dismounts, and again the squeeze technique is applied, followed by re-mounting, etc.

Masters and Johnson claim that 15-20 minutes of lasting power is a fairly average achievement after only a few days with this method. After the acute phase of the treatment, the couple is advised to use the lateral position and to continue ejaculatory control techniques for another year or so. A total of 98.7 per cent of Masters and Johnson's (selected) population have achieved lasting cure. M. and J. warn that a transient period of erection difficulties following such cures is common and should cause no alarm. The cost of this treatment at Masters and Johnson's Institute in St. Louis ($2,500) seems to be somewhat out of proportion, both with the attention required and the results obtainable elsewhere.

'Systematic desensitization'

Another quite successful approach which also requires a great deal of cooperation by the woman has been advocated for 14 years by Dr. Joseph Wolpe[9] of the Department of Psychiatry at the University of Virginia. He calls the method 'systematic desensitization,' and bases his approach on the fact that while erection depends on a parasympathetic response, ejaculation responds to sympathetic stimuli such as adrenalin, and is thus precipitated by anxiety. Wolpe instructs the couple to engage in sexual activity without either of them expecting intercourse.

As in Masters and Johnson's later variation on this method[5] (the 'sensate focus' technique, and not the one that was discussed in this paper), the object is sensual discovery over the total body surface. The man especially must rid himself of any feeling of pressure, of any expectation that he has to perform. He is instructed to concentrate on the pleasure of the moment and to do only as much on each occasion as he can, without feeling the slightest anxiety. As he becomes increasingly relaxed, he is soon overcome by pleasurable sensations. As a result, he finds that he is able to engage in more and more intensive sexual activity without ejaculation. Wolpe often combines his own method with that of Semans.

Although total body surface as well as penile desensitization were combined in Wolpe's treatment records,[10] only a record of the latter will be reproduced here. The reader's attention is directed at the precise documentation of the minutes lasted on subsequent trials – obviously the patient was asked to go on with as many trials on each occasion as 30 minutes or so will permit. This documentation is, in itself, a powerful treatment device: the patient can follow his own progress and be encouraged by it. The record indeed shows that while there is a tendency for lasting power to decrease within the trials during any one occasion, the overall trend between occasions is one of definite increase. (Each figure refers to the number of minutes of manual stimulation of the penis by the patient's partner that brought him just short of ejaculation for each successive sequence of stimulations.)

'*First occasion* (Saturday) 8, 6, 6, 6, and 3 minutes.

Second occasion (Saturday) 11, 7, 3, 4, and 4 minutes.

Fourth occasion (Sunday) 17 minutes.

Fifth occasion (Monday) 33 minutes. At this juncture he felt confident enough to have Mrs. I. stimulate him as he sat astride her. The time to "pre-ejaculation" on two successive sequences was two minutes and three minutes.

Sixth occasion (Monday) lying face to face sideways the pre-ejaculatory point was reached in 10 minutes and was maintained for 20 more minutes, when Mrs. I. desisted because of fatigue.

After this occasion, Mr. I. declared that he had never before been able to reach and maintain so high a level of excitement; but this became the norm subsequently.

Eighth occasion (Tuesday) Same as sixth occasion but "pre-ejaculation" was reached in 12 minutes and maintained to 30 minutes.

Ninth occasion (Wednesday) Penile stimulation while astride: 5, 12+, and 9+ minutes.

Eleventh occasion (Thursday) Penile stimulation while astride: 12½, 12, and 23 minutes. After the last, Mr. I. inserted just the glans of his penis into the vagina, maintaining it there for 5 minutes.

Twelfth occasion (Friday) Partial insertion (glans penis) for 20 minutes during which Mrs. I. alone moved and in this way gradually manipulated the penis deeper. At the end of the period Mr. I. withdrew as he felt ejaculation imminent.

Thirteenth occasion (Friday evening after meeting with therapist) Partial intercourse lasted 30 minutes.

Sixteenth occasion (Sunday) Ejaculation after four minutes.

Seventeenth occasion (Monday) Forty minutes, varying between one-quarter to half insertion of penis. Ejaculation was several times imminent, but Mr. I. averted it by relaxing each time.'

To show a couple this typical record at the beginning of their treatment can be quite therapeutic in itself by instilling the confidence that is necessary to carry through until the end of treatment.

All methods discussed here (with the possible exception of the Wolpe method) are recommended only for the sthenic type of prematurity. The asthenic patient who presents with both premature ejaculation and weak erection will be hindered rather than helped by most desensitizing methods. Diverting attention away from sex will be equally counterproductive, of course, to the elderly man whose problem lies in too weak rather than too strong drive pressures. As a matter of fact, most of these methods (with the possible exception of thioradizine which is not yet generally used, however) may backfire even in cases of sthenic prematurity, if overdone. The path between too quick and too slow sexual response – or no sexual response at all – is sometimes a rather narrow one.

PSYCHOLOGICAL FACTORS

Although all the methods discussed in this paper focus on sexual technique (which is indeed crucial in most cases where the problem is a purely sexual one), psychological variables such as attitudes are, of course, important and may defeat the treatment if they are overlooked. A man who thinks of intercourse as his duty or a performance in which success is the key word, will feel very much on the spot when approaching even the most understanding woman, with the memory of his past failures still fresh in his mind. These are the expressions the family physician should watch for in his first interview. Gentle correction should be supplied: sex should be relaxed pleasure, full absorption in sensuous impressions of the moment without any expectation of things to come. Just as in cases of erection difficulties (the almost opposite type of common sexual problem) the performance-oriented attitude will lead to a typical vicious circle in which, just because of the anxiety, the same experience is more and more likely to be repeated. And, of course, results will not be good with the patient who is unable to grasp this simple truth because his real problem is not prematurity but chronic neurotic lack of confidence in himself, and a consequent need to continue proving himself by competing with some imaginary ideal norm or even with his own earlier record. In stubborn cases referral to a psychologist or psychiatrist may be indicated.

INTERPERSONAL CONSIDERATIONS

Many of the techniques discussed here depend on the relationship of the couple to each other, since these measures require the female partner's active and sympathetic cooperation. However, all methods will fail if the wife harbours hostility and resentment towards her husband. Anxiety, tension, and anger are all important (sympathetic) components in lack of ejaculatory control. A loving woman can be a great asset in reducing these discomforts by showing understanding and affection; a hostile one is sure to aggravate the situation by ridiculing her male partner. Sometimes the family physician has been aware of these problems from his earlier contacts with the family; in other cases he will pick up

the tension between the couple while discussing the treatment with both partners – as he always should. (Actually, I suggest seeing husband and wife separately at first; together afterwards.)

If the family doctor forms the judgment that tension comes from non-sexual
areas, or if the problem, while originally a sexual one, has spilled over to other
areas of the marriage to the extent that an honest truce cannot be arranged for
the duration of treatment, it is best to postpone therapy for the sexual problem
until the couple can work through their power struggles and communications
problems with the help of a qualified marriage counsellor.

'Premature ejaculation' is, however, in the overwhelming majority of cases, the
easiest of all common sexual problems to treat. The condition is eminently treatable even among the usual pressures of family practice. Once the assessment is
done and the treatment strategy selected and explained (60-90 minutes at the
most), no more than 10-minute follow-up sessions are necessary in which the couple accounts for progress made, and the physician offers encouragement and may
suggest a few corrections in technique. Emphasis on non-coital techniques as well
as the Semans and the Wolpe methods offer the best promise of lasting success.
Regardless of which method is chosen, however, a very great deal of misery can
be eliminated with relatively little effort. All the more reason why the family
physician should not deprive himself of this most rewarding opportunity to help.

NOTES

1 Kelly, L.G. in: Ellis, A. and Abarbanel, A., eds., *The Encyclopedia of Sexual Behavior*, New York: Hawthorn Books Inc., 1961, (vol. I p. 519-520).

2 Kinsey, A.C., Pomeroy, W.B., and Martin, C.E., *Sexual Behavior in the Human Male*, Philadelphia and London: W.B. Saunders Company, 1948.

3 Masters, W.H. and Johnson, Virginia E., *Human Sexual Response*, Boston: Little, Brown and Co., 1966.

4 Ellis, A., *The Art and Science of Love*, New York: Lyle Stuart, 1960.

5 Masters, W.H. and Johnson, Virginia E., *Human Sexual Inadequacy*, Boston: Little, Brown and Co., 1970.

6 Pillay, A.P., 'Common Sense Therapy of Male Sex Disorders,' *Int. J. Sexol.*, 1950, *4*, 19-22.

7 Hirsch, E.W., *Modern Sex Life*, New York: New American Library, 1957.

8 Semans, J.H., 'Premature Ejaculation: A New Approach,' *Sth. med. J.*, *49*: 353-357, 1956.

9 Wolpe, J., *Psychotherapy by Reciprocal Inhibition*, Stanford: Stanford Univ. Press, 1958.

10 Wolpe, J., *The Practice of Behavior Therapy*, New York: Pergamon Press, 1969.

STEPHEN NEIGER

Some new approaches in treating the anorgasmic woman*

The 'frigid' or anorgasmic woman may or may not visit with this overt complaint in the family physician's office. I suspect that 'unspecified pelvic discomfort,' and possibly 'nervous tension' would be more frequent disguises in which this condition (in its early form) is brought to the attention of the busy family practitioner who, rightly or wrongly, is not always thought of by his female patient as a 'good listener.' Perhaps this is why, by the time a woman perceives herself as 'frigid,' she will seek out a psychologist or psychiatrist – often quite unnecessarily – and not her family physician, or even her gynecologist.

I use the term 'anorgasmic' deliberately in this paper instead of the much better known term 'frigid.' Although most of us think we know what we mean when saying 'this woman is frigid,' it takes little re-thinking to realize that the term has many possible meanings. It ranges over a wide quantitative continuum from the woman who is completely anorgasmic to the one who is able to achieve satisfaction only occasionally.

Moreover, frigidity may refer to such qualitatively completely different conditions as the woman who gets excited during intercourse but is unable to reach orgasm (this is the condition which leads to unspecified chronic pelvic complaints most frequently); or the woman who is completely cold and indifferent to intercourse (a stronger form of negative early conditioning than is the former type); or even the woman who is violently disgusted by the thought not only of intercourse but by the touch of her husband or any other male as long as his touch carries the implication of sexual advances (a condition that is usually superim-

*Reprinted from *Canadian Family Physician*, 17 (May 1971), 52-56.

posed on one of the two above original pictures). I have even heard the term 'clitoral frigidity' used to describe the problem of a very large group of women who are able to achieve orgasm through external but not through internal (intercourse) stimulation. ('Clitoral frigidity' is a rather confusing term introduced by some psychoanalytically-oriented marriage manuals to describe a frequent result of essentially normal individual conditioning.) Not only the origins but also the methods of treatment may be quite different in the different conditions mentioned above which are often lumped together under the term 'frigidity.'[1]

Thus, frigidity is as vague a word as are its male counterparts 'impotence' and 'premature ejaculation.' Yet it is deeply entrenched in the literature and its early disappearance from medical terminology is therefore most unlikely, although Masters and Johnson[2] made a good start by completely refraining from using this 'term' in *Human Sexual Response*.

Almost all cases of disturbance in female sexual satisfaction are psychologically or psychophysiologically based, and we trust the family physician to recognize the very few exceptions that may be partly or fully influenced by some congenital or acquired local condition (e.g. clitoral adhesion, vaginal injury or infection); debilitating systemic illness, gross malnutrition, etc.); or drug abuse (barbiturates as well as many modern 'non-addictive' tranquilizers and antidepressants are well known suppressors of sexual desire if abused – as is alcohol).

FRIGIDITY

Let us discuss, first of all, the 'simple' anorgasmic woman, that is the woman who just cannot reach orgasm without, however, producing additional symptoms of 'freezing' and/or disgust (i.e. real frigidity) on contact with her husband. In the great majority of cases this type of patient is not even indifferent towards – let alone disgusted by – sexual intercourse. She reaches a point of excitement beyond which she cannot rise, however, and she is most frustrated by her inability to reach orgasm. In the absence of relief by orgasm, the pelvic vasocongestion, which is the physiological response to sexual excitement, will take hours to dissipate.[3] No wonder that this is the type of anorgasmic woman whom the family physician most often encounters in his office, where she presents with vague complaints in the pelvic area. This condition is especially typical in early years of marriage, before continued frustration yields to resignation, fear of the situation and, eventually, complete aversion to intercourse. What is the initial cause of such lack of orgasm?

There are many possible answers and therefore we have to admit that we do not yet really know. Some writers believe that every woman is potentially capable of orgasm and that individual and/or social conditioning suppresses this ability more or less permanently in some. Other authors blame the husband's technique instead of, or in addition to, early childhood influences; yet others the couple's *total* relationship, and so forth.

Yet another, perhaps the most interesting, school of thought insists that it is wrong to ask why some women are anorgasmic and the *opposite* question should be asked instead: why do some women have orgasm, while others do not? This school points out that female orgasm is by no means a universal ability throughout all cultures and peoples around the world – nor even through all periods of our own culture.

Less than 70 years ago, it was possible for a famous British gynecologist to declare without fear of contradiction that any married woman who receives pleasure in the act of marital duty is no better than a prostitute.[4] Indeed, during that period, the anorgasmic woman was the cultural norm and the few women who did have orgasm were 'cultural deviates,' and did their best to hide this fact from all but their most intimate friends – a behaviour pattern remarkably similar to that shown today by the anorgasmic woman.

We know from Margaret Mead[5] that there are still a number of cultures in which it is against the norm for the woman to have an orgasm. Indeed, in these cultures, female orgasm tends obligingly to disappear.

A number of researchers[6,7,8] have shown that, with a very few exceptions, there is little evidence of female orgasm among mammals, including anthropoid apes. They also point out that without *male* orgasm (which is almost inevitably connected with ejaculation) no mammalian species would survive – but it could very well survive without *female* orgasm. The female sexual drive in mammals compels the animal to 'present' – i.e. to remain still while the male inserts. It does not compel the animal to orgasm. Margaret Mead concludes that the very fact that whole human cultures could bring the female orgasm to disappearance shows that it has a very much lesser biological basis than has the male orgasm.

EVOLUTIONARY ADVANTAGE

Why then do some females – and indeed in our culture most females – have an orgasm and why do most anorgasmic females strive to have one? It appears that, at some fairly recent point of human evolution, the responsive female has gained an evolutionary advantage because she was selected with preference by most males. What may have happened at that point was that probably more and more responsive mothers gave life to (and reared in a more sex-affirming climate) more and more potentially responsive daughters, or, so this school of researchers points out.

But this transition from the anorgasmic sub-human female to the fully orgastic human female is far from completed yet, as can be seen, among others, in the many cultures (including phases of our own) in which the responsive female is unwelcome. The 10 per cent or so stubbornly anorgasmic women of our own culture may be looked at, therefore, as an evolutionary remnant of this transition – or in other words an ever decreasing rearguard of the 'original' anorgasmic human female, who has not developed the faculty of enjoying intercourse to the fullest.

The attractiveness of this theory notwithstanding, my own bias is that the lack of orgasm in women can be sufficiently explained by individual and social conditioning (i.e. learning) and that at least potentially every woman (or, at least, *almost* every woman) is capable of orgasm. In other words I believe that it is the culture – and within the culture some parents more than others – which is responsible for the suppression of an otherwise universal potential ability in women.

After all, the 65 or so years that have passed from the end of the repressive Victorian phase in which women were practically forbidden to have orgasm to a sexually half-approving period in which they are required to have orgasm (but only under certain conditions), represent a very short period in human history. Undoubtedly, there are still many remnants of Victorian thinking in our own philosophy which cannot but affect the sexual potential of our female children. As Albert Ellis[8] points out, it is quite illogical to raise girls with the ideal of absolute virginity (i.e. non-responsiveness) up until marriage, and then expect them to turn into raving nymphomaniacs within one night just because official cultural approval is now suddenly given. Of course, it is quite possible that this state of affairs is slowly changing now; for example, there seems to be, in some circles at least, greater acceptance of petting that may or may not lead to orgasm; perhaps even some grudging acceptance of intercourse among the engaged.

PREVENT EMOTIONAL WEAR

Kinsey's sample,[9] less than a generation ago, showed that while 75 per cent of women could perform this feat within one year of marriage, at the end of the first year still about one woman in four was unresponsive. The same data seem to indicate that this 25 per cent decreased to 10 per cent some time between the first and the 15th year of marriage. While this in itself is encouraging since it shows that, in most cases without any therapeutic intervention, most of those who couldn't achieve orgasm before, eventually will be able to, the job of the family physician, gynecologist, psychologist, or whoever, in attempting to help the anorgastic woman, is to prevent the emotional wear and tear, and the development of secondary symptoms that are bound to occur between the first and the 15th year, by abbreviating this time period and by restoring the woman to as full an orgastic capacity as swiftly as possible. How can this be done?

Orgasm is a reflex, dependent on a reflex arch, as is the patellar reflex, vomiting, or bowel movements. Like many other reflexes, and perhaps even more so, female orgasm can be very substantially influenced and even completely suppressed by cortical control. We all know patients who have so consistently suppressed their bowel movements that they are now capable of responding only to the most drastic artificial aids. Since orgasm is by no means as powerful or essential a reflex as most of the others mentioned (because of its evolutionary novelty), it is far more subject to individual and cultural conditioning. There is a substantial and still growing body of evidence[10] showing a rather clear relationship between how early in life female orgasm was first elicited (e.g. by petting or masturbation); how regularly it was then elicited, and the ease and frequency with which it can be achieved later in marriage. If female orgasm has been consistently and drastically suppressed during the first decades of life, it later becomes increasingly difficult.

Obviously, one will approach such a suppressed 'rusted in' reflex arch with maximum, rather than minimum, stimulation. And here is the first difficulty the practical sexologist usually encounters. As we have learned only recently from Masters and Johnson, but as we know all too well now, sexual intercourse, strangely enough, is minimum stimulation, especially for the inexperienced human female. 'She needs much more time to achieve a climax than her husband,' as the marriage manuals told us for half a century now, but in the light of data from research[3] this must be rephrased to read: 'Much more time – but in intercourse *only*.'

What are stronger stimuli? Masters and Johnson's work shows that almost anything else is. In my 15 years experience, I have found that the following should be discussed with the couple (in increasing order of effectiveness): manual and oral stimulation by the husband; self-stimulation (masturbation), where the woman herself is able to regulate the pressure, the pace, the speed of stimulation on various parts of her body; most efficient, however, self-stimulation (and stimulation by the husband), aided by such powerful gadgets as vibrators. Especially with the help of the latter two methods most women can achieve orgasm within a time period that is remarkably close to the average North American male (two to three minutes).

BARRIER OF INHIBITIONS

As for the anorgasmic woman, in most cases even one of these methods (preferably, however, two or more in combination), if patiently and skilfully practiced, will break through the barrier of inhibitions within days or weeks at the most, often even after 20 years of anorgasmic marriage in women aged 40 and older. Which of the methods should be tried first depends on individual taste; and this is a very important point. All too often one or the other method will be strongly rejected by the husband, by the wife, or by both. If this happens, the point should not be pressed, of course. Amazingly, the method completely rejected by couple A may be completely accepted by couple B, and vice versa. Fortunately, in most cases at least, one or two methods are found acceptable by both partners.

Manual stimulation by the husband is often acceptable but very frequently insufficient. In most cases the couple had experimented with some inadequate form of this type of stimulation for a long time and think they know all the 'tricks' by now, but are convinced that these did not help them. It is very difficult to explain just where they went wrong, and if they wish to do better just how and when to apply more effective stimulation and on what parts of the female anatomy. The wife, who alone knows and would be able to guide her husband's hand, often refuses to: communications are most often blocked in sexual matters between the partners in such situations as a result of romantic insistence on 'spontaneity or nothing at all'; often aggravated by the many years of pent-up frustration due to repeated failures in lovemaking.

If the husband and the wife can be induced to accept the idea of oral lovemaking then this, especially if combined with intravaginal fingerplay, can be an extremely powerful new stimulus. I usually instruct the husband to play with his lips and tongue on the clitoris and the upper vulva area including especially the upper parts of the labia minora (an anatomical atlas is always necessary for this type of explanation) while simultaneously inserting two of his fingers into the anterior one third of the vagina and performing various operations there which go far beyond the possibilities of what can be done with the penis.

If this process can be clearly communicated to the husband and accepted by the wife, it usually results in a very powerful orgasm sooner or later, if not on the first attempt then on the second or third. Very soon after this happens, a series of multiple orgasms may be elicited in this way in the wake of one of which – Masters and Johnson's 'plateau phase'[2] – it is the best time for the husband to penetrate with his penis for one, final, big and usually simultaneous orgasm. This is the easiest way, then, usually to 'transfer' orgasm sensations in the woman from non-coital loveplay to actual intercourse.

Unfortunately, and despite rapidly changing cultural norms in this type of sexual behaviour, the idea of oral stimulation is still often unacceptable to one or the other partner. Also, if accepted, the process of communication is not clearcut, and 'failure' of the attempt to bring about orgasm by this means is not infrequently reported on follow up. Especially in such a situation self-stimulation, if acceptable to the female, can help clear the way for a breakthrough. I have managed to induce orgasm in women after 3 to 20 years and more of anorgasmic marital life by doing nothing more than to encourage them to masturbate whenever they had sufficient privacy to do so, and handing them the female Kinsey report[9] which details the different methods that are used by women for effective self-stimulation. Not surprisingly, a woman who has just achieved her first, second, or third orgasm by masturbation, can guide her husband's manual and oral lovemaking efforts with increasing effectiveness. Unfortunately, the idea of masturbation is often unacceptable to the woman.

VIBRATORS MORE EASILY ACCEPTED

Strangely enough, and contrary to what one might expect, vibrators tend to be more easily accepted than either of the above two recommendations. There are two types of vibrators – external and internal. The external vibrators are the more useful and should be tried first. There are at least two different types of external vibrators. Although most readers will probably have seen these, I will describe them for the benefit of the minority.

The most economical and most efficient of these gadgets looks something like a large revolver with an electric cord and various removable attachments, some made of bakelite and some of rubber. The bakelite attachments are good for general massage of deep muscles but unsuitable for sexual purposes. From the rubbery attachments the most frequently favoured ones look like a cup and a saucer. Each of these can be used alternatively for pressure, suction or fine stimulation, the latter by using the sharp edges of the saucer.

A completely different type of external vibrator is known to the male reader from his local barbershop where it is used for massage of the scalp. It looks like a rather big (about hand size) bug with metal straps attached to its bottom. The person who does the massaging can insert his full hand through one of the straps and a few fingers through the other. As a result of this he retains a very great degree of mobility in his fingers while the powerful motor inside the gadget keeps vibrating these at a pace which he could not possibly match by his own motor activities. His own manipulations, however, are very effectively added to the vibrations of this little machine. This gadget, although it combines the touch of human hands with machine power, is the more expensive and generally the less effective of the two external vibrators.

Until recently I used to believe that internal vibrators were completely useless. An article published one year ago by a renowned U.S. gynecologist and sexologist, Dr. LeMon Clark[10] claims differently. Dr. Clark reports using with excellent results a vibrator constructed from an electric toothbrush and a rubber vaginal dilator in combination with an external vibrator, on women who were resistent to stimulation by external vibrator alone.

Until fairly recently, vibrators used to be viewed with some suspicion and alarm by most marriage counsellors and sexologists, not only because they were looked at as 'taking the human element out of lovemaking' but also because there was thought to be a danger that the woman might become addicted to the strong stimulation of the vibrator and would then no longer be as sexually interested in her husband. However, the official attitude of the medical profession to vibrators has undergone a drastic change during the past few years.

In addition to LeMon Clark's endorsement,[10] both external and internal vibrators have been strongly endorsed most recently by such authorities as Dengrove,[11] who is also a gynecologist and a past president of the Society of the Scientific Study of Sex. These two join earlier authorities, such as Masters and Johnson, who recommended the use of vibrators (personal communication 1963). Furthermore, in independent recent conventions of the American Association of Marriage Counsellors and the Society for the Scientific Study of Sex,[12] gynecologists, marriage counsellors, and sexologists who have used vibrators for 10 years and more in their practices have spoken up one by one and have agreed that they have yet to see a genuine case of addiction to such a gadget.

Admittedly, stimulation by vibrator is extremely strong and the release equally powerful. Both, however, are very short-lived, about two to three minutes in duration. Practically every woman prefers to have the slow build-up of natural lovemaking over many more minutes and up to half an hour and more, followed by an equally powerful release by the husband's skillful lovemaking.

STRICTLY LEARNING DEVICES

It cannot be sufficiently emphasized that all the methods discussed so far, including especially masturbation and vibrators, are strictly learning devices. The idea is not simply to give orgasm by *any* means. The purpose is instead to *teach* the woman the sensation of orgasm and the feelings that accompany the build-up towards orgasm so that she can more easily recognize these; so that she can become aware or more aware of her body and her sexual sensations; so that she can more easily distinguish between effective and less effective stimulation by her husband, and can guide him.

Another way of putting the same point is that, especially in the case of the unused, inhibited, or 'rusted in' reflex arch, maximum stimulation has to be applied first in order to unblock the reflex and make it capable of responding to the much more subtle stimulation of intercourse later. It appears very much as if each time we succeed in eliciting a reflex at all, by whatever stimulation, its elicitation becomes somewhat easier the next time, still easier the next, and so forth. This finding is quite consistent with what we know of how learning occurs at any level of the nervous system.

It is generally postulated that synaptic gaps shorten with the repeated elicitation of a reflex; in other words the reflex arch becomes 'run in' in a manner not too different from restarting the motor of a car after it has run for some time and then was shut off. Again, this is emphasized to show that such devices as vibrators are strictly for teaching their users how to respond to subtler stimulation and not substitute methods in their own right. Typically, after the learning process has ended, they are put away and used only as occasional methods to increase marital variety.

The three methods discussed before will, in my experience, bring about orgasm in 90 per cent or more of anorgasmic women who are motivated for treatment; even after many years and sometimes decades of marriage without orgasm. No psychological or psychiatric treatment is necessary with this group, no skills and no time investment are needed beyond that which is available in family practice.

This still will leave, however, a hard core of about 10 per cent of anorgasmic women who usually can be recognized in the first interview by either a complete lack of interest in sex or even a direct aversion to the sexual act, and even the touch of the husband. They come to the office not of their own will, but under strong pressure from the husband. These are cases in which a gross neurotic condition was either induced by very powerful early repression of all sexual thoughts, feelings, and needs in the parental home; or else where such an anesthesia or revulsion has been superimposed on the original simple anorgasmic condition by repeated clumsy and frustrating attempts on the husband's part. In such a situation it is no use trying techniques of more powerful stimulation – it is the basic fear that manifests itself in vaginal anesthesia or revulsion which must be attacked first. Here then is a real role for the specialist in psychotherapy.

SYSTEMATIC DESENSITIZATION

In my experience the best method of dealing with this type of patient is not traditional psychotherapy but a form of behaviour therapy called systematic desensitization.[14]

Systematic desensitization, like other forms of behaviour therapy, is a relatively modern approach to various types of neurotic disturbance, and, unlike psychoanalytically-oriented psychotherapy, concerned not so much with the past, but with the present. All behaviour therapies are based on the assumption that neurotic symptoms are pieces of learned behaviour which, given the proper methods, can be unlearned and replaced by more adequate behaviour patterns.

Behaviour therapy methods are relatively short-term treatments. For example, systematic desensitization, while admittedly not a two or three session counselling affair like the methods discussed before, will still be of much shorter duration than most other methods of psychotherapy.

Essentially, systematic desensitization begins by establishing the conditioning history of the symptom while teaching the patient to relax more thoroughly. After the history is complete and relaxation is mastered, the patient is faced with the concrete situations in which the symptom has first developed and now tends to develop – but not before she is put in a thoroughly relaxed condition.

Systematic desensitization, also called 'reciprocal inhibition therapy,'[13] is based on the antagonism between the sympathetic and parasympathetic parts of the automatic nervous system. Since relaxation is the most complete parasympathetic-dominated condition that can be achieved in a wakeful state, minor sympathetic, anxiety-arousing stimuli are just unable to break through and to result in adrenalin outpour. As more and more of the weaker, and later increasingly stronger images that have earlier led to fear responses are now tolerated and become associated with comfort, calm, safety, relaxation, and protectedness in the therapist's chair, so the effect will begin to generalize outside the therapist's office.

Vaginal anesthesia and revulsion against touch by the opposite sex are not the only symptoms that are treatable by systematic desensitization, but they are among the most responsive ones.

Like the shorter methods discussed at the beginning of this paper, systematic desensitization does not rely on the one or two sessions per week in the office, but insists on home assignments. One of the most successful methods of self-desensitization that can be practised at home by the couple has been brought into the limelight lately by Masters and Johnson,[2] although it was originally proposed and practised for many years by Dr. Joseph Wolpe[14] of Philadelphia Temple University, the father of behaviour therapy, and his followers.

This method is based on the assumption that the neurotically anorgastic woman is, in most cases, terrified not so much of sexual stimulation, but of penetration by her husband which she expects to be the inevitable result of his advances and preliminaries. In consequence, the treatment consists of instructing the couple to lie in close contact with as much of each other's nude body surfaces exposed as possible and engage in loveplay for hours, concentrating on the sensuous pleasure of the moment only. All intercourse and thought of 'any duties yet to be performed' is strictly forbidden during the first days.

This phase may last up to a week or even two, until the behaviour therapist has had an opportunity to have a report of the couple's feelings during these encounters which, devoted entirely to the process of self-discovery, must be free from all expectations. Until the wife requests differently, even touch of the vulva and mons areas is to be strictly avoided and caressing is to concentrate mainly on the upper body. Usually within a couple of weeks, if not earlier, strong desire for heavy petting and then for intercourse is reported. Even then the couple is cautioned by the therapist to proceed very slowly and gradually.

NOT ORGASM WORSHIP

Nothing that has been said above should be interpreted as condoning 'orgasm worship'; the pursuit of orgasm as the all important, supreme value in marriage. In fact, I have consistently maintained that orgasm is far from being the only important part of the sexual act and sex is far from being the only aspect of marriage. No urologist, cardiologist, neurologist, or ophthalmologist would make such exclusive claims for their organs or systems of specialization – nor does the sexologist.

Some marriages are quite happy with a minimum of sexual expression, or even none at all. No attempt should be made in these situations to disturb the balance. Those who are not motivated to change, or those who are unsuccessful no matter how hard they try, should be reassured about just how much of their marriage remains to be enjoyed without full sexual expression – just as there is so much of art and culture that is open to those who are colour blind.

On the other hand, there is no point in giving in too early if both partners wish to go on trying. And precisely because sex is no cure-all for a bad marriage and because love and orgasm are two different things, the reverse also applies. The most perfect relationship will not cure sexual inadequacy by itself. When removal of sexual symptoms is desired by the couple, these symptoms must be attacked directly if there is to be any hope of success. No amount of 'relationship' or 'communication'-oriented therapy will do. Technique is certainly no substitute for love. But love without any technique will not help the woman who genuinely desires to be a responsive and satisfied sexual partner to her husband.

NOTES

1 Masters, W.H. and Johnson, Virginia E., *Human Sexual Inadequacy*, Boston: Little, Brown and Co., 1970.
2 Masters, W.H. and Johnson, Virginia E., *Human Sexual Response*, Boston: Little, Brown and Co., 1966.
3 From Rubin, I., *Community Acceptance of the Responsible Teacher.* Symposium on 'The Uncertain Quest: The Dilemmas of Sex Education.' U. of California, San Francisco Medical Center, Apr. 10, 1965.
4 Elkan, E., 'The Evolution of Female Orgastic Ability,' *Int. J. Sexol.* 1948, *2*, 1-13, 1948, *2*, 84-92.

5 Mead, Margaret, *Male and Female*, New York: New American Library, 1955.
6 Shuttleworth, F., 'A Biosocial and Developmental Theory of Male and Female Sexuality,' *Marr. Fam. Living*, 1959, *21*, 163-170.
7 Terman, Lewis M., 'Correlates of Orgasm Adequacy in a Group of 556 Wives,' *J. Psychol.*, 1951, *32*, 115-172.
8 Ellis, A., *The American Sexual Tragedy*, New York: Twayne Publishers, 1954.
9 Kinsey, A.C., Pomeroy, W.B., Martin, C.E., and Gebhard, P.H., *Sexual Behaviour in the Human Female*, Philadelphia and London: W.B. Saunders Co., 1953.
10 Clark, L., 'Is There a Difference between a Clitoral and a Vaginal Orgasm?' *J. of Sex Research, 6,* 1, 25-28 Feb. 1970.
11 Dengrove, E., 'Mechanotherapy of Sexual Disorders,' *J. of Sex Research, 7,* 1-12 February 1971.
12 Rubin, I., 'Helpful and Harmful Sex Devices,' *Sexology, 36,* 9, 14-16 April, 1970.
13 Wolpe, J., *Psychotherapy by Reciprocal Inhibition*, Stanford: Stanford University Press, 1958.
14 Wolpe, J., and Lazarus, A.A., *Behaviour Therapy Techniques*, Oxford: Pergamon Press, 1966.

PART THREE

SEXUAL BEHAVIOUR AMONG SELECTED GROUPS

BENJAMIN SCHLESINGER

Sexuality and the physically handicapped*

The general approach of our society towards handicapped people is to deny their existence. When that is not possible we fund institutions and agencies to house and care for them, to keep them out of sight and out of mind.

Although the only differences between handicapped and 'normal' people are the specific disabilities of the handicapped and the adjustments these disabilities necessitate, the majority of the physically handicapped are hindered from becoming fulfilled human beings by the fears, guilts and misconceptions of a society that denies them two basic needs – a realistic and positive identity as sexual beings and the opportunity for sexual expression and fulfilling sexual relationships.

SEX EDUCATION

At a time when efforts are being made to normalize or humanize the handicapped, sex education for these people is particularly important. The trend away from institutions and toward community living in group homes, hostels and halfway houses is strong. Socialization programs offer greater opportunity than before for heterosexual contacts and for developing loving relationships. Our 'sex-oriented society' and permissive policies place greater temptations before the young of this generation than before those of previous generations.

Bass[1] views sex education as particularly important to the handicapped because of the following points:

*Reprinted from *Canadian Medical Association Journal*, 114 (May 8, 1976), 772-773, 809.

1 It must be assumed that they have less information and more misinformation than the nonhandicapped.

2 They often have poorer judgment and fewer social skills because of overprotection and isolation. Training must be directed towards acceptable social behaviour. Much can be taught within this context and the handicapped person usually accepts rules more readily than the normal person.

3 Their sexual development may be delayed and they may be inhibited. There may be more homosexuality than normal, especially if they are in residential schools. Teachers should realize that, during the phase of peer group interests, there may be expressions of homosexuality; severe correction and punishment may fixate such behaviour. If homosexuality is explained to these young people and they have an opportunity to talk about it and participate in substituting other expressions of sexual feelings, homosexual behaviour will usually diminish, particularly when heterosexual interests develop.

4 Severe handicaps may make marriage inadvisable or unlikely. Individuals with such handicaps must be helped to understand that it is not necessary to marry to be happy – many people choose not to marry, many others wish they had never married.

5 While competency for parenthood should be considered by all young persons, it is particularly important for the handicapped, who may be able to care for themselves but cannot bear the added burden of parenthood. Substitutes for parenting must be explained. The responsibilities of parenthood must be broken down into tasks they can understand. The reasons for wanting a baby are often neurotic: we hear much about the joys of parenthood, but the sacrifices and disappointments are seldom mentioned. There are advantages to the child-free marriage. Marriage is a difficult adjustment for the handicapped so it is important that they wait about 2 years before having a baby.

6 Genetic factors must be explained so that these individuals know what the chances are of passing on their handicap.

7 The educational content must be presented simply and repeated often. For those who have difficulty understanding, human reproduction should be taught first to avoid the confusion of shifting from birds to people. Pictures should be used whenever possible.

SEXUALITY

A child's attitude towards his body greatly affects his sexuality; this is especially true of the handicapped. The handicapped adolescent is apt to be self-conscious about his body and may have many sexual concerns. Parents should be prepared for this and should voice questions for those who are shy. Body changes should be discussed with the orthopedically handicapped even more than with the normal child. The handicapped child, Spock[2] advises, will be better adjusted if allowed to engage in sex play and to masturbate without punishment. If the parent feels compelled to stop this behaviour, it should be done without threat of physical harm or guilt since the child may associate sex play with his handicap.

Ayrault[3] has pointed out that only if handicapped children are loved and accepted for what they are can they develop self-love and self-acceptance, and if they have self-acceptance they can be more readily accepted by their peers.

The handicapped teenage girl has many disadvantages compared with the normal child, but this should not prevent her from being as feminine as possible. Parents, particularly the mother, can place realistic demands on the girl by helping to feminize her environment – her room, appearance, make-up, clothes, crutches, etc. A handicapped girl should learn how to conduct her own toilet and menstrual care so as to establish some independence.

Because a physically handicapped boy has so many of his needs looked after by a woman, there is danger that his masculinity will not develop fully. This can be partially alleviated if the woman (usually his mother) treats him in a masculine way. The father should help in taking care of his son's physical needs and spend recreational time with him, thus serving as a masculine model.

Though there is little proof, most authors agree that the handicapped need as much sex-role modelling as the nonhandicapped, if not more.

SEXUAL NEEDS AND OPPORTUNITIES

Many parents, trying to cope with their guilt for bearing a handicapped child, deny the sexual desires of their child,[4] and many institutions and agencies have also followed this approach.

Research has demonstrated that orthopedically handicapped children have a sex drive at least as strong as the average individual but they do not have the same opportunity for sexual release as their peers. Much of this is due to their feelings of inferiority and lack of confidence.[5] Loneliness is a part of the lives of many physically disabled teenagers, not because of a lack of friends but because they are denied the type of boy-girl relationships that normal teenagers enjoy. It is commonly believed that the handicapped are not eligible for marriage, although there is no strong evidence that they have any more difficulty adjusting to heterosexual relationships than the general population.[6] Nordquist[7] reported that orthopedically handicapped children masturbate, reveal themselves, investigate each other's genitals and ask questions about sexual behaviour to the same degree as children without handicaps. Dating is a major problem for the disabled.[7-9] In a study in Denmark on this problem, quoted by Nordquist,[7] 50 per cent of the handicapped men and women included in the study had little social intercourse with others in their leisure time, compared with only 10 per cent of the nonhandicapped.

The handicapped person with a normal sex drive, deprived of the normal emotional, physical, intellectual and sexual outlets, may have permanent feelings of frustration and anxiety, which may only be relieved by masturbation. While Ayrault[10] has warned that the disabled teenager often engages in 'excessive and psychologically damaging' masturbation, Spock[8] and Nordquist[11] have advocated masturbation; its only danger is guilt, which can only be externally induced.

Physiologically, what are the possibilities of physically handicapped persons engaging in intercourse and other sexual acts? Most disabled persons are able to engage in sexual acts but may require special education, and in some cases special help.[12] Most research on this topic has been done on paraplegics.

Sexual intercourse, from a technical perspective, is easier for a disabled woman than for her male counterpart, because our culture emphasizes the performance by the male. The woman, unlike the man, does not need to be sexually excited in order to engage in intercourse. Although some handicapped women are not technically capable of intercourse, the greater problem is what pregnancy would mean to them.

The paraplegic woman is usually able to have intercourse and even to conceive and give birth. Although many such women are not able to have orgasm, most can still gain sexual pleasure through breast stimulation or other forms of lovemaking. Even if intercourse is impossible a woman can stimulate her clitoris manually or with a massage apparatus. (This is true only if she has control of her arms.) If the woman's partner is a paraplegic and cannot achieve erection, he can still satisfy her by stimulating her clitoris with his fingers, mouth or massage apparatus.

The paraplegic male has more problems with intercourse, although many achieve good erections and some can ejaculate. Many male paraplegics can satisfy their partner, provided she is sufficiently active. Thus, the woman must often take the initiative and be the active, leading partner. Because this entails a reversal of sexual roles, such couples would benefit from counselling on this subject.

Like a woman, a man can achieve orgasm without intercourse. His partner can stimulate his penis manually, orally or with a massage apparatus or he can do this himself if he has control of his hands. While many of these findings have come from studies in paraplegics, much information is relevant for other disabled groups such as those with cerebral palsy.

Some handicapped couples could have intercourse with the aid of a third person but this opportunity is denied them because of the prevailing attitudes of society. Despite the adjustments involved, most handicapped people feel that any effort to improve their sex life is valuable because it increases their worth as men or women.

SEXUAL COUNSELLING

Because sex instruction does not achieve all its educational goals and barely attempts to deal with personal and emotional problems, the counsellor must fill the gaps. The professional can help the disabled youth with dating problems by instilling in him a greater confidence in human relationships. It is important that the professional working with handicapped people should make them comfortable with their sexual feelings. Sexual questions should be dealt with at length and in depth. If the standard method of intercourse is not possible because of the individual's handicap, then the counsellor should help the patient find the position or sex act that will best suit the couple's needs. The couple should feel at ease about any changes they must make from the basic intercourse position.

The handicapped person often does not receive counselling on contraception and the problems of having children. This is especially true of children with cerebral palsy or muscular dystrophy living in residential homes.

Masturbation, the most common method for sexual release for the physically handicapped, is often complicated by feelings of anxiety or guilt. Counsellors can be instrumental in making a teenager feel comfortable about masturbation.

Ayrault[13] has stated that homosexuality, masochism and exhibitionism are more prevalent among the disabled than within the general population. She has claimed that a major cause for this is the person's reaction against his disability, and stresses that counsellors should be prepared for this.

INSTITUTIONAL LIFE

Only a few of the severely handicapped are able to live in their own homes, because society's services to the physically handicapped outside institutions are so poor.

It is extremely difficult for a couple to maintain a satisfactory sex life in an institution because of the lack of privacy. Fortunately 'privacy rooms' are being introduced into institutions. In the Netherlands, in England and in Cincinnati, apartment units have been designed for handicapped couples and are staffed by professionals. In a few institutions masturbation has been prescribed and stimulation is being provided for those unable to masturbate.[14]

CONCLUSION

I have presented selected highlights of the topic of sexuality and the handi-capped, and can only echo the statement by Bidgood.[15]

If we are sincere in wanting to help handicapped persons to become all they are capable of becoming, to lead fulfilling lives, and to enjoy all the aspects of their God-given humanity, then we as professionals cannot evade this issue. We must invest ourselves – our talents, our knowledge, and our energies – in working for the acceptance of the fully human, fully sexual nature of handicapped people, so that some day soon millions of other handicapped around the world will not have to beg acceptance, but can state proudly: We are like other people.

NOTES

I am indebted to Niki Galloon and Mark Creedon, students at the faculty of social work, for their assistance in the review of literature.

1 Bass, M.S., 'Sex Education for the Handicapped,' *The Family Coordinator,* 23: 27 1974.
2 Spock, B., Lerrigo, M.O., *Caring for Your Disabled Child,* Riverside, N.J.: Macmillan, 1965, p. 237.
3 Ayrault, E.W., *Helping the Handicapped Teenager Mature,* New York: Associated Press, 1971, pp. 86-97.
4 Bidgood, F.E., 'Sexuality and the Handicapped,' *Siecus Report* 11: 1, 1974.
5 Ayrault, E.W., *op. cit.,* pp. 100-101
6 Wright, B.A., *Physical Disability: A Psychological Approach,* New York: Harper and Row, 1960, pp. 189-90.
7 Nordquist, I., *Life Together,* Stockholm, 1972, p. 31.
8 Spock, B.M., Lerrigo, M.O., *op. cit.,* p. 246.
9 Kershaw, J., *Handicapped Children,* London, Heinemann (William), 1966, p. 60.
10 Ayrault, E.W., *op. cit.,* p. 130.
11 Nordquist, I., *op. cit.,* p. 28.
12 Lassen, P., *Sex and the Spinal Cord Injured: A Selected Bibliography,* Paralyzed Veterans of America, Washington, 1973.
13 Ayrault, E.W., *op. cit.,* pp. 134-39.
14 Bidgood, F.E., *op. cit.,* p. 2.
15 Idem: *op. cit.,* p. 3.

BERNARD GREEN AND RENA PAUL

Parenthood and the mentally retarded*

In this paper we examine the problem of the expression of sexuality of the mentally retarded from the perspective of their parents. Although we consider the
utility and legality of various methods of birth control available to the retarded,
we focus on one: sterilization. Our concern is even narrower; we examine only
the problems associated with voluntary sterilization. Our discussion will show
there are many difficulties – legal and social – facing conscientious parents seeking sterilization for their retarded child.[1] For this reason we conclude with the
draft of a model statute.

MENTAL RETARDATION AND METHODS OF BIRTH CONTROL

The development of retarded persons is permanently and (so far) irreversibly
arrested. They are unable to learn or to mature, physically and socially, at the
rate considered usual for their chronological age. Although now, with sophisticated training methods, they acquire skills never before thought possible, mentally retarded adults do not attain the degree of knowledge, understanding, and
adaptive discrimination necessary for independent survival.[2] This statement may
sound pessimistic but it is one of the realities we must face in providing services
to meet their needs.

In recent years, the philosophical pendulum in the care of the mentally retarded has swung from institutionalization to community-based services.[3] The
aim now is to help the mentally retarded lead lives as close to normal as possible,

*Reprinted from *University of Toronto Law Journal*, 24 (1974), 117-125.

approximating the patterns and conditions of everyday life and the norms and life styles of other members of society.

Full implementation of this policy would mean that approximately 11,000 persons now in institutions in Ontario would move out into the community to join the estimated 200,000 already there. But this move means living in a world in which sexual expression is an accepted and acknowledged form of adult behaviour. What are or should be, our expectations of the mildly retarded in this sphere of human activity?[4] We contend that they need personal human contact, companionship, sexual participation, and marriage just as much as other members of our society,[5] albeit their needs and aspirations may sometimes be awkwardly articulated and inappropriately expressed.

Sexual intimacy between willing partners is a private matter, and rightly so; but when one or both partners are mentally retarded the possibility that children will result should be of concern. This point of view is based on three major considerations. First, the concept of normalization – the view that retardates should be able to lead lives as similar as possible to those of ordinary members of the community – has important consequences. We have referred to the deinstitutionalization that will take place; of more significance is society's understanding that the retardates will have the same right to express their sexuality as the rest of us. The result is that there will be a greater number of mentally retarded individuals in the community engaging in sexual activity, thus increasing the population at risk greatly. Second, a 1965 study by Reed and Reed, involving an investigation of over eighty thousand persons, led them to conclude that '... the 1 to 2 per cent of the population composed of fertile retardates produced 36.1 per cent of the retardates of the next generation, while the remaining 98 to 99 per cent of the population produced only 63.9 per cent of the retarded persons of the next generation'[6] and 'The fact that about five-sixths of the retarded have a retarded parent or a retarded aunt or uncle is of great significance because it demonstrates the large extent to which transmission is involved in the etiology of mental retardation.'[7]

Third, we contend, as others have, that mentally retarded persons who experience severe difficulties in the management of their affairs make inadequate parents,[8] not from any lack of affection for their children, but because they are unable to cope with the pressures of parenthood. Compulsory and universal schooling, reinforced by various community resources, does not protect the offspring of the mentally retarded from this parental neglect and cultural deprivation.

Many of the retarded parents are unmarried. The single retarded mother known to us bears no resemblance to the emancipated bachelor Ms who, after considering all the alternatives, decides upon motherhood outside the framework of the conventional family. The pregnancies of retarded mothers are not planned, they simply happen – the unthought-of outcome of sexual activity. But marriage does not seem to be the solution. In many of the cases that we are familiar with the parents are married to each other but nevertheless the children and the family suffer; it is not unusual to have five community agencies helping the retarded parent: the social service department of the local Association for the Mentally Retarded, the Children's Aid Society, the Child Adjustment Services of the local Board of Education, the public health nurse, and a voluntary family agency.

In all cases that we know about, the parents indicated fondness and concern for their offspring, yet the children suffered from neglect and deprivation. We have concluded, therefore, that the neglect stems from inability to cope rather than from unwillingness to provide the necessary care. Furthermore, this inability to cope is so pronounced that even the supervision provided by several social agencies has failed to alter the living conditions of these families. Clearly, eliminating the problems which parenthood poses to the mentally retarded and their children is not an easy task.

The introduction of an adequate income supplement to augment the individuals' earnings and the provision of supervised living arrangements, such as group homes and small residences, would improve this grim situation. But the turnover of residential personnel is high, and sharing a household with other retarded individuals or families poses its own problems. While these measures are attractive alternatives to putting the children in a foster home when parenthood is a *fait accompli* and the family needs immediate help, they are no substitute for planned parenthood.

In our opinion, the real solution is birth control. For the retarded, we need a method that does not require the conscious participation of the user at the time of intercourse. This rules out condoms, coitus interruptus, foams, creams, and diaphragms; even IUDs have drawbacks. The alternatives are: abstinence, which demands great if not impossible self-control; the pill, which offers almost one hundred per cent protection if taken properly, but which cannot be left to the individual's memory and discretion; abortion, which is hardly the birth control method of choice; and finally sterilization, which is one hundred per cent effective but which raises a number of legal and, of course, ethical questions.

THE LEGALITY OF VARIOUS BIRTH CONTROL METHODS

Methods of contraception fall into two groups: those which require no surgical action and those which do. The non-surgical methods, whether mechanical or chemical, are now legally available to all adults.[9] In our discussion of the surgical methods we consider the legality of their use first for the non-retarded and then for the retarded.

Use of surgical methods for the non-retarded

One of the surgical methods of birth control – abortion – is expressly restricted by law. If the conditions set out in the Crminal Code are not satisfied, the person who performs the abortion as well as the person who is aborted are guilty of criminal offences.[10] And it is well known that the restrictions imposed by the Criminal Code have been strengthened by the actions of some publicly funded hospitals.[11] A woman may seek an abortion because she is afraid that the child she will deliver will be retarded.[12] If she lives in an area of Canada which has established the machinery required by the Criminal Code,[13] and if the hospital in which the operation is to be performed has a liberal abortion committee, she may receive a certificate: carrying the child, childbirth, and caring for the child may be extremely disturbing to the woman. But we have suggested that abortion is hardly the birth control method of choice: aside from aesthetic, religious, philosophical, and economic problems, it is not permanent.

Sterilization, though sometimes reversible,[14] must for legal purposes be considered permanent. Doubts concerning the legality of sterilization have been raised,[15] but they seem to be without substance – at least in relation to the sterilization of a normal adult.

Criminal liability can be imposed only for an offence expressly set out in the Criminal Code; in Canada there are no common law offences.[16] The Code contains no provisions expressly penalizing parties to a sterilization. Only two sections could be even remotely relevant to the problem: s 244, which declares assault to be a criminal offence; and s 228, which penalizes any person 'who, with intent (a) to wound, maim or disfigure any person ... causes bodily harm in any way to any person ...'

It is implicit in the definition of assault contained in s 244[17] that the consent of the alleged victim precludes criminal liability. Moreover, s 7(3) of the Code expressly declares that common law defences are still applicable; consent is a defence to an assault charge. That parliament intended this result is evident from the express provisions in the Code excluding consent as a defence in cases of euthanasia[18] and various sexual activities involving children under 14 years of age.[19] This analysis seems equally applicable to a maiming charge under s 228.[20]

Perhaps the only qualification to our suggested analysis is that the courts have held that a person could not consent to his own disablement that would prevent him from being an effective fighter.[21] But even if we assume that the English judges of the seventeenth and eighteenth centuries viewed women as potential soldiers, it is difficult to see how sterilization reduces one's ability as a warrior.[22]

If voluntary sterilization were criminal, courts might impose civil liability on the person who performed the operation even if it was done competently. In fact, there is no reported decision in any English-speaking jurisdiction imposing liability for sterilization of a consenting adult. There may be liability – even assuming a lack of negligence – if the operation is performed on a minor without the consent of his or her guardian,[23] just as there may be civil liability imposed on the physician who performs an abortion on a minor without the consent of the guardian.[24]

Use of surgical methods for the retarded
The retardation of a person will be legally significant only if a surgical method is to be used. Two different stiuations must be distinguished: one, an adult retardate seeking abortion or sterilization for herself or himself; the other a normal parent seeking sterilization, for example, for a child considered to be retarded. In the first situation the wise surgeon will obtain the consent of a responsible adult since any operation is an assault unless there is consent to the operation; if the retardation is of a sufficiently severe character the retardate will not be able to give a valid consent.[25]

For the parent of a retarded child the problem is that sterilization of an adult retardate can be emotionally disturbing.[26] From the perspective of this parent the ideal solution would be sterilization of the child before puberty.

Unfortunately, this ideal solution may not be legally available.[27] It is clear law that the consent of the parents to ordinary operations for their child is sufficient to exculpate any person or institution involved in the operation unless there has been negligence.[28] But there is an unexpected difference between sterilization and other operations. Sterilization is a truly elective procedure in the sense that the physical health of the person whose sterilization is sought will not suffer if the operation is not performed. This is also true of cosmetic plastic surgery. But sterilization is not only elective but also permanent.[29] A child who has had plastic surgery can often alter its effects later; a child who has been sterilized will never be able to have children.[30]

A LEGISLATIVE PROPOSAL

Our proposed statute is designed to remove these doubts concerning the legality of the sterilization of a retarded child.[31] It is based upon the following assumptions: first, sterilization is non-criminal and should remain so; second, such an operation should be performed on a person who lacks the capacity to provide a valid consent to it only when it is objectively necessary or desirable. We need not examine the first assumption; it is the second that requires discussion.

We have sought a means to ensure that only the truly retarded child will be sterilized and then only if the operation is considered beneficial by a person whom society recognizes as having the best interests of the child in mind. This control is necessary because there are children who have been diagnosed as retarded who later showed ordinary intellectual competence.[32]

Various protective procedures are available. In at least one jurisdiction sterilization of a minor is allowed only upon an order of the court in response to a petition from the minor's parents or guardians if the court finds the operation to be in the best interests of the minor.[33] But judicial intervention is an unnecessary invasion of the family's privacy. Any application to a court, even in camera, means an embarrassing examination of the problems of the family which should be avoided if possible.

If judicial supervision would be useful, the embarrassment to the family would be a minor issue. But we are unable to see how it could be useful. The judicial process in this context would work in a vacuum. In custody cases the best interests of the child test could be given content by courts and commentators; for the problem with which we are concerned it is impossible to formulate relevant factors to help guide decisions. A layman, asked to decide several custody cases, will probably refer to factors that the law considers relevant. What factors could be considered relevant in deciding whether sterilization of a retarded child is in that child's interests? Would any parent who sought sterilization for his retarded child be able to *prove* that it was in that child's best interests?

The alternative of leaving the decision solely to the parent or other guardian of the child does not adequately protect the child. Too much is at stake. In a society that professes to believe in the autonomy of the individual, that autonomy should be allowed to prevail to its utmost limits, but only in relation to that individual. In ancient Rome parents had the power of life and death over their children. We doubt that any of our readers - even true believers in planned parenthood and zero population growth - would be willing to allow parents of non-retarded children the right to have them sterilized because the parents believed that the world was threatened by people pollution.

If the parents are seeking sterilization for their child because he is retarded, society should ensure that the child is in fact retarded. This can be done by requiring that the child be certified as mentally retarded by experts.[34] To meet the need for protection of the child we would require certification by a second expert at least one year after the initial certification and within six months of the sterilization. No sterilization would be permitted in the absence of two certificates.

To some extent, the problem of enforcement and sanctions in this context is reduced because the operation has to be performed by a licensed professional. Our controls would be directed to him: any physician who sterilized a child in the absence of the required certificates would be guilty of medical malpractice and subject to the sanctions of his professional organization. He would, in appropriate circumstances, also be subject to criminal penalties.

Neither licence-suspension nor criminal conviction is of direct benefit to the person who has been sterilized without the proper safeguards. Although we provide an action for damages to remedy this defect, two questions trouble us. Since there will be no objective basis upon which to estimate the damages, the action may ultimately prove to be useless.[35] Our solution is to provide for a set award subject to proof by either party to the action.

The other question is who should have standing to institute the action. Clearly, the person who has been sterilized improperly should have standing; if he lacks legal capacity then his parents or guardian ad litem will be able to represent him. We leave open the issue of whether the welfare authorities should have this right.

Our proposed statute follows.

Sterilization of the Retarded Act
1 A licensed physician may sterilize a person if
A he has the consent in writing of that person to the procedure or, if that person is unable to provide a valid consent, the consent of that person's parent or guardian and
B he has at least two certificates in a form prescribed by the regulations by mental retardation experts that the person for whom the sterilization is sought is retarded;
i the latest certificate shall be made not more than six months before the operation and
ii the certificates shall be made at least one year apart.
2 Any person who contravenes any provision of this Act shall be
A liable in any action at the suit of the person who has been sterilized illegally or of his parents or of his guardian for damages in the amount of $10,000, unless either party convinces the Court that this amount is unjust in which case the Court shall award such larger or smaller sum as seems just in all the circumstances, and
B guilty of a summary conviction offence if he knew the requirements of this Act.
3 Nothing in this Act shall effect the legality of sterilizations performed or sought to be performed for reasons other than the alleged retardation of the person.

Our topic is important; we recognize that the issues are difficult. We welcome comments.

NOTES

1 'Child' refers to a biological relationship unless the context indicates the contrary.

2 The heyday of the IQ score has passed, and today it is rarely the sole factor in diagnosing mental retardation; emotional control and social adaptability also influence overall competency. Subject to this caveat, persons with IQs from 68-83 are considered 'borderline,' those between 52-67 'mildly retarded,' those between 36-51, 'moderately retarded,' those between 20-35, 'severely retarded,' and those whose IQ was less than 20 are 'profoundly retarded.' See US Department of Health, Education, and Welfare, Office of the Secretary, Secretary's Committee on Mental Retardation. *The Problem of Mental Retardation* (Washington: US Government Printing Office, 1969. Cf the slightly different classification used in Ontario Government, *Community Living for the Mentally Retarded in Ontario: A New Policy Focus*, The Honourable Robert Welch, Provincial Secretary for Social Development, Table I-1, p. 25 (1973) (hereinafter *Community Living for the Mentally Retarded*).

3 The government of Ontario has accepted the philosophy of community-based services: *Community Living for the Mentally Retarded*, supra note 2.

4 The reader should recognize two important facts: 1/ there are a sizeable number of retardates presently in the community with an IQ range of 36-67; 2/ with deinstitutionalization, the size of this group in the community will increase significantly. We should emphasize that we are not concerned in this paper with the problems posed by the borderline retardates.

5 Hagerty, Kane, and Udall, 'Legal Rights of the Mentally Retarded' (1972), 6 *Fam. L.Q.* 59, at 64: 'In the related area of sexuality, heterosexual contact among the residents of a typical retarded institution is forbidden ... [The result is a] ... greater degree of illicit sexual activity among members of the same sex ... In a California institution for victims of cerebral palsy, there is a weekly "touch session." To us this minimum random human contact may seem sad; to them it is an all-too-rare moment of sensual pleasure, even though non-intimate.'

6 Reed and Reed *Mental Retardation: A Family Study* (1965) 78. This study was a project of the Minnesota Human Genetics League.

7 Ibid. These views are not to be accepted without question. See Berg, 'Heredity and Mental Retardation,' a paper presented at the Conference on Sex Education and Community Living for Mentally Retarded, Toronto, 8 April, 1972: 'From a practical point of view ... severely retarded individuals are, to a large extent, infertile ... (O)n the whole, amongst the mildly retarded the chances of having retarded children is greater than it is amongst the general population. However ... there is a tendency for those who are mildly retarded to have children who on the average are brighter than themselves.' Support for the sceptical views of Berg can be found in Vokowich, 'The Dawning of

the Brave New World: Legal, Ethical and Social Issues of Eugenics' (1971), *III. L. Forum* 189.

8 The views cited in the text are supported by Woodside, *Sterilization in North Carolina* (1950) 24-5 cited in Williams, *The Sanctity of Life and the Criminal Law* (1957) 85. However, Ferster, 'Eliminating the Unfit: Is Sterilization the Answer?' (1966), 27 *Ohio S.L.J.* 591, at 604 and 624, refers to the scepticism of Diamond, *Report on Mental Health Legislation in British Columbia* (1960) and Kanner, *A Miniature Textbook of Feeblemindedness* (1949), 4-5. Kanner summed up his experience thus '... (T)o a large extent independent of the I.Q., fitness for parenthood is determined by emotional involvements or relationships.' See also McWhirter and Weiger, 'The Alberta Sterilization Act: A Genetic Critique' (1969), 19 *U.T.L.J.* 424, at 426.

9 The restrictions on the dissemination of birth control information were removed by parliament in 1969. Stats Can. 1968-9, c 41, s 13.

10 Criminal Code, s 251

11 Toronto *Globe and Mail*, 13 April 1973, p. 1

12 This term may be realistic. See supra note 7. Some forms of retardation may be detected by drawing amniotic fluid from the pregnant woman. It is beyond the scope of this paper to explore the extremely difficult social-ethical issue of whether the state should have the right to require a woman who will be delivered of an individual who will be permanently helpless to have that foetus aborted. For a discussion of some of the jurisprudential and other factors involved in state intervention in birth control and population planning see Friedmann, 'Interference with Human Life: Some Jurisprudential Reflections,' (1970), 70 *Col. L. Rev.* 1058, and Note, 'Legal Analysis and Population Control: The Problem of Coercion' (1971), 84 *Harv. L. Rev.* 1856.

13 Criminal Code, s 251

14 The problem is that the surgeon cannot guarantee reversibility.

15 Williams, supra note 8, at 103-11

16 Criminal Code, s 8

17 Ibid, s 244: 'A person commits an assault when, without the consent of another person ... (a) he applies force intentionally to the person of the other ...'

18 Ibid, s 14

19 Ibid, s 140

20 Note also s 45 of the Criminal Code which provides that 'Everyone is protected from criminal responsibility for performing a surgical operation upon any person for the benefit of that person if (b) it is reasonable to perform the operation, having regard to the state of health of the person at the time the operation is performed and to all the circumstances of the case.'

21 See authorities cited in 1 *Russell on Crimes* 625 (12 ed. Turner)

22 See Williams, supra note 8 at 1103, citing *R* v *Donovan*, [1943] 2 K.B. 489, 507. *Donovan* would not seem to be relevant for our problem. There a man who obtained sexual gratification in inflicting physical violence on a consenting woman was held criminally responsible notwithstanding the woman's consent. We suggest that there is a substantial distinction between a doctor performing a sterilization operation and a person who engages in sexual activities that the majority profess to find distasteful.

23 See text accompanying note 28 infra for a discussion of the problem of consent in relation to a minor. Williams, supra note 8, at 111 suggests, 'The probability is that the courts would not regard as lawful any operation upon a mental defective unless it is for his benefit and with the consent of his parent or guardian ... A voluntary sterilization statute is highly desirable.'

24 It is unlikely that this liability would be imposed if the operation were necessary to save the girl's life. In the Abortion Cases the United States Supreme Court left open the issue of consent: *Doe* v *Wade* (1973), 93 S.Ct. 705, *Doe* v *Bolton* (1973), 95 S.Ct. 739.

25 See supra note 23. Various situations can arise: 1/ the surgeon sterilizes a person who is retarded to such a degree that he is unable to give a valid consent. The surgeon, without any negligence on his part, does not discover the retardation. In the absence of negligence in the sterilization procedure the surgeon would not be civilly liable. 2/ If the person seeking the sterilization is known to be retarded to the surgeon, the surgeon cannot validly perform the operation unless there has been a committee of the person appointed under such statutes as the Mental Incompetency Act, R.S.O. 1970, c 271, s 12. But even then the committee of the person of the retarded would have no greater legal powers than the parent of a retarded child. See text accompanying note 27.

26 See Dodds, 'Modern Approaches to Birth Control,' a paper presented at the Conference on Sex Education and Community Living for the Mentally Retarded, 8 April 1972.

27 See note 15

28 See supra note 20

29 Cf *Strunk* v *Strunk* (1964), 445 s.w. 2d 145 (Ky Ct of Appeals) where the court by a single vote authorized a kidney transplant from a donor in an institution for the retarded for the benefit of the donor's brother. The emotional reaction of judges to irreversible operations not necessary to the physical well-being of the person being operated on is well illustrated by the dissenting judgment in this case which begins: 'Apparently because of my indelible recollection of a government which, to the everlasting shame of its

citizens, embarked on a program of genocide and experimentation with human bodies ...'

30 It is true that he or she will have the possibility of adopting children; most people prefer having their own children.

31 We have not examined the problem of the adult retardate seeking sterilization for himself. If the government carries out its decision to implement a special program of guardianship for all the mentally retarded adults in the community (*Community Living for the Mentally Retarded* 22), then presumably the consent of the guardian will be necessary and sufficient. Until then we would argue that if the concept of normalization is to be given effect the retardate should be able to obtain this procedure in the same circumstances as other members of the community. This means that he should be able to give a valid consent to this operation as he does to any other. The role of the professional in this context is not to be envied; but we see no solution. Consider for example, the difficulties involved in counselling the young pregnant girl who is undecided whether to place the child that will be delivered for adoption or to keep the child. See Green, 'Re Mugford: A Case Study in the Interaction of Child-Care Agency, Court, and Legislature' (1971), 1 *R.F.L.* 1.

32 See McWhirter and Weiger, supra note 8

33 Va. Code Ann., s 32-424 (1969) cited, in Tierney, 'Voluntary Sterilization: A Necessary Alternative' (1970), 4 *Fam. L.Q.* 373, at 382 n. 48.

34 In our model statute we do not define who is the 'expert.' Among the disciplines that are relevant in diagnosing retardation are psychiatry, psychology, and social work. The problem is simply that a person qualified in any one of these disciplines is not necessarily qualified to make the diagnosis.

35 Cf cases cited in Kemp and Kemp *The Quantum of Damages* (3rd ed 1900) 432 and in 2 Belli *Modern Damages* (1960), 230, 231, 279.

SUSAN HANLEY, BENJAMIN SCHLESINGER
AND PAUL STEINBERG

Lesbianism: knowns and unknowns

HISTORY AND BACKGROUND

Homosexuality is as old as humanity itself. Lesbianism has been with us from
the beginning of recorded time and no doubt even earlier, in primitive societies
and sophisticated ones – in ages known for rigorous moral standards and in
others equally renowned for their sexual liberality. Often in the corridors of history the lesbian's presence has been overshadowed by male-loving males who,
more numerous in almost all instances and more apparent as well, have attracted
greater attention. The female has, nevertheless, not been absent from the scene.
Furthermore, female homosexuality has, for a number of reasons, been met with
more acceptance or less condemnation both in the past and at the present time.
Kinsey lists approximately eleven reasons for this, some of which are [13]: the
superior status of males historically, frequency of incidence, the nature and type
of sexual contact, and religious outrage and objection concerning 'the wastage of
semen in all male activities that are noncoital.' The advent of Christianity and
the Justinian code and later Mohammedanism perpetrated the idea that male
homosexuality was a sin as semen was viewed as a precious life-giving fluid whose
waste was contrary to divine law. Therefore lesbianism was regarded as less sinful because the female had 'nothing to waste' [6].

Perhaps the most well-known, important, and influential seat of culturally
recognized and approved female homosexuality appeared in Greece. Its advocate
was the celebrated poetess, Sappho, who lived on the island of Lesbos in the
Aegean Sea. It is Sappho who has traditionally been hailed as the founder of lesbian love and in fact, lesbianism is a term derived from the name 'Lesbos,' the

island where Sappho was born in the village of Eresos [5]. Sappho lived from 630 to 530 B.C. and at her home, 'The House of Muses' she gathered a circle of young girls around her. There, they devoted their time to the cultivation of poetry, music, and dancing almost in defiance of the prevailing attitude in Greece, which at the time held women in low esteem. They were granted little recognition and considered far inferior to men – hardly human in some cases. Sappho was clearly a rebel and ardent feminist.

In Roman history lesbianism was frequently mentioned, and it is said that female slaves were available to gratify women citizens at the bath. These slaves were called 'fillators,' a strange name indeed. Bassa, Aggripina, and Livia were three notorious lesbians among the aristocratic women of ancient Rome [5].

In ancient China a woman could indulge in affairs with another woman without shame. Moreover, a rose-coloured penis could be purchased by women without embarrassment. Lesbianism was common in the harems of Egypt and India where women were herded together, often seeing no other males but eunuchs, while awaiting their turn for a night with the husband-master. Female homosexual practices were even reported to be carried on in the small but highly populated islands off the coast of Asia. Here, where Japanese civilisation flourished, women were reported inserting ball-like objects into their vaginas in the presence of each other and sharing in the masturbatory pleasures derived therefrom [5].

The Dahomeans, an African people, attribute frigidity among married women to their practice of and interest in homosexuality, and the Haitians state that 'The frigid woman who cannot please her husband seeks another woman as a sex partner' [6].

In France during the eighteenth and nineteenth centuries a homosexual society, 'The Vestals of Venus,' flourished throughout the country and was particularly popular with women in the upper classes. Initiation rites were severe for women entering the society and required rigorous examination of the new converts by other lesbians. If accepted, the candidate had to swear an oath never to have intercourse with men nor to betray the secrets of the order.

Religion has had various views and opinions on homosexuality throughout the ages. In India, not only was homosexuality represented in the sculptures on the temples, but also in religious ceremonies. In fact, many ancient gods were considered homosexuals. During various services artificial phalli (*lingams*) were used. In Greek rites, 'during the offerings to Demeter at Pellene, not only all men but even male dogs were excluded from the temple, so that no male element may disturb the sanctity of the female homosexual rites' [6].

Lesbianism was regarded as a trivial obscenity in the Talmud of the ancient Hebrews. In the Holy Scriptures there are only a few references that may be interpreted as suggesting lesbianism. In Paul's Epistle to the Romans we find the passage: 'God gave them unto vile passions: for the woman changed the natural use into that which is against nature: and likewise also the men leaving the natural use of the woman, burned in their lust one towards another, men with men working unseemliness.'

Does 'vile passions' refer to oral-genital relations, and does 'likewise' suggest tribadism? The answers to these questions are left to interpretation. During biblical times male homosexuality was an offence subject to capital punishment, whereas women's transgressions were looked upon as too unimportant for such punishment. It is not known whether this was a reflection of the lesser frequency with which such activities took place between women or the lesser threat to society.

RELIGION

There are no biblical proscriptions against homosexuality, rather, it has been a matter of interpretation by scholars in each age. Hence, today there is no one church position on homosexuality. Attitudes and sanctions differ within denominations and depend on how orthodox or liberal a particular sect, or even a particular sector, is. For example, after the Wolfenden Report was published in England in 1957, many of the high-ranking bishops in the Church of England supported the recommendations publicly. Many denounced it publicly, stating that the Scriptures, rather than academic discussion, should be the guiding force. More recent 'breakthroughs' include public statements by the Lutheran Church of America (not necessarily Canada) and the Unitarian Universalist Association (including the Canadian counterpart) in support of homosexual rights. While the Presbyterians see homosexuality as incomplete and not a valid lifestyle, they do grant that the homosexual, like the heterosexual who has strayed, is reconcilable to God [1].

The Reverend Troy Perry of Los Angeles was first to set up a church for homosexuals. He also authored a book, *The Lord's My Shepherd and He Knows I'm Gay*. Many groups have followed suit. For example, there is now a gay synagogue in Brooklyn.

For the lesbian who does not have access to these institutions, there is nothing. She must come to grips with her lesbian identity and her religious feelings by herself. Most move away from the church, becoming agnostics. Some are able to arrange a personal belief system within their faith, while for others, their self-hatred and self-punishment becomes more severe.

THE LAW

Although the courts turn to the psychiatrist as the authority in pronouncing the female homosexual 'sick,' it has direct jurisdiction over a number of aspects of the individual's life – in particular, her job opportunities and her children.

Canadian law is based on English law which at no time proscribed lesbian behaviour [15]. Male homosexuals are charged under the rubric of gross indecency, an indictable offence. Whatever indecency or gross indecency may be, it is concerned with the improprieties between men, not women. A lesbian may be charged under indecent assault but it must be shown that the act is hostile, with circumstances of indecency [8].

American law did make a provision for 'lesbian sexual practices,' hence one may be a lesbian but not practise it. Needless to say, this law is next to impossible to enforce, except in cases of overt homosexual acts and in the US Armed Forces where suspected behaviour or guilt by association is sufficient to charge the individual person [14].

In Canada, if a lesbian is discriminated against because of her sexuality, she has no recourse to appeal. Homosexuals are not recognized by the Civil Liberties Association.

The major issue for the law is whether or not its jurisdiction should extend to morality or not. For certainly it is an ethical issue if a woman who is fit and competent to care for her children is denied this right on the basis of her sexuality. A number of cases are cited by Martin and Lyon who devote a whole chapter to lesbian motherhood [14]. They include instances of mothers who lose children to fathers who don't want them, and children in lesbian households who grow up 'straight.' They point out that all the homosexuals they know grew up in heterosexual households. Not all lesbians want children, for this greatly restricts their freedom to pursue careers, etc. However, for those who do, having the right to legal marriage would make the lesbian couple more eligible as adoptive parents. This point brings up many questions, particularly about the rights of children, and these would require a knowledge of the lesbian beyond her sexuality, in order for the law to reflect justice to all parties concerned.

PSYCHOLOGICAL THEORIES AND RESEARCH

In the past there has been much research and thinking on the identification and labelling of the sources that supposedly induce homosexuality [20]. This labelling, of course, has been reinforced by the tremendous guilt- and anxiety-reducing function it serves. Explanations which postulate a biological etiology for homosexuality or early seduction by an older person allow parents of homosexuals to experience a sense of relief in avoiding the terrible question, 'Where did I go wrong?' Other explanations allow the homosexual to counter societal rejection and self-rejection with an 'It's not my fault' posture [17]. It seems that a society in which homosexuality is most commonly repressed by non-rational punishment requires one to view the behaviour as pathological.

The homosexual is told that he is 'sick.' As we shall see, most of the literature we surveyed for this paper considered lesbianism almost invariably as a sick, neurotic, personality disorder, caused by a malformed psyche. We feel that it is crucial for counsellors to see how these myths have been generated and perpetrated, how they have shaped our thinking, created our biases, and how totally ridiculous they now seem.

In 1869 Dr. Westphal, a professor of psychiatry at the University of Berlin, made one of the first scientific inquiries into lesbianism. His most famous conclusion was that it was a 'disease of inversion,' a view still held today. He referred to it as an anomaly, a term that has been popular ever since. It is important to note that at this time, insanity was regarded as a hereditary taint or as possession by the devil. Westphal referred to the lesbian as having a form of 'moral insanity' and hence of 'contrary sexual feeling.' It is not known to the authors whether any exorcisms were performed on lesbians during Westphal's time.

Around this time Montegazza, an Italian investigator whose works are still widely read, found female homosexuality to be an error in nature caused by a physiological difficulty in practising normal intercourse and by immoral pleasure-seeking. It should be noted that we have here the beginning of two very influential lines of thinking about lesbians: on the one hand they were conditioned from birth (Montegazza), and on the other they were moral degenerates (Westphal).

In the 1880s a school of French investigators published their findings on the subject. One of these distinguished scholars was Charcot, a hypnotist who was later to be a very great influence on Freud. Charcot saw homosexuality as being caused by some form of inherited degeneracy – an organic hermaphroditism in which elements of both sexes were found in the lesbian. This view was sharply challenged by a colleague of Charcot's named Chevalier who stated that factors other than hereditary were of major importance in causing lesbianism namely: lust, prostitution, fear, and necessity. The term he coined to explain lesbianism was 'acquired artificial inversion.' Thus two types of lesbian were clearly delineated: acquired and congenital.

In 1886 a scholar named Richard von Krafft-Ebing published his powerful masterpiece *Psychopathia Sexualis* which was and remains today one of the main vehicles for spreading the doctrine of various kinds of sexuality as disease. His thoughts spread from country to country and from generation to generation. Krafft-Ebing regarded both of the above two classes as being hereditary in origin – signs of degeneration. He believed that an inherited neuropathic or psychopathic state was the cause of lesbianism. However, it seems that the subjects he investigated appeared to have few or no significant differences from the general Viennese population – other than, of course, their sexual proclivities [4].

In the 1890s a German physician named Magnus Hirshfeld estimated after many kinds of inquiry that about 2.3 per cent of German males were predominately homosexual. Hirshfeld (himself a homosexual) spent thirty years gathering information and performing cross-cultural studies. He was one of the only theorist-researchers of his time who protested against discriminatory legislation and who sought to raise the self-image of those people personally involved. He concluded that the homosexual urge was congenital, inborn, and perhaps hereditary.

Next in line of the pre-Freudian contributors was Havelock Ellis, whose ten-volume series, *Studies in the Psychology of Sex*, first published in 1897, was an unsurpassed contribution. He pointed to heredity as cause and to the futility of cure. His case histories, on the other hand, have been said to suggest that there might be environmental, psychogenic, and even sociological factors involved [6].

It seems that early researchers, working with a paucity of cases and possessing no conceptual framework into which to fit them, became extremely interested in the stories of the girls they saw and in their intense erotic attraction toward other girls, or in their preference for playing with guns and soldiers and even dressing like boys from earliest childhood. If children of three or four manifested both strong identification with the other sex and displayed its characteristics being physically attracted to their own, then it is no wonder that early theoreticians postulated that lesbianism was definitely congenital.

Perhaps more than any other theoretician Sigmund Freud was to have a profound influence on the world's view of sexuality. Indeed, he presented a new shocking theory of sexuality, which he saw as beginning in infancy. He postulated that a homosexual component could be found in the sexual development of every human being and that in every individual could be found residual manifestations of bisexuality (by the very fact that every individual is procreated by a union of the two sexes). Freud hypothesized that preference for homosexual activities was due to an arrest of sexual development at an early age, hence the term 'fixation.' Adult homosexuality was considered by Freud to be a retrogression to an early stage of sexual development and therefore had to be regarded as an expression of sexual immaturity due to a deep-seated neurosis. The lesbian was thought by Freud to be suffering from a father fixation, or 'Electra Complex' as he termed it. This was a strong neurotic and incestuous attachment to father.

The lesbian was portrayed by Freud and his followers as a deeply disturbed person with an unresolved incestuous drive toward the father. In order for her to repress this horror-inciting urge, the growing girl turned away from *all men*, who, by being men, represented her father. Hence her libidinal urge could be best and safely fulfilled by being directed toward other women. In Freud's eyes the lesbian was a sick, unhappy person who needed to be cured.

To see how closely Freud's outlook resembled the prevailing view, one need only reflect that what was illegal in his day became 'neurotic' or 'perverted' in psychoanalytic terminology. Thus sodomy, buggery, oral-genital contacts, homosexuality, all widely punishable by law, were classified by psychoanalysis as perversions.

Recent researchers like Bieber [3], whose work is widely disseminated and discussed, are still clinging to the almost ridiculous notion that homosexuality is a sickness. This is so even after Kinsey has reported homosexuality to be on a continuum ranging from predominately heterosexual to predominately homosexual. Bieber and his research group reject the viewpoint supported by the authors of this paper, that homosexuality may be viewed as 'one type of expression of a polymorphous sexuality which appears pathologic only in cultures holding it to be so.'

Instead Bieber has taken the stance that homosexuality is a psychopathological state. The assumption he made was as follows: 'Our conception of the genesis of homosexuality gave minimal attention to hereditary, chemical or organic-genetic theories. We assumed that the dominant sexual pattern of the adult is the adaptive consequence of life experiences interpenetrating with a *basic biological tendency toward heterosexuality*' [3]. Bieber is taking the stance that humans are launched at birth onto a path towards heterosexuality and anything that leads one away from this pre-ordained path is learned. Furthermore, in his eyes such deviant learning is pathological.

We feel that this line of thinking is absurd and for the most part unsubstantiated. Recent research has clearly indicated that as we ascend the evolutionary ladder all sexual behaviour becomes less and less determined by biological blueprints, and more and more influenced by the learning experiences of the individual [2]. Notable sex researchers no longer take for granted that heterosexuality is a 'biological norm.' The only definitive statement one can make at present is that heterosexual behaviour is most frequent [20].

Homosexual acts are deviations from prevalent *social norms* and in this light may be interpreted by some as sick. But to term the homosexual 'sick' because he deviates from a *biological norm*, as Bieber has, seems to the authors to be a disguised moral judgment, stated as a clinical observation [24].

SOCIETAL VIEWS

Weinberg [22] sums up public opinion in one word: homophobia. Many of the stereotypes accompanying homophobia have already been discussed. The following are the motives postulated by Weinberg:

1 Religious motive – taboos against non-reproductive sex and sex that may be 'unduly pleasurable';
2 Secret fear of being homosexual – or reaction formation;
3 Repressed envy – remnants of the puritan ethic which says 'They're deviant but they may be enjoying it more';
4 Threat to values – the deviant, by virtue of rejecting one norm in the society, is seen as being opposed to them all;
5 Existence without vicarious immortality – children counteract the fear of death, people without children are considered misfortunate; homosexuals, while potentially fertile, undermine this investment in children by heterosexuals.
In sum, Weinberg states that the homophobic reaction is a form of acute conventionality; ultimately it condemns on the basis of difference alone.

The mass media have done much to popularize and promote psychological and psychiatric theories and opinions. Results of studies are usually in abbreviated and sensational forms for a public that has no way of evaluating the merits of such reports. While Fluckinger [7] did a thorough and devastating analysis of Bieber's study, the Bieber study had already been printed in paperback.

It is perhaps in the area of entertainment that the media have had the greatest effect. For example, because pornography includes lesbians, many consumers assume that the reverse is true [14]; that lesbians indulge in a myriad of sexual perversions with the other sex. David Reuben's book, *Everything You Always Wanted to Know About Sex but Were Afraid to Ask*, subscribes to many of the myths and stereotypes about lesbians. His attitude seems to be that there is no 'real' sex without a man and a woman, despite the findings of Kinsey which suggest that female homosexuals are better lovers of women than men are. Reuben's attitude is implicit in the following capsule description about a new film: 'a futuristic fantasy about a sexless society of lesbian women and effete men in the year 2293.'

It is the feeling of a number of authors that much of what goes on in the field of mental health is merely a reflection of conventional values. Although this situation is not bad in and of itself, when such opinions and theories are taken as justification of the predominant beliefs, it can be very damaging and destructive to the person on the other side of the psychiatric label. Note, too, that this is a self-perpetuating situation. Many lesbians considered their feelings to be natural and good, until they found out they were held to be 'sick.' Now they fear that if people know about their homosexuality they will shun them.

A vast amount of public education must be done on all levels of society in order to bury the stereotypes and allow lesbians to live as people first. Many courageous women have risked their jobs and professional careers to declare their sexual preference. As people are confronted more and more with homosexuals living comfortable and productive lives, their opinions will surely change. Public opinion is not only shaped by, but itself shapes, the prevailing beliefs of religion, jurisprudence, and psychology-psychiatry. As public opinion moves ahead, these institutions will gradually change with it.

SEXUAL SOCIALIZATION

The lesbian in today's society faces many problems; she is clearly an oppressed person. Whether or not and how to tell her parents of her homosexual career perhaps remains the single greatest issue she will have to deal with. Psychiatrists, psychologists, and writers have not helped her in this area either, for they have spread volumes of misinformation about homosexuality and have poisoned millions of parents against young adults who have embarked on homosexual lives. We feel that this is a strategic area for the potential involvement of social work – in helping homosexuals work out how they can best tell their parents of their sexual life and in simultaneously working with families to sort out their feelings about their homosexual son or daughter. Needless to say, this will require a great amount of perseverence on the part of the social worker, for he or she will almost have to re-educate parents and families about the truths and facts of homosexuality, while breaking through the thick jungle of myths and hearsay they learned to accept as fact.

Two of the most common conceptions parents seem to have when they learn their son or daughter is a homosexual are: (1) that this means that his/her parents are at fault and also sick themselves; (2) that homosexuality is likened to criminal behaviour in that it is called the result of botched job by parents [22]. Hence, upon hearing the news that their son or daughter has opted for homosexuality, many parents ask themselves (and the social worker, if present) the age-old question 'Where did we go wrong?'

One of the prerequisites for the counsellor of such parents is that he deal thoroughly with his feelings around homosexuality in males and in females and make an inventory of his beliefs, fears, and prejudices. Without this precaution the counsellor may very well intentionally or unintentionally make matters far worse than they are by reinforcing the parents' already misconceived notion that their daughter is a sick girl because they failed to bring her up properly. We feel that all too often parents and counsellors do not have a clear perspective from which to view female sexuality and its development. Clearer understanding of this matter will hopefully reduce anxiety and misconceptions for the counsellor and the parent.

It is generally understood that the lesbian differs from other women in the gender of the object that engages her sexuality. Unfortunately, as mentioned before, the significance of this difference tends to consume nearly all of the researcher's attention. Consequently what is generally neglected is the degree to which the lesbian's commitment to sexuality reflects general female patterns of sexuality, notwithstanding the difference in gender selection.

It is generally accepted by social scientists today that in most cases the female homosexual follows conventional feminine patterns in developing her commitment to sexuality and in conducting a sexual career [17]. This finding will not be particularly surprising if we consider that, apart from the specific experiences (if any) that influenced gender selection, most lesbians are exposed to the numerous diffuse and subtle experiences and relations that generally serve to promote conventional sex-role identification in this society. 'Moreover, many of these experiences and relations occur prior to the emergence of sexuality as something explicit and salient and there is little reason to assume that these sources of sex-role learning are not assimilated in much the same way as occurs with females who are more exclusively heterosexual' [17].

One of the main features of the socialization of the female in North American society is the degree to which it is devoted to a single outcome – the domestic pattern. No matter if she desires glamour, a colourful career, or a romantic companionship, the most pervasive commitment of the society within which the female lives is to the production of wives and mothers, and from this she can neither escape nor be immune. No matter what the psychoanalysts may tell us, society neither conceives of nor trains – except by inadvertence – females who will have roles more complex than those of wife and mother. In the course of her socialization process, the female child is taught to inhibit patterns both of aggression and assertion as well as those of sexuality so that she will be acceptable and conforming to the needs of the male.

It is now almost accepted as fact that the patterns of overt sexual behaviour of homosexual females tends to resemble closely those of heterosexual females and to differ radically from the sexual activity patterns of both homosexual and heterosexual males [12].

This similarity between females (regardless of gender choice) and the differences between women and men seem to be explained by the fact that women and men have different natural introductions to sexual activity. For males it seems that the major organizing event in their sexual lives is puberty, for nearly all males within two years after puberty have their commitment to sexuality reinforced by the experience of orgasm. As Kinsey indicated, many males masturbate at a fairly high rate during early adolescence.

Females on the other hand, tend to begin overt sexual activity (that is, behaviour that has a reasonable probability of culminating in orgasm) much later, during late adolescence or the early years of adulthood. For females, the initial experience of orgasm is nearly as likely to occur during precoital petting or coitus as during masturbation. Indeed, according to Kinsey, half or more of the women who report masturbation as a source of sexual outlet 'discovered' this outlet after achieving orgasm from precoital petting or coitus. In this pattern of male-female difference, female homosexuals do not appear to differ significantly from heterosexual females.

Hence, males develop commitments to sexuality before involvement in complicated, emotionally charged interpersonal relations, that is, before developing a commitment to the cathexis of love. In females, lesbians included, the reverse appears true, training in love precedes training in sexuality. Women do not seem as much to pursue sexual gratification as something separate from emotional or romantic involvement. In fact for many, including lesbians, it may be impossible. Only 29 per cent of the lesbians interviewed by Kinsey and his associates had sexual relations with three or more partners, and only 4 per cent had contact with ten or more partners. These figures closely approximate the figures for females as a whole. These figures are far below those reported for heterosexual males and dramatically low when compared with those of homosexual males.

Moreover, an essential part of learning to be female in our society is the repression of sexuality, learned by hetero- and homosexual women alike. Her particular sexuality is usually taken as the salient feature of the lesbian. If it is more self-conscious in the lesbian, it seems so only in that her commitment is to a deviant pattern. However, we hope to have shown that the more general character-moulding processes of society appear to be the dominant factors in forming her sexuality.

PERSONALITY FACTORS

From the reports of the women interviewed in recent literature [1] as well as the conclusions found in other studies [23], the lesbian's awareness of her attraction to other women comes late in adolescence. At first she does not understand her strange feelings and may in fact deny them. A trip to the library reveals that she is a lesbian and arouses two feelings: (1) relief upon discovering that she is not alone and upon obtaining a fuller understanding of her inclinations, and (2) horror, disbelief, and fear of rejection by others, and quite possibly self-rejection as well. Until recently, the only material on homosexuality in libraries consisted of medical books which speak of perversions, inversions, and unnatural acts. Often it is a number of years after this that the lesbian has her first sexual encounter. For many women, the recognition of their homosexuality comes later than adolescence, even after they are married and have children. For both groups there is a tremendous amount of guilt and shame associated with these feelings. Further, the mother and wife is torn between her desire for other women, her indifference towards her husband, and her children whom she loves and does not want to lose. Needless to say, self-acceptance for the lesbian is extremely difficult. She is in a hostile environment, that is, a society which offers only heterosexuals rewards, support, confirmation of their identity. Because of her sexual preference, the lesbian knows she is different; indeed, her desires are despicable and degenerate according to books she may have read. The lesbian finds that the stigma of her sexuality follows her even in the non-sexual aspects of her life: 'The lesbian who simply wants to live her life as most people live theirs is frustrated by a net of social expectations. She herself comes to feel that she cannot have an ordinary life, and that normalcy is stolen from her more by these expectations than directly by her sexual preference. She feels pushed more and more toward a bizarre identity as she internalizes society's concept of herself' [1].

How does the lesbian cope with her new identity with its attendant negative values and anxiety. She may deny that she has homosexual feelings for women; denial may be so great that she joins others in open hostility and ridicule of another lesbian. Such an adjustment is personally costly but socially rewarding in that the lesbian is treated as a heterosexual woman.

Other women acknowledge their homosexuality to themselves but continue to feel that their way of life is perverse – a crime. These lesbians constantly feel unworthy yet indebted towards society and often work hard to compensate for their deviance. She is the 'good nigger' of the homosexual world [1].

A third way of coping is to give in and act out to the fullest all the attributes associated with her deviant behaviour. She is irresponsible, promiscuous, and tough. She becomes ultra-butch, accepting the heterosexual stereotype of lesbians and hence is doubly damned, for she remains only on the fringes of the gay world. Underneath this bravado and gaiety is a profound insecurity and sense of worthlessness.

Those who cannot face the implications of lesbiansim, the rejection, the thought of being different or 'queer,' are filled with guilt, self-negation, and self-hatred and they seek oblivion through alcohol, drugs, and/or suicide. While findings differ on the prevalence of alcoholism and excessive drinking [18] (as do personal reports) [1]. Saghir and Robins found that female homosexuals in their sample had significantly more suicide attempts than both male homosexuals and the female heterosexuals [18]. This finding is corroborated by the personal experiences of Martin and Lyon. Attendance at college often coincides with a period of intra- and interpersonal conflict and is thus a time of 'high risk' for the lesbian. This could be a crucial time for intensive, supportive counselling.

All too often it is the lesbian's deviant sexuality that is focused on to the exclusion of their non-sexual attributes. Marylee Stephenson [19], in her study of eleven female homosexual couples, questioned her subjects on numerous non-sexual areas, debunking the stereotype of lesbians as 'sick.' She states: 'I have shown that these couples meet societal criteria of adequacy in their work, in the stability of their relationships, in their acceptance and application of the dominant values of the society, and as such can be usefully characterized as mentally ill only by the moral entrepreneur.'

Another piece of research that focused on factors other than sexual behaviour is that conducted by Saghir and Robins. This study consisted of fifty-seven homosexual women and forty-three single heterosexual controls, none of whom had been confined to a psychiatric or penal institution or was judged psychiatrically ill. One of his conclusions was: 'Being a homosexual seems to be compatible with functional and personal productivity although the risk of having a psychiatric and intrapersonal conflict seems to be greater in the homosexual than in the single heterosexual' [18].

Tentative as this conclusion may be, it seems to come from one of the few objective, experimental studies using a relatively normal sample and exploring aspects other than sexuality *per se*. From the literature written by lesbians and the interviews conducted by us we conclude that lesbians come in as many shapes, sizes, colours, and mentalities as do 'straights.' 'The Lesbian looks, dresses, acts, and is like any other woman' [14].

COMMUNICATION WITH PARENTS

An understanding of female sexuality, its onset, and development is crucial for the dissemination of valid information to the lesbian and her parents. That disturbed parents are the cause of homosexuality is clearly a myth. Nevertheless the counsellor should be prepared to answer parents' queries as to their involvement in their daughter's lesbianism.

It seems very possible that parents themselves have almost nothing to do with their daughter's homosexual career. In a study conducted by William Simon and John H. Gagnon [17], it was found that in almost every lesbian interviewed there was a strongly expressed preference towards one of the parents, and attitudes towards the other parent or substitute parent ranged from condescending neutrality to open hostility. However, the preference for the male or female parent was almost equally divided. Furthermore, while extreme relations with parental figures in any direction appear to predispose individuals to deviant patterns, the very same 'predisposing' factors are equally evident in families that do not produce homosexuals. The question then becomes one of these 'predisposing' factors plus those unknown variables that lead to lesbian commitments. This question may never be answered, nor in our view, need it be.

One may speculate that perhaps when the mental processes are somehow impressionable and receptive they may in the child's development become imprinted with pleasurable experiences of a homosexual nature. These in turn may motivate the desire for more of the same. What we are proposing here is the speculation that the intricate web of coincidences can take so many forms that parental influence (or lack of it) is only one in a thousand factors.

The counsellor is bound to be confronted with a lesbian client who claims that she would like to tell her parents of the joy of her new life but feels that friendship with her parents would be irrecoverable if the disclosure were made. This excuse warrants further exploration in our opinion, for, as Weinberg points out, it can be used 'as an excuse for withdrawing from their parents, when the real reason was that they were ashamed of being homosexual, and felt too weak to withstand even a single word of rebuke' [22]. If this is the case, perhaps the counsellor could impart to the lesbian that the prospect of a few unhappy interludes should not be a deterrent to discussion with parents, if the possible outcome is a continuation of a love relationship with them. Moreover, one would think that the lesbian could use all the love she could get from her parents in a society which she finds scornful and perhaps disappointing.

Parent's reactions to the news that their daughter or son is a homosexual can be viewed as a crisis for them in deciding whether to give precedence to love or conventionality. Conventionally *their* children just don't grow up to be homosexual. What it seems to boil down to is the question of whether the parents simply want their child to accomplish in society what they themselves failed to do, or whether the parents really want their child to find happiness and meaning in their lives. If they choose the latter, their son or daughter is simply a pawn for achievement, an embellishment. As Weinberg points out '... the ultimate attitude of the parent tells us the parent's dominant motive: love or conventionality' [22].

The lesbian will very probably have a more difficult task in telling her parents than the male homosexual. It is easier for boys than girls to prevent inquiries by parents into their private lives. A male may be able to overcome his father's inquiries into his personal life by a simple wink, indicating that he is having his share of 'good fortune.' The same device could hardly apply to the lesbian. Furthermore, women are expected to have nice confidential chats with their mothers. It will be remembered that when we were discussing female sexuality we mentioned social pressures on the women to follow the domestic pattern of marriage, wifehood, and motherhood.

In this light then, if the woman quite frankly announces to her parents that she is happy and that marriage is not on her agenda, it is apt to be assumed that she is pretending satisfaction while being inwardly discontented. In addition, if disclosure to parents is contemplated, it should be remembered that lesbianism is even less familiar to the average person than homosexuality in men. All in all, the lesbian has much more to contend with, much more to explain, much more stupefaction to overcome, and needs much more support. She and her counsellor should be well aware of this before any attempt at disclosure. For these reasons we recommend that role-playing and behavioural rehearsal be used to ease the anxiety and help the lesbian become more aware of what she may expect and hence more confident about her ability to deal with her parents' reactions.

In a case where a young lesbian tells her counsellor that she has decided not to let her parents know because they would be right to feel revolted, special attention is needed. This girl is probably experiencing a severe amount of inner turmoil, guilt, and shame, and precisely on this account there is a special reason to tell the parents. Besides the fact that disclosure would reduce inner turmoil, by telling her parents she is acting on the premise that her being homosexual should not disqualify her from enjoying the full backing, love, and support of people who care about her. If the parents strongly oppose their daughter, at least her struggle has been externalized and she is free to be an advocate of her own rights.

If a person decides not to trust in their parents and not tell them about their homosexuality because of their own misgivings about being homosexual, she should do so remembering that secrecy tends to reinforce these painful and uneasy feelings. The more you conceal any trait that embarrasses you, the more you increase your sense of shame over it. Indeed, after a time one's homosexuality, if veiled, may seem even reprehensible.

Up until now, we have been stressing the fact that the counsellor should help the homosexual client tell her parents about her preference, if she so desires. It should be made very clear that this is not always the case. Sometimes there are destructive motives for making this disclosure. Such motives are well worth searching out, and if present should be counteracted. One of these motives is the desire to punish oneself, or as Weinberg calls it 'moral masochism' [22]; the other is hostile defiance.

When the first motive is at work, the client hopes that her parents will be shocked, recommend therapy, disapprove, and do anything but sanction the homosexuality. In this case she wants to make the parents appear as decent as possible, placing them on a pedestal and assigning them the role of high priests who will punish or forgive. This creates possibilities for relieving her guilt, if retribution is made by her parents.

Where defiance is the predominant motive, the homosexual wants a violent confrontation with the parents. Guilt can be the activating force here as well. In this case, the person is attempting to prod the parents into making foolish statements, into making them appear ignorant. By discrediting the parents, she hopes to depreciate the importance of the attitude *thought* to be taken by them. This thinking is greatly in error, for the much more likely result is that parents' ideas or preconceived notions are reinforced and hence even more fervently defended against.

FAMILY RELATIONSHIPS – THE LESBIAN COUPLE

Further stereotypes of female homosexuals concern their partnership which is thought to replicate the heterosexual union with a rigid role-polarization based on what they see as traditional male/female attitudes and divisions of labour: the butch-fem, active-passive delineation [21]. Although butches and fems do exist, they constitute a minority of homosexual women, though a visible one. This role-playing goes on among the older lesbians and indicates a generation gap, according to Martin and Lyon [14]. Stephenson in her study of eleven couples found that lesbians have not adopted the familiar modes of heterosexual couple behaviour; the 'butch-fem' description is most inappropriate. Rather, they forge their own expectations along practical lines. Both women work therefore. There is an equal sharing of household tasks and financial aspects of maintaining a household. Further, 'The women studied see themselves as women, and their concept of that role does not include looking or acting as they understand men to look or act' [19]. This statement holds for the majority of lesbians in other literature reviewed as well, except for lesbians in prisons. Of the estimated 75 per cent of women who engage in homosexual activities in prison, most are heterosexuals who return to their heterosexual relationships on release. Becoming a 'jail house turnout,' as they are called, is a way of adjusting to a stressful situation and meeting not sexual needs primarily but emotional ones – comfort, support, and reassurance. In prison, one of the reasons women try to appear masculine and butch is to attract primarily heterosexual women who, as fems, can assume similar roles to those they played with their fathers, husbands, or lovers [9].

There have been a number of theories and misconceptions about lesbian lovemaking, for example that lesbians have a longer clitoris which functions like a penis. The work of Kinsey and of Masters and Johnson did much to dispel these notions. Two facts reported of significance in understanding female homosexuality are: (1) 'the body goes through certain physiological changes during the sexual cycle whether the initiator of the cycle is you, a partner, or an inanimate object' [14]; (2) a penis is not essential for a woman's sexual gratification. Few lesbians ever use a penis substitute with their partners, except possibly those caught up in the heterosexual stereotype of lesbian lovers.

Martin and Lyon cite mutual masturbation, cunnilingus, and tribadism as the three most common techniques in lesbian lovemaking [14]. Another technique is anilingus. It should be noted here that mutual masturbation, cunnilingus, and anilingus are also practised by many heterosexual couples. Tribadism, although it connotes lesbianism, actually refers to a particular sexual practice (from Greek 'to rub') and not to lesbianism as a whole. Hence, according to its derivative meaning, tribadism may be said to be common among heterosexual couples as well. The methods of lesbian sexual gratification, therefore, are not any more or less deviant than those of heterosexuals. A tentative conclusion, then, is that lesbians deviate only in the gender of their sexual choice and, intercourse aside, not in lovemaking techniques. Kenyon goes on to say that sadomasochistic practices, for example, the use of a whip, are not all that uncommon [11]. It is our contention that, while this may or may not be the case, it is likely that this statement is based on research done on highly biased samples and that sadomasochism is a result of psychosexual disturbances (discounting lesbianism as such a disturbance), not of lesbianism per se.

Involvement in marriage arrangements is common among lesbians. Hedblom found in his sample of 65 that 71 per cent had had such an arrangement and 75 per cent had had two or fewer such relationships [10]. Stephenson's criterion for her sample selection was two years of living together [19]. In the actual sample seven couples had been together three years (shortest), and one couple twenty years (longest). Because a homosexual marriage is not legally binding, the women feel that what holds them together is their love and their ease with each other. 'What keeps us together is not a piece of paper or words. What keeps us together is feelings of love, commitment and mutual respect.' There are certain pragmatic aspects of legal marriages, however, that homosexuals are denied. These are community property and home-owning, joint income tax returns, inheritance rights, family insurance policies, and family fares. Further, a legal marriage would serve to validate the couple wishing to adopt a child.

In California there is a law that allows a common-law liaison to be formalized by a religious ceremony and that provides for a church certificate of marriage as sufficient proof of legality of the marriage without a marriage licence. In Los Angeles in June 1970 the Reverend Troy D. Perry, pastor of the Metropolitan Community Church, performed the first religious marriage, legally binding together two persons of the same sex.

Such innovations, however, do not approximate the social supports and sanctions that are afforded heterosexual marriages. There are women who feel a genuine, deep, personal need for public and religious recognition of their union and are working for the legalization of homosexual marriages. Although the couples in Stephenson's study cited advantages they had over heterosexual couples, such as freedom with their own time and money, absence of role expectations and freedom from rearing children, the couples missed aspects of living that would fit under the category of social acceptance. Further, couples did not like having to be secretive about the most important relationship in their lives. Lesbian couples would like to be able to be open and honest about their commitment to each other. Martin and Lyon point out that lesbians have their marital problems too [14], and often see a need for marriage-counselling.

FRIENDS, NEIGHBOURS, AND JOBS

Friendship is a very important source of support for the lesbian, who, as a member of a stigmatized minority group, would generally encounter discrimination and hostility if her sexual proclivities were known. There are different ways of dealing with the question of friendship: many lesbians choose friends from the homosexual community exclusively. This has the advantage of enabling the lesbian to be open about herself and serves to validate her lifestyle. Further, she is spared the tensions of trying to combine the two worlds, and the anxiety of discovery by straight friends. Having heterosexual friends who know is also of great support but requires managing two lives simultaneously.

Lesbians' and lesbian couples' relationships with neighbours is marked by constraint and distance. Stephenson reports that most of the couples in her sample were unsure about the neighbours' knowledge of the couples' homosexuality and lived so that any doubts could not be turned into substantiated fact [19]. Couples were not unfriendly but avoided close, frequent contact, such as drop-in visits, with neighbours. The degree to which some lesbians feel constrained to maintain a heterosexual façade is evidenced by the fact that they will date heterosexual males.

Employment is another realm in which the lesbian must often hide, posing as a heterosexual. For the lesbian employee, fear of losing her job is rarely unjustified [14]. 'Homosexuals and other sex perverts' are barred from civil service jobs and the military in the United States [16]. They are considered security risks. Nevertheless, there are lesbians holding such jobs. Lesbians face other problems on the job; they may be pressed for dates by single male employees. Dressing 'butch' helps to discourage this. There may be solicitous co-workers who try to fix them up with dates.

For these reasons, lesbians remain aloof from others on the job. This often extends to those people at work whom the lesbian may know to be homosexual as well. Unlike the heterosexual married woman for whom a job or career is secondary to home and family, the lesbian carries the responsibility of maintaining herself. Hence, not only is it essential that she have a job, but that her work also be a primary source of reward and gratification. 'In some cases it is this more serious involvement with work that adds to the public misconception of the masculine character of lesbians, for, in our society, work still predominantly remains the masculine sphere' [16].

The necessity of living a dual life, of denying the existence of part of her life, of being bypassed for promotion because she is a woman, is, understandably, a source of frustration and resentment. However, the stigma attached to being a lesbian has been sufficient not only to suppress these feelings but, in concert with other factors (fear of disclosure and loss of job, commitment to work for a livelihood and satisfaction), works to make lesbians employees with relatively stable work histories and high motivation.

MEETING-PLACES AND CLUBS

The gay bar provides the lesbian with a meeting-place. For some time it has been the focal point of the homosexual subculture or the gay life. Bars perform a number of functions. Here, the lesbian may 'freely act out her self-definition' [16], thus consolidating her identity. They facilitate sexual unions by providing a range of attainable partners to choose from and reducing the risk of 'falling for a straight girl.' The bar subculture also supplies social support through the sharing of common feelings and experiences. 'It is an environment in which one can socialize one's sexuality and find ways of deriving sexual gratification by being admired, envied, or desired, while not necessarily engaging in sexual behaviour' [16]. Finally, it provides a language, an ideology, and a justification for homosexual behaviour itself. There are gay bars to be found in most major cities in Canada, the United States, England, and many countries in Europe.

Nevertheless, the gay bar and the gay life do not meet the needs of all lesbians. Many lesbians do not wish to be associated with the gay life because they feel they can manage without it, or they feel that it would further alienate them from conventional society. Others fear exposure, while many couples fear that their present union will be threatened.

Homophile organizations are more recent than gay bars and provide two more important functions in addition to the ones outlined above. First, they provide a public image of the homosexual by producing literature and homosexual newspapers and providing speakers. The homophile organizations also provide counselling, a round-the-clock 'distress' number, and an information service.

Even more recently, much more politically active and socially aggressive organizations have arisen representing increased solidarity and a greater collective identity. These groups are not asking for equality and integration into the existing community but rather seek a radical change in the whole structure of the capitalist society. They state that the patriarchal family perpetuates the myths of femaleness, maleness, and male superiority. The family is seen as the key to bourgeois society and is the arch-oppressor. The Lesbian Collective is one such group in Toronto.

CONCLUSION

The latest study by David Rosen [15a], in which he interviewed twenty-six lesbians, points out that lesbianism is not a psychiatric disorder. After reviewing existing studies and his own findings he states: 'The majority of female homosexuals are mentally healthy and do not desire to be heterosexual. Female homosexuals have the same or a lower incidence of psychiatric disturbances when compared with matched heterosexual controls. No significant difference in the prevalence of neurotic disorders exists between female homosexuals and heterosexuals. These findings have been well documented by numerous nonpatient studies.'

In our view, further understanding and study of the sources of lesbianism and all homosexual behaviour will reveal a complex, multivariate process in which there is great variation in the combination of attributes that produce seemingly similar outcomes. We strongly feel that future research should be aimed at the lesbian for whom sexual preference has not obstructed her functioning as a normal, healthy, and productive adult. This would serve not only to illuminate ways in which these women come to grips with the stigma attached to lesbianism and serve to educate the helping professions, but also to counter-balance the great quantity of research and conclusions based on highly biased samples, such as institutionalized lesbians.

We should mention the fact that very recent research has tended to break away from concerning itself with a never-ending and, in our view, futile search for the etiology of homosexuality. Much of this new research has focused on the homosexual bar or tavern and the homosexual community.

The prevalence of female homosexuality is very difficult to determine because it is not visible in most women and because of the low-profile maintained by most lesbians. Therefore no attempt was made here to estimate the incidence except to suggest that it is more widespread than it is thought to be by most people and that, as such, the need for public education and understanding is even more urgent. Further, there is need for understanding and acceptance of homosexuality by the helping professions, not only as the servants of those seeking counsel, but as agents of change in public opinion.

In 1975 the governing body of the American Psychological Association voted to oppose discrimination against homosexuals and to support the recent action by the American Psychiatric Association which removed homosexuality from that association's official list of mental disorders. It adopted the following resolutions:

Homosexuality per se implies no impairment in judgment, stability, or general social or vocational capabilities;
The American Psychological Association deplores all public and private discrimination in such areas as employment, housing, public accommodation, and licensing against those who engage in or have engaged in homosexual activities and declares that no burden of proof of such judgment, capacity, or reliability shall be placed upon these individuals greater than that imposed on any other persons;
The American Psychological Association supports and urges the enactment of civil rights legislation at the local, state and federal level that would offer citizens who engage in acts of homosexuality the same protection now guaranteed to others on the basis of race, creed, color, etc.;
The American Psychological Association supports and urges the repeal of all discriminatory legislation singling out homosexual acts by consenting adults in private.

It appears that the helping professions are joining with society to bring homosexuality 'out of the closets.'

NOTES

1 Abbott, Sidney and Love, Barbara, *Sappho Was a Right-on Woman*, New York: Stein and Day, 1972.
2 Bandura, Albert, *Principles of Behaviour Modification*, New York: Holt, Rinehart and Winston, 1969.
3 Bieber, Irving, *A Psychoanalytic Study of Male Homosexuality*, New York: Basic Books, 1962.
4 Brecher, Edward M., *The Sex Researchers*, New York: Signet Books, 1969.
5 Caprio, Frank S., *Female Homosexuality*, New York: Grove Press, Inc., 1954.
6 Cory, Donald Webster, *The Lesbian in America*, New York: MacFadden-Bartell Co., 1965.
7 Fluckinger, Fritz, 'Through a Glass Darkly: An Evaluation of the Bieber Study on Homosexuality,' *The Ladder*, 10 (1966), Nos. 10, 11, 12.
8 Gigeroff, Alex. K., *Sexual Deviations in the Criminal Law*, Toronto: University of Toronto Press, 1968.
9 Gross, Leonard H., 'Lesbians in Prison,' *Sexology*, February 1968, 478-481.
10 Hedblom, Jack H., *The Female Homosexual: Social and Attitudinal Dimensions*, Research founded in part by The Bio Medical Research Foundation State University of New York at Buffalo.

11 Kenyon, F.E., 'Homosexuality in the Female,' *British Journal of Hospital Medicine*, February 1970, 183-206.

12 Kinsey, Alfred C., *et al.*, *Sexual Behaviour in the Human Male*, Philadelphia: Saunders Co., 1948.

13 Kinsey, Alfred C., *et al.*, *Sexual Behaviour in the Human Female*, Philadelphia: Saunders Co., 1953.

14 Martin, Del and Phyllis Lyon, *Lesbian/Woman*, New York: Bantam Books, Inc., 1972.

15 *Operation Socrates Handbook*, Federation of Student Inc., University of Waterloo.

15a Rosen, David H., *Lesbianism*, Springfield, Ill.: Charles C. Thomas, 1974.

16 Simon, William, and John H. Gagnon, 'The Lesbians: A Preliminary Overview,' in Simon and Gagnon, eds., *Sexual Deviance*, New York: Harper and Row, 1967.

17 – 'Femininity in the Lesbian Community,' in *Social Problems*, 15 (2), 1967, 212-221.

18 Saghir, Marcel T., and Eli Robins, 'Homosexuality I: Sexual Behaviour of the Female Homosexual,' Reprint: *Archives of General Psychiatry*, February 1969, XX.

19 Stephenson, Marylee, 'Living with a Stigma. A Study of Eleven Female Homosexual Couples,' An abstraction of the author's M.A. Thesis, completed at the University of Essex, U.K., January 1971.

20 Tripp, C.A., 'Who Is a Homosexual?' *The Ladder*, 10 (3) 1965, 15-23.

21 Ward, David A., and Gene G. Kassebaum, 'Lesbian Liaisons,' *Transaction*. January, 1964, 28-32.

22 Weinberg, George, *Society and The Healthy Homosexual*, New York: St. Martin's Press, 1972.

23 Wolff, Charlotte, *Love Between Women*, London, England: Gerald Duckworth and Co. Ltd., 1971.

24 Wolbram, Bonnie, and Kathye Gentry, 'Homosexuality IV: Psychiatric Disorders and Disability in the Female Homosexual,' Reprint: *American Journal of Psychiatry*, 127 (2) August 1970.

25 Wyden, Peter, and Barbara Wyden, *Growing Up Straight*, New York: Signet, 1968.

Male homosexuality*

What is a homosexual experience?
A homosexual experience is any physical arousal you feel in response to some-one of your own sex. This can range from just thinking about someone and be-ing aroused, to actually experiencing orgasm with that person. You can have a homosexual experience without being predominantly homosexually oriented. Most people have a homosexual experience at some point in their lives.

How common are homosexual experiences?
According to Kinsey in 1949, 37 per cent of American men have had at least one homosexual experience to the point of orgasm and 13 per cent were predomi-nantly homosexually oriented (4-6 on Kinsey's scale). For women the percent-ages were 20½ per cent and 7 per cent respectively. This means that when you walk down the main street of your town or city, approximately one out of every three people you pass has had a homosexual experience and one out of ten is predominantly homosexually oriented.

Will one homosexual experience cause me to be homosexually oriented for the rest of my life?
Most people have at least one homosexual experience during their lifetime. This experience can range from a thought or a dream, to actual sexual contact. These

*Excerpts from the University of Waterloo handbook on homosexuality, *Operation Socrates Handbook*, 1973.

experiences may or may not be related to your general sexual preferences. You may be predominantly heterosexual, bisexual or homosexual in your orientation; one homosexual experience cannot determine this and should not be feared.

What sexual activities occur between women?
The most common techniques in female lovemaking include: mutual masturbation (manipulation of the clitoris, caressing the labia, and/or penetration of the vagina with the fingers until sexual excitation or orgasm occurs), cunnilingus (stimulation of the clitoris, the outer lips of the genital area, and sometimes penetration of the vagina with the tongue), and tribadism (one partner on top of the other followed by rhythmic movements to stimulate the clitoris). All of these may be done one to the other or by both at the same time. Another activity is analingus which entails use of the tongue in and around the anal area and penetration with the finger. It is important to note that a penis is not necessary for a woman's sexual gratification (see Masters and Johnson) and the use of penis substitutes (e.g. dildo) is rare among lesbians. The dildo is more commonly used by heterosexually oriented women during masturbation.

What sexual activities occur between men?
Men do a number of things in bed. As well as hugging and kissing, they may masturbate each other. They also suck each other's penis to the point of orgasm (called fellatio or in slang, 'a blow job'). They may swallow the sperm if they want to, it is not harmful. Sometimes men will do a '69' where they lie in such a way that they can suck each other's penis at the same time. Another activity is analingus (see sexual activity between women). Men also have anal intercourse, which requires a lubricant such as 'K-Y' or vaseline. There is no set pattern of behaviour; it all depends upon what the couple prefers.

Can a homosexually oriented person have heterosexual sex?
Yes, a homosexually oriented female or male is not built differently than anyone else. She or he has the same genitalia which function in exactly the same manner as heterosexually oriented people. The difference lies only in the preference of having sexual relations with a member of the same sex.

Who is the husband and who is the wife in homosexual relationships?
In many such relationships there is no need to define one person as husband and one as wife. Household duties and sexual activities are not based on traditional marriage roles. But, just as in heterosexual marriages, there are some homosexual relationships in which one partner will assume the dominant role and the other the passive role.

Has homosexuality always been frowned upon?
No; in the past homosexuality was an accepted part of Greek and Roman cultures. It was only with the acceptance of Judaeo-Christian teachings that these attitudes changed. When these religions began the tribes were struggling to survive and so it was important to produce children. To make sure this occurred, all forms of sexuality and sexual acts which did not lead directly to the birth of a child were outlawed.

How do other cultures react to homosexuality?
Although our own Western culture does not approve of homosexual activity, many in the Near and Far East do. Drs. Ford and Beach report that of the societies they sampled, 49 of the 76 (64%) considered homosexual behaviour to be normal for members of the community. Homosexual activity in these societies is often a part of the normal growing up process that all teenagers go through and does not lead to one exclusive sexual orientation (either heterosexual or homosexual). In fact exclusive sexual orientations are only found in the Western world.

Isn't homosexuality a sign of a society breaking down?
The best answer to this question comes from 20 Questions about Homosexuality by Gay Activists Alliance (see Suggested Reading List).
   'The Persian empire declined quite nicely along with strong antihomosexual taboos. Homosexuality flourished freely at the zenith of the Roman Empire, but the decline was accompanied by an increase in antihomosexual restrictions. Homosexuality thrived during the heights of Periclean Greece, Renaissance Italy and Medieval Japan. And some cultures in which homosexuality has been accepted, like those of certain African and American Indian tribes, neither rose to nor fell from world-dominating heights. The acceptance or non-acceptance of homosexuality had nothing whatever to do with the rise or decline of any culture, and no reputable historian since the 18th century has taken this theory seriously.'

Do homosexually oriented people really want to be heterosexually oriented?
No, homosexually oriented people are by definition primarily attracted to people of their own sex, that is where they find most fulfillment. Many have wishes for the acceptance they would get if they were primarily heterosexually oriented. Some have even tried a heterosexual life style, but in many cases they have not been willing to keep up a pretense. If society did not condemn homosexuality and homosexual experiences, people would be more comfortable with their sexuality, no matter where they were on the sexual spectrum.

Why do the experts claim that all homosexually oriented people are emotionally disturbed?
A careful look shows that psychiatrists and counsellors make their judgments from their experiences with homosexually oriented people who come to them for help. If their only contact with the heterosexual world was through their clients, they could draw the same conclusions about heterosexually oriented people. Professionals in these fields seldom see the healthy homosexually oriented individual because she or he does not need counselling.

Can a homosexual orientation be changed [cured]?
Some individuals have undergone attempts to change their homosexual orientation. In some cases, the person's enjoyment of homosexual relationships has been removed, but in very few cases has this resulted in a satisfying adjustment for the individual. Why attempt change (cure)? Homosexual behaviour, being natural needs no curing. It is not a disease or a sickness and thus the term 'cure' really does not apply.

Are there fewer females than males who are homosexually oriented?
No. According to recent statistics there are not only as many females as males who are homosexually oriented, but probably more. Since there are more women than men in the population, then statistically there are more lesbians. In the past and present a shield of invisibility was maintained by lesbians in order to get and keep a job. Of all the homosexually oriented women in North America 20 per cent have children and since these women are considered to be unfit mothers they hide in order to keep their children. As well, men don't believe that two women can actually achieve sexual satisfaction and therefore do not recognize homosexually oriented women and for much the same reasons there are very few books that have been written about lesbians.

Do lesbians hate men?
Lesbians have an erotic preference for their own sex. This does not mean that lesbians seclude themselves from contact with men. Lesbians can relate to men emotionally and intellectually but they generally do not want to have a sexual relationship with them. Since for lesbians the sexual attraction is not necessarily a main factor in their relationships with men, lesbians and men often have good and relaxed friendships.

Do women who are homosexually oriented want to seduce every woman they meet?
Homosexually oriented women have a sexual preference for women but that does not mean 'every' woman. Like anyone else, homosexually oriented women

are only attracted to certain women and then some interest must be shown on the part of the woman before any move is made.

How can you spot a homosexually oriented person?
Generally, you cannot spot a 'homosexual' any more than you can pick out who is a doctor or a secretary. Most gay people just look average. Many go out of their way to avoid acting or dressing in any of the ways which might associate them with the stereotypes most straight people have of gay people. The idea that all homosexually oriented men are swishy and effeminate, and that all homosexually oriented women are butch truck drivers is simply not true. In fact, many effeminate looking men and masculine women are heterosexually oriented.

Why do we only hear about homosexually oriented people in the arts?
This is probably because the arts (theatre, fine arts, interior design, etc.) hold the most liberal attitudes on sexuality thereby allowing the homosexually oriented person to acknowledge her/his sexuality with little or no discrimination.

Why are there no homosexually oriented people in the professions?
According to the Kinsey statistics, about one out of every ten professionals is predominantly homosexually oriented. Because they are afraid they might lose their jobs or clientele, many professionals do not admit their sexuality. Because of this we get the impression that there are no homosexually oriented professionals.

Do homosexually oriented women prefer men's jobs?
Since the idea that a woman who is attracted to other women must want to be a man is so common, it is natural to think that homosexually oriented women prefer men's jobs. However, this is not the case. Because of women's liberation, job equality is becoming a reality and lesbians can be found in any type of job or position from model to mechanic.

Can homosexually oriented people successfully raise children? Where do the children come from?
Homosexually oriented people are capable of producing children. A person might have been married before realizing her/his sexuality; lesbians can also be unwed mothers.

A certain sexual orientation is not a prerequisite for child raising. Children need love and understanding and homosexually oriented people are perfectly capable of giving them these things. Since children are not isolated from the rest of the world, they will not necessarily be pressured into growing up with a homosexual orientation.

Because I don't date, does it mean that I am homosexually oriented?
Not at all. Many people have trouble dating and feel awkward with members of the opposite sex. Sexual preference usually takes some time to develop, so don't categorize yourself too soon.

If I associate with homosexually oriented people will I become homosexually oriented?
No! People don't catch a homosexual orientation. You have probably been associating with homosexually oriented people throughout your life without even being aware of it. If 'you associate with gay people, there is a possibility that you might have a homosexual experience, if you want one, but it does not mean that you will become homosexually oriented.'

Why don't animals do it?
Many people are unaware of the fact that animals of all species engage in homosexual acts. Wainwright Churchill states that homosexual behaviour has been observed by scientists to occur between 'monkeys, dogs, rats, bulls, porcupines, guinea pigs, horses, donkeys, cats, racoons, baboons, apes and porpoises.' These acts are more frequent and observable between males than females.

Don't 'homosexuals' molest little boys?
This idea has not been supported by facts. Gerhard, Gagnon, Pomeroy and Christenson report that child molesters more frequently victimize girls than boys and that their personalities and behaviour do not resemble those of typical homosexually oriented persons. Most child molestations occur in the child's home, in a neighbour's home or in a relative's home and are committed by either a relative or a friend of the family. Like the vast majority of heterosexually oriented people, homosexually oriented individuals have no sexual interest in children.

Are gay people trying to take over?
This idea may have resulted from a misunderstanding about Gay Liberation. What gay people want is equality not supremacy. If homosexually oriented people were allowed to live as openly and honestly as heterosexually oriented ones, there would be no need for things like Gay Liberation and homosexual demonstrations. Homosexually oriented people don't want everyone in the world to be gay; they simply want to be allowed to be themselves.

Are homosexually oriented people more promiscuous than heterosexually oriented people?
This may be the case for some, because for homosexually oriented people there are no pressures to settle down with one partner. Also there are fewer prelimi-

naries to a sexual experience in the homosexual world. Many people have a series of affairs which may or may not lead to a long-term relationship. Homosexually oriented people, like heterosexually oriented people, can be true to one person or play around with many.

Do homosexually oriented men try to seduce every man they meet?
This is untrue. Like heterosexually oriented men, homosexually oriented men are only attracted to some people and if the men they are attracted to are not interested in sex, they will not force the issue. Homosexually oriented men do not go out of their way to 'make' straight men. There are plenty of homosexually oriented men to chose from.

Do homosexually oriented men hate women?
Homosexually oriented men can relate to women emotionally and intellectually, but they generally do not want to have sexual relationships with them. While some men (of all sexual orientations) dislike women, the majority have good friendships with them. For homosexually oriented men the sexual attraction is not necessarily a major factor in their relationships with women; homosexually oriented men and women often have good and relaxed relationships.

Are homosexually oriented people bad job risks?
Homosexually oriented people are just as responsible as heterosexually oriented people. Those who are homosexually oriented are sometimes believed to be security risks. If their sexuality were known, they would lose their positions; therefore, these people are liable to blackmail. If their sexuality made no difference to the employers, then homosexually oriented people could not be blackmailed and would not be security risks.

THE CHURCH

There are many quotes in the Bible concerning homosexuality, but Christ does not say anything for or against it in any passage. Christ made it obvious that His message was to all, no matter who or what they were. Today, many churches leave it up to one's own conscience and do not outrightly condemn homosexuality.

The Roman Catholic Church
Officially, the Roman Catholic Church says that being homosexually oriented is not a sin. However, performing a homosexual act is. Now many priests say that determining whether you are right or wrong is strictly a matter of conscience.

Judaism
If members of the Jewish Orthodox Church find out that someone in their family is homosexually oriented, according to custom, they would 'sit shiva' (formal mourning of the dead). Reformed Jewish families, on the other hand, are not bound by these rigid rules and may act as they wish.

Anglican Church
At the 1967 General Convention in the USA, the Anglican Church passed a resolution to study the topic of homosexuality. The report's conclusion was that as long as homosexual activity is carried on between consenting adults, the persons involved may be acting as normally as anyone else in society.

United Church of Canada
Through a resolution approved on April 12, 1969, the United Church regarded private acts of homosexuality between consenting adults as acceptable. They oppose discrimination by the law, civil service and employment. The resolution does, however, approve of prosecution and dismissal where homosexual practices occur in public, against children or minors, and where force is used.

Lutheran Church
The Lutheran Church of America voted on July 2, 1971, at its Biennial Convention in Minneapolis that: 'In relation to this private concern [homosexuality], the sexual orientation behavior of freely consenting adults in private is not an appropriate subject for legislation or police action ...'

Unitarian Universalist Association
Recognizing that homosexually oriented people represent a significant minority and that they are found in the clergy as well as the laity, the Association resolved on July 4, 1970, that all discrimination against homosexually oriented people must end and urged all churches and fellowships to begin meaningful sex education programmes.

THE LAW

See: The Criminal Code RSC 1970 Chapter 43, sections 155, 157, 158. The Ontario Human Rights Code RSC 1970 Chapter 318.

Any sexual act is now legal in Canada if performed in private by two consenting adults. The legal age of consent between unmarried people is 21, but usually the law does not bother anyone who is over 18. If one of the partners is not consenting or is under age, the older person can be charged whether or not she/he is the initiator.

Although these laws apply to everyone, they are usually only enforced against homosexual acts. For instance, 'public' is considered to be any place that people can enter either by right (e.g. parks) or by invitation (e.g. bars); while a man and a woman who are making love in a parked car will be told to go home or to move on, a couple of the same sex will be charged with 'gross indecency.'

It is not illegal to ask someone to go to bed as long as offensive language is not used, it is clearly understood that a private place (e.g. your home or a hotel) will be used, and no payment will be made. However, one can be charged with indecent assault (male) if a man touches a man between the knee and the naval without his invitation. The same law applies to a woman if she is touched between the knee and the breast without invitation, but it is difficult for any woman to press a charge on these grounds.

Sex in washrooms, parks, or with more than two people present is deemed 'public.'

Those charged with an indictable offense (punishable by more than 2 years in prison), will be taken to the police station (or told to appear the next day) to be fingerprinted and photographed; they will then be released on their own recognizance until the trial date. Whether or not a person is convicted, these records remain on file at the RCMP headquarters and in the United States (the FBI computer). If a person is convicted of an indictable sexual offense, then she/he can be charged with 'Vagrancy E' if caught loitering in or about parks, school grounds, or public bathing areas. Theoretically after anyone has served a sentence (paid fine etc.), she/he is free; but in this case there is punishment for life because she/he is now liable to repeated charges for just being in certain areas.

Civil law is a little more vague as far as homosexuality is concerned. According to the Marriage Act, any two people may marry within the sanction of the law, but it is inferred that the people are of the opposite sex. To get around this, homosexual couples may incorporate themselves, thereby having a legally binding agreement between them. This does not entitle the partners to the lower taxation bracket, or give the mother benefits that a male and female couple receive.

Wills can only be contested on the grounds of mental illness. Homosexuality as such is not considered mental illness in the eyes of the court. However, death taxes are extremely high if the estate has been left to a friend (or same sex lover) because the law considers this type of beneficiary to be unrelated and a stranger. If the couple has an incorporation contract each is entitled to half the estate automatically, a will covers the rest.

Homosexual orientation can be used as grounds for divorce action. If children are involved, there usually are complications in terms of custody. The courts tend to look upon homosexually oriented individuals as immoral and poor examples for children. There is also the belief that a homosexually oriented parent

will condition a child to be a homosexual. These attitudes make adoption difficult. A single person may be suitable in every way to be a good parent but if it
is suspected that she/he is homosexually oriented there is usually an automatic
refusal of the application.

The Human Rights Code which lists everyone's basic rights does not include
the words 'sexual orientation.' Therefore, a homosexually oriented person can
be discriminated against on the job, or in housing situations. In reality, it is difficult to prove discrimination on any ground but the majority of people think
twice before actually discriminating when the Human Rights Code protects people's rights.

The Immigration Act, Sec. 5, E&F, states that anyone who enters Canada 'for
the purposes of practising homosexualism, pimping, or prostitution' is excluded
entrance and that anyone who is subsequently discovered to be 'a homosexual,
a pimp, or a prostitute' will be deported. Officials seldom ask if a person is a
'homosexual, pimp, or prostitute,' but deportations and denials are usually carried out under the clause which states that anyone having a criminal record cannot immigrate to Canada.

There is no official law which states that a homosexually oriented person cannot be employed by the government as a civil servant or a member of the armed
forces. Many homosexually oriented people are employed in such areas. However, if someone is suspected or found to be homosexually oriented, then that
person is considered a security risk. The only reason homosexually oriented people in government are likely prospects for blackmail is the fact that they will lose
their jobs if their sexuality is discovered; therefore, they are security risks. This
circular reasoning has caused a lot of unhappiness and confusion for homosexually oriented individuals.

VENEREAL DISEASE

Venereal disease is as much of a problem in homosexual sex acts as it is in heterosexual sex. It is possible to contract pubic lice, vaginitis and venereal warts as
well as the two most serious of the sexually transmitted diseases: gonorrhea and
syphilis.

Gonorrhea
Gonorrhea is the less serious, but the more widespread of the two infections.
The gonococcus bacteria dies within a few seconds of being outside of the mucu-
ous membranes of the body.

A male can contract gonorrhea through anal intercourse where either the
penis or the rectum may become infected. Both the penis and the rectum are

mucous lined and allow for the survival of the bacteria. With the penis infection (gonococcal urethritis) a thick creamy yellow or white discharge seeps out of the end of the penis two to five days after anal intercourse with an infected person. A few days later there will be pain and burning on urination. After two weeks these symptoms will begin to disappear, but the infection remains. Left untreated gonococcal urethritis can result in sterility. If the infection is rectal (gonococcal proctitus) there are rarely any symptoms. There may be a slight anal mucous discharge and blood or pus in the feces. Left untreated gonococcal proctitis has no effect on the body but allows for the continuous passing on of the infection to new partners. A man can also contract gonorrhea through oral-genital contact (fellatio). The mouth and throat are lined with mucous membranes. There are usually no symptoms but one may experience a sore throat and low fever a few days after the oral-genital contact.

It is very unusual for a female to contract gonorrhea from another female. She can only contract it if she inserts her tongue into the vagina opening of her partner during cunnilingus.

Syphilis
Syphilis is the most dangerous sexually transmitted disease. If left untreated it can cause blindness, heart failure, paralysis, sterility and brain damage.

Ten to ninety days after infection a small painless sore appears in the area that the bacteria entered the body (mouth, anus, penis, vagina). This sore will disappear with or without treatment.

The second stage begins within three months, and symptoms may be rashes, sore throats, headaches, patchy hair loss, and slight fever and/or swollen glands. During this phase syphilis is highly contagious and can even be contracted through kissing.

The disease then goes into the latent stage which may last for years and during which the person may feel quite well.

The final stage may occur twenty years or more after the initial infection. With this stage comes the blindness, heart failure, sterility, paralysis and brain damage.

Other sexually transmitted diseases
For further information on pubic lice, vaginitis and venereal warts refer to the *McGill V.D. Handbook,* copyright 1972.

PROBLEMS GAY PEOPLE HAVE

Coming out of the closet
Self-acceptance is a major part of growing up. For the homosexually oriented person, there is the added hurdle of overcoming myths and misconceptions and

accepting oneself as a valid, worthwhile human being. Local gay liberation groups can often assist in this process because the members understand the problems and hassles of coming out.

Coming out is different for every individual; there are no rules or 'how to' manuals to follow in order to become a well adjusted person. It is helpful to know that gay people can and do lead productive lives.

Telling friends
The fear of rejection can make telling friends as difficult as telling parents of one's sexual orientation, but close friends are often willing to listen and to learn. Sharing a major part of one's life-style can enrich friendships. Good literature is available for friends and family; this may help them to more fully understand the spectrum of sexuality.

A job and homosexual orientation
Sexuality does not play a part in the way one performs on the job. The homosexually oriented person who is overly worried about being found out often makes it possible for others to believe that there is something terrible about homosexuality. Secrecy breeds curiosity.

There are those who are afraid they will lose their job should their sexual preferences become known. This fear may be ill-founded; in the small survey that *Operation Socrates* carried out among employers, 76 per cent do not care what the employee's sexuality is, and are concerned only with performance and ability to do the job. Being straightforward about one's sexual orientation, when appropriate, is the only way to find out exactly what the response would be and also the only way people's attitudes are going to change.

Blackmail
Blackmail only becomes an issue when an individual hides her/his sexual orientation because she/he would suffer loss of job, friends, etc. This fear may or may not be realistic. If our society were more accepting of homosexuality as a part of the sexual spectrum these fears would be groundless.

Keeping a gay relationship together
Gay relationships are difficult to maintain because they do not have the legal cement, social approval or family support that most heterosexual relationships have. In most gay relationships, there are no children to add permanence to the 'marriage'; its stability is dependent on the strength and commitment of the two people involved. This is probably as it should be for any relationship but in the gay 'marriage' the partners find not only the internal hassles to deal with but also the outside social pressures that discourage such a relationship. For those

homosexually oriented couples who are still 'in the closet,' a superficial appearance of being heterosexually oriented must also be maintained and this causes additional strain. In the face of these obstacles it is surprising that so many long term gay relationships do exist.

Falling in love with a heterosexually oriented person
For the homosexually oriented person, this problem is very similar to that of falling in love with *anyone* who is not equally interested in you. People of every sexual orientation have become interested in someone who cannot return their affection. This can be true of those of your own sexual preference or of another sexual preference. People who have difficulty accepting their homosexual orientation may sometimes separate themselves from contact with other homosexually oriented people, and this prevents them from having the opportunity to develop a relationship with someone of their own sexual orientation.

Telling parents
Homosexually oriented people may wish to tell their parents about their sexuality for a number of reasons: if they are happy with their sexual orientation, they really won't want to hide or to continue to live a life of half truths. They may be afraid that their parents will accidentally find out from some source other than themselves. They may have someone they love and wish to share this happiness with their parents.

Telling one's parents requires some forethought and planning and must include educating them about homosexuality. Abruptly confronting them with the facts more often than not will assure the individual of a negative response. It is much wiser to introduce the topic to one's parents by including it in everyday conversation and offering good books on the subject for their reading. Having accepted one's own sexuality usually makes it easier for parents to accept and adjust to it. If their child seems happy and contented with her/his sexual orientation, there will be less reason for them to become anxious about the well-being of their daughter or son.

How does one deal with parents' responses to the fact that they have a homosexual daughter or son? There is the possibility that they will be very accepting of the fact and happy that their child is comfortable in her/his sexual orientation. If parents are very upset and/or angry, then their child has some more educating to do. Even if this is the response, the individual is at least now free to carry on her/his sexual life without deceit and lies. Questions which in the past have assumed heterosexuality may no longer come up and be an embarrassment, and if they do the person can now respond to them honestly. Once parents know, one can be much more open with them about friends and interests. Hopefully parents' attitudes about homosexuality may change.

If the parents are accepting of their sexuality, the homosexually oriented person may be able to answer a lot of the questions that parents may have and may be able to deal with a lot of their anxieties. Follow-up education is as important as the actual fact of telling them. There are a number of good books available for reading. Most Gay Liberation Movements are willing to talk with parents or suggest good people in the area who may be of assistance to them.

Before telling one's parents that one is homosexually oriented, it would be a very good idea to read Weinberg's *Society and the Healthy Homosexual*, and Fisher's *The Gay Mystique*. These books contain chapters which may help.

J. HOENIG

The management of transsexualism*

Transsexualism has attracted a great deal of interest, far beyond any practical clinical need as the number of patients involved is relatively small. Extrapolating from Swedish (35) and British (15) figures, about 222 males and 71 female cases in the whole of Canada would be expected, the prevalence figures being one case per 34,000 population for males, and one per 108,000 for females. The interest in transsexualism derives mainly from the light which the study of these rare cases will throw on the general nature and development of gender identity. Why a boy comes to consider himself a boy, or a girl a girl, is hardly ever questioned until the uncommon deviant from the norm comes to our attention. A better understanding of gender identity, its roots, the factors influencing its permanence and so on, will in turn find a practical clinical application in cases of hermaphroditism where the question of gender reassignment quite often arises.

GENDER REASSIGNMENT SURGERY

Since Hamburger's (11) case of Christine Jorgensen the procedure commonly called 'sex change operation' has come to be more and more accepted (22) after initial opposition (3,8). There is perhaps even a danger that the pendulum may now be swinging too much in the opposite direction and that this treatment is given without due assessment of the indications, and sometimes to the wrong type of patient. There are a few cases on record where haste and wrong judgment

*Reprinted from *Canadian Psychiatric Association Journal* Vol. 19, No. 1 (February 1974), 1-6.

have led to regrets and tragedy (2,21). The increase in acceptance of the operation is due to the empirically assessed results which were good in the great majority of cases (2,13,22,23). Earlier resistance was largely based on theoretical preconceptions, or on ethics. The theoretical speculative preconceptions gave way to therapeutic empiricism. Religious and moral issues have often been raised, but without reaching a consensus (10,27). The medico-ethical issues, which are of course quite apart from therapeutic results, resolve themselves into three questions: is the treatment carried out in good faith to serve the interest of the patient; is it carried out with due skill (including the methods of selecting patients); is it within the law of the country? In most discussions of the medical ethics of the operation the first two are not questioned. The third point is complex, and all legal aspects surrounding the operation have by no means been resolved.

LEGAL ASPECTS OF THE OPERATION

The question of the legality of the operation itself is subsumed under the legality of all operations leading to castration and sterilization. A number of lawyers have concerned themselves with these problems and have published reports (20, 27,31). Strauss (31) reviews a number of cases which have come before courts, and although in Argentina in 1966 judgment went against one doctor who performed such operations, another case there in 1969 led to acquittal. Yet another in Belgium in 1969 led to acquittal.

Smith (27) gives an admirable summary of the legal status of the operation in various countries. In brief, Belgian, Swedish (34), Danish (32), British, Dutch and Swiss law make the operation legal, subject to varying conditions. In Germany it is illegal although it has been performed. In the United States the situation varies from state to state, and the existence of mayhem-statutes need to be taken into account. The mayhem-statutes, originally enacted in England, were designed to prevent men from dismembering themselves or others so that they would be unable to fight in the service of the Crown. To establish an offence under that statute specific intent to maim would be required, and this could not be established in well-considered surgery. On the other hand consent is not a defence. Mayhem-statutes vary from state to state and caution is counselled for anyone contemplating the operation (26).

In Canada there have been no test cases, but it is suggested that gender reassignment surgery would be legal under Section 45 of the *Canadian Criminal Code*, provided that it can be shown that the patient is in distress and would benefit from the treatment. (Edwards 'Recent Developments Concerning the Criteria of Sex and Possible Legal Implications,' 31 *Man. B. News 104*, 1959). The distress of these patients is illustrated, not only by a high suicide rate, but also by self-mutilation of genitalia, which is frequently reported, as Standage *et al.* (28) remind us in the discussion of their unusual case report in this issue.

Recently there have been suggestions that gender reassignment operations should not be covered by the provincial insurance schemes in certain provinces. The reasoning behind such a restriction is obscure as the operation is entirely therapeutic, and the saving would be trivial in view of the small number of cases – an inception rate of 4 to 5 cases could be expected (15). In Britain the operation is covered by the National Health Insurance scheme.

Strauss (31) concludes that: '... if it is assumed that the performance of conversive surgery upon transsexuals, subject to certain conditions, is lawful, not all juridical problems connected with transsexualism are solved.'

POSTOPERATIVE LEGAL ASPECTS

The legal problem concerning the postoperative status of the patient is indeed very much in question (16,26). Smith (27) states: '... completing surgical reassignment marks the beginning, not the end, of the transsexual's encounters with the legal system. His name is inappropriate and must be changed; his birth certificate states the wrong sex; his passport has the wrong picture and name in it; his Social Security card must be changed so that he may secure employment in the new sex.' The most difficult hurdle will be a change of entry on the birth certificate. Glaus (7) reports a successful case from Switzerland. In Britain such a change can only be effected if it can be shown that a mistake had been made at the time of original registration. So far only 'marginal corrections' have been allowed. In Germany the personal status remains unchanged by the operation (33).

In the United States fifteen states have permitted postoperative changes in the birth records (16,27). In the remaining states the position is not so sympathetic to the plight of the patient, who then has to go through life with a female gender identity, 'female' external genitalia, but an embarrassing basic personal document describing 'her' as a male. Court rulings are usually based on chromosomal sex.

MARITAL STATUS

The legal status of marriage contracted after surgery is very problematic indeed, notwithstanding the fundamental civil right of every person to marry. One such case came to court in Britain (Corbett *versus* Corbett) in which both parties sought an annulment on the grounds of incapacity or wilful refusal to consummate the marriage. Judge Ormerod found that there had not been a marriage. He reasoned that since marriage is: '... essentially a relationship between a man and a woman, the validity of the marriage in this case depends, in my judgement, upon whether the respondent is or is not a woman.' The criteria chosen by him to decide that question were chromosomal, gonadal and external genital sex; and operative interventions as well as psychological criteria, such as gender identity, were ignored (17). The judgment has been critically discussed (4,27) and the question was subsequently debated in the Commons on April 2, 1971 when the *Nullity of Marriage Bill* was before the House (*Hansard Vol. 814*, No. 118, 1827ff). The member for Pontypool (Mr. Leo Abse) said: 'We are addressing ourselves to the problem of those who have a male sex but a female gender. Their personal identity problems are replete with anguish and their social relations bathed in agonizing ambiguities. They live under a law which is too hidebound, too rigid ... Nature does not obey man made laws and ... we would be unjust and unfair if we persisted in continuing to believe that nature is not often shamelessly untidy. We have in our community a small group of people on whom nature has played a tragic trick ... We would indeed be an insensitive Parliament if we allowed the passing of this Bill without amendment, for that would push these people yet further into a bewildering limbo.' Although the case he quoted was that of a hermaphrodite he realized that his amendment would permit marriage with a transsexual. Mr. Abse's amendment was not passed and the Bill received its third reading, upholding the judgment in the case Corbett *versus* Corbett.

In Canada no case has arisen so far.

PREOPERATIVE LEGAL ASPECTS

Most doctors recommend that the operation should not be considered before the age of 21, when the patient can assume full responsibility for consent, and unless the patient has lived in his cross-gender role for at least one year. In order to do that a number of legal hurdles have to be taken. A change of name can be effected with relative ease, and the social insurance card can usually be changed provided a medical certificate assures the officials of the *bona fides* of the case. Sometimes the Department of Welfare, before issuing a female social insurance card, requires the applicant to sign a document that he waives his rights to maternity benefits!

Cross-dressing is an offence in many countries and patients often fall into the hands of the police for that reason. The fierceness with which conformity in clothing is enforced is matched only by the importance cross-dressing assumes for the patient in his gender role play. Both seem equally unreasonable. Patients discovered by the police while cross-dressing can be charged with soliciting, causing a public annoyance, disorderly conduct or loitering with intent. In some countries such as Denmark, Germany or Switzerland the police, on medically supported applications, can issue permits which protect the patients, but the safest protection for the patient is simply not to become conspicuous.

Homosexuality is another charge which can be brought if any kind of intimacy takes place in public, such as can be readily observed going unheeded by the police among heterosexual couples any Sunday afternoon on the village green.

AVAILABLE TREATMENTS

The syndrome once established presents an endstate, and reversals if they occur at all are rare. A 'cure' in the sense of changing the psychosyndrome itself cannot be achieved by methods so far known. Conventional psychotherapy has not achieved any results of that kind, and although psychoanalysis has been tried (3) there is only one case on record where psychoanalysis (of the existential type) has succeeded (25). This case was followed up successfully for three years after termination of therapy. More than half of the 30 eminent psychotherapists who expressed their views in a public debate conceded that surgery was not contraindicated, although that debate took place long before the empirical results of operation (in a large number of cases) were known (14).

Behaviour modification therapy has not fared any better (6). An important reason for the failure of all types of psychotherapy is probably the poor motivation of the patient.

Whereas castration by hormone therapy affects erotic abnormalities by reducing the sexual drive, the transsexuals actually seek out this treatment and the condition thrives rather than diminishes (2,14). As the core of the transsexualist syndrome is a 'conviction' on the part of the patient that he is a person of the opposite sex, neuroleptics which are effective in conditions with paranoid features have been tried, but again without success.

There is then no 'cure' known at present and the sheet anchor of therapy is management rather than treatment. Surgery by itself is not enough but it can be an important help to the patient as part of an overall plan of management, which is to help the patient to a better social as well as inner adjustment. That this can be achieved in over three-quarters of the cases has been established in several studies (2,14,22,23).

ORGANIZATIONAL NEEDS

It is clear that the assessment of cases and the management preoperatively and postoperatively are complex, and require multidisciplinary teams including psychiatrists, surgeons, endocrinologists, social workers, psychologists, lawyers, clergy and others. In view of this, gender identity clinics have been established which can provide this kind of service and, by concentrating the work in one centre, they can give researchers access to the necessary case material (12). There are now fourteen such clinics in North America, including the one in the Clarke Institute of Psychiatry in Toronto, which is described in this issue by Steiner *et al.* (29). Research in Canada is not confined to this clinic, as is shown by Martel's paper in this issue (19), and reports from Montreal which have appeared elsewhere (18,36).

SELECTION OF CASES FOR SURGERY

Although surgery can help many transsexuals, provided they are reasonably stable and do not suffer from psychotic illnesses, it can do damage and lead to regrets if applied to the wrong person. The type of patient to avoid, but who is sometimes difficult to recognize, is the transvestite who says he feels himself to be both male and female and has to give expression to both these aspects of his personality. His cross-dressing may have begun for erotic purposes but is later continued for other reasons. He takes hormones to enlarge his breasts. But he differs from the transsexual in lacking the conviction that he is of the opposite sex. Most such patients do not want 'sex change' surgery, but the diagnostic difficulties increase when they do request such operations – reminiscent of the Münchhausen syndrome (1) – which, if granted, they regret (21). Insistence on prolonged preoperative observation will help to eliminate such errors.

Some progress has been made in bringing more order into this field of study which is confused by a terminology reminiscent of the Tower of Babel and by preconceived notions and premature theorizing (24,30). Many theories further blur the issues rather than clarify them. Some hold that the conditions lie on some kind of continuum of masculinity/feminity often imprecisely defined, or that they are all the same disorder, differing only from each other in severity; for example, transsexualism is regarded as more severe than transvestite fetishism or homosexuality. Other theories presume that the syndromes are all due to an arrested development and that the variety of forms merely reflect the level of arrest. Very few of these authors attempt to test their theories. Rather than rush ahead with such theories, for the time being it would be better to work patiently, trying to more precisely circumscribe transsexualism and the other syndromes joining it on the list of differential diagnoses, supporting clinical studies by a statistical item analysis, as was attempted by Freund *et al.* (5), to arrive at the categories which can be secured. It would be better to look to experimental work such as that done by Green (9) and others, making longitudinal studies of children with gender identity problems.

There is still a great deal to be discovered before we can feel confident in our management of transsexualism. Premature theories can mislead us into a false confidence, possibly to the detriment of our patients.

NOTES

1 Asher, R.: Münchhausen's syndrome, *Lancet 1*: 339-341. 1951.

2 Benjamin, H.: *The Transsexual Phenomenon*, New York, The Julien Press. 1966.

3 Boss, M.: Umwandlungsoperation, *Psyche* (Stuttg) *4*: 230-233. 1950.

4 Dewhurst, C.J.: 'Sex and Gender,' Correspondence, *Lancet*, March 7, 517. 1970.

5 Freund, K., Langerin, R., Nagler, E., Zajac, A. and Steiner, B.: Measuring feminine gender identity in homosexual males, *Arch. Sex. Behav.* In press.

6 Gelder, M.G., and Marks, I.M.: 'Aversion Treatment in Transvestism and Transsexualism' in *Transsexualism and Sex Reassignment*, Ed. Green R., and Money, J., Baltimore, Johns Hopkins Press, 1969.

7 Glaus, A.: Operative Geschlechtsumwandlung und nachträgliche gerichtliche Anerkennung des weiblichen Personenstandes. *Schweiz. Med. Wschft.* 76-79. 1963.

8 Green, R., Stoller, R.J., and MacAndrew, C.: Attitudes toward sex transformation procedures. *Arch. Gen. Psychiat. 15*: 178-182, 1966.

9 Green, R.: Childhood cross-gender identification, *J. Nerv. Ment. Dis. 147*: 500-509. 1968.

10 Green, R.: 'Attitudes Toward Transsexualism and Sex Reassignment Procedures' in *Transsexualism and Sex Reassignment*. Ed. Green, R., and Money, J. Baltimore, Johns Hopkins Press, 1969.

11 Hamburger, C., Stürup, G.K., and Dahl-Inversen, E.: Transvestism, hormonal, psychiatric and surgical treatment, *J.A.M.A. 152*: 391-396. 1953.

12 Hastings, D.W.: 'Inauguration of a Research Project on Transsexualism in a University Medical Centre' in *Transsexualism and Sex Reassignment*. Ed. Green, R., and Money, J. Baltimore, Johns Hopkins Press, 1969.

13 Hoenig, J., Kenna, J.C., and Youd, A.: Surgical treatment for transsexualism, *Acta. Psychiat. Scan. 47*: 106-133. 1971.

14 Hoenig, J.: The rationale and myth of the surgical treatment of transsexualism, *Med. Aspects of Human Sexuality, 2*: 7-13. 1972.

15 Hoenig, J., and Kenna, J.C.: The prevalence of transsexualism in England and Wales. *Br. J. Psychiatry. 123*, February 1974.

16 Holloway, J.P.: 'Transsexuals and their "legal sex"' in *Transsexualism and Sex Reassignment*. Ed. Green, R., and Money, J. Baltimore, Johns Hopkins Press, 1969.

17 *Lancet*; Sex and Gender, Correspondence, Feb. 21: 405-407, 1970.
18 Lowy, F.H., and Kolivakis, T.: Autocastration in a male transsexual. *Can. Psychiatr. Assoc. J. 16*: 5, 399, 1971.
19 Martel, P.: Etude d'un cas de transsexuel male. *Can. Psychiatr. Assoc. J. 19*. 13-16. 1974.
20 *Maryland Law Review, 31* 'Transsexuals in Limbo: The search for a legal definition of sex.' 236-254. 1971.
21 Money, J., and Wolff, G.: Sex reassignment: male to female to male, *Arch. Sex. Behav.* 2: 245-250. 1973.
22 Pauly, I.: Current status of the change of sex operation, *J. Nerv. Ment. Dis. 47*: 460-471, 1968.
23 Randall, J.: 'Preoperative and Postoperative Status of Male and Female Transsexuals' in *Transsexualism and Sex Reassignment*. Eds. Green, R., and Money, J. Baltimore, Johns Hopkins Press, 1969.
24 Roth Martin, and Ball, J.R.: 'Psychiatric Aspects of Intersexuality' in *Intersexuality of Vertebrates, Including Man*. Eds. Armstrong, C., and Marshall, A. London, Academic Press, 1964.
25 Schwöbel, G.: Ein transvestitischer Mensch, die Bedeutung seiner Störungen und sein Wandel in der Psychoanalyse, *Schw. Arch. Neurol. Neurochir. Psychiat. 86*: 358-382. 1960.
26 Shervin, R.V.: 'Legal Aspects of Male Transsexualism' in *Transsexualism and Sex Reassignment*. Eds. Green, R., and Money, J. Baltimore, Johns Hopkins Press, 1969.
27 Smith, D.K.: Transsexualism, sex reassignment surgery and the law, *Cornell Law Review, 56*: 963-1009, 1971.
28 Standage, K.F., Moore, J.A., and Cole, M.G.: Self-mutilation of the genitalia by a female schizophrenic. *Can. Psychiatr. Assoc. J. 19*. 17-20, 1974.
29 Steiner, B.W., Zajac, A.S., and Mohr, J.W.: A gender identity project. *Can. Psychiatr. Assoc. J. 19*: 7-12, 1974.
30 Stoller, R.J.: The term 'Transvestism,' *Arch. Gen. Psychiat. 24*: 230-237, 1971.
31 Strauss, S.A.: Transsexualism and the law, *Comp. Int. Law. J. South Africa 3*: 348-359, 1970.
32 Stürup, K.G.: 'Legal Problems Related to Transsexualism and Sex Reassignment in Denmark' in *Transsexualism and Sex Reassignment*. Eds. Green, R., and Money J. Baltimore, Johns Hopkins Press, 1969.
33 Uhlenbruck, W.: Transsexualität und Personenstand, *Med. Klin. 64*: 1178-9, 1969.
34 Wålinder, J.: 'Medicolegal Aspects of Transsexualism in Sweden,' in *Transsexualism and Sex Reassignment*. Eds. Green, R., and Money, J. Baltimore, Johns Hopkins Press, 1969.

35 Wålinder, J.: Incidence and sex ratio of transsexualism in Sweden, *Br. J. Psychiatry 119*: 195-196, 1971.
36 Warnes, H., and Hill, G.: 'Gender Identity and the Wish to be a Woman,' in press.

ANDREW I. MALCOLM

The influence of drugs on sexual behaviour*

The Romans worshipped Venus as the Goddess of Love; but in English the word venery means sexual intercourse. The Greeks adored Aphrodite as the Goddess of Love; but in English the word aphrodisiac is applied to any food or drug that excites to venery.

In spite of the passionate claims of shamans, charlatans, and old wives there is probably no drug that specifically stimulates sexual desire. There are, however, numerous drugs that alter mood and perception in such ways as to bring about a receptive attitude toward sex. No doubt the most famous of these is alcohol, a central nervous system depressant that serves to allay anxiety, dispel self criticism, and block the intrusion of inhibiting ideas.

Alcohol in moderate amounts is almost an aphrodisiac. In larger amounts, it passes from tranquillizer to anesthetic until in the end the drinker is not just unable to engage in venery; his incapacity is such that he cannot even pronounce the word!

A few years ago a patient told me that, for him, sex was a most agreeable diversion. It was like stepping off the second lowest step. Sex with alcohol, however, was even more interesting because extraneous thoughts and feelings somehow failed to distract him. It was like jumping from the top of the flight. Sex with marijuana, he said, was like leaping from the front door right onto the sidewalk, if he could only remember that it was his intention to engage in such an exercise. Sex with LSD, said my patient, was like flying headlong from the top of

*Reprinted from *Medical Aspects of Human Sexuality* Vol. 3, No. 11 (November 1973), 30-33. (Canadian edition)

the chimney, except that the roof was hard to find, and the view was so confusing that it usually did not occur to him that he was supposed to jump.

There are three variables that will determine the effect of a drug on sexual behaviour. The first of these is the drug itself, its pharmacologic properties, and the size of the dose in relation to body weight. The second is the user himself, including the state of his maturity, his philosophical position, and his mental and physical condition. The third is the influence of the milieu in which the drug is taken.

THE INTOXICATING DRUG

Such depressant drugs as the barbiturates, the newer sedative-hypnotics, and alcohol all tend to bring about an attitude of abandon; and they produce, moreover, such tubular vision that the person intent upon coition may single-mindedly address himself to the pursuit of this particular pleasure. He may be more clumsy but he is not distracted by the events of the day, the restraints in his mind, and the peripheral stimuli in the environment.

Heroin has a very different effect. Following the injection of this drug there is a marked reduction in sexual desire and indeed in any urge to be physically active or aggressive. This is also true of morphine, methadone, and all of the other narcotic drugs. Perhaps this is one of the reasons why so many prostitutes regularly use this vicious drug. Once they have secured their mark they may become quite passive and detached, quite uninvolved in any service they are required to provide.

Marijuana is an illusionogen. It distorts perception, dissolves the boundaries of the self, interrupts normal thought processes, diminishes the capacity to comprehend reality, and increases suggestibility. Depending on the dose, this drug may bring about everything from a degree of euphoria to a completely disorienting hallucinosis. It is important to note, however, that the user ordinarily consumes as much of the drug as is necessary to achieve intoxication. In this respect, marijuana is very unlike alcohol. Most drinkers do not seek to become drunk; and they can measure the amount of alcohol consumed in gross quantities to check the onset of this undesired state. Most marijuana smokers intend to become stoned on every smoking occasion; and they are inclined to regard any condition other than that as being disagreeable. Cannabis brings about an altered state of consciousness in which thoughts and sensory stimuli are interpreted in odd and often surprising ways. [The user] might, in such a condition, be more easily aroused; but the fragmenting influence of the drug might just as easily draw his attention to some other perception a moment later.

In the case of marijuana the periphery is assigned as much value as the centre. Incongruities co-exist, the inessential is as significant as the essential, and time, place, and person are increasingly less well defined. In such a circumstance the cannabis smoker might never get around to sex even if the circumstances were propitious, but if he did, he might experience sensory and emotional effects that would seem, at least for the first few times, altogether novel.

The effects of LSD are related to those of cannabis but they are markedly exaggerated. Thus, while it is true that the sexual experience under its influence might be extremely bizarre, it is far less likely that the intoxicated person would be sufficiently well organized to relate effectively to another person or to concentrate his interest in the sphere of sexuality.

PERSONAL VARIATION

The second variable is that of the personality of the user. A person who is ordinarily rather suggestible is more liable to set aside his critical judgment and be [affected by] the upsurge of elemental emotion that is released by the intoxicant. Thus, people who are immature or poorly integrated will be affected by relatively smaller doses of any of these drugs. Furthermore if a person feels lonely and alienated, or if his self esteem is particularly low, he will be more receptive to the belief that a drug will benefit him in some magical way. His mental set will be such as to greatly facilitate the power of the drug to disinhibit and confer euphoria.

THE ENVIRONMENT

Most of the drugs that bring about an altered state of consciousness are used in social settings. The milieu in which the drug is taken is, therefore, of the greatest importance. This is particularly true of groups that have added marijuana to their battery of psychoactive drugs. In this sub-culture, gratification of the senses is frequently held to be the primary goal of social life; and much emphasis is placed on behaviour that is considered to be unrestrained and therefore natural. Marijuana, the sexual urgency of youth, the conviction that rebellion against established patterns of behaviour is virtuous, and a system of values that emphasizes emotional experience in the here and now, all come together in this sub-culture to produce a variety of sexuality that is uninhibited, polymorphous, and curiously lacking in mystery. But it is certainly not the drug alone that is responsible for the creation and diffusion of this generally unsatisfying sexual style. It is, rather, the interraction between the pharmacologic properties of the drug, the philosophy of neo-transcendentalism, and the vulnerable personalities of people caught in the process of maturation.

There is no such thing as an aphrodisiac. There are only certain drugs that alter consciousness, certain people who crave the high, and certain environments that favour sexual expression. It is the combination of all three that leads to the behaviour named in honour of Venus.

PART FOUR

SEXUALITY AND THE LAW

LORENNE M.G. CLARK

Rape in Toronto: psychosocial perspectives on the offender*

Because of the pervasive and deeply rooted attitudes toward the legitimacy of sexual coercion in our society, our conceptions of 'normal male and female' derive from taking *coerced* sexuality as the *natural* standard. And given that this is true, it is scarcely surprising that it should be considered to be 'normal' for men not to like women at least to some extent, since they must perceive women as being misers and hoarders of a commodity they are led to believe they desperately desire and need. Nor is it surprising that they should identify themselves as 'true men' in accordance with the degree to which they are aggressive and dominant. Aggressive and dominant men get what they want; it is merely the forms of aggressiveness and dominance which vary, and is only when the forms resorted to involve the use or threat of violence that we are prepared to call it 'rape' and to punish those who commit it.

What all those involved in this process take for granted is that in society as we know it, men are expected to apply a certain amount of pressure in order to have women submit - called 'agree' - to sexual acts of various kinds, including intercourse. Women, on the other hand, are expected to resist such pressures, whatever their actual desires might happen to be. Men are supposed and expected to be sexually dominant, to initiate sexual activity, and women are supposed and

*The results discussed in this unpublished paper are based on research carried out in Toronto. Beginning in the fall, 1973, all rape complaints reported to the Metropolitan Toronto Police Department during 1970 were examined and analyzed. This work was carried out jointly with Ms. Debra J. Lewis, and all of the results are discussed in *Rape: The Price of Coercive Sexuality*, to be published in the spring, 1976, The Canadian Women's Educational Press, Toronto.

expected to be sexually passive, and to give the final 'yes' or 'no' as to whether or not sexual activity of any very serious nature is to take place. This pattern of behaviour exists at all levels of society and between persons who are variously placed in the socio-economic scale. There are, among different groups, different 'norms,' as to what constitutes 'acceptable' methods of male coercion and acceptable and appropriate female responses. Difficulties arise because what is regarded by the male as 'standard practice' is not so regarded by his female companion. One woman in our study who complained of rape, a young woman classified as 'idle,' and who was 'known as' a frequenter of the old Yorkville area of Toronto, disagreed about the standard. She felt that the man 'had gone too far,' whereas his reply was 'that he had used no more force than is usual for males during the preliminaries.' In another case, again involving a young woman, the woman rather sagely remarked that 'usually guys stop when you tell them to. This one didn't.' It is significant too that in both of these cases the men were middle-class, one a businessman and the other a semi-professional, and the women involved failed to conform to the stereotyped image of the 'real victim.' If the cases had come to trial, they are not the sort of men likely to have been judged to have resorted to unacceptable tactics, or who would be sent to jail for what they did because the women involved were not 'real victims.'

These men, in common with most accused rapists, did not see anything wrong in what they had done. What the victim experienced as rape, they believed to be seduction. Early on in the study we were struck by the fact that virtually none of these offenders believed that they were doing anything wrong; they did not see themselves as acting any differently from other men in society, and did not see, and resisted seeing, themselves as men who had broken the law. Almost all of them either saw, or went to quite incredible lengths to see, their behaviour as 'normal' and acceptable. The extreme case simply believes everything he does in relation to women is acceptable, and after that there are subtler shadings in self-deception.

The basis for these findings was made possible by the fact that Metropolitan Toronto Police Officers often carefully recorded any conversation which took place between victim and offender. An analysis of these conversational exchanges revealed some striking features. Such conversation was reported present in 22.4 per cent of the cases, and it is possible that it was present but unreported in more. Some police officers are more meticulous than others, and of course their own perceptions vary as to what is important enough to be painstakingly copied out on a General Occurrence Report. In 22.7 per cent of the cases in which conversation was recorded, some reference to a girlfriend or wife was made, but it was impossible to calculate statistically other kinds of data.

However, what emerges very clearly from a composite of these conversational exchanges is a continuum of attitudes, in which the individual variations can be explained by reference to the degree to which the male identifies with the need to be aggressive and dominant in order to display 'true masculinity.' First there are those men who simply do not think that what women think or desire is of any relevance whatsoever. In one case, the rape of an employee by an employer, the victim struggled away from the encounter calling him a 'stupid damn wop' (which, I might add, he was not, that is, he was not an Italian), and he just laughed at her. So sure of himself was he that he took no pains whatsoever to conceal his identity or to absent himself. She did lay a complaint, and the police acted on it, arresting him, thoroughly unperturbed, shortly thereafter at his home. No doubt he had been indulging in such behaviour for years but none of his victims had thought it worth the trouble to themselves to attempt to have him arrested. In another case, a man known to the victim, and known by her to be of a somewhat vicious disposition, dragged her to the floor saying, 'You don't want to fuck but you are going to fuck, you son of a bitch.' In still another case: 'When the offender tried to put his penis in her, "I told him that I was menstruating and he said that was alright that I was only a pig anyway."' Earlier in this encounter – they had met at a party and she had accepted a ride home from him, 'When the victim told the suspect to keep his hands to himself the offender slapped her across the face several times and called her a bitch and a slut.'

More commonly, however, the offender tries to see the situation in more generally acceptable terms. Protestations of love are quite common. In one case, a woman of forty-four was asleep in her bedroom when attacked by a stranger some fifteen years her junior; she stated to the police officer that, 'During the struggle the assailant stated he loved her ... All the time that he was trying this he kept saying to her that he loved her very much.' In another similar case, one would have thought they were old friends. On standing over the victim with a knife, the man remarked, 'This is my lucky night. I was trying doors and found yours open.' In another stranger-to-stranger case involving a young woman in a heavily wooded area, 'The offender fondled the victim's breasts and tried to kiss her, asking her if she loved him ... This man shouted "goodbye" as he ran off when he was finished.' In another stranger-to-stranger hitchhiking case, the man, after the rape, asked for the victim's telephone number and stated that he would pay her $500 if she would sleep with him again. In another hitchhiking case, the man again took down the address of the victim, drove her home, shook her hand, and said goodbye as he drove off into the night.

In another apartment break-in case, the suspect established an atmosphere of severe violence and then proceeded as if the situation were one between new lovers, where, indeed, the female was a virgin: 'He informed the victim that he had done this many times before, and no harm would come to her if she cooperated. "There was only one woman that resisted and I broke her neck" he told me.' And then: 'I am only going to make love to you, not hurt you,' he said. In this case, the offender wished the victim to engage in what would be quite usual and acceptable forms of foreplay, including fondling and kissing his penis. Following this, '"He told me that he would be very gentle with me." When she refused to insert his penis into her vagina, "he then sunk his teeth into the fleshy part of the upper left breast, cutting the skin, and leaving teeth marks." With this, she complied, and on complaining that it hurt her, "he then asked me, 'Do you want me to go all the way?'"'

The offender frequently wanted the victim to participate pretty actively in his fantasy. He often asked whether or not the victim was enjoying the situation: 'He then undid his pants and pulled them down enough to expose himself and got on top of the victim and inserted his penis in the victim's vagina and said, "Do you like it?"' Moreover, he, and most aggressors usually wanted and demanded positive confirmation, having an underlying belief that if the victim admits to liking it, then he is not doing anything wrong. I quote further from the case above: 'She did not reply. He then asked again in a louder voice, "Do you like it?" Again the victim did not reply. He then asked in a very fierce voice "Do you like it?" and then pushed on the victim's shoulders. At this time she repeated "Yes."' Here it is interesting too, that as soon as she made the requisite 'admission,' the offender ejaculated. In another stranger-to-stranger case, the pattern was virtually identical: 'He then inserted his penis into her vagina. He said "Do you like it?"'

In yet another case, the offender wanted the victim to assure him that his penis was bigger than her husband's. And in still another, from which I shall quote at length later, the offender carried on a virtual running patter, wanting to know whether the victim liked intercourse, had difficulty achieving a climax, and whether she smoked or drank.

In another violent rape involving an abduction off the street, the rapist exhibited the same kind of pattern as that noted in an earlier case, of having first to establish an atmosphere of very real danger and then trying to minimize this as much as possible. In this case, the offender was clearly having difficulty maintaining the two points of view, though it seems clear which he wished to prevail: 'He raped her in his car, following which he put his hand over her mouth and then placed his other hand on her throat and said he was going to kill her ... He then dragged her, nude, out of the car to a grassy area about 50 ft. away where he had the victim sit nude on the wet grass. He got her clothes and told her to sit and talk, asked her to light him a cigarette which she did. He talked about being married, having a wife and six kids. He then raped her again by placing his hands on her throat and threatening her with death.'

These cases illustrate very clearly that the offender tries to pretend to himself that the situation is normal. He tries to see the victim as someone he loves, and hopefully as someone who loves him. He expects, and wants, the usual preliminary gesture of kissing, fondling, and other forms of foreplay. During the rape he wants to be thought a good performer, and likes to be assured that he is. He also wants the victim to be enjoying herself. Following the event, he wants a normal parting; idle chit-chat, a cigarette or two, an exchange of phone numbers, and friendly goodbyes. He would appear often to restrict his violence only to what is necessary to achieve a sufficiently coercive situation to facilitate his objective of sexual satisfaction, but he will try to minimize the obviousness of the violence, and clearly in many cases wants sexual communication as much as mere sexual satisfaction. The threat or reality of violence sets the stage, but, once it is set, the offender often pretends that this was not so and proceeds as if it were a perfectly normal encounter between a more rather than a less willing female. At the outer limit, it is for him a seduction rather than a rape.

However, there are clearly variations within the general pattern of attempting to normalize the situation. Those cases which seem to show extraordinary callousness on the part of the offender, where he engages in abusive behaviour of varying sorts, verbal as well as physical, seem to indicate a belief on the part of the offender that he must act in this way, that he must manifest hostility and demonstrate real power over the victim in such a way as to make her fear and perhaps even dislike him in order for him to exhibit real manliness and so appear to himself as the embodiment of true masculinity. In other cases, such as the one discussed immediately above in which there seems to be an atmosphere of more violence and threat created than the situation demands, but in which, at the same time, the offender tries to engage in 'normal' conversation and other forms of unexceptional behaviour, we seem to be dealing with an offender who sees the reality of power created through the threat of force as an element in his behaviour but not as the sole motive or objective of his actions. He seems to need the reassurance of both the effectiveness of power and, virtually simultaneously, the non-necessity of it. He seems to need to know that he can get what he wants by using the threat of severe violence, and to try to promote real fear of it in the victim, while at the same time not wanting to believe that he really has to rely on this in order to get what he wants.

Other studies have indicated behaviour of the sort we are characterizing as attempts at normalization, though none have drawn the inferences from it that this demonstrates a range of attitudinal variations on the part of offenders. MacDonald (see References) mentions the fact that many offenders demand co-operation and affection from their victims and that many of them talk at length with them. He comments that 'touching solicitude may be shown for the victim's welfare' and he discusses one particularly revealing conversational exchange which clearly illustrates the rapist's unwillingness to recognize that he is doing anything wrong. 'A victim asked her assailant, "Is that always the way you have to get a girl, by rape?" He became very angry saying, "Did I rape you?" reaching for his knife and adding, "In that case, I'll have to kill you." The girl quickly told him that he did not rape her.'

But even here, MacDonald makes no inference from this that the offender obviously does not want to see his behaviour as wrongful or as to the possible psychodynamics lying behind this process. He also comments that many offenders afterwards express what MacDonald sees as remorse: 'A grateful offender paid a florist to send roses to his victim.' MacDonald assumes that actions such as this are expressions of remorse, but it seems to me that the expression of remorse must necessarily involve some recognition of wrongdoing. Sending roses is certainly not a clear-cut case of this and seems more obviously an attempt to normalize the situation. This is the kind of thing one does to show appreciation to a lover, the sort of thing which is appropriate for someone who feels pleased at having accomplished a pleasurable seduction and not for someone who feels sorry about having raped someone. Expressions of guilt and remorse are not unheard of, but they are much less ambiguous than a gesture such as this.

McCaldron attempted to assess the offender's attitude to the offence and found that the offender 'admits' his offence in 33 per cent of the cases, 'denies' it in 27 per cent, and 'rationalizes' it in 33 per cent. He comments that, 'rapists ... have a tendency to avoid a full admission of guilt with an appropriately contrite attitude. Instead, in two-thirds of the cases, one hears – 'I'm here on a phoney beef' ... or 'So I might have been a little rough, but she was asking for it,' or 'I might have done it, but I was too drunk to remember.' Thus his conclusions certainly support our contention that most rapists do not see their behaviour as morally wrong.

In a small number of cases, five in our study, the offender shows some clear awareness that what he is doing is wrong. In one case it was difficult to escape the feeling that perhaps the offender did what he did in order to get help. Here, it was a stranger-to-stranger apartment break-in case: 'He came through a window, threatened the victim with a knife, slightly cut her throat on the right side, raped her, and took her purse. When she said she needed the money he returned it ... Conversation ensued and the suspect told the victim to tell the cops he lived in ———— and that he had a motorcycle parked on Queen Street East. He told her he couldn't help what he did. He'd been brought up with bad people and no girls would go out with him.' This suspect was subsequently arrested where he said he could be found. This case also exemplifies what is more usual where there is some awareness, and admission, of wrong-doing, namely, an attempt to present some excuses and to portray the behaviour as uncontrollable.

In two cases, the offender stated that prison was the cause of his problems: 'He then told me what a terrible life he had had, and that he had been in and out of jail.' Further, 'He stated that he had been in prison for two years and he didn't usually do this.'

Sometimes rather more sophisticated explanations are offered:

The suspect never stopped talking. His wife was a nurse, that he had been a homosexual at age 12-14 years, that this was the sixth time he had done this, that the first time had been to a young woman in a suburban area ... He had received a 'dose' from this woman. He had never beaten anyone to the point of submission, asked if she was a virgin, asked her name and address, asked her if she had trouble reaching a climax. He stated that he didn't drink, that he didn't smoke, and didn't hang around bars. This was going to be his last time, that he knew he was a pathetic case, that a hospital couldn't help him, that his relations with his wife had been better lately, and that this would be the last time he would have to do this ... The suspect stated that he was emotionally disturbed, also that victim would be crushed emotionally, that he wanted to keep a good relationship with his mother-in-law. When he let the victim out of his auto, he said he never did have a knife, and that he was sorry he had raped her.

This confession is all the more startling in light of the circumstances of the case. The offender abducted the victim from the parking lot of a large downtown Toronto motor-hotel, at two o'clock in the afternoon, with a great deal of struggling, and with several witnesses who attempted to stop him. The victim was bound and gagged and kept literally underfoot under the front seat of his car until the offender had driven well out into the country. Neither had he not used considerable violence, nor was this his 'last time.' This suspect was apprehended later in 1970, following the commission of two more rapes, one of them exhibiting a rather high degree of violence, and on arrest, was charged with six counts of rape, two counts of attempted rape, and one count of assault causing bodily harm.

This case illustrates two further problems, however, which suggest future research. First, some of the alleged facts about himself which the offender recounted to this particular victim were not true on the basis of facts verified by arrest. Some of the false statements were no doubt the product of self-deception, but some of them would appear to be deliberate attempts to mislead the victim. Some of them may well have been calculated simply to make detection difficult, but some of them appear to have been calculated to elicit the victim's sympathy, and may have been attempts to turn the event into a genuine seduction, by trying to gain the victim's willing co-operation through her sympathy. Succeeding in such a situation, of course, furthers the offender's belief that he is really seducing, and not raping, the victim.

Second, rapists may not exhibit a univocal pattern of response. That is, they may tend to display more aggression and hostility, more need to demonstrate and confirm their power openly, with some victims than with others. The extent to which the offender shows or has the need to accomplish sexual intercourse through the use and/or threat of force, and has this as one of his objectives, may be a function not only of his own psychosocial features, but of his perceptions of particular victims. His conception of what is necessary to be truly male may vary with particular situations and particular victims. These are possibilities that can be verified only by further research designed to elicit information about the offender's attitudes to his own sexuality, male sexuality in general, to the sexuality of women in general, and to that of particular women. In this way it may be possible to assess the extent to which his responses vary with other factors.

In one case the simplest of all explanations was offered for behaviour which the offender clearly believed to be wrong and indeed which he did not want to commit. This was a group rape, in which the victim was abducted off the street into a car by six offenders. When the other five had raped the victim, this suspect commented, 'He didn't want to do it, but if he didn't, the others would "beat the shit out of him" ... They talked of having done this to other women.'

These data also seem to shed some light on what has been another controversial aspect of past rape research. The findings that most alleged rapists were 'normal,' which led to the conclusion that what they had done wasn't then 'real rape,' was also fostered by the view that the act committed by the rapist is normal in that it does not proceed from any abnormal motivation. It is seen as the expression of the universal desire for the (in itself harmless) act of sexual intercourse. The alleged rapist is simply a man who seeks satisfaction of perfectly normal desires for sexual gratification. This is an assumption which has been severely criticized by many feminists. It has been their contention that rape is motivated at least as much by the need to dominate and to degrade women as it is by the normal desire for sexual gratification. The rapist is the man who *must* exercise power over women in order to satisfy both his sexual needs and his emotional need to be seen, and to be perceived by himself, to be a super-masculine male. Thus, forcible intercourse accomplished by at least the threat of violence is, it is alleged, necessarily the sexual act of first choice for some men. Intercourse of this type is all that can confirm the male's image of himself as the dominant, aggressive man that 'real' men are supposed to be. The rapist is, then, power-motivated and must rape in order to confirm his own self-image. This view has even been endorsed and verified by some rapists. One convicted rapist volunteered that 'You don't want to rape someone just for the orgasm. You want to hurt a woman.'

There seems little reason to regard behaviour which is so motivated as normal. But what the data from the present study illustrate is that while some rapists clearly are motivated almost purely by the desire to exhibit total domination, not all are. In those cases discussed which seem to exhibit more violence and threat than is necessary to accomplish the intercourse, it is almost impossible to say whether it is sexual intercourse accomplished by means of the threat of violence or more simply sexual intercourse, which is the objective of his behaviour. In still other cases, it seems much clearer that the offender really just wants sexual intercourse and that he keeps both the use and the threat of force to a minimum as he really does not want to believe that this is basically how he is managing to secure what he wants. These are the cases which seem to involve the clearest fantasizing in order to obscure to himself what he is in fact doing to accomplish his ends, and would seem to indicate that the desire to see power as necessary for the accomplishment of his objectives is not only not necessary but indeed is something which the offender absolutely does *not* want to see as causally related to the satisfaction of his desires.

This seems to suggest that it is as misleading to see every labelled rapist as a 'super-power-tripper' as it is to see him as 'normal.' All men are conditioned by a society in which coercive sexuality is the norm rather than the exception, but not all men respond to it in the same way or to the same degree. Thus rapists are 'normal' in so far as many of them exhibit no more sexual aggression than most, or many, other men in society who do not get labelled rapists, and some rapists who exhibit more need to be sexually coercive and dominating than seems characteristic of most men in society are no more coercive and dominating that some other men in society who are not labelled rapists. Rapists exhibit the same *range* of identification with sexual aggression and domination as is exhibited by men in general. Some of them are super-power-trippers as are some men who are never, and would never be, labelled rapists; some are just men with the same need for sexual gratification, and the same desire for it to be with a more rather than a less willing participant, than are other men who are not, and would never be, labelled rapists. There is no one set of characteristics which differentiates the rapist from other men because although all men are shaped by the same conditioning, there are individual variations in the extent to which, and the precise ways in which, they are affected by it.

Mainly because of differences in cultural and socioeconomic backgrounds, some men will identify more strongly with the need for aggression and domination than others. Also, some will have legally and socially acceptable ways of expressing that aggression and dominance. Men who have other means whereby they can accomplish their objectives, who have strategies available to effect sexual coercion without having to report to the use of threat of violence, will not be labelled rapists despite the fact that their motivation is no different from those who are so labelled. Some rapists are as 'normal' as most other men in society, and some rapists are no more 'abnormal' than many other men in society who are not labelled rapists. 'Normal' and 'abnormal' are defined within a framework of pervasive sexual coercion and within an economic system that provides many men with the means to purchase the sexual commodities they want without having to commit or threaten violence.

Within our society, the only sexually coercive males labelled rapists are those who have nothing to offer but physical force. They are, by and large, men who have gained no status in the social structure, and who are powerless to effect their ends other than by physically coercive means. The greater the extent to which the particular defendant can be seen as a 'born loser,' the more likely he is to be convicted and labelled as a rapist. The labelled rapist is simply the man who cannot make it any other way, often for reasons over which he has very little control. Those who seem to present the appearance of confidence, competence, and sophistication are not likely to be perceived as men who are likely to have fallen below the minimum standard of acceptable behaviour. While the phenomenon of rape is a direct function of the fact that we live in a sexually coercive society, just who is labelled a rapist is a direct function of the economic structure. The findings emerging from the present study indicate clearly that those men who become labelled as rapists are physically unattractive and of low socio-economic status.

As we were particularly anxious to see to what extent the stereotyped picture of the 'real rapist' was borne out by the facts, we attempted to amass as much information as possible pertaining to a physical description of the suspect. This was, however, difficult. The most reliable information was that obtainable from Record of Arrest forms, as these have the virtue of being objective. However, not all rapists are arrested, and, even where they are, the descriptive data supplied are very scanty, giving only the offender's age, racial origin, occupation, and place of birth. However, we used the data supplied by victims in an attempt to build up something like a physical profile of the rapist, though these data must be understood as reflecting the victim's beliefs about her assailant and cannot be taken as absolutely definitive. Clearly, these data are more unreliable with regard to such things as precise height and weight than with regard to such things as colour of eyes, hair, and general descriptive characteristics. For these reasons, we felt justified in tabulating this information, and what emerges is a rather interesting picture.

Of the 104 'founded' or 'unfounded/possibly founded' cases which formed the data base of the study, some information as to a description of the offender was available in 38 (48%) of the cases, for a total of 50 offenders (38.7%). In 19 cases information was missing, or specified only very generally, with respect to height. Of the remaining 31 cases, 6.4 per cent were estimated to be 5'5" or less; 19 per cent 5'5"-5'7"; 40.6 per cent 5'8"-5'9"; 19.0 per cent 5'10"-5'11"; and 15 per cent, 6'0" or over. Thus, the vast majority (66%) were estimated to be not more than 5'9". This is particularly significant as one would expect the subjective bias of the victim to run in the direction of seeing her attacker as taller rather than shorter than his actual height. Thus, the average rapist appears to be on the short side. Of course, 5'8"-5'9" may well be the average height of men in Canadian society, but certainly, so far as the stereotyped images of men are concerned, these men clearly come out 'short to medium' at best, and 'short' at worst.

Nor are they particularly well built. Precise data on weight were missing in 27 cases, though of these, 85 per cent had general descriptions ranging from 'slim' or 'slight' to 'medium' build; 2 per cent were described as 'well-built,' and 3 per cent were described as 'fat.' No data were available on the remaining 10 per cent. Of the 24 cases where more specific information was offered, 12.5 per cent were estimated to weigh 130-139 pounds; 20.8 per cent 140-149; 12.5 per cent 150-159; 20.8 per cent 160-169; 12.5 per cent 170-179; 16.6 per cent 180-189; and in only one case (4.3%) was the offender estimated to be over 200 pounds and he was described as 'fat.' Thus, in one-third of the cases (33.3%) the offender was estimated to be not more than 149 pounds, or definitely on the small side; in almost half the cases (45.8%) he was estimated to be not more than 159 pounds, still not a large male; and in fully two-thirds (66.6%) to be not more than 169 pounds. Again, while the average weight based on these figures may well be the average weight of the Canadian male, it does not conform to the image of a muscled, well-built he-man, like the men in the television advertisements. And once more, this is somewhat surprising in that one would expect the subjective bias of the victim to see her attacker as somewhat bigger than he is in reality.

So far as other general descriptive characteristics are concerned, data on hair length were available in 25 cases, and of these 16 (64%) had short hair, 24 per cent medium-length, and 12 per cent long hair. Some were dressed in suits and ties (20%); others (30%) in casual clothing such as sports jackets and tailored trousers, occasionally running to see-through shirts and vinyl raincoats. About another 20 per cent presented an appearance consistent with what can best be described as that of a 'greaser' - lots of tattoos, unkempt dirty hair, body odour, and so on. The remainder are mixed, with little data available, but on the whole appeared 'clean,' 'neat,' and beardless. Thus, they seem to be males who conform, on the whole, with the basically middle-class, 'straight' image of the Canadian male.

But judging from other specific comments made in 24 per cent of the cases, they are not an especially handsome lot. Indeed, most of those about whom such comments were made would definitely not be considered attractive: 'definitely large bulging blue eyes'; 'square face, small nose, tobacco-stained teeth, front teeth crooked, running at an angle, slightly overlapping one another'; 'thin face and lips'; 'thin'; 'very fat lips'; 'balding, bags under eyes, very pale, looked sick'; 'small-appearing eyes, possibly from the use of alcohol'; 'prominent nose'; 'freckles'; 'high forehead, very pointed and large nose.' However, we could not of course conclude that all rapists conform to this rather unattractive picture. Doubtless comments of this kind were made precisely where the unattractiveness was obvious. On the other hand, it is significant that these characteristics were as common as they were, and significant, too, that in no case was there any comment giving what could be described as a positive account of the suspect's physical appearance.

Among the most interesting data, however, are those having to do with the occupation of the offender. Without exception, all offenders came from lower socio-economic groups, with almost one-quarter (24.1%) classified as 'idle' or 'unemployed.' Of the remainder, 24.1 per cent were truck-drivers, 13.8 per cent labourers, 6.9 per cent clerks; 20.7 per cent were 'semi-skilled' (e.g., service-station attendant, baker's helper, metal cutter); 6.9 per cent were 'skilled' labour (e.g., optical grinder, barber, welder); and 3.4 per cent were 'self-employed' (e.g., landlord, small shop operator). Among those classified as 'idle,' only one was a student. These findings compare favourably with Mohr's, in which 75 per cent of offenders were of low socio-economic status, 9.4 per cent semi-skilled, and 12.5 per cent skilled (3.1% students). McCaldron does not give a precise breakdown of the employment background of the offenders in his study, but classifies them only as to 'socio-economic status – upper, middle, lower.' Within these classifications, 0 per cent are 'upper,' 59 per cent 'middle,' and 41 per cent 'lower.' Thus, his study would appear to show more rapists within the middle-class range than does ours, though the general trend to middle-to-lower class status is clear, and, as he himself comments, these figures appear to represent a certain bias in classification.

The results of our study demonstrate clearly that of those who become labelled as 'rapists' the vast majority are from the lower economic strata, and these data are confirmed virtually universally. This finding reflects, we believe, not the fact that male persons from this strata are more likely to commit rape, but merely that those who are tried for rape are more likely to be convicted if they come from this strata. They are more likely to be perceived as the sort of men who likely would have exceeded the bounds of legally acceptable sexually coercive behaviour. They demonstrably do not have many prospects and consequently are not perceived as having much to offer in return for the sexual favours they solicit. It is, of course, true as well that men from such backgrounds are more likely to rely on the threat or use of physical violence as a strategy for settling disputes. It is a bare sociological fact that middle-class men do not resort to violence in any sort of conflict situation as readily as do males from less enriched environments. The legal definition of 'rape' itself reflects a bias against the strategies of sexually coercive behaviour more typical of lower-income groups. Or, put from the point of view of the middle-class perspective, the methods of sexual coercion typical of middle- and upper-income groups are not believed to be unacceptable (and certainly not seen as legally unacceptable), and so they are not included within the ambit of a definition of 'rape' which articulates the basic standards of unacceptable sexually coercive conduct.

Thus, it is entirely possible that such men are being punished for modes of behaviour quite acceptable within their own subcultural socio-economic level but not judged acceptable by those outside that level. It is also true that their physically abusive behaviour may not be acceptable to the women who share their subcultural milieu, and in suggesting that there is a middle-class bias at work in punishing them for behaviour that their peers regard as acceptable, I am not suggesting that they should be judged only by the standards of their own male peers. What I am pointing to is that the perspective of the woman who is the victim of such behaviour is not the standard used to convict the offender. What she thinks is simply not relevant to the judgment. These men are being judged by other men who are not their peers, and who are applying standards which are acceptable to them. It is not even the case that those doing the judging are somehow operating *in loco parentis* on behalf of the female victim. The man is convicted because the other men who are judging him do not like him and his kind of behaviour.

Thus what distinguishes those we label rapists from those we do not are characteristics which simply show him to be socially and economically marginal. They are men who have no real status in society, and no assets which give them access to desirable commodities within society, including that of female sexual property. The labelled rapist is socially inadequate, and displays a range of attitudes which vary in accordance with beliefs about the need to demonstrate power over women as a characteristic of masculinity. The majority of such offenders do not appear to be motivated by the desire for sexual intercourse with violence as a single clear objective, but seem instead, to desire a sexual relationship which they can believe to be 'normal,' that is, as not necessitating or displaying unacceptable levels of sexual coercion. In order to make such beliefs credible to themselves, they will often go to (from our perspective) quite incredible lengths to see what they do as 'normal' and to minimize recognition of the real nature of their actions.

Our study provides yet one more piece of evidence to substantiate this picture. Once a picture of the labelled rapist as a social inadequate and a loser, began to emerge, we started to wonder to what extent his sexual competence was affected by his other psychosocial features. No previous studies of rape have considered the question as to whether or not the offender encountered any difficulty in achieving an erection or in achieving orgasm, although MacDonald mentions in passing that erection is sometimes a problem and he links it with the offender's demands for co-operation or affection, stating that 'demands for affection take the form of requests for a loving response.' This finding would seem to substantiate the hypothesis that the offender is attempting to normalize the situation and that at least some offenders encounter difficulty in achieving erection unless they can believe that what they are engaged in is, from their perspective, a seduction rather than a rape. McCaldron attempted to assess what he calls 'heterosexual adequacy' and judged that it was 'good' in 56 per cent of the cases in his study, 'fair' in 33 per cent, and 'poor' in 11 per cent. His own comments about this assessment must, however, be kept in mind in attempting to evaluate his findings. He says that 'This amounted to a rough guess in each case as to how well he managed in an adult heterosexual relationship. Comments about wives or girlfriends were most revealing and relied upon. This rating probably represents, not a high proportion of perfect adequacy amongst the rapists, but rather their reluctance to admit to sexual inadequacies, plus the apparent aggressive normality of their usual sexual behaviour.'

Thus, MacDonald's findings seem consistent with our hypothesis, namely, that for many rapists their sexual behaviour, even with those with whom they have some continuing sexual relationship, is not markedly different from what it is in the rape situation. If they characteristically believe that a high degree of power through threat or use of force is necessary to demonstrate masculinity, then this element will be present in all their relationships and accounts for their beliefs about the lack of moral wrongdoing in what is in fact a rape situation. It goes without saying that such men will not be likely to admit to any sort of sexual inadequacy. It is doubtful that they even assess adequacy in terms of their ability to satisfy their sexual partners, and to the extent that they assess it at all, it is likely that they do so only in terms of their own ability to achieve erection and orgasm.

In the present study, it was difficult to extract this information from the reports, and indeed in only the 'founded' cases was there sufficient information to indicate some trends. In many cases, there was simply no information one way or the other. In the 42 cases held to be 'founded,' there was no reference to orgasm in 26 (61.9%). Of the remainder, there was an unqualified 'yes' as to orgasm in only 7 per cent of the cases. Orgasm was *not* achieved in 20.9 per cent of the cases, and only with difficulty in a further 10.2 per cent. Thus, in fully a third of the cases in which it is mentioned, the offender encountered some difficulty achieving orgasm. On going over the reports in the light of these statistical findings, a fairly clear picture emerges. In a significant number of cases, 50 per cent, where difficulty with orgasm occurred, the offender's problem began with an inability to achieve a satisfactory erection. In the remainder of the cases, the problem seemed to lie in achieving orgasm. While there is some evidence to suggest that it is sometimes the offender's conscious or unconscious awareness of the real nature of this situation which is the cause of his problem, this does not seem to be the usual pattern. Thus, a significant proportion of those labelled 'rapists' turn out to be incapable of achieving satisfactory orgasm or orgasm within the normal limits of sexual activity. There is, obviously, a certain amount of irony in this.

Unfortunately, however, it is frequently a very bitter irony for the victim, because it is in precisely these situations that the victim is frequently forced to undergo further sexual acts and in which the period of her forcible confinement is extended. It is most often in cases of this kind that the offender resorts to fellatio, and/or cunnilingus, masturbation, both by himself and by the victim, more fondling of the victim, artificial lubricants, anal intercourse, and other rather more bizzarre acts, such as, in one case, the insertion of a wooden bed leg into the vagina of the victim, and the use of Reddi-Whip sprayed over the genitals of both victim and offender, in an attempt to achieve a satisfactory erection or to reach orgasm when vaginal intercourse fails to achieve it. In some cases, this results in far more serious physical harm to the victim than would otherwise be the case, and certainly leads to far more psychological shock and mental anguish.

The ironies inherent in this grotesque situation do more than anything else possibly could to convince one that there can be no solution to the problem of rape until we cease to live in a social, political, and legal system which consistently treats the female as inferior, and forces the male to achieve superman heights in order to be considered, and to be able to function, as an 'adequate' male, whether that be in the area of employment or of sexual relationships. Because coercion is so characteristic of our 'normal' sexual relationships, rape is an unavoidable phenomenon of our lives, and until women cease to be regarded as the property of individual men and of having nothing other than a sexual/reproductive role and value, there can, and will be, no solution to the problem. As the data from the present study make clear, men are also victims of the concepts and attitudes which shape our culture. The picture of the labelled rapist which emerges from the study clearly indicates that those men who are losers in every other respect are also losers in terms of their ability to achieve satisfactory sexual identities that do not depend either on the use or threat of violence to create the conditions in which they can be sexually adequate, or on the illustory justification of fantasy to create an atmosphere of 'love.'

Within the present framework, we certainly do nothing for such men in convicting them. But we certainly do nothing for women unless we convict them. Clearly new approaches to treatment must be found in order to afford women better protection than is at present offered by having nothing better to rely on than automatic remission with the mellowing of time. But before that is even possible, we must acknowledge the framework within which rape is an offence, and which explains why and how it comes about. Definitions of 'normality' with respect to the adult male must be developed apart from the framework of coercive sexuality in which they are currently embedded. It has first to be accepted that misogyny *is* a mental disorder and that those suffering from it, and who commit assaultive acts against women as a result of it, must be regarded as suffering from a treatable mental illness and as creating a potential risk to the well-being and life of others in society. Their punishment is justified because their actions always and necessarily create such a risk; but their treatment must be directed toward removing the causes of their behaviour rather than at simply penalizing them for damage they have already caused.

Rapists, whether detained or diverted, must be given psychiatric treatment based on the theoretical assumption that men can learn to see themselves as 'adequate' males without having to exercise aggression and domination over women. And societal definitions of 'masculinity' must be made dependent on this concept of 'adequate male.' Men must learn to accept women as their equal partners in society, and as entitled to all the rights and freedom of other persons under the law. This necessarily includes the presumption that women are, and ought to be, as sexually self-determining as males, and that unprovoked attacks on their sexual organs are no more to be tolerated than attacks against any other of their bodily parts. Men must learn to accept themselves as the equals, and as no more than the equals, of women and unless we start from that assumption we cannot hope to get anywhere in solving the problem.

The old concepts of 'real rape,' and the concepts and attitudes which underlie it, lead to the belief that rape is an inevitable reality of human life, a natural liability given the aggressivity, dominance, and uncontrollable or insatiable sexuality of the male. But rape is not a 'natural' fact: it is a *social* fact, a product of a particular kind of social relations, based on concepts of sexual inequality and the legitimacy of sexual coercion. As such, it can cease to be a fact if the conditions which create those particular social relations are altered. The fundamental principle that has to be accepted is that the sexes are equal and that concepts of 'normal male and female' sexuality should reflect that equality and the equal right of members of both sexes to be sexually self-determining. Once all men learn to perceive women as people, as persons who are more similar than dissimilar to themselves, we shall be well on the way to eliminating, rather than merely ameliorating, the problem as we know it. But new psychiatric concepts must be developed within this framework in order to provide new therapeutic approaches to the convicted rape offender. Since it is the offender who is both the source and the symptom of the problem, this is clearly the place at which we ought to begin.

REFERENCES

Amir, Menachem, *Patterns in Forcible Rape*, Chicago: University of Chicago, 1971.
– 'Victim Precipitated Forcible Rape,' *Journal of Criminal Law, Criminology and Police Science*, LVIII (1967), 493-502.
Chappell, Duncan, Gilbert Geis, Stephen Schafer, and Larry Siegel, 'Forcible Rape: A Comparative Study of Offenses Known to the Police in Boston and Los Angeles,' *in* James M. Henslin, ed., *Studies in the Sociology of Sex.* New York: Appleton-Century-Crofts, 1971, pp. 169-90.
Clark, Lorenne M.G., 'Politics and Law: The Theory and Practice of the Ideology of Male Supremacy: Or, It Wasn't God Who Made Honky Tonk Angels.' A paper delivered at the Annual Spring Lectures, Osgoode Hall Law School, York University, Toronto, February 1975, to be published in the Proceedings of the Series.
Cleaver, Eldridge, *Soul on Ice*, New York: Dell Publishing Co., 1968.
Dixon, G., 'Corroboration of the Complainant's Testimony in a Sexual Offense,' *Alberta Law Review* (1969), 156-60.
Drapkin, Israel, and Emilio Viano, eds., *Victimology*, Lexington, Mass.: D.C. Heath and Co., 1974.
Gebhard, P., J. Gagnon, W. Pomeroy, and C. Christenson, *Sex Offenders: An Analysis of Types*, New York: Bantam Books, 1967.
Giffin, P.J., 'Rates of Crime and Delinquency,' *in* W.T. McGrath, ed., *Crime and its Treatment in Canada*, Toronto: Macmillan of Canada, 1965, pp. 59-90.
Gigeroff, A., and J.W. Mohr, 'A Study of Male Sexual Offenders,' *Canada's Mental Health*, XVI, No. 3 (1965).
Griffin, Susan, 'Rape: The All-American Crime,' *Ramparts Magazine* (December 1970).
Hibey, R.A., 'The Trial of a Rape Case: An Advocate's Analysis of Corroboration, Consent and Character,' *American Criminal Law Review*, XI, No. 2 (1973), 309-34.

Karpman, B., *The Sexual Offender and his Offenses: Etiology, Pathology, Psychodynamics and Treatment*, New York: 1954.

McCaldron, R.J., 'Rape,' *Canadian Journal of Corrections*, IX (1967), 37.

MacDonald, John M., *Rape Offenders and their Victims*, Springfield: Charles C. Thomas, 1971.

Margolin, D., 'Rape: The Facts,' *Women: A Journal of Liberation*, III, No. 1 (1973), 19-22.

Medea, Andra, and Kathleen Thompson, *Against Rape*, New York: Farrar, Straus and Giroux, 1972.

Mohr, J.R., 'Sexual Behaviour and the Criminal Law,' *Rape and Attempted Rape: Preliminary Report*, Forensic Clinic, Toronto, October 1965.

New York Radical Feminists, *Rape: The First Source Book for Women*, edited by Noreen Connell and Cassandra Wilson, New York: New American Library, 1974.

Pascal, G.R., and F.I. Herzberg, 'The Detection of Deviant Sexual Practice from Performance on the Rorschach Test,' *Journal of Projective Techniques*, XVI (1952).

Perdue, William C., and David Lester, 'Personality Characteristics of Rapists,' *Perceptual and Motor Skills*, XXXV (1972).

Radzinowicz, L., and the Cambridge Department of Criminal Sciences, *Sexual Offences*, London: Macmillan and Co., 1957.

Ringrose, C.A. Douglas, 'Sociological, Medical, and Legal Aspects of Rape,' to be published, *Trial Lawyers Journal for Canada* (Fall 1975).

Schafer, Stephen, *The Victim and his Criminal*, New York: Random House, 1968.

Schultz, G.D., *How Many More Victims?* Philadelphia: J.B. Lippincott, 1965.

Statistics Canada, *Crime Statistics*, Ottawa, 1971.

Svalastoga, 'Rape and Social Structure,' *Pacific Sociological Review*, XLVIII (1965).

Von Hentig, Hans, *The Criminal and his Victim*, New Haven, Conn.: Yale University Press, 1948.

Wolfgang, M.E., *Patterns in Criminal Homicide*, Philadelphia: University of Pennsylvania Press, 1958.

Wolfgang, M.E., L. Savitz, and N. Johnston, eds., *The Sociology of Crime and Delinquency*, second edition, New York: John Wiley, 1970.

Wood, Pamela Lakes, 'The Victim in a Forcible Rape Case: A Feminist View,' *American Criminal Law Review*, XI, No. 2 (1973), 335-54.

G. ERLICK ROBINSON, JAMES OLDHAM
AND MARLAINA SNIDERMAN

The establishment of a rape crisis centre*

From 1967 to 1973 there was a 76 per cent increase in the number of reported rapes occurring in Metro Toronto. Some authorities estimate that ten times as many are not reported to the police. The woman who complains of rape must then undergo examinations, interrogations and finally a court process which may prolong the original trauma. The other woman who does not complain may have to resolve her feelings about this incident alone and forgo even medical attention. Feeling the need in this community to provide a service to aid these assaulted women, the Community Psychiatry Team of the Toronto General Hospital decided to organize a Rape Crisis Centre.

The basic component of this centre consists of a group of volunteers operating a 24-hour telephone answering service. Volunteers are sent out to pick up any victim of an attack and take her to the Toronto General Hospital. The hospital provides a smoothly running program whereby the woman can be checked by family practice physicians and give specimens, be seen by the psychiatry resident to assess mental status and questioned by the police in a setting a little less intimidating than a police station. The volunteers remain in touch with the woman, with consultations with the Community Psychiatry Team, for as long as needed; they accompany her to court. The other aims of the Centre include extensive research of the rape victim, the rapist and the crime itself, together with education of the public regarding understanding and decreasing the incidence of this crime.

A group of about 40 women volunteers were assembled. Educational sessions with the police, lawyers, gynecologists and the Community Psychiatry Team

*Reprinted from *Canada's Mental Health* Vol. 23, No. 5 (September 1975), 10-12.

were organized. Importance was placed on bringing to light any fears, biases or fantasies of the volunteers. Contacts were made with the hospital administration, gynecology department, police, crown attorney's office, emergency department and nursing staff. A mixture of encouragement, support and strong opposition was encountered.

The Community Psychiatry Team responded to a perceived community need for such a service. It acted to initiate this program, assembling workers, enlisting cooperation between various departments and providing educational sessions. As the volunteers became organized it withdrew more into a consulting capacity with responsibility for any problems occurring in the hospital's part of the service. In this way they followed the precepts of sound community psychiatry intervention.

THE VOLUNTEERS

In order to find active, interested women who would be prepared to act in the capacity of lay volunteers, we initially approached a centre for women's rights: 'Women's Place.' We had an initial enthusiastic response from some of the leaders there concerning the philosophy of such a centre, but they were not ready to take action at that time. Some of these women did end up, however, in the final volunteer group. The other women were recruited largely from the student and professional staff of the University of Toronto under the supervision of Professor Lorenne Clarke of the Centre of Criminology. We felt as a Community Psychiatry Team that our role should not extend to direct supervision of the volunteers' organization. We did feel, however, that we were responsible for setting up educational sessions for these volunteers. Sessions were organized with the police, lawyers, gynecologists and the Community Psychiatry Team.

While the basic goals of these sessions were to cover the psychological (9,12, 15,17,19), medical and legal aspects of rape, a number of facts became apparent during these meetings with the volunteers. Although this is a service for women, we did not want it to be characterized by an anti-male feeling as we felt that the dealings with the assaulted women would be highly biased and it would be more difficult for the staff to get cooperation with the doctors and the police. For example, a great many women turned out for the session with the gynecologist; some of them were not very interested in what the gynecologist had to say about his part in the collection of evidence for a rape victim, but instead, were anxious to re-educate him in his attitude towards women. Some of the more radical members of this group assumed that as soon as any male had anything at all to do with the Rape Crisis Centre, it was doomed. The one man on the Community Psychiatry Team had a great deal of work to do to break down this kind of resistance. He continued to be present at all educational meetings, and not bow to covert pressure to have him removed. When specific attacks were made on men, either as doctors or generally, an attempt was made to show this person's real point of view rather than allowing the woman to retain stereotype images.

Another problem concerned the conceptions often present concerning the role of psychiatrists. We emphasized that we saw our contact with the patient as being of a preventative nature. We wished to assess her mental status to see if she needed any immediate help and provide a contact should the woman later get into difficulties. Many of the women seemed to fear we would immediately try to psychoanalyze each rape victim or that we might twist the facts to make the woman appear responsible for the whole event.

The topic of rape was discussed at great length (1,2,3,5,7,8,10,11,20,21). Many fantasies associated with this were made explicit, and women's reactions to these fantasies examined. Some talk was started about the problem of over-identifying with the victim. We also tried to be very clear about the possibility of the victim being seriously wounded. We hoped to scare away at the beginning volunteers who we thought would be unable to cope with the rape victim's stress without falling to pieces themselves. It was emphasized that ongoing groups would be available for volunteers to discuss their reactions to cases as they occurred.

LIAISON WITH THE POLICE

At an early stage in the establishment of the centre, we contacted the police to work out the most effective way of helping the rape victim without impeding the work of the police. The senior police staff we contacted were most helpful and seemed to wish to facilitate our efforts. They were particularly concerned that the apprehension of rapists was not as high as they wished, considering the violence of the crime, and furnished us with statistics (16) and details of the requirements of a court of law to prove the crime of rape (4,6,11,18). They were also able to furnish us with a detailed list of the type of medical specimens required to corroborate the fact that the rape had occurred.

We also made contact with the director of Crown Attorneys of the Province of Ontario who was very eager to assist us in any way possible.

LIAISON WITH THE HOSPITAL

Having given the volunteers instruction in the kinds of things that would be expected of them, we then felt our only problem would be to work with the hospital staff so that they would understand the volunteer and would not be hostile to the presence of a lay person in the middle of a busy Emergency Department. Because the core of the system involves a volunteer being present with the rape victim from the time she is initially called in to the time she appears in court, it was also hoped to have this volunteer present during the medical examination. It was felt that some doctors might be uncomfortable with this idea and so we organized sessions for them. In fact, the opposition encountered proved to be more than we expected.

There is a great deal of resistance to doing an examination of the victim of a rape. There seems to be several reasons for this. There was a fear that our program would lead to the Emergency Department being swamped with rape victims thus keeping the gynecology residents extremely busy. (In fact, by involving the Department of Psychiatry, we hoped to relieve much of the work of the Department of Gynecology and minimize their involvement with a rape victim to merely having to do the clinical examination.) There was concern about the amount of time that might have to be spent testifying in court. Some of the resistance, however, seemed to be due to a rather surprising attitude on the part of some of the gynecologists. This generally tended to be that very few rapes were legitimate, many women were faking or lying and merely causing extra work for the Emergency Department for no good reason. Over a period of several months, we had many sessions with gynecologists at various levels in the Department. Several times we thought the problem was solved but it would always crop up again when the next patient was seen in Emergency. This resistance on the part of the gynecologists was obviously interfering with the smooth reception that we hoped the victim would get in the Emergency Department of the hospital. Finally, we were able to make arrangements with the Department of Family and Community Medicine to take over the work of examining these women. They participated with a spirit of enthusiasm and a feeling that this was a necessary and a worthwhile task. Things have gone much more smoothly since then.

It should also be mentioned that there was some initial reluctance on the part of the psychiatry residents to become involved with this. Again, there was also the feeling that they would be over-burdened. Some of the same negative attitudes towards the victims of rape seemed to come from some of these residents. They, as well as the gynecology residents, did not feel this fell into their sphere of responsibility. Emphasis on the preventative nature of the work we were asking them to do resulted in a change in their attitude such that they agreed to assist in the program.

PUBLICIZING THE RAPE CRISIS CENTRE

There was very little difficulty getting publicity for the Rape Crisis Centre. In fact, we had to fend off the media until we were ready to make some public statements. Rape is a sensational subject and we were determined to avoid stressing the sensational aspects of this, such as allowing the rape victims to appear on radio or television. We did have some difficulties with the hospital administration who wanted to keep a low profile on such a controversial issue. They were afraid we would be overwhelmed by the number of victims who would suddenly present themselves to the Emergency Department.

THE ROLE OF THE COMMUNITY PSYCHIATRY TEAM
IN SETTING UP A RAPE CRISIS CENTRE

Conventionally, a Community Psychiatry Team does not initiate the establishment of a community agency, but waits for the community to approach them for help. Because we felt there was an urgent need, we did take an active role in initiating this project. As soon as we catalyzed the initial reaction of introducing the volunteers to one another and to the services of the hospital, we attempted to extricate ourselves from the day-to-day organization of the volunteers and concentrate on the smooth functioning from the hospital side of things. The Community Psychiatry Team does not take direct responsibility for the patients going through the Rape Crisis Centre. We remain in a consultative role to the workers of the agency, discussing problems with cases as they arise. From time to time, should a patient seem to require therapy, appointments are made for them in the Psychiatric Out-Patient Department.

CONCLUSION

It took nine months of continuous effort to establish a smoothly functioning Rape Crisis Centre. We had to deal with organizational and administrative problems, as well as biases of the lay worker towards the professional worker and vice versa and many fantasies and negative feelings towards the victim of a crime such as rape. At present, the centre seems to be functioning smoothly and the hospital involvement is being efficiently handled. The Community Psychiatry Team now acts in only a consultative capacity. We feel fairly confident that this organization is an effective one and can be used as a model for other hospitals concerned with the care and treatment of the rape victim.

NOTES

1 Amir, M., 'Victim precipitated forcible rape' *Jrl. of Criminal Law, Criminology and Police Science* 58: 493-502, December 1967.
2 Amir, M., 'Forcible rape' *Federal Probation* 31: 51-57, March 1967.
3 Anon, 'Sexual assaults on children' *Brit. Med. J.* 2: 1146-1147, 1963.

4 Anon, 'Medical testimony in a criminal rape case showing the direct and cross-examination of the bacteriologist and psychiatrists and including the court's instructions to the jury' *Med. Trial Technique* Quar. Annual (1963), pp. 287-355.

5 Barnes, J., 'Rape and other sexual offenses' *Brit. Med. J.* 2: 293-295, April 29, 1967.

6 Bornstein, F., 'Investigation of rape: medico-legal problems' *Med. Trial Technique* Quar. Annual (1963), pp. 229-234.

7 Burgess, A.W. and Holmstrom, L.L., 'The rape victim in the emergency ward' *Amer. J. Nurs.* 73: 1741-1745, October 1973.

8 Evrard, J.R., 'Rape: The medical, social and legal implications' *Amer. J. Obstet. Gynecol.* Sept. 1971, 15: 197-199.

9 Factor, M., 'A woman's psychological reaction to attempted rape' *Psychoanalytic Quarterly* 23: 243-244 (1954).

10 Foxe, A.N., 'Rape, rats and reflection' *Corrective Psychiatry and J. of Social Therapy* 14: 213-223 (1968).

11 Graves, Jr., L. and Francisco, J., 'A clinical and laboratory evaluation of rape' *J. Tenn. Med. Assn.* 55: 389-394 (1962).

12 Halleck, S., 'The physician's role in management of victims of sex offenders' *JAMA* 180: 273-278 (1962).

13 Hayman, C.R. et al. 'A public health program for sexually assaulted females' *Public Health Rep.* 82: 497-504, 1967.

14 Hayman, C.R. et al. 'Sexual assault on women and girls in the District of Columbia' *Southern Med. J.* 62: 1227-1231, 1969.

15 Lipton, G.L. and Roth, E.I., 'Rape: A complex management problem in the paediatric emergency room' *J. Pediat.* 75: 859-866, 1969.

16 Lynd, Det, P., 'Rape statistics in Ontario' Compiled by Police Personal Communication November 1973.

17 Massey, J.B., 'Management of sexually assaulted females' *Obstet. Gynec.* 38: 29-36, 1971.

18 Sutherland, D., 'Medical evidence of rape' *Can. Med. Assn. J.* 81: 407-408 (1959).

19 Sutherland, S. and Scherl, D.J., 'Patterns of response among victims of rape' *Amer. J. Orthopsychiat.* 40: 503-511, 1970.

20 Tappan, P., 'Some myths about the sex offender' *Federal Probation* 19: 7 (1955).

21 Weiss, E.G. et al. 'The mental health committee: Report of the subcommittee on the problem of rape in the District of Columbia' *Med. Ann. D.C.* 41: 703-704, November 1972.

JOHANN W. MOHR

The pedophilias: their clinical, social and legal implications*

Of all forms of sexual behaviour, sexual acts between adults and children are least acceptable in our society. Such acts arouse strong public concern and account for a major proportion of all sexual offences, especially of those arising out of deviant impulses. Legal prohibition is expressed in several charges under the Criminal Code of Canada as well as the Juvenile Delinquency Act. Since this form of sexual behaviour and the underlying impulses, desires and phantasies are not considered to be 'normal' in adults, they must be considered as pathological and are a subject for the field of psychiatry, which has given this phenomenon the name of pedophilia, literally 'love of children.'

Despite its legal and social significance, pedophilia has received relatively little attention in the psychiatric literature. In the area of sexual deviation as such, with the exception of homosexuality, there is an inverse ratio of the importance of the deviations and the amount of literature available. There are many more contributions on fetishism and transvestism for example than on pedophilia and exhibitionism.

The comparative lack of knowledge is further intensified by insufficient organization and differentiation which leads to apparently contradictory conceptions.

DEFINITIONS

Unfortunately it is not possible to discuss the literature in any detail in this paper (1). However, it may be useful to refer shortly to the standard psychiatric texts.

*Reprinted from *Canadian Psychiatric Association Journal* Vol. 7, No. 5 (October 1962), 255-260.

Mayer-Gross, Roth and Slater (2) and Henderson and Gillespie (3) make no specific reference to pedophilia, although Mayer-Gross et al. note sexual acts with children in old age. Noyes (4) sees pedophilia as a variant of homosexuality, apparently ignoring the heterosexual pedophilias. The American Handbook of Psychiatry (5) devotes half a page to the subject. Friedman's definition there is: 'Pedophilia is the term applied to sexual activity, involving a sexually immature object. A pedophile may be homosexual, heterosexual, or both in his choice of objects, and theoretically, his activity can take almost any of the forms characteristic of heterosexual or homosexual activity with an adult partner.' One may want to extend this definition by the one Cassity gave in 1927 (6): '... pedophilia implies an erotic craving for the child of the same or different sex on the part of an adult, which is distinctly asocial only when it attains overt proportions.'

Within the frame of these broad descriptive definitions, pedophilia can be discussed from many aspects; as a concept of disease, deficiency, mal-formation; as a symptom of intra-psychic dynamics or interpersonal relations; or as an endemic feature of the socio-cultural system. These aspects in turn can be approached in terms of various theoretical structures, as psychoanalytic theory, behaviourism, learning theory and so on.

However, before an attempt of any kind of etiological clarification can be made, it is necessary to examine the phenomenological structure of pedophilia, since it is not reasonable to assume that the fondling of a small child by an impotent old man (7) and the rape of a girl in puberty by a young man (8) are based on the same set of causal factors.

BACKGROUND

The major part of the material for this paper was derived from the following sources: A Follow-up Study of Sexual Offenders Referred to a Forensic Outpatient Clinic (9) which included the analysis of 55 pedophiles; A Short Survey of Sexual Offenders in Kingston Penitentiary (10); A Survey of Sexual Offenders in the Millbrook Reform Institution (11) with a specific reference to pedophilic offenders; and the professional literature on the subject as well as statistical information from the police and various other sources.

Although we have attempted to broaden our experience, it has to be stated, that the main part of our information is derived from patients of an out-patient clinic. Even if great care is taken to adjust one's generalizations from setting-determined samples, our experience with other researches and studies show us that certain biases are difficult to detect and will colour one's generalizations and conclusions.

The study of empirical data suggests the following phenomenological approach:

There are three significant items to be considered: *the agent* (offender), *the act* and *the object* (victim). For the purpose of discussion it is advantageous to reverse the order.

The object

The object in pedophilia is obviously a child. However, social, legal and clinical definitions of a child may vary widely. Since our theme is of a sexual nature, the logical break-off point would be the onset of puberty. This delimitation would exclude most cases of statutory rape or in Canada cases charged with intercourse with a female between 14 and 16 years of age. For this group Bernard Glueck suggested the term hebephilia (12) (literally, love of youth). The object of pedophilia can be a boy or a girl, and accordingly we can speak of homosexual and heterosexual pedophilia.

The act

In regard to the act, two facets have to be distinguished: the act itself and the intentionality of the act. By the latter we mean the position of the act in the urge-gratification dimension. For instance, the act of showing the male genital can have various intentionalities or purposes; it can be the final preferred aim (exhibitionistic), it can be done with the intent to be fondled as the final preferred aim (truly pedophilic) or it can be a foreplay to coital activity.

This example also furnishes us with the three major classes of final preferred aims: (a) *Immature gratification*, which consists predominantly of touching, fondling, looking, showing and at the most in masturbation, activities which are commonly found among children; (b) *Deviant acts* (as final preferred aims) as exhibitionistic, voyeuristic or fetishistic acts and finally (c) *Genital union.*

Genital union is largely excluded by our definition of the object as a pre-pubertal child. The remaining cases, with whom we have little experience, should be excluded from the definition of pedophilia. Not only are the social and legal consequences of child rape different, but we suspect that these cases also constitute a different group clinically.

Deviant aims should be seen in the context of the specific deviation rather than in the context of pedophilia. This is especially important in regard to exhibitionism. The exhibitionist who exposes to a child does so at safe distance without the intentionality of further contact. As a matter of fact, the close contact which is desired by the pedophile would in most cases be frightening to the exhibitionist.

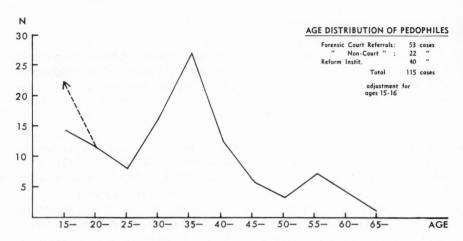

The lack of this one differentiation alone, we find, renders the majority of statistically grouped observations on both deviations useless.

We can so far summarize that we consider pedophilia as an expressed desire for immature sexual acts with an immature object. Depending on the sex of the child, we can distinguish between heterosexual pedophilia or homosexual pedophilia.

The agent

Concerning the agent or offender now, we find that in the great majority of cases the object is fixed, namely either a male or a female child. Only a small group, in our study about 10 per cent, will engage with both sexes. This undifferentiated group, as we call it, is the most regressed and most pathological one of the three, and shows a tendency towards generalized multiple perversion. The two major groups, the heterosexual and the homosexual pedophiles seem to appear in rather equal numbers.

Another classification, namely age of offender, arose out of an unexpected finding in our studies. In plotting the age distribution of the 55 pedophilic follow-up cases, we discovered a distinct trimodal distribution, which was quite unlike that of the other deviations (Homosexuality and Exhibitionism). In order to assure ourselves that we were not dealing with an artefact, we drew another sample of 22 cases which came to us from sources other than the courts, and found the distribution confirmed. A prison sample of a later substudy finally convinced us that we were dealing with three forms of pedophilia, one culminating in adolescence, another one in the mid-to-late thirties and the classical old age one which usually dominates the descriptions of pedophilia, although it appears less frequently than the other two.

HETEROSEXUAL PEDOPHILIA

Heterosexual pedophilia in adolescents indicates a lack of sexual maturation as well as a strong deficiency in differentiated object relations. The average age of victims in our studies is 6 to 7 years. The offenders have no experience with adult sexual relationships, nor does there seem to be a real desire for such. Since adolescent pedophilia tends to disappear towards the early twenties, time can be assumed to be an important factor. Growth in interpersonal relations and greater skills in the general social adaptation should be the major clinical considerations.

The next group, culminating in the middle to late thirties represents regression rather than lack of progression or fixation, which we have noticed in the former group. Most of these people are or have been married, or at least had significant adult sexual experiences. The group is characterized by severe marital and social disorganization, with alcohol playing a major role. Another feature of this group are quasi incestuous strivings. This is the largest of the three groups in the reform institutions, partly because of their age which deprives them of the special considerations afforded to the young and the old, and partly, it seems, because of their generally disorganized situation. Therapeutic intervention should be directed towards restoration and strengthening of ego-functions and their extensions, especially in regard to family relationships.

The old age pedophile has most often been described in the literature. He is characterized by loneliness and isolation, impotence or concern about impotence, and his court appearance after an incidence is in most cases a sufficient shock to prevent further occurrences of acting out.

One should, however, not overlook that there is a small number of chronic cases who remain prone to acting out throughout their lives.

HOMOSEXUAL PEDOPHILIA

It was interesting to find that the age distribution of the homosexual pedophile follows that of the heterosexual pedophile and not that of the homosexuals who choose adult objects. There are a number of other characteristics in which the homosexual pedophile is similar to the heterosexual pedophile and dissimilar to the adult homosexual. Unfortunately there is not enough time to elaborate on these similarities and differences. Suffice it to say that the average homosexual is no more a seducer of children than the average heterosexual man, with one qualification which is linked up with the distribution of the ages of victims, to be mentioned later.

One further difficulty of the homosexual pedophile is his position as a double deviant. His acts are neither accepted by the heterosexual society he lives in nor by the other homosexuals. There is more chronicity in this group than in the heterosexual one and their acts are far less incidental and situational and more phallic and orgastic in nature.

However, similarities in the age groups remain, as adolescent exploration, a pseudo-parental attitude (as compared with the pseudo-incestuous) in the middle age group, and loneliness and isolation in old age.

THE VICTIM

Pedophilia cannot be discussed without taking some cognizance of the situation of the victim. The literature is small but well founded with studies of Rasmussen (13), Bender and Blau (14) and Rogers and Weiss (15). Together with the findings of our own studies we can form the impression that many children are psychologically and socially predisposed to such acts and some are openly seductive. This, of course, does not exonerate the transgressor, because being an adult he has to carry the social and legal responsibility for his acts.

Our data suggest the following main trends: The preferred object of the heterosexual pedophile is between the age of six to eleven, with the peak at eleven and then sharply decreasing (the mean age of victims for the adolescent group of offenders being around 6 years and for the two older groups around 10 years). The victim lives in the closer environment and tends to be acquainted or even related to the patient. The situational character of the act is quite obvious in many instances and important to consider, because the deliberate seeking out of a strange child would point towards chronicity.

The age of objects of homosexual pedophiles unfortunately does not show the same decrease of distribution but increases right up to the legal break-off point of 16. If one assumes a further increase of what would then be adult homosexuality, one would have a gradual transition in this respect, which would only allow an artificial break-off point. The relationship of the offender to the victim tends to be less close than is the case with the heterosexual pedophile, the incidences less situationally determined, and the acts, as we have mentioned, more orgastic in nature.

LEGAL IMPLICATIONS

A pedophile may contravene the law under the following sections of the Criminal Code of Canada and the Juvenile Delinquents Act:
Contributing to Juvenile Delinquency – (JDA s.33)
Indecent Assault – (CCC s.141, s.148)
Indecent Act – (CCC s.158)

Gross Indecency – (CCC s.149)
Sexual Intercourse with a female under 16 (CCC s.138)
Incest – (CCC s.142)
Rape – (CCC s.135, s.137)

The first two charges, namely Contributing to Juvenile Delinquency and Indecent Assault are the most common ones and represent almost all pedophilic patients referred to the Forensic Clinic. They also apply to the majority of pedophilic offenders in the Millbrook Reform Institution. Unfortunately in both charges common statistics cannot be assessed, since they also include other acts; the contributing charge may refer to a number of non-sexual offensive acts, and indecent assault also applies to adults. We have already stated our bias in regard to the acts in which actual intercourse occurs and would like to see this charge together with actual incest and rape treated separately.

From our study of the Millbrook Reform Institution, Court observation and information from probation officers, it appears to us that the young and the old group receive special considerations by the courts. Recidivism in sexual offences is generally low and studies in various countries show a constant rate of 14-16 per cent, excluding studies done on prison groups which have a higher rate of recidivists by the very nature of the sample. Homosexual pedophilia has the highest recidivism rate after exhibitionism (about 20 per cent), whereas heterosexual pedophilia is much lower at around 6 to 10 per cent and virtually absent in the old age first offender group. The chances of repeating a sexual offence for all first offenders who came to the clinic was only 1 in 20 whereas for previous repeaters it was 1 in about 4.

SOCIAL IMPLICATIONS

It is therefore important that the likely repeater is differentiated from the incidental offender to prevent social consequences beyond all proportions. It is understandable that society demands that children be protected from sexual molestations. It is our task to translate this demand into rational procedures to assure the proper combination of maximum protection of society with a minimum of the kind of senseless punitiveness that changes nothing.

CLINICAL IMPLICATIONS

The implications for the field of psychiatry are obvious. They consist in consultation to the community and the courts, in differential diagnosis and in treatment (16,17). This indeed, applies to all psychiatric conditions that have a specific legal and social consequence. The community and the courts are more and more ready to receive clarification and help in these problems, to arrive at more rational and adequate decisions. In regard to diagnosis, the social and legal consequences will be of great importance, in order to determine whether treatment is necessary and can be best carried out in an outpatient clinic, in a hospital or in a correctional institution. Treatment itself will have as an important goal the strengthening of ego controls, since in many cases we cannot hope at the present time to achieve a primary resolution of the deviant impules.

ACKNOWLEDGMENT

The study from which most of the data for this paper were derived, was in part supported by Federal Mental Health Grant 605-5-216: Principal Investigator: R.E. Turner, MD, Research Officers: J.R.B. Ball, MB, M. Jerry, MA; the author is also indebted to Dr. K.G. Gray for his kind encouragements, to Dr. R.E. Stokes for his material on the subject and to Mrs. M. Jerry for editorial assistance.

NOTES

1 For a discussion of the literature see: Stokes, R.E., A review on Pedophilia. Seminar No. 66, Forensic Clinic, Toronto Psychiatric Hospital, October 1961.
2 Mayer-Gross, W., Slater, Eliot, Roth, Martin, *Clinical Psychiatry*, London 1960, p. 539.
3 Henderson, Sir David, Gillespie, R.D., *A Text Book of Psychiatry*, Toronto 1950, p. 225.
4 Noyes, Arthur P., Kolb, Lawrence C., *Modern Clinical Psychiatry*, Philadelphia 1958, p. 559.
5 Friedman, Paul, 'Sexual Deviation,' in *American Handbook of Psychiatry*, Basic Books 1959, p. 596.
6 Cassity, John H., 'Psychological Considerations of Pedophilia,' *Psychoanalytic Review* 1927, *14*, p. 189.
7 Mayer-Gross et al., op. cit.
8 Karpman, B., *The Sexual Offender and His Offences*, N.Y. 1957, p. 345.
9 Mohr, J.W., A Follow-up Study of Sexual Offenders. Forensic Clinic, Toronto Psychiatric Hospital; Part I, Sept. 1960; Part II, First Section, Feb. 1961; Part II, Second Section, Nov. 1961.
10 Mohr, J.W., A Short Survey of Sexual Offenders in Kingston Penitentiary. Forensic Clinic, Toronto Psychiatric Hospital, March 1961.
11 Mohr, J.W., A Short Survey of Sexual Offenders in the Ontario Reform Institution Millbrook. Forensic Clinic, Toronto Psychiatric Hospital, Sept. 1961.

12 Glueck, Bernard C., Final Report. Research Project for the Study and Treatment of Persons Convicted of Crimes Involving Sexual Aberrations. June 1952 to June 1955, p. 13.
13 Rasmussen, A., 'Die Bedeutung Sexueller Attendate auf Kinder unter vierzehn Jahren, fuer die Entwicklung von Geisteskrankheiten und Charakteranomalien, *Acta Psych. et Neurol.*, 1934, p. 351.
14 Bender, L., Blau, A., The Reaction of Children to Sexual Relations with Adults, *Am. J. of Orthops*, vol. 7, 1937, pp. 500-518.
15 Weiss, Joseph, Rogers, Estelle, et al., A Summary of the Study of Child Victims of Adult Sex Offenders, in *California Sex Deviation Research, Final Report*, Department of Mental Hygiene, State of California, March 1954.
16 Gray, K.G., Tuchtie, M.D., Atcheson, J.D., Turner, R.E., A Symposium on the Sex Offender, *Criminal Law Quarterly*, Vol. 3,4, Feb. 1961, pp. 443-472.
17 Hartman, V., Some Observations of Group Psychotherapy with Pedophiles, *The Canadian Journal of Correction*, Vol. 3,4, Oct. 1961, pp. 492-499.

EDITORIAL NOTE

Although this article was originally published in 1962 and followed by extensive further work leading, among others, to the publication of *Pedophilias and Exhibitionism* (with R.E. Turner and M.B. Jerry, University of Toronto Press, 1964) the basic characterization and description in the article was essentially borne out by subsequent studies. Some of the findings such as the tri-modal description of the age of pedophiles were introduced into the literature for the first time in this article and assisted greatly in clarifying clinical observations which tended to be contradictory in the past because they were not related to specific sub groups. The findings also addressed themselves to some persistent myths such as the child molester as a stranger and dangerous person. Although these cases exist they do not represent the majority of pedophiles who tend to be in an ongoing relationship with the child and who are characterized by passivity rather than aggression. The low recidivism rate, especially of heterosexual pedophiles, is well established now and has led to the opening up of non-institutional measures as a penal response. Of the many publications which emanated from the Toronto Psychiatric Hospital and subsequently the Clarke Institute of Psychiatry in this area, the article represents somewhat of a model of the kind of investigation undertaken and the kind of approach used. Selected subsequent publications: J.W. Mohr, R.E. Turner and M.B. Jerry, *Pedophilia and Exhibitionism. A Handbook*, Toronto Univ. of Toronto Press, 1964; J.W. Mohr and K.G. Gray, 'Follow-up of Male Sexual Offenders: Empirical Data and Their Implications,' in *Sexual Behaviour and the Law*, Slovenko, R. (ed.), Springfield, Ill.: Charles C. Thomas,

1964; J.W. Mohr and R.E. Turner, 'Sexual Deviations: Implications for Office Management,' *Applied Therapeutics* Vol. 9, Nos. 1-4 (Jan.–Mar. 1967); J.W. Mohr, 'A Child Has Been Molested,' *Medical Aspects of Human Sexuality*, Vol. 2, No. 11 (November 1968); J.W. Mohr, 'Evaluation of Treatment,' in *Sexual Behaviours: Social, Clinical and Legal Aspects*, Resnik, H.L.P. and Wolfgang, M.E. (eds.), Boston: Little, Brown & Co., 1972.

JOCELYN DINGMAN

Incest: the cover-up crime*

Little Red Riding Hood is a real person, who turns up occasionally in psychiatric practice. When she was little, her mother often sent her on errands to her grandmother's house, and when her grandmother was out she would play games with her grandfather, who liked to feel her under her dress. She never told her mother, because she was afraid her mother would scold her and tell her she was lying.

When she grows up, she spends her life running errands for other people, meeting a lot of dirty old men whom she enjoys frustrating (filling up wolves' bellies with stones, as in the fairy story) but can't seem to get interested in anyone her own age. According to psychiatrist Eric Berne, who described her in What Do You Do After You Say Hello?, she often owns and wears a red coat.

Another woman goes through life saying 'But the emperor has no clothes.' She always knows which people aren't nearly as nice as they pretend to be, but when she points it out to them and their friends and relatives, nobody ever believes her. She causes herself a lot of trouble this way, and gets labeled 'emotionally disturbed.'

Eventually she finds a therapist who can read her riddle, and remembers that the original emperor who had no clothes was none other than her daddy, who attacked her sexually before she could talk well enough to tell her mother what had happened.

In recent years we have been paying more attention to child-battering, the real physical violence against children which takes place in too many homes, but a wall of silence surrounds the subject of the sexual abuse of children. The fact

*Reprinted from *Chatelaine* (August 1974).

that some parents not only have sexual feelings toward their children, but act them out, seems to arouse great repugnance, and articles on child molesters usually slide hastily over the fact that most incidents of sexual interference with children take place in their own homes. Though there are no reliable statistics, the clinical experience of psychiatrists and social workers suggests that parental sexual abuse may well be more common than outright violence. (Barbara Chisholm, project director of the Canadian Council on Children and Youth, said recently that as many as fifty per cent of girls now in training school may have been subjected to initial rape by their own fathers.)

Yet the Toronto chapter of Parents' Anonymous (a self-help group for abusing parents) has never had a parent admit to this problem, though their literature lists two kinds of sexual abuse, active and passive (the parent who looks the other way and condones the act, rather than protect the child, is guilty of passive abuse).

People tend to feel that sexual abuse happens somewhere else – in another neighbourhood, another province, another ethnic group. In fact it cuts across class and economic lines, and happens in the most outwardly conventional, respectable families; though families that are marginal, socially and economically, are more subject to exposure by social workers and the courts, while better-off families can hush things up.

Ever since Freud, middle-class therapists have been aware, from the stories their patients have told them, that a lot of unpleasant sexual things happen to female children in nice families, with their fathers, brothers and uncles. But too many of them, especially male therapists, have backed away from the implications, dismissing real incidents of rape or molesting as exaggerated fantasy, or taking the attitude that 'no great harm has been done anyway.'

Phyllis Chesler, author of *Women and Madness*, is one woman who is made angry by this clinical approach. 'Female children whose fathers rape them are seen as "seductive" – or the mothers are blamed for not preventing the rape-incest, or for secretly "wanting" it,' she says. 'The few cases of maternal seduction and incest reported are all seen as the cause of the male child's ultimate "schizophrenia."'

Doctors working in the burgeoning field of primal therapy, however, take the sexual abuse of children much more seriously. Primal therapy is a method of getting patients to recall, and relive, the painful things in their childhoods that make them emotionally disturbed as adults. One of the leading practitioners in Canada is Dr. Tom Verny of Toronto, who has been specializing in primal therapy for the last few years. Verny says that sexual abuse is a factor in the childhoods of about one in four of his primal patients, though the memory of it has often been completely suppressed before therapy. He adds that when he thinks of what he didn't know about his patients when he was doing conventional psychotherapy, he thinks it is to their credit that any of them got better.

'*Now* I know what the awful secret was,' a woman may say, after recalling her father coming over to her crib and putting his penis in her mouth. Or, '*Now* I know why I want to cut men's penises off and stuff them down their throats.' Or, 'So it wasn't true that my hymen got broken when I fell off the garage roof.'

Just as physical abuse can range from the occasional too-hard slap to outright mayhem, sexual abuse can range from the seductive teasing of small children to outright incest. The amount of damage to the child also varies; rape of a three-year-old may result in psychosis, while milder forms of abuse may lead to a woman who mistrusts men and never really enjoys sex.

Girls are much more likely than boys to be subjected to active sexual abuse, and most of the perpetrators are male. Small boys, too, are sometimes interfered with by adult males; but on the whole boys are likely to be subject to more in-direct abuse – usually overstimulation, as with a mother who allows her eleven-year-old boy to sleep with her.

Abuse can begin in the crib; adults may believe an old wives' tale that you can quiet a boy baby by stroking his penis (actually it doesn't soothe the baby, it makes him angry). Fathers, and sometimes mothers, may amuse themselves by playing with the clitoris of a girl baby. There may be incidents of fellatio (oral sex) or sodomy (anal sex) with very small children. This is sadistic behaviour, and is done by parents who were themselves treated cruelly as children; there is something in such parents that wants the child to feel as bad as they did.

Parental interference of this kind violates deeply rooted cultural taboos, taboos which most clinicians working with sexual problems regard as healthy. Children around the ages of two and three begin to become aware of themselves and their bodies. They experience pleasure in examining and playing with their genitals, and become mildly exhibitionistic; they also become aware of romantic feelings (which are sexual in origin) toward the parent of the opposite sex. In 'normal' families this phase passes smoothly. Parents treat masturbation, exhibi-tionism and curiosity with matter-of-factness. They avoid reactions of puritanical horror, which make the small child unnecessarily ashamed; they resist the temp-tation to enter into his budding sexuality in a prurient way, as by making fun of the small boy's erections, or actively stimulating the girl child's genitals. They treat the child of the opposite sex with warmth, while making it clear that sexual love is reserved for adults, and that Mummy and Daddy are married to each other. If they have fleeting sexual impulses toward the children (not 'normal,' but not so very uncommon either) they repress them.

One commonsense rule for preventing trauma in young children is that the child should not sleep in the same room as the parents beyond a few months of age. (Dr. Spock suggests a screen between the beds if no other room is available.) Seeing parents having sex is frightening to babies and young children.

REASONABLE MODESTY

Nor are clinicians enthusiastic about the kind of modern 'permissive' home in which children are frequently exposed to their parents' nudity; they feel this causes confusion and over-stimulation, though one psychiatrist points out that what is exhibitionism in one family may be matter-of-factness in another – a lot depends on the parents' attitudes. Generally they feel that while there's no need for the parents to express embarrassed horror if a child sees them naked, a reasonable modesty should be the general rule. An adult can answer the small child's questions about adult genitals, but politely discourage exploration of the adult's body.

It is natural for parents to be on physically intimate terms with little children, to be with them in the bathroom, and to take them into the parents' bed. What is not a good idea is to have the child spend the night in bed with the parents or sleep with the parents of either sex – this is different from an early-morning visit, or from letting a small child who has had a nightmare come for comforting.

Most children, by the time they reach school age, begin to express a desire for more privacy. They don't want the parent of the opposite sex in the bathroom with them, and they stop asking to come into bed. This desire should be respected, and not overridden by parents. Most parents automatically put an end to practices that seem unsuitable to the age of the child, but Tom Verny suggests that parents with blind spots have to take their cues from the children.

For many immature adults, unfortunately, the sexiness of young children is an invitation to abuse; it is a peculiarity of all types of abusing adults that they see the child, at least for the moment, not as someone small, helpless, and in need of protection but as an adult, with adult desires. While no sensible male would think that a girl of five or six would really enjoy masturbating him, an abusing father can manage to convince himself that she does.

There are many borderline types of abuse in which the adult pretends to himself that he is a child too, and that adult and child are simply playing childish games. The father may engage the little girl in games in which her head frequently brushes against his genitals, or he may fool around in a playful way with her genitals, perhaps under the pretext of giving her a bath. The parent of the opposite sex may continue to bathe the child, or take him into bed and cuddle him, into adolescence, when the child is beginning to feel adult desires. Overt mother-son incest is rare, but seductive behaviour, as for a mother to be careless about covering herself in front of a boy who is approaching puberty, or to ask him in a flirty way to rub her back or brush her hair, is not uncommon, and causes frustration and anger in the child, who does not know what to do with the feelings aroused. A mother may permit or encourage the touching of her breasts by boys into the age of adolescence.

Young children tend to feel any strong physical excitement sexually; 'playful' tickling or an angry beating can arouse sexual feelings in both adult and child. This is especially true when the atmosphere between parent and child is so sexually charged that the beating almost comes as a relief; the beating of adolescent children is likely to contain strong sexual elements. (There may be a lot of subtle stimulation going on, but it is cut off short of actual physical contact, which arouses frustration in both parties.)

Adolescence is the age at which brother-sister incest is most likely to occur; it can begin with the boy lying beside his sister, pretending that he is 'helping her go to sleep,' and go as far as conscience permits. Some families are surprisingly lax about brother-sister sexual contacts, and seem to look on them as 'natural.' They don't in fact seem as emotionally traumatic as parent-child contacts – the degree of damage depends on how large the age difference between the children is, and how much force and exploitation is involved.

'THE CHILD SEDUCED ME'

'The child seduced me' is a common defense of adults who commit these offenses, and is also a common theme in clinical literature. It is, according to Tom Verny, 'hog-wash.' Children from families where there is a lot of prurient interest in sex may indeed become seductive, but they have been taught to be that way. Some children play the piano to please their parents, some do well in school, and some become seductive, Verny says. The parents send hidden messages about the kind of behaviour that pleases them. Perhaps the little girl learns that hugging her father in a certain way excites him, and she goes on doing it. (Although if you ask one of these fathers *what* the child did to seduce him, he is apt to say something like 'Well, she came into the bathroom while I was shaving.')

If genital sexual play with an adult is a regular occurrence, over a long period of time, the child learns that this is one way to get attention from adults; the child may even 'enjoy' the physical sensations involved, but the feeling of being exploited by the adult is never far away. And sexual overstimulation in childhood affects adult life; it is hard for such a person to believe that adults can love each other sexually in wholesome ways.

More incidents would probably come to light if the children involved did not also receive strong messages about the adult's shame, and take these messages into themselves. The father who molests his child knows he is doing something society disapproves of, and does it furtively and without joy. The child feels his guilt, feels guilty herself and is afraid to tell her mother. Sometimes the fear is justified: 'You're old enough to know better' is a mother's common reaction to an eight-year-old's hesitant story. Or, 'You must have done something' – a reflection of the programming females in our society receive from an early age.

The terrible confusion produced in young children by the sexual advances of adults was described by Sándor Ferenczi, a disciple of Freud. A little girl, say, loves an adult in a tender way, and indulges in the harmless fantasy that she is his mother. The adult allows himself to be carried away by passion; the child, caught off guard, feels not only terror and pain, but also the guilt and shame of the adult. 'When the child recovers from such an attack,' Ferenczi wrote, 'she feels enormously confused, in fact split – innocent and culpable at the same time – and her confidence in the testimony of her own senses is broken. Moreover, the harsh behaviour of the adult partner tormented and made angry by his remorse renders the child still more conscious of her own guilt and still more ashamed. Almost always the perpetrator behaves as though nothing had happened, and consoles himself with the thought: "Oh, it is only a child, she does not know anything, she will forget it all."' In fact, the adult may become self-righteous and moralistic, and try to save the soul of the child by severity. There may be only one such traumatic incident, especially if it occurs when the man has been drinking, but some men, having once broken the taboo, find it easy to repeat the offense.

If the father uses force, the child feels terrified and helpless; the emotional damage to the child is probably greater than if she consents, though it is hard to assess 'force' when the man is saying something like 'All fathers do this to their daughters.' Kinsey, in a study of incest offenders against children under twelve, found that coitus took place in only about ten per cent of cases; most used either genital manipulation or mouth-genital contacts.

In Kinsey's study (which was only of men imprisoned for incest offenses) the most common type of incest offenders against children were rather ineffectual men, emotionally and often financially dependent on their wives, and in the throes of marital discord. Such men tended to drink heavily, work sporadically, and be preoccupied with sex, he found.

One of the most damaging results of sexual abuse may be the little girl's loss of confidence in her mother. A young child of two or three, say, just cannot believe that her mother does not know all about it. She blames her mother for not protecting her. In many cases, it has never entered the mother's head, or she suspects, but looks the other way, out of her own guilt feelings about not being a better wife and mother.

Psychiatrists point out that there is usually a lot of marital discord in such families. The parents are apt to be people who have been deprived of real parental love in childhood, and both want the other partner to be a mother to them. When this hope is disappointed, they become dissatisfied. Probably neither of them is very interested in adult sex - what they really crave is physical closeness and maternal warmth. Sometimes the mother seems to be unconsciously pushing the daughter at the father - 'Aren't they sweet together,' she will say - because she doesn't feel up to being a real wife. The father, for his part, is likely to be the kind of man who becomes frightened and passive with a mature woman; he actually feels more comfortable playing immature sexual games with his child.

A kind of subtle seduction - in which the father and little girl act as if they are married to each other and in collusion against the mother - is not uncommon in families, and puts an unfair emotional burden on the child. But when actual sexual contact is introduced into this fantasy, it adds an unpleasant note of reality which is even more damaging to the child, who still needs and wants her mother's love and protection, and tends to feel betrayed by both parents.

Otto Weininger, psychologist at Browndale, in Toronto, who deals with disturbed children and their families, says that the man who molests his child is himself the product of a very disturbed family. He has probably had an absent father, and a demanding but ineffective mother. He identifies with the girl baby, and acts out his own passive homosexual desires; he is doing to her what he feels he would have liked his father to do to him. He is also, by hurting her, expressing his anger against women.

Weininger says that such a man suspends, for the moment, his normal thought processes, saying to himself things like 'It really doesn't matter.' 'She won't remember.' 'It's my own daughter, anyway,' and 'I won't do it again.' If his child comes into treatment for emotional disturbance, the father does not admit, at the first, second, or third interview that he has ever molested her. However, if someone can win his trust, he may eventually admit it, and he can be helped. Not, says Weininger, by behaviour therapy, which simply treats the behaviour, but by being helped to understand his own psychological makeup, and change his attitudes to his family. The mother needs help, too. This doesn't need to take ten years of psychoanalysis, but it does take a therapist or counsellor who can offer warmth and understanding for the unmet needs which cause the parents to act in ways that damage the children.

Unfortunately, when sexual offenses come to light in a family, an atmosphere of blame and horror is apt to surround the event. The child's reason for not 'telling' may be an instinctive sense that to 'tell' will make the situation worse; if her mother becomes angry with her, or angry with the father, the child's security is even further threatened; as long as she protects him, she has the hope of some affection, however distorted.

This is unfortunate, because if abuse is caught in its early stages, it can often be stopped before so much damage has been done that the family can no longer remain together.

Most of the people involved in sexual encounters with children stop once they have been discovered, according to Dr. Clive Chamberlain, director of the Family Court Service of the Clarke Institute in Toronto. If the abuse was relatively mild, the horror of outsiders can be more traumatizing to the child than the event itself. When psychiatrists say this kind of thing, Dr. Chamberlain adds, they are apt to be accused of being too permissive, of putting up with anything. But you have to try to see things from the child's point of view, not your own, and the child may prefer to forget an unpleasant incident rather than submit to a lot of probing questions that feel like another sexual assault.

When outside agencies enter the picture, bringing with them the force of the law, and the righteous horror of society, the family situation may deteriorate even further. The child may have to tell the story over and over to social workers. It is a characteristic of many incestuous families to have few ties outside the nuclear family, either to other relatives or to people in the community. And in fact, it may simply not occur to the father, when he is dissatisfied with his marriage, to seek either friendship or adult heterosexual contacts outside the family.

HELPLESS MOTHERS

There are many mothers who, having discovered that a husband is abusing one of their children, insist on separation, and no sane therapist would try to deter them, Dr. Chamberlain says. But in other cases the mother feels helpless. She does not want the situation to come to light because she does not know what the family would do without the father's earnings. To the outside observer, the father may seem to be 'sick,' or some kind of monster. His wife and children often describe him as kind, affectionate and hard-working – except when drunk.

It is to help such families rehabilitate themselves – since they are going to remain together anyway – that many observers now believe that the specific crime of incest should be removed from the criminal law. Alex Gigeroff, a Toronto legal scholar who has specialized in the study of sexual offenses, recently coordinated a study group which has recommended to the federal Law Reform Commission that perhaps incest (which in Canadian law means specifically intercourse) should be regarded as a family matter, rather than a crime. (It would still be covered by the laws against assault, and rape of a child.) Gigeroff feels that fear of the law deters many mothers from seeking help before it is too late. He points out that incest has been a crime throughout Canada only since 1890; before that it was regarded as a sin that could be dealt with by the church. If it were no longer a crime, family courts could steer families in the direction of help without the immediate threat of imprisonment for the father.

'Society is locking families into these patterns through fear of social condemnation and the law,' Gigeroff says.

At the present time, whatever direction the outside intervention takes, it tends to focus on the needs of the adult, whether for help or punishment, and to overlook the needs of the child.

The damage to her sense of self-worth is apt to be permanent. She grows up with a fear and distrust of men and she tends, if she isn't put off sex entirely, to seek out men who will mistreat her. If she marries a man who is violent and abusive, like her father, she is unhappy, but the situation seems familiar. If she marries a decent man who has no desire to hurt her, she may find life boring and dull. Social workers point out that while girls who become delinquent or promiscuous frequently report sexual abuse by their families, there is no way to know how many marry happily and become good mothers. No doubt most do marry, and become responsible citizens, but they are apt to carry unhealed wounds which distort their relationships with their husbands and sons, and they pass their old unhappiness on to their children. While some parents abuse their children sexually, as they themselves were abused, others go to the opposite extreme, and are afraid to show normal physical affection toward the child of the opposite sex. Thus are the sins of the fathers visited on the sons, unto the third and fourth generations.

This unhappy pattern does not have to continue into eternity, however, because with outside help and support parents can break the vicious circle of abuse and neglect. Just as child-beaters can stop beating their children, though they are not going to turn overnight into happy, fulfilled adults, the mother who suspects or knows that her children are being subjected to sexual abuse can stop looking the other way. And mothers who were themselves interfered with as children can take a clear look at their own fears, which may be interfering with the normal development of their children. Good therapy, though not easy to find, can be very helpful.

Much sexual abuse of children could be prevented if parents were more careful about the people they choose to look after their children in their absence. Too often a wolf is left in charge of the sheep. If a woman knows that her husband or boyfriend is an angry, hostile person, especially when drunk, she should not leave a small child alone with him. (One study of child-battering shows that nearly one reported case in five occurs while the child is left with a male caretaker, and often coincides with sexual assault, drunkenness, and 'sadistic gratification of the perpetrator.')

Parents should also listen carefully when their children tell them about incidents that upset them, and not immediately dismiss them as lies or the products of a vivid imagination. While adolescent daughters have been known to invent stories of incest in an attempt to get rid of a father, this is much less likely with a younger child. Little Red Riding Hood's life might have turned out differently if she had felt free to tell her mother about Grandpa the first time he played games with her. If an incident of sexual abuse does occur, it is important not to panic. The child needs warmth and support. Too many children in these situations get not support but anger for causing trouble.

Children who have been sexually abused do not carry visible wounds, like the victims of child-beaters. They can't be easily spotted by family doctors, and nobody thinks improved 'reporting' procedures would help very much. But they have wounds, and even if they 'forget,' they carry scars. The onus is on their parents to realize that the 'terrible secret' is one they share with many other people, and that they can find help before their children grow up and continue the family tragedy. There is also an onus on their friends, relatives, teachers, clergymen and doctors not to look the other way, or recoil in self-righteous horror, but to speak their minds plainly and help them face the problem squarely and humanely.

JOHANNA STUCKEY

A feminist looks at prostitution

INTRODUCTION

Prostitution is, as I see it, the basic, the central, the raw experience of women in our society. It is the core of our female experience, for, it is my contention that, at some level, most women in Canada today have at some point prostituted themselves - not necessarily for money, but often for that or its equivalent.

As I define it, prostitution is the use of sexual stimulation to gain non-sexual ends. The woman who gives her body to her husband as soon as she gets something she wants is doing what a prostitute does to live. A woman who gives in to a casual Saturday night date because she does not want to become a social misfit or be rejected is being paid not in cash but in emotional or social currency. A married woman who contracts in law to pay for her keep with her sexual favours is at that level little different from the prostitute. Of course, we all know that in marriage what is basic may be tempered by love and generosity, but the law *is* the law. Love and generosity ameliorate individual situations, it is true, but they do not basically make marriage any the less what it is - exchange of sex for keep. When love and generosity are absent, or limited, what essential difference is there between the married woman (or the single woman on an evening out) and the prostitute? At least the prostitute is involved - directly, honestly, and openly - in a cash transaction!

When I began this research, I started from a basic premise - that radical feminist political analysis would help me approach and understand prostitution; and, since prostitution is one of the simplest forms of direct exchange between men and women, the study of prostitutes and their attitudes would help me clarify my feminist analysis.

Radical feminism maintains that the cause of female oppression in our society is not, primarily, the capitalist system, though economic oppression clearly has something to do with it. Rather, it puts the proposition that, in Shulamith Firestone's words, 'the end goal of feminist revolution must be, unlike that of the first feminist movement, not just the elimination of male *privilege* but of the sex *distinction* itself: general differences between human beings would no longer matter culturally.'[1] Hence, radical feminism attacks, first and foremost, our system of sex-role stereotyping, seeing 'feminist issues not only as *women*'s first priority, but as central to any larger revolutionary analysis. It refuses to accept the existing leftist analysis not because it is too radical, but because *it is not radical enough*: it sees the current leftist analysis as outdated and superficial, because this analysis does not relate the structure of the economic class system to its origins in the sexual class system, the model for all other exploitative systems ...'[2]

What radical feminism is, then, opposed to (both personally and politically) is what Kate Millet has called 'sexual politics.' Millet defines 'politics' in the following manner: 'The term "politics" shall refer to power-structured relationships, arrangements whereby one group of persons is controlled by another.'[3] The one remaining 'ancient and universal scheme for the domination of one birth group by another' is 'the scheme that prevails in the area of sex';[4] 'the birthright priority whereby males rule females.'[5]

Sex-role stereotyping is the main means our society uses to effect its patriarchy. 'The limited role allotted to the female tends to arrest her at the level of biological experience. Therefore, nearly all that can be described as distinctly human rather than animal activity ... is largely reserved for males.'[6]

One of the main institutions of patriarchy is, of course, the nuclear family, in that it is chiefly responsible for the socializing of children. In itself, the nuclear family in our society is usually a microcosm of the patriarchal macrocosm – the state. In both, male authority is the norm, in that women and children are essentially considered dependents, giving in return for their keep, emotional and domestic support and, in the case of women, sexual accessibility.

Our society, idealizing as it does monogamous marriage and the nuclear family, holds up to women the norm of wife and mother and the ideal of 'the good woman.' At the same time, if the system of sex-role stereotyping and the nuclear family is to work, society must deny most women the psychological, emotional and social training to allow them to be independent. Now in our society (and indeed in most patriarchal societies) few women, except the very wealthy, are in fact ever to achieve the ideal; married or not, they must work outside the home for the bulk of their lives in order to help or totally support themselves and/or a family. Since society still sees female work outside the home as secondary, women are forced into the lowest available work in terms of pay and status.

Prostitution seems to me to be the inevitable corollary of such a concatenation of circumstances. First, it is a paradigm of the master-slave relationship. Upon the payment of a fee, the buyer has sexual access to the seller for an agreed period of time. It is the rock-bottom example in our society of sexual politics, the domination of one group, women, by another group, men. The male-dominated institutions that harrass and condemn prostitutes even use a knowledge of accepted sex roles against the women. Second, prostitutes by nature of their 'pariah' position in our society are the type *par excellence* of woman as victim. The ideal of 'the good woman' holds society's imagination, and the prostitute is condemned as deserving of her situation.

Her situation is indeed paradoxical. She of all women has gone directly to the crux of the sexist society and, perhaps unconsciously, has seen that, in our society, it is only the sexual difference of women that gives them value. Since she cannot refuse to use her assets (after all, she must live), she sells her body. And for this blatant (and even logical) acceptance of the very point of sexism, she is castigated.

Indeed, a woman who wishes independence has rarely been able to make enough money to make that possible. Through history, since the time of the 'virgin' (i.e., independent) prostitutes of the Mesopotamian and ancient Greek temples, prostitution has not only been for the destitute woman her only solution but has offered the badly paid woman an 'independent' status. So society unintentionally encourages her to exploit this saleable commodity.

Our sexist society has to 'keep women in their place': first, by making it almost impossible for them to choose a career other than that of wife and mother (and still be 'respectable') and, second, by setting women against each other – madonna vs. whore, good woman vs. bad. (Until recently we have all had, essentially, to opt for one or the other.)

I hope that what I have to say in this article will help not only to ameliorate the situation prostitutes find themselves in – there is little hope of changing the basic situation for them until we change it for all women – but also to 'bridge the gap' that has been artificially created to separate the so-called 'good woman' from her own alter ego – the so-called 'bad woman.' We must recognize that, though our life experiences differ widely in detail, our basic realities are yet the same and will continue to be as long as sexism and sexual politics remain the system by which our society is organized.

PROSTITUTION IN TORONTO TODAY

Today in Toronto, according to my sources, prostitutes vary from young girls who prostitute themselves in the backs of cars for a few dollars (as little as $2.00, according to the police) to high-class call girls who say they earn between $100.00 and $250.00 an evening. Depending on how old they are and how long they have been in the business, they are either setting limits to how long they will stay in it or they are resigned to it. I have talked to (among others) a 'kept woman,' a street hooker (and a drug addict), a bar girl, and a female homosexual pimp. I have talked to the police (members of the Morality Squad); and I have talked to officials at Street Haven, a drop-in centre for female drug addicts and prostitutes.

The prostitutes I talked to generally fall into two groups: first, those who are prostitutes because of economic need, who could not, given their lack of education and training, make even a decent living legitimately; and, second, those who are prostitutes because they want the good things of our materialistic world, want what the consumer society has to sell, want those things badly enough to prostitute themselves for them. In other words, the prostitutes I talked to are women who *have to* exploit their bodies either from need or from greed – ones who cannot survive in any other way and ones who have 'bought consumerism,' one of the prevailing myths of our society. Needless to say, those among the women who prostitute themselves from economic necessity are usually 'lower-class' women, from poor families and/or broken homes and from backgrounds of drugs and alcoholism, poor education, even (in some cases) of mental retardation, and (occasionally) of crime. The others who prostitute themselves to be able to consume are usually (but not always) 'middle-class' in origin, not mentally or even educationally inferior, though (occasionally) from disturbed family backgrounds.

This second group does not immediately seem as sympathetic as the first group, for the latter's plight is immediately clear and unambiguous, and it underlines one of the central problems of women in our society – the need for equality of opportunity, equal chance to earn a respectable living wage and not be condemned to earning a second-class wage – the position of most women in our society.[7] There is, however, no question in my mind that the second group is also deserving of understanding, and perhaps more so, for its members have done only what many middle-class women in our society have done. They too have joined the faceless consumers who keep our economy of increasing production in business. The only difference between a middle-class homemaker, who 'goes shopping' for fun and the prostitute who spends most of her money on clothes is how each gets her money – one through promiscuous selling of her body and the other by the selective, and sometimes highly calculated, selling of herself – in marriage – to the 'most eligible' man available, often the best 'bread-winner' she can find.

THE WOMEN THEMSELVES

When I began to try to talk to women in Toronto who practised as prostitutes at one level or another, I was at a real disadvantage. First, how was I to meet prostitutes? Well, I solved that in part through a friend who had a male friend who knew where prostitutes could be found. We arranged a meeting, and he took me around town. He did the actual approaching for me. He explained that I wanted only to talk and negotiated how much I should pay for the woman's time (I felt that, since I was asking her to talk to me when she could be working, I had to offer payment). Then the woman and I would talk, very informally; I usually took notes. I was advised not to use a tape-recorder. And I asked questions which I had prepared beforehand to try, not always successfully, not to 'lead' the respondent, to try not to influence her answer too much. I also encouraged considerable free exchange of information (unguided by me) when on occasion it was possible. My data are, then, very unscientific, very subjective – but in a way, random. I had to rely for my subjects on mainly chance encounter in bars, hotels, and restaurants.

My second disadvantage was that I was a woman – and a 'square' one at that. My companion had to convince one or two women that I really wanted only to talk; they were adamant that they would not 'go with' a homosexual. And, further, as a 'square' woman, I did not know the jargon of the 'round' subculture. I had to learn that clients were 'Johns' or 'tricks'; that the world I lived in was 'square' and that the subculture was 'round.' Quickly, however, I dealt with that problem, but it took a while even to begin to overcome the fact of my being square.

After I had talked to a number of women, I realized that they were all speaking in much the same way about their lives, their work, their hopes. So consistent was it that I wondered even then whether the subculture had a 'line' it gave to outsiders. They almost all explained their getting into prostitution in economic terms: most saw it as a problem of lack of education and, hence, lack of ability to earn adequately. Most said they did not like the job and they especially disliked their clients. Most wanted eventually to marry. Many told me that what they were doing was socially valuable and justified themselves in these terms.

I have tried to present the views of my subjects with as few of my value-judgments as I could and, wherever possible, I have tried to quote their exact words and tried to capture their presence. Nevertheless, the reader should be aware that the material to follow is highly idiosyncratic in its compilation. I make no claim of truth for it. The reader must judge whether or not it rings true. It is safe to say that I was not always sure that people were telling the truth. Indeed, as I have pointed out, everyone could have been giving me 'a line.' I had no way of knowing. Some of the women I really believed; others I took with a grain of salt. But I did seem to get a reasonably consistent picture: is it that the subculture has its own rules, its own justifications, its own version of reality, 'the illusion which makes life possible,' which it serves up to outsiders?

As to my ordering of the selected (and drastically shortened) interviews with women and my own reactions to them and to places, I begin with the consumers and end with the economically oppressed. Joan is clearly middle class, well educated, well off, aware and sensitive; Shirley is also intelligent and articulate but has only a grade ten education; and Mary, a 'reformed' drug addict with a grade eight education, is only just (and for the time being) keeping herself out of the environment I encountered at Streethaven and the all-night Snack Bar.

Joan, a 'kept woman,' juggles three men, all of whom pay for her favours. 'I am not answerable to these men for any action. I can do what I want.' She justifies her situation: 'If women have to work too much, they become bitter because they get tired and depressed. Most jobs don't pay well.' Joan had a marvellous job; it paid well, but she 'worked like a slave.' Now with her three men and part-time occasional jobs, she's comfortable.

'I'll have a tough time remarrying, because it's hard to put up with a man, and now I'm so independent. I wouldn't stop working if I remarried. A legitimate job is nice and I like it. It keeps me in contact with the outside world, though I like to stay at home and do homey things, cook.' She goes on, 'Any man who works hard resents the fact that his wife "has nothing to do." He doesn't feel housework is hard. He doesn't realize how hard it is to run a house. Anyway, resentment builds up because he feels his wife does nothing.'

Joan enjoys sex, even with her 'clients.' 'I am more to them than just a body. If I were just a body, I'd feel seedy. If it is a strong personal relationship, it is not seedy.' Joan has recently fallen in love. 'I get nothing from him. I wouldn't ask him for a nickel. I like to have a man around.'

Joan concludes that the main reasons she lives the life she does are money, sex, and variety. She needs the money; she likes the sex; she likes going places, 'places I wouldn't go to in a million years if I was married.' But all these things are important because they give her independence. 'I am not answerable to anyone. If I'm sick, I have someone to call on. I have no job; so I have independence and free time for the kids.' Joan says she has no guilt about money. She 'sees women around who aren't good wives and mothers. They are looked after but they don't *give*.' 'There is no difference between me and the others except the legal aspect, and I *give*. Men think that they are paying their wives. They complain all the time about wives who take and don't give.' For Joan, 'life is easier this way.'

Shirley has been in the business for three years and plans to stay for three more only. She wants to get married. She has one child already (a girl) by a pimp she loved. She says she makes $100–$200 a night. Some she saves; the rest she spends on clothes. She has a grade ten education. After she leaves the business, she plans to go to school to improve her education. 'I stay in it for the money.' It is important for Shirley to be independent. She was originally with a man, a pimp, but she didn't get enough money because he took it all.

On pimps – 'girls must love the pimp. It's the only way girls go on working.' Some pimps have two or three women – called 'wife-in-laws.' They know about one another; they don't mind, because 'the money is going the same place,' and they like the man. Shirley doesn't like this scene. She got tired of it. 'They take you all out the same time.' Sometimes the pimps are just money-hungry and mean. They beat a girl if they do not get enough money from her. But, Shirley points out, 'I don't down'em cause they're getting money.'

Getting warmed up now, Shirley begins to talk about tricks. 'I can't stand them touching me.' She says she doesn't enjoy sex with tricks. She goes to hotels with them. 'At home I forget them.' She goes on, 'If I feel he's not right [safe], I won't go with him, or I get dressed first, or something.' 'I don't do all the things,' she assures me, 'not everything, only certain things.' She never has an orgasm with a trick, but she does with her 'special friend' (a man). Tricks 'are nothing but money.' They smell; they are in other ways offensive. Being in love means to Shirley 'getting into a closer relationship.' Shirley is not interested in women sexually, except to put on a show for a trick, and then she is acting.

On the subject of square women, Shirley gets pretty hot. She is particularly angry at the ones in nine-to-five jobs, who get $100 a week, who go out on Friday nights, get drunk, and go to bed for nothing. Then 'they scorn us because they don't get paid. They think they're better, but they aren't – only stupid!'

The police – 'they bust you but then you're out and at the business again.' Shirley says, 'I don't like the police.' They can 'queer the pitch.' Often for a whole evening, if they just hang around, the girls can't do anything. Girls recognize them and tip one another off. She has experienced no violence from the police, though occasionally from tricks. 'They beat you up to get their money back. If you stand up to them, they back down.'

If prostitution became legal, it would lower prices and that would be bad. 'There would be more young ones available' and thus less for Shirley. She adds, 'If it wasn't for us, there'd be more rapes.' Around the bars most of the girls are between eighteen and twenty-seven or -eight. 'It's fine if you look OK. Then you can go on longer. You must keep your looks.'

She wants to marry and be a mother again. 'Women have a need to be mothers, but I don't want a trick's child. You'd want to know who the father is.' Shirley has no square friends. Her friends are 'all getting money somehow.'

Shirley talked finally about how she got into the business. 'I got into the business when I met a guy who told me how much money I could make. I was in a bad job; so I tried it. I got more money than I could ever make working.'

Mary is thin, too thin. She looks much older than her avowed twenty-five years. She is ill at ease (because I'm square? because of the man who is present?). She hangs around downtown restaurants with about forty 'girls,' of whom about ten are 'gay' (homosexual); about fifteen of these women are under twenty years old. The ages of the forty women range between fifteen and thirty. Mary assures us that she is off heroin now (she seems to be – she shows her arms). She has a grade eight education, she says. She got into the business eleven years ago at fourteen years of age because she got the heroin habit from her sister, a junkie who supported her habit by prostitution. At first her sister gave her heroin, but eventually she told her to make her own money to buy it. Mary became a prostitute at fourteen. She needed, she says, $125.00 a day for heroin. She has been in jail. She tells us that she was living with a man common-law and has two kids, who are now with the Children's Aid. She gets on fine with her kids, but she wouldn't want a man around. Mary doesn't want to get married because, she says, she likes her independence.

The other women she hangs around with are, she thinks, really 'hard.' Some tricks are, she says, nice; some are nasty and beat her up. She doesn't have orgasm ever with a client, but she does with other girls or men who are not tricks, if a 'relationship develops.' Around the restaurants there are fifteen or so pimps, who handle one girl each. She doesn't say whether she has a pimp.

Of the police Mary says, 'The police are just doing their job; but sometimes they beat girls up and take their money.'

In Mary's opinion 'square' women are lucky. If she had to do it again, she'd get more education. She is in the business, she assures us, because it is not possible to make a good salary if a woman has only a grade eight education.

At Street Haven, I did not talk to any of the drop-in women. I was asked not to, and I agreed. However, I did conduct an in-depth interview with the director.

Many of the women who come to Street Haven, she tells me, are on drugs, and when they are on hard drugs, such as heroin, they are usually prostitutes or involved in criminal activities of some sort. The Street Haven project was set up, in the director's words, 'to give emergency help to the woman offender.' Often these women are on drugs or alcohol or both. Those who support their addiction by prostitution solicit along the streets; in the evening the neighbouring streets are clogged with cars. It makes the director angry that in these cases only the woman is charged. The men come looking; the 'girls' do the approaching. In her opinion, until the law is changed, the client ought to be dealt with too.

The women feel, according to the director, that prostitution is a business; there is 'no love lost between the girl and the client.' The women 'come to have an intense dislike of men.' For them, men are 'no source of pleasure.' They 'come to mistrust men and in many instances they hate men.' Many become homosexual. If they live with someone, they choose a woman. But, the director believes, they are 'not "true" lesbians; their lesbianism is purely psychological, not physical. If they get on top of their problems and meet a man to whom they can relate, they become heterosexual again. In prison they often relate sexually to women; when they get out, they become heterosexual. There is nothing hereditary.' The director went on to explain that everybody, in her opinion, has latent homosexuality. 'What you do with what happens to you is what counts in what you become.'

The women who come to Street Haven have very bad self-images, 'right down on the ground. They put on a brash front but have lost any shred of dignity they might have had. They detest themselves. They hate what they do to themselves, but they can't get out, because it's a vicious circle.'

'Most of our girls carry knives to protect themselves.' They fear the clients, but have no respect for them. 'It's a case of get money – get sex over and on to the next trick.' For the majority 'it is a continual parading in and out of rooms. If a woman has a big habit, she needs about $125.00 a day. So she is continually stealing or hustling.' 'Any girls we get who are prostitutes are on drugs or alcohol; most have mixed addiction.'

As far as the director of Street Haven is concerned, economic difficulties are a large factor in prostitution. 'In this area women on welfare trying to raise families often become prostitutes and sometimes even put twelve- or thirteen-year-old daughters out to hustle and steal to get a little extra money.' The majority of women who come to Street Haven have backgrounds of illegitimacy or broken homes (usually when they were babies) and 'sometimes as many as twelve foster homes.' And then they produce their own illegitimate children. They cannot be relied upon to practise birth control.

Another reason for going into prostitution is 'their own personal needs for some kind of attention. So they become prostitutes. Because of the insecurity in themselves, they become promiscuous to gain attention. It's better to be beaten up than ignored ... Sometimes women come in to show us where they have been beaten and hurt. Yet they want to go back.' The Street Haven director sees it as a bit of sado-masochism as well as the need for attention.

The average age of the women who drop in at Street Haven is late twenties; they are as young as sixteen and as old as sixty. But if the women there continue 'this way of life, their life expectancy is very low. The oldest is an exception. She has been on the corner since twenty.'

The director of Street Haven particularly asked that I record her 'strong feelings about the business of only women being charged ... If it is illegal for a woman to solicit, it should be illegal for a man to look for her.'

Finally, she pointed out that 'if a person persisted in this type of life for any length of time, they'd have to feel pretty poorly about themselves. They have to get rid of their guilt feelings and see the thing as business. Our girls have guilt feelings, but sometimes they get beyond the point of knowing right from wrong.'

Around two-thirty, after an evening of roaming around bars and hotels, I ended up near Street Haven in a small, crowded snack bar. My first impression was that it was in an advanced state of physical deterioration. I soon realized, however, that, though the bar itself was utterly filthy, the feeling of deterioration came from the people not the place. It was the most depressing, degrading place I think I have ever been in. Physically the bar was gray-black with filth, which I soon discovered was sticky, heavily sugared coffee which had been spilled. Sticky, half-dried, blackened sugar coated the counters. The floors were black also. I was told that drug addicts, who flock to the place, need large quantities of sugar for energy. That made sense, but I did not pursue it.

The people were fascinating but also revolting, like characters in a Fellini movie. They were a strange mixture – a young and very beautiful transvestite; many old, hag-like women; some, who were obviously Indians, male and female; a number of other men, young and old, dressed in ragged, patched-together clothing. Two or three times while I was there, a policeman entered and questioned people. Once the police came to look at a woman on 'bombers' (some sort of pill), and there was a minor flare-up of temper. The police were gentle, considerate, but they were obviously hated. One woman muttered beneath her breath 'pigs.' Tension was high.

Outside, a police-cruiser was stopped at the curb. People loitered. Cars cruised up and down. Women went out, came back.

I was there about an hour, talking to a woman (I'll call her Bernice), who was, according to my information, a pimp. She told us she had been off drugs for six months and out of the business as long, since she had fallen in love. But the man Bernice had loved was now dead. So there she was – in a junkie bar, thin, taut-faced, attractive, and well groomed. She looked out of place, but she obviously was not. She knew the crowd. In the middle of our discussion, she left for a few minutes. We watched her, outside talking to another woman, who seemed to be working for her. My informant said, 'She's back on junk now, though she won't admit it. She's very thin; she used to be fat.' Anyway she agreed she was back in the business.

I will never forget that snack bar – its filth, its decay, its despair. It was the lower depths, what the director at Street Haven had been talking about. I began to feel ill. When we left, the bar was still crowded.

The police describe prostitutes in Toronto as mostly independent, in the business to supplement their incomes. According to the police, prostitution is not a big problem in Toronto. Most of the women are in business because they need money to live 'the good life.' Their motivation is solely economic. Prostitution is a job for which a woman needs no training. She can work through a bar or a girlfriend or, occasionally, through a pimp. According to the police, about 75 per cent of all Toronto prostitutes work alone, and the average fee is $20.00, the highest $50.00. If the demand is for 'weird sex,' the fee is higher. 'The trade now takes place in bars. The streets are clean.'

If the police raid, the male client is charged as a 'found-in' and is usually fined $25.00. The woman is fined $100.00 for a first offence, $200.00 for a second, and so on. Male homosexual prostitutes, of whom there are many in Toronto, are charged with 'gross indecency.' According to the police, the laws have been changed because they want to be able to arrest male prostitutes too. However, it is harder for a policeman to spot a male prostitute as soliciting because his masculine role allows him to approach another man. The police say that they use their knowledge of the feminine role to arrest female prostitutes. No 'nice woman' would approach a man on the street!

The police agree that Toronto's prostitutes are generally lacking in education. 'Most are not too bright. The odd one has grade thirteen.' They also find that 'the girls expect physical punishment as part of the trade. This is part of their character. They are masochists before they get into the trade.' The officer said, 'There is a greater percentage of lesbianism among prostitutes because of their hatred and distrust of men. And they hate themselves as much.'

CONCLUDING REMARKS

Generally, prostitutes I talked to confirmed what my research had told me. With a few exceptions, they distrust and dislike men. At the same time they despise them. As do all women the man they are attached to, they defended 'their man,' if they had one, by asserting that he was 'different from the rest,' but they are clear about what they think of the rest!

My investigations support my research again in that these women make a clear distinction between sex with love and sex without it. They could not 'love' the Johns, the marks they take advantage of, no matter how much they tell 'the suckers' they do.

Whatever their economic and educational background – both generally very low – they are, with very few exceptions, in it for the money, either from need or for the good life. Some say they want to get married and plan for that almost idyllic time when they can quit the business and join the 'square' society they say they loathe; others assert that they value their independence and see independence as clearly related to economic stability. They became prostitutes to get money to buy independence.

Usually, prostitutes despise 'square' women for doing what they do in relation to men. They seem very clear-sighted when it comes to assessing the position of most 'straight' women in our society. They see marriage as a socially accepted but badly paid form of prostitution. As evidence, the prostitutes cite the behaviour and words of men who come to them for sex, usually for something they couldn't ask their 'pure' wives to do or for phony love and understanding which the men often say they don't get in their square marriages. They complain that their wives are not carrying out their part of the bargain. Prostitutes generally despise square women, but they despise their clients, men, much more.

Finally, pretty generally, when pushed far enough, prostitutes are vaguely aware that they have low self-images, are lacking in self-esteem. In many, what happens to them is, I think, that they play out their own conditioned masochism, the masochism that our society tries to programme in *all* its women. They represent the extreme of reification of self. They even often regard their sexual organs as their weapon, their economic equipment, their 'money box,' as one put it.

All this is no surprise to a feminist. Since females in our society are trained to be dependent on males and to 'suck up' in order to be supported, they must see their sex and sexuality as a bargaining commodity – and that from a very early age. The logical extension of this attitude, an attitude which our society assumes will fit girls for marriage, is prostitution. No wonder prostitutes think married women are legalized prostitutes, and stupid to boot! Why sell your commodity for less than the market will bear – and get stuck in a boring rut at the same time?

As I see it, prostitution is the logical and ultimate development of our society's treating its women as sex objects and the relationship between the sexes as power politics based on economics. The degrading of one person into 'sex object' is absolute when the person so degraded is denied the right to reciprocate and is fobbed off instead with payment of some sort or another. When the payment implies, as it usually does, a situation in which the payer is superior and the payee inferior, the circle is complete – and we are describing not only prostitution but legalized marriage!

At the level of sexual politics, prostitutes are indeed, as Kate Millet says, 'the political prisoners of the Women's Movement.' All who are concerned about the position of women in our society must fight not only against sexual politics generally, but against the particular manifestation of it which the prostitute's situation represents. We must all press to have removed from the legal code all laws which can be used to harrass and degrade prostitutes. Above all, we must vigorously oppose any move to legalize prostitution. If prostitution were legalized in Canada, it would be, like the present marriage laws, just another step in legalizing the degradation, the reification, of women.

Since the beginning of male-dominated societies, patriarchy has profited from having women classed as either good or bad, madonna or whore. And women have accepted these divide-and-rule definitions. Now, however, feminism has shown that there are only women – some more nearly liberated than others. What is more important, it has shown that women can and do gather strength from the recognition of their sisterhood. Indeed, prostitutes are no other than the 'political prisoners' of all women in sexist society. Women are all in it together, square and round, and they are beginning to realize that the only way out is together.

Literature on prostitution
There is very little Canadian material on prostitution. What there is, is usually out of date or of limited value. Historically interesting are two books, one first published in 1898 and the other in 1972. In 1898 C.S. Clark's book, *Of Toronto the Good*, appeared (reprinted Toronto: Coles, 1970); at least part of its aim was the legalization of prostitution. In a very biased argument (on behalf of respectable women and against the emancipation of women, whom he labels as 'largely fools') Clark presents some useful and revealing data on prostitution in Toronto between 1895 and 1898. The other historically interesting book is *Red Lights on the Prairies* (Toronto: Macmillan, 1972). Its author, James H. Gray, examines prostitution in prairie cities such as Winnipeg, Brandon, Regina, Calgary, and Edmonton, from the early settlement days to about the 1920s. Though prostitution was not then legalized, it flourished as a result of an unofficial zoning system. The only book that I know of on recent prostitution in Canada is that by Thérèse Limoges, *La Prostitution à Montréal. Comment, pourquoi certaines femmes deviennent prostituées* (Montréal: Les Editions de L'Homme, 1967). A sociological, psychological, and criminological study, the book examines the lives and motives of twenty French Canadian women, all Roman Catholic and all under twenty-seven years of age. Limoges explains what sort of woman becomes a prostitute (anti-social, lacking in moral conscience, hating men, homosexual in tendency), and she examines why women enter the profession (defective family background, educational and consequently economic inferiority, and ease of entry). *Deviant Behaviour and Societal Reaction* (eds. Boydall, Grindstaff, and Whitehead, Toronto, Montreal: Holt, Rinehart and Winston, 1972) is a general and useful book on deviance.

Following is a list of non-Canadian books which I have found useful for this study: Carol Andreas, *Sex and Caste in America* (NJ: Prentice-Hall, 1971); Judith Bardwick, *Psychology of Women* (NY: Harper and Row, 1971); George Battaille, *Death and Sensuality* (NY: Walker, 1962); Dinitz, Dynes, and Clarke, eds., *Deviance* (NY, London, Toronto: OUP, 1969); P. Durban, *La Psychologie des prostituées* (Paris: Maloine, 1969); Kate Millet, *The Prostitution Papers* (NY: Avon, 1973); Rubington and Weinberg, eds., *Deviance* (London: Collier-Macmillan, 1969); Mary Jane Sherfey, *The Nature and Evolution of Female Sexuality* (NY: Vintage, 1972).

NOTES

1 Shulamith Firestone, *The Dialectic of Sex* (London: Cape, 1971), pp. 11-12.
2 *Ibid.*, p. 42.
3 Kate Millet, *Sexual Politics* (NY: Doubleday, 1970), p. 23.
4 *Ibid.*, p. 24.
5 *Ibid.*, p. 25.
6 *Ibid.*, p. 26.
7 *Labour Canada: Women in the Labour Force. (Facts and Figures 1973 Edition).* Ottawa: Information Canada, 1974. passim

Obscenity*

THE MEANING OF OBSCENITY

What is obscenity? Clearly something hard to talk about constructively. For one thing there is a problem of good faith. 'Obscenity,' said George Orwell, 'is difficult to discuss honestly – people are too frightened of seeming to be shocked or of not seeming to be shocked.' For another, there is lack of agreement about the definition of obscenity.

After all, what makes a thing obscene? Take a theatrical performance for example. Some college students once put on a play to open their college theatre. The opening had been widely publicized, the house was full and a lot of local dignitaries were present. The play itself passed off without remark until the final scene, which showed a burning at the stake: the stage completely dark, a solitary spotlight on the centre, and in the midst of the flames the victim standing absolutely naked. Some students giggled, some dignitaries walked out, one middle-aged woman told newspaper reporters afterwards: 'I didn't know where to look.' The college authorities made the students change the scene for subsequent performances.

But was the play obscene? Should there have been a prosecution and conviction with all this would have involved? Or if there had been a prosecution, should there have been an acquittal on the ground that the play was not obscene?

*Reprinted in extract from Law Reform Commission of Canada, *Limits of Criminal Law: Obscenity: A Test Case*, Working Paper No. 10 (Ottawa: 1975).

We come back to the question: what is obscenity? Something too vague perhaps to be defined, one of those elusive terms we use but can't explain - like civilization. 'What is civilization?' said Kenneth Clark; 'I don't know: I can't define it in abstract terms - yet. But I think I can recognize it when I see it.' Some say the same about obscenity: 'I know it when I see it,' said Justice Stewart in an American case.

But different people often see things differently. Some see obscenity in nude pictures, statues, ballets and so on. Others find less obscenity in these things than in the way the affluent nations live in a world where millions are dying of starvation. 'Obscene' is clearly a pejorative term.

All the same, 'obscene' isn't the same as 'wrong' or 'bad.' Was it obscene of Cain to murder Abel? Or was the great train robbery obscene? Clearly obscenity is not identical with evil; it only covers a single segment of it. But what is that segment?

A look at the words 'obscenity' and 'pornography' suggests that it is a segment that didn't worry people very much till relatively recently. Take the word 'obscenity.' The original Latin meant 'ill-omened, inauspicious,' as did its English counterpart at first apparently. In Shakespeare's day, however, it meant primarily 'offensive to the senses, filthy, foul, disgusting.' Only secondarily did it refer to what was offensive to modesty or decency. Compare the word 'pornography,' derived from two Greek words meaning 'harlot' and 'writing.' Unlike 'obscenity,' the word 'pornography' is of later currency and doesn't appear until the nineteenth century. It primarily referred to literature about prostitutes and their patrons, but slightly later came to embrace literature about 'unchaste or obscene subject-matter.'

If language suggests that obscenity is a relatively recent worry, our law provides corroboration. Though censorship was known in English law quite early on, it wasn't for obscenity but for heresy and sedition. Nor was obscenity prosecuted in England till the eighteenth century and even then the cases were limited to sexual material in the context of anti-religious works. Not till the beginning of the nineteenth century do we find prosecutions for obscenity by itself, nor did the common law define obscenity till the *Hicklin* case in 1868 - itself a case about an anti-religious pamphlet with sexual contents.

In earlier times, then, people were disturbed, not by obscenity but by heresy. What worried them was not attacks on sexual decency but attacks on religion. Today the very opposite is true: the problem isn't heresy but obscenity.

What lies then at the root of our present notion of obscenity? Two things, it seems. Obscenity somehow has to do with sex. It also has to do with revealing things we don't like seeing, for reasons which perhaps we can't explain - it just offends, we feel it inappropriate.

Not that such revelations are always inappropriate. Nudes in art gallery paintings or in anatomy textbook illustrations don't offend. Is this because art and science have some redeeming value? Or is it that art and science both seek truth, while obscenity and pornography both distort the truth? Take pornography for example. Ostensibly it deals in sex. But sex is highly personal and therefore hard to market. So what pornography provides isn't real sex but an *ersatz* product. And what about the pornography world - a world where men are always virile and erect, where woman never menstruate, where love and individualism are conspicuously lacking? Is this a true picture of reality or is this what makes it 'undue exploitation of sex?'

'Undue exploitation of sex' is what criminal law in Canada prohibits. This is how our criminal law defines obscenity. In doing so, however, it overlooks some other distinctions. It doesn't for instance differentiate between 'ordinary obscenity' and 'hard-core pornography,' the first denoting the ordinary run of 'girlie' magazines and the second denoting pictures, literature and so on that deals with rape, sadism, masochism, bestiality, necrophilia and other perversions. The distinction may be important, though, since many people object far more to hard-core pornography than to ordinary obscenity. Besides, hard-core pornography tends to be available only under the counter or through the mail.

Another distinction overlooked by our criminal law is the distinction between isolated instances of obscenity and the products of vast commercial enterprise. Quite clearly today's obscenity problem isn't the occasional Fanny Hill, it is the continuous outpouring of a multi-million dollar industry. The 'pornography explosion' has swept pornography beyond the horse and buggy stage.

INAPPROPRIATENESS AND DISTORTION

But why does obscenity offend? Can it be simply because of inappropriateness and distortion? Take the college students' play. Some in the audience found the burning scene inappropriate and false - inappropriate because the nudity distracted from the action, and false because the darkened stage highlighted the victim's private parts in a way a real execution wouldn't. Some took a different view: they found the nudity appropriate and realistic - appropriate in that the protagonist was stripped to the nakedness with which his life began, realistic in that this was how it really would have happened. The fact is, as so often with obscenity, the case is borderline.

But even suppose the nudity was inappropriate, what's wrong with inappropriateness? 'In Prague last night,' reported a music critic before the war, 'we heard a little boy of three sing with a perfect bass voice but with no proper sense of the fitness of things.' Should that have been a crime?

Alternatively, suppose the nudity was a distortion of reality, should such distortion be a criminal offence? Look where that would lead! We'd have to outlaw operas – whoever heard of people talking in song? And ballets – what adult ever pirouettes in real life? Plays too – where can we find off-stage a three-walled room? Yet no one wants to outlaw operas, ballets, and plays. No one would dare: they're too much in demand. So is obscenity!

Obscenity is very much in demand. It's very much in supply as well – supplied by a large and growing industry. This makes for economic growth, presumably, and helps create employment. Does this conclude the matter? Or can we ask a further question: is this a worthwhile allocation of resources – a suitable avenue for channelling labour, money and materials? Or is this further question best left to the market?

THE IMMORALITY INVOLVED

Is obscenity wrong? 'An interesting but irrelevant question,' you may say; 'for though some think it's wrong and therefore ought to be a crime, and others think it isn't wrong and therefore shouldn't be a crime, most people think it doesn't matter whether it's wrong or not. Wrongfulness isn't enough to make an act a crime. With obscenity, as with homosexuality, its morality or immorality is immaterial.'

But how can this be? Morality can't be utterly irrelevant to criminality. As Helvetius said two hundred years ago, 'laws draw their strength from common morality.' An act that isn't wrong in any way is one we should be free to do – it shouldn't be a crime.

'Not even if it harms others?' But then the act is wrongful: one of the best reasons for holding an act wrongful is its tendency to cause harm to other people. 'But what about the converse? What about an act that is wrong but has no tendency to harm others? Surely the immorality of this sort of act isn't enough to make it a crime.' Why not? For what sort of act could be wrong without harming anyone?

'An act known to be offensive to the Deity perhaps. Or one unworthy of a human being. That sort of act is wrong but doesn't deserve to be a crime. That sort of act falls within an area of private morality that isn't the law's business. "There's no place for the State in the bedrooms of the nation." Everyone is entitled to go to Hell in his own fashion so long as he does no harm to others.'

But can you go to Hell in your own fashion without a risk of harm to others? Mightn't you drag others down with you? As John Donne said, no man is an island. Sin against God and you may infect others and make them do the same. Or – to take the alternative approach – fall short of human standards and you may lead others to do likewise. Once grant that any act is wrong – in theological or other terms – and how rule out the possibility of harm to others? That's why so many thought we needed criminal laws against homosexuality. To show that 'mere immorality' shouldn't be a crime we need a stronger argument.

Such argument is available. Take an act known to offend the Deity. How do we know this? We don't even know there is a God, let alone what offends him. These things are matters of belief, and no one, we hold in Canada, is entitled to impose his religious beliefs on others.

Or take an act considered as falling short of human standards. Here too we are concerned with belief and attitude, not knowledge. For those condemning the act do so because of their own personal ideals. But these are strictly personal. Each of us is entitled to his own ideals so long as they involve no demonstrable harm to others. Or at least, we hold in Canada, no one is entitled to impose his own ideals on others.

So whether we believe obscenity wrong on religious or idealistic grounds – and many do – this isn't enough to warrant making it a crime. Religions and ideals are matters of personal commitment. They are insufficient grounds on which to base the criminal law.

THE HARM FEARED

But what if obscenity were wrong, not simply on religious or idealistic grounds, but in that it causes harm? Would this warrant making it a crime?

But does obscenity cause harm? This is a difficult question. The answer doesn't just depend on evidence. It also depends on a value-judgment – it all depends on what we choose to count as harm. For 'harm' is not just a descriptive term, it's also an evaluative one. What then is harm? What sort of thing do we categorize as harmful? Things, we suggest, that make life poorer, nastier, less agreeable.

But these themselves are value-laden words. Whether you reckon something harmful depends both on the circumstances and on your preferences. Suppose I cut your leg off, do I do you harm? It all depends: not if I'm a surgeon and your leg needs amputating – here I perform a beneficial operation, for a life is generally considered more worth saving than a leg. But what if you're a ballet-dancer who would rather live a week with both legs than a century with only one? In this case you might well regard the act of amputation as a harm.

Or, to take another example, would something causing blindness always qualify as harmful? Surely sight is an advantage and blindness a misfortune. Yet take Brentano's case. The philosopher, Brentano, in his later years went blind. His friends commiserated with him. 'Blindness,' he replied, 'is a blessing in disguise –

it makes me concentrate more fully on my philosophy.' To him external sight meant less than inner vision.

All the same, the ballet dancer and the philosopher Brentano are exceptions. The rest of us will usually agree on what makes life poorer and on what we count as harm. Violence, for example, is a paradigm case of harm – it causes pain and physical suffering. But there can be non-physical suffering too. And this is why we also count as harmful those traumatic occurrences – like black-mailing – which give rise to anxiety and reduce the ability to cope with life; as well as those acts – like theft and fraud – which cause distress through *loss* of something of value. A third type of harm, some would argue, consists of injury to sensibilities. So we may count as harmful such things as offensive smells, unpleasant noises and so on, which most of us can't tolerate because they nauseate, disgust and distract from other more interesting and more enjoyable aspects of life. A further kind of harm consists of things adversely affecting personal interaction. Since man is physically and spiritually a social creature, he must communicate and interact with other men. Anything, therefore, that impedes this by worsening personal relationships – for example, the lies Iago told Othello or, the hate propaganda against minority groups – must count as harmful. Lastly, things adversely affecting society in general constitute harms. These may be things that threaten the very existence of a society or things that make that society less worth living in.

But does obscenity cause these kinds of harm? First, take violence. Does exposure to sadistic literature make a man a sadist and make him put his reading into practice?

To start with, how do we find out? Some say we need empirical research. Such research was done at enormous cost by the us Commission on Obscenity and Pornography, which reported that no evidence of any causal link between obscenity and violence had been found. Some social scientists, however, have criticised that research as inadequate, and other critics have pointed out that failure to find a causal link doesn't prove there isn't one.

Yet others remain unconvinced by any empirical research. They say it's only common sense that obscenity might lead to violence. Couldn't it have been exposure to obscenity, they ask, which led to the Manson murders? After all, we know that man is by nature imitative. We also believe that good literature has a civilizing influence. So why should it be surprising if bad books have a detrimental influence? Such people would dismiss the Commission's Report in Lincoln's words and say: 'People who like this sort of thing will find this the sort of thing they like.'

The question about obscenity and violence, then, can't easily be settled. So what about the question whether obscenity causes non-physical harm? Some argue that it does so by causing sexual arousal or by giving rise to libidinous thoughts. And, not surprisingly, studies conducted for the US Commission showed, that sexually explicit material can and does cause sexual arousal or stimulation in adults. But is such sexual arousal harmful? Some think, on religious grounds, that libidinous thoughts are harmful in themselves and a danger for salvation. But this of course rests on religious belief – belief not shared by all in our society, and therefore, as we said before, not sufficient ground for criminal law.

But does obscenity result in psychological harm? Does it lead people to withdraw from reality into fantasy, to use pornography as a substitute for sex, to prefer solitary masturbation to sexual intercourse? In short, does it arrest development? On this the evidence is inconclusive. Again, we can look to the US Commission. Their studies show that exposure to sex stimuli increased the frequency of masturbation only among minorities of various populations and that the increase died down within forty-eight hours after the exposure. In other words, so far as adults go, there's little evidence that obscenity causes psychological harm.

What about children? Because of ethical considerations the US Commission didn't fully study the effects of erotica on children and juveniles whose sexual behaviour was not yet fixed. It isn't that the evidence is inconclusive, it's rather that there is no evidence. Perhaps there is a risk to children. Who knows? Parents may well fear there is one: they did so in the following incident.

Not long ago an Ottawa variety store, quite close to several schools, installed peep-show machines. Pay twenty-five cents and you could see the sex show of your choice – normal sex, abnormal sex, sadism and even incest. The message of the incest item seemed to be: 'You too can get your Daddy to do this with you.' Some parents vigorously objected. They sent for the police. The police investigated and got an order from the court, authorizing seizure and destruction of the machines. Clearly these parents were afraid of what exposure to such peep-shows might do to their children. They were afraid that it might give them a distorted view of sex and that this might militate against a healthy personal development. Can we be sure the parents weren't correct?

So does obscenity have a tendency to cause physical or psychological harm? The answer seems to be: we don't know. Some suspect it does, maybe with good reason. On the other hand, there isn't much empirical evidence. At any rate the evidence there is doesn't provide too firm a basis for calling into play the criminal law. A firmer basis must be sought elsewhere.

Is obscenity wrong by being harmful in a less direct and individual way? By being harmful in a more indirect and social way? By adversely affecting sensibilities, personal interaction or society in general? In other words, does it threaten our values?

THE VALUES THREATENED

But why are threats to values worrying? Because, as Aristotle pointed out, man is a social animal. Physically he needs society to procreate, rear young and maintain the species. Spiritually he needs the company of other human beings. He has a natural need, then, for society. But what is society, if not a co-operative venture? As such it can't succeed unless its members are committed to doing what will make it succeed and to avoiding what will make it fail. They have to be committed to certain values.

What are these values? It depends on the society in question, but only partly. Certain values are essential to any society. Without them no society could survive. Take, for example, the value of 'non-violence' or 'peace': without some acceptance of the notion that violence and killing are 'off limits,' a society would simply become a group of frightened, hostile individuals. Or take the value of truth: without some acceptance of the notion that lying and falsehood is 'out,' a society would turn into a group of separate non-communicating entities, for communication needs language and language only works on the basis that people are telling the truth – lying itself is a parasitic activity and only possible because we normally speak the truth. Then again, in any society there has to be some vestigial respect for property rights: whether a society holds all its property in common or is wedded to private ownership, it couldn't make satisfactory use of land and other items of property unless the user were given some security of possession – some confidence that he won't suddenly lose the clothes off his back, the food on his plate and the spade in his hand. Finally, no society would be possible without some respect for order and regularity – some preference for orderliness over anarchy. These are the basic values necessary for society. Without them there can be no real co-operation and hence no real society.

Small wonder then that in most societies we find such basic values underlined in criminal law. This after all is society's fundamental law about right and wrong, and this is what lays down the groundrules of society. In any criminal law, then, we expect to find crimes of *violence* like murder, wounding and assault; crimes of *dishonesty*, like fraud and perjury; 'crimes against *property*,' like theft; and crimes of *disorder*, like riot, sedition and treason.

The value of peace
Which of these values does obscenity threaten? The prime possibility is the value concerning violence. Obscenity can't be shown to result in increased violence, but certain brands of obscenity – the sado-masochistic brands – quite clearly run counter to our notion that violence should be restricted. At worst they glorify violence, at best they anaesthetise us to it, for the everyday becomes the normal

and the normal becomes the norm. In this way violence comes to be accepted. Can this be healthy for society?

The value of individual liberty

And what about other values? Some values there are which, though not absolutely necessary to society, are nevertheless worth treasuring. Take for example the value of individual liberty. This clearly isn't essential to society: there have been, and still are, unfree societies. But liberty is one of the things that makes a society worth living in. Not simply that we resent being subject to the will of others. Rather there is a need to be free to experiment, to try new things, to be different, since this is what makes people individuals, each one unique instead of all the same like minted coins. 'It takes all sorts to make a world' is more than a plea for tolerance – it is a tribute to the virtue of variety. To this variety individual freedom is essential.

Does obscenity threaten individual liberty? Public obscenity quite clearly does. So does obscenity distributed to children.

Public obscenity

No question but that obscene matter arouses powerful feelings of shock, shame, disgust and revulsion in many who are exposed to it. We know this from our own experience: a lot of people strenuously object to having obscenity thrust upon them. We also know this from research: the US Commission studies found evidence that many people who have had experience with erotic material react with feelings of disgust. They object to being made involuntary viewers of obscenity, on billboards and on other materials on public display in public places. Obviously obscenity offends.

But, we might argue, isn't this just a matter of taste? Some like obscenity, some dislike it – isn't that the long and the short of it? There's no accounting for tastes. As Shakespeare said,

Some there are love not a gaping pig;
Some that are mad if they behold a cat;
And others, when the bagpipe sings i' the nose,
Cannot contain their urine.

So why discriminate against those who like obscenity in favour of those who don't?

To this two answers can be given. The first is that to outlaw obscenity in public places isn't discriminatory. The second is that it is the only justifiable solution to a problem of incompatible and conflicting aims.

First, it isn't really discriminatory. For one thing, those who want to show or see obscenity in public may not want to do so all the time: they too may sometimes want an unspoiled view of a natural country vista or a city's streets; they too, therefore, could benefit from these laws. For another, public obscenity is in fact a type of public nuisance, and public nuisances arrive in many forms. Some forms annoy some members of society, others annoy others: those who like obscenity may detest the noise of 'souped-up' motor cars, and *vice versa*. So public nuisance laws, which aim to prevent all these kinds of annoyance, can confer a benefit on everyone. And public obscenity laws, which can be looked on as laws against one type of public nuisance, can therefore play their part in conferring a benefit on everyone.

Secondly, the problem of incompatible aims. How weigh against each other two incompatible aims? We do it often enough in ordinary life: I want the television on, you want it off; I want to use the lake for fishing, you for water-skiing. What principles do we use to weigh them? The following principles, we suggest:

1 freedom should be maximized;
2 the desires of the conflicting parties are not conclusive but must be justified;
3 preference of either party's aim depends on its effect on those of others.

1 First, *freedom should be maximized*. In any free society this principle is axiomatic. Unless an activity causes serious harm – something beyond mere trivial discomfort – people should be free to pursue it. The scales are tipped in favour of allowing an activity, against restraining it.

2 Next, likes and dislikes aren't enough to tip the scales the other way. If mere dislike on anyone's part was sufficient ground for restricting your activity, then individual liberty and happiness would soon be at an end. At best we'd be at the mercy of puritanism; and 'puritanism,' said Mencken, 'is the haunting fear that someone, somewhere, may be happy.' At worst we could be prey to some more vicious ideology: the Nazis disliked Jews being around and killed them. As Shaw remarked, the ultimate form of censorship is assassination.

So mere dislikes are not enough to tip the scales against an activity. What's needed is some *justified* dislike. Dislikes can be justified on two different grounds. They may be grounded in some physical fact of human nature: we object to certain smells because our make-up is such that they nauseate. Or else they may be based on reasons: we may object to excessive advertising on the television because it interrupts the programme and this is what we really want to watch.

3 Yet, even justified dislike is not enough to tip the scales against an activity. Where one man's aim is incompatible with another's, isn't the aim that should prevail the one that least conflicts with other aims? Suppose I want to fish, you

want to water-ski, the lake's too small for both. If fishing is compatible with other activities, like swimming, paddling, boating and so on, but water-skiing rules out all other activities, then shouldn't my aim - fishing - take precedence? Giving priority to the aim compatible with the greatest range of alternative aims is simply maximising freedom: other things being equal, it leaves the greatest number of people free to pursue their own activities.

How do these principles apply to the problem of public obscenity? First, the objection to it isn't just a matter of taste. We can support it rationally. Obscenity offends because it conflicts with values those objecting to it seriously hold: the value they set on sex, on privacy, on human dignity, in short on man as something more than mere flesh and blood. Secondly, the desire for public obscenity would preclude many legitimate activities - quiet strolls, enjoyment of the view, and so on; the desire to frequent public places without exposure to obscenity would preclude but one thing - obscenity in public places. Meanwhile since obscenity could still be seen in private, doesn't this tip the scales against public obscenity and in favour of restricting it?

There is, however, a further aspect - the question of degree. How serious is the harm prevented by the law? Is it a significant affront to the values it conflicts with? Or is it just a trivial disregard of them? Whistling in a church, for instance, is far less serious than urinating on the altar. The greater the affront, then, the greater the justification for the use of criminal law.

Children

But obscenity conflicts with freedom in another way. This has to do with children. In our society we consider that children should be brought up and educated in their own best interest - the welfare of the child is paramount. We also consider that when it comes to choosing the type of education, most suited to the child's best interest, the proper person to judge and make that choice - since the child is too young to do so - is the parent. Unless the parent's choice is demonstrably contrary to the interest of the child, society doesn't interfere.

Now when it comes to sex and similar matters, it follows that the proper person to decide how children should be introduced to such things is the parent, not the pedlar of obscenity. Public obscenity conflicts with this approach by exposing children to influences which their parents may well prefer them not to be exposed to. So does the sale and distribution of obscenity to children.

In these two ways obscenity lessens liberty. Those who protest in the name of freedom against any restriction on obscenity should reflect that freedom here works in two opposite directions. Freedom *for* obscenity is one thing, freedom *from* it is another. Which is the more important?

Human dignity
But are there other highly important, if non-essential values that are threatened by obscenity? What about the value we set on human dignity? One heartening feature in our present society is a growing recognition of the dignity of man – and more particularly the dignity of *woman*. It is no accident that some of the strongest protests of women's lib have been against the use of women as sex-objects in advertisements, in obscenity and in pornography. To view women as mere objects of sexual gratification, such protestors rightly argue, is to degrade not only the women being used but also the men making use of them: it is to look on both as less than persons. And this, some say, is symptomatic of a general cultural and moral decline in values.

But has there been any such general, moral and cultural decline? Has there been a change in general values? Has it been for the worse? And is it due to obscenity?

Changing values?
First, are our values changing? There is certainly a change in the way we talk, the kind of books we read, and the kind of plays and movies we see. Take language: four-letter words, once taboo and never used in polite conversation or mixed company, are now used widely. 'Not bloody likely' – Eliza Doolittle's famous line in Shaw's *Pygmalion*, the original of *My Fair Lady* – caused a sensation in its time: today's audiences wouldn't lift an eyebrow.

Or take literature, 'Bad money drives out good,' says Gresham's law. Is there a similar law regarding books? Will obscene books drive less obscene ones from the marketplace? Not long ago *Lady Chatterley's Lover* sold like hot cakes; today it can't be found in sleazier bookstores – they're all too full of spicier wares like sodomy, flagellation, bestiality and other vices.

But what about our moral values? Has there also been a change in attitude to marriage, sex and privacy? Free love is more openly accepted, co-habitation without formal marriage more common and group sex more widespread. Privacy is less jealously protected: parts of the human form once kept hidden are now revealed in public; acts once considered strictly private are now performed in public view. And sex is increasingly commercialised. Not that sex hasn't always been on sale – the oldest profession is the prostitute's. All the same, wasn't there once a generally accepted, if unarticulated view, that certain things like friendship aren't really for sale? And didn't this to some extent apply to sex? Today we see sex or its counterfeit increasingly exploited, packaged and commercialised.

A change for the worse?
Is this change in moral attitudes and values a change for the worse? Are art and language any the poorer for the increase in sexual elements and in four-letter

words? Or was our previous art and language unnaturally emasculated? For instance, was there something ridiculous about the way yesterday's adventure
heroes, paling beneath their tan, used euphemisms because 'bloody' was taboo?
What about literary taste? 'Good taste,' as Emile Faguet pointed out, 'develops
through reading bad books so long as you read good ones too.' And what about
the earlier view on marriage and sex? Was it a sounder one, or was it on the contrary too imbued with hypocrisy? Are present day attitudes more liberated and
more healthy?

Take first of all obscenity in language. The problem with four-letter words,
for instance, is that their constant use impoverishes language. Sparingly used,
words denoting sexual and excretory functions can serve two useful purposes:
they can refer to the activities themselves or can be used to shock. Employed
more frequently, they lose their purpose and simply distract from what is being
discussed. Used constantly, as nowadays increasingly, they degenerate into boring ritualistic noises preventing more discriminating use of language. Our language has a million words. How sad to only use a mere half a dozen all the time!

Or take obscenity in books and plays and movies. The trouble is not that it
exists, but that its success seems to require all other books and so on to conform
to this particular pattern. Some authors have complained of being forced to include obscenity in order to get published. 'Today,' said Shaw, 'it is the sexless
novel that should be distinguished; the sex novel is now normal.' This militates
against variety, for if sex novels have their place, then so have sexless ones, or
literature is impoverished.

What about ordinary morality? Do changes in our attitudes to sex, privacy
and so on affect society for the worse? Lord Devlin, in a famous paper, argued
that a society owes its existence less to its institutions than to the shared morality that binds society together, and therefore anything that affects that shared
morality adversely is seriously harmful to society.

The thesis, though, is only partly true. As we have argued earlier, society
couldn't exist without accepting certain basic values, principles and standards.
On things like violence and truth a shared morality is essential. But this doesn't
mean that all the values in our shared morality are basic and essential, or that
decline in one value spells decline in all the rest. First, not all our values are
essential. Our rules about property, for instance, aren't: some principles about
property we have to have, as we have seen, but no society need have those very
property principles we have – the principle of private ownership, for instance. A
society could own all property in common without ceasing to count as a society.

What about values concerning sex, marriage and privacy? Are these essential
values? Some rules and principles about these things are clearly necessary. In
order to continue its stock of members a society must take some provision for

procreation and child-rearing, but not necessarily the provision we make. Again, sex is such a driving force that some rules and standards are needed, but again not necessarily the ones we have. Or again, maybe some principle of privacy is essential to our well being: maybe each person has a need for private space and private time, but again not necessarily in those matters where we want it. Societies could exist and have existed with quite different attitudes from ours to all these things. On these our shared morality is less essential than our shared morality on truth and violence.

But does a change in non-essential values bring about a similar change in fundamental values? There's little evidence, in fact, that change in attitude to sex necessarily results in change in attitude to truth and violence. A loosening of older attitudes to sex is quite compatible with holding fast to older attitudes to these other things. Would those who constantly decry the present decline in moral values prefer earlier societies with their insensitiveness to violence, poverty and suffering? Our shared morality, as Professor Hart pointed out in criticism of Devlin, is not the seamless web this thesis makes it out to be.

All the same, the Devlin thesis isn't without appeal. Decline in moral attitudes to sex may be symptomatic of a general moral decline. We may today set less moral value on sex, not just because of change in attitudes to sex, but because we set less moral value of *anything*. Sincere change in moral attitude is one thing, mere growing indifference is another. And indifference about moral values generally, including those concerning truth and violence, is detrimental to society.

But is our change in attitude to sex in any case a decline? Perhaps not, but some would say that the pornography industry's view of sex as something devoid of individuality, personality and intimacy, as something seen in standardized and purely physical terms, would, if taken seriously, reduce something magical to something at best animal and at worse mechanical. And this would be to lessen human dignity. Yet the less respect we have for human dignity, the less is our society worth living in. In the long run human happiness depends on self-respect and respect for others as individual persons. Obscenity and pornography, then, could produce a change for the worse in our attitudes regarding human dignity.

A change due to what?
But in so far as there is such a change in attitude, is it due to increased obscenity? Or has the increased obscenity resulted from our change in attitude? It's hard to tell. It's difficult to determine the relationship between obscenity and change in moral standards. So many complex factors influence these standards that we cannot isolate the impact of obscenity. Theory suggests, as we said earlier, that if decent books can inculcate acceptable attitudes and moral values,

then equally, a person can acquire perverse attitudes and values from obscene writings. Empirical evidence however is inconclusive. The US Commission's researches show that exposure to pornography makes people see less harm in such material and be less anxious to restrict it, and that those with more recent experience of erotic material tend to tolerate homosexuality, pre-marital intercourse and the non-reproductive functions of intercourse more than do those without experience. All the same, they don't prove that this is a consequence of that experience.

There is, however, another aspect of obscenity. The whole point of obscenity is either to shock or else to titillate. Chances are, the more obscenity we see, the more indifferent to it we become: familiarity breeds contempt. We know this from our own experience: loud music makes us deaf – we have to turn the volume up; brash advertisements makes us blasé, so they must grow increasingly aggressive; and obscenity dulls the capacity for shock, disgust and titillation. 'Extensive exposure to sexually explicit material,' the US Commission's research confirmed, 'leads to a satiation effect and a diminished desire for further viewing, even though the material is fully available.'

Obscenity and pornography, then, are self-defeating. To keep on shocking or disgusting us, purveyors of obscenity must constantly extend the margin of the shocking and disgusting. To all things, though, there is a limit. Shock, disgust and titillation are no exceptions. Pornography, then, blunts our sensitivity to obscenity and leaves our appetite jaded. In one way, perhaps, this is no bad thing. Perhaps the Danes' increased lack of interest in obscenity since they legalized it is to be welcomed. Yet all the same, is lack of sensitivity – an inability to be shocked, disgusted or stimulated by obscenity – something to be complacent about?

PART FIVE

EDUCATION FOR SEXUALITY

ANN BARRETT, BONNIE BEAN AND MARILYNN RYAN

A short course on sexuality for ten-to-twelve-year-olds

'What would happen if we ran a sex education course for ten-to-twelve-year-olds in small, mixed groups?'
'How much anatomy and physiology do grade six students need?'
'Will the students open up about their concerns?'
'Will parents support us?'

These were some of the questions that kept arising as we set out to design and present a course on sexuality to grade six children as part of an after-four program at Oriole Park School in North Toronto. This paper discusses some of the problems resolved during planning and presentation of such a course to twenty-seven students. We will also describe student concerns, level of knowledge, peer interaction, and general reactions to the various topic areas explored, along with our own impressions. Our aims for the program were:
1 To help students develop positive attitudes towards their sexuality by exploring attitudes about masculinity and feminity and by giving correct factual information. This would include both physical and emotional aspects of changes that take place. We felt it was important to help develop a positive self-image for both sexes and reaffirm that bodily changes and the anxieties about them are natural.
2 To help students develop decision-making skills as a basis for intelligent, fulfilling behaviour.
    One of our first concerns was that parents know what we were doing, support our aims, and be confident of our ability to present the course. Some parents who knew of our interest and experience in the area were strongly behind us and

obtained the backing of the Parents' Association for such a course. Not surprisingly, many school administrations are hesitant to introduce programs in potentially sensitive areas without strong parental support. In this case, the parent organizations indicated their support and interest and the administration, taking the lead from this obvious positive response, then endorsed the plan. The idea for such a course, called 'Growth and Human Relationships,' was first introduced to all parents by means of a letter which briefly described the course content and invited parents to meet the three presenters at an evening get-together.

At this meeting, attended by thirty parents, we introduced ourselves, outlined the course, and answered questions. Parental concerns centred on course design and logistics; they wondered how their own children would be affected by the course and how they as parents could supplement or reinforce what was being done. Questions arose such as 'Would leaders keep the same group each week?'; 'What resource materials would be used?'; and 'How will an only child feel in a mixed group?' These led to more general concerns about the bathing of children together and parental nudity. The parents held very strongly that their children needed to talk about feelings, and therefore agreed with the small group approach.

Although we were confident that the students could benefit from such a course, another area of concern was whether they wanted it. In announcing the course to the students we wanted to attract their attention, stimulate interest, and have them think of the course as fun. Any association with school or formal classwork had to be scrupulously avoided. Our choice of advertisement was a colourful flyer. It got a positive response, and twenty-seven of thirty possible grade six students signed up.

Our third area of concern was how most effectively to accomplish, in eight one-hour periods, our heroic aims, particularly with students who had already spent a full day in school. We planned each session so that blocks of small-group work would be broken up by some diversion such as a movie or a game and tried to set a relaxed, open climate by having a popular record playing ten minutes before each session started as we were setting up the room. We chose records currently popular with this age group and in addition left out a number of books such as Peter Mayle's *Where Did I Come From?*. The students soon learned that it was acceptable to come in early, browse through the books, chat with us or help set up the audio-visual equipment. This activity helped to produce a comfortable atmosphere.

In the process of planning the course, the three of us spent at least sixty hours in discussion and preparation, plus unmeasured other time previewing movies, reading books, and mulling over ideas in our heads. We came up with the following course.

Our first session was called 'What is sexuality all about anyway?' We first met in our groups which had been organized with suggestions from a teacher who knew all the students. We attempted to split up cliques and have an equal number of boys in each group. We ended up with three or four boys in each group of nine students. Each group talked about the basic ground rules they felt would make the group run most effectively. They came up with the following suggestions: no talking when someone else is; everyone has the right to his/her own opinions; everyone should have a chance to be heard; no one can be forced to talk if he/she feels uncomfortable. They seemed amazed to hear from the adults that it was all right to disagree with the adult. Although the groups often needed reminding about the ground rules, from time to time a student would recall one of them in order to facilitate progress.

Feeling that we needed something relevant to start the course that would also catch their attention, we put together an eight-minute slide show. We claimed that the show was about sexuality, and included slides of young children, teens, families, and older people. A few of the slides were taken from professional pictures – several from old masters and one from a Rodin sculpture. Most, however, were borrowed from family, friends, or any source. We accompanied the slide show with a record. Before starting the show, we asked our groups for their definition of sexuality. They came up with such ideas as growth, talking about yourself, how your body works, feelings. The one term they hesitated to use, and brought forth with giggles, was the term sex. During the slides, they giggled at ones showing naked children but paid close attention to the entire show. In discussing the slides in the groups, they expressed easily how such pictures as naked children, teenagers holding hands, and a wedding scene illustrated sexuality. More discussion was generated by pictures of an old person hugging a doll and a man standing alone on a beach.

The students decided that sexuality was 'how we feel about our body, ourselves, friends, and people.' They expressed curiosity in the whole area but admitted to feeling embarrassed about talking about their bodies. One group said that they were ready and mature enough to deal with the topic, but that younger children should not be told about sex. They felt in a way they shouldn't laugh about the subject 'because it is serious stuff.' Some of the students spoke very openly about their feelings, others were more reluctant but joined in by head shaking or nodding. The atmosphere in the groups became progressively more relaxed.

Session two dealt with acceptable and inacceptable feelings. We felt it was important to spend time on this topic at this point since the students had expressed some feelings about the idea of sex. We also planned to talk about their bodies from the point of view of the changes that were taking place, and their feelings about these changes.

To start them thinking about feelings as opposed to ideas, we played an animal game. Each person was to jot down on a scrap of paper the name of the animal he would most like to be and the one he would least like to be. Each person then named the animals and explained their choices. After listing the animals chosen, we talked about the feelings related to each choice. One girl wanted most to be a monkey because they are show-offs. She said this made her feel happy and joyful. Someone else said that being a show-off made him feel uncomfortable. Several students listed such animals as minks, deer, and pigs as 'least liked,' on the grounds that they were hunted or raised to be killed. The feeling they related to was fear. We listed all the feelings, then divided them into two groups which we decided to label as 'OK' and 'Not-OK.' We felt that the former are those that make us feel good about ourselves and the latter the opposite.

Two of the three groups entered into the game with enthusiasm, whereas the third group needed a bit of prodding. Some of the students had trouble differentiating between a feeling and an idea, and as in many situations some of the group members tried to answer for others when they hesitated.

As our change-of-pace attraction we had a short movie *The Daisy*. This cartoon shows a man who wants to destroy a daisy and a little girl who loves the flower. The three characters show a range of feelings that the students found easy to identify. They related easily to the nice daisy and sweet little girl, but had to stop and consider whether there might not be some justification for the man's frustration.

In session three we introduced the body. When the people entered the room, each group found it had a full-sized cardboard cut-out of a person, in this case complete with ping-pong balls, dixie cups, balloon, and coloured string, to represent the male reproductive system. When they perceived what the various parts represented, there were great giggles from the girls. It did not take the boys long to see that Henry would easily become Henrietta next week, and then the teasing stopped. By the time we got around to talking about the testes and the penis, no one was visibly embarrassed.

None of the students knew the meaning of the word puberty, and they were vague about many of the changes that happen at this time. They admitted to feeling uncertain about these changes, although several girls and boys said they were looking forward to this time. We talked about the changes taking place inside the male body, pointing out structures on Henry. We used the correct terms but did not emphasize terms like 'epididymus' (a tube). After mentioning the name of parts other than the testes and penis, we used simpler terms such as 'tube.' We believe that children should know and be able to use correct terms for common body parts, but felt we would lose some of our audience by overwhelming them with only the medical terms for obscure parts. Our concern was to help them understand what is happening in their bodies. In general, the students were attentive through this part but had few questions. They knew very little about the structure and function of the male reproductive system. One child, being convinced penis was spelled 'penus,' tried to look it up in the class dictionary. Although other parts of the body appeared to be defined in it, reference to this part of the male anatomy could not be found!

Our visual presentation was a ten-minute movie called *Puberty in Boys* which reviewed what we had talked about and showed visually how sperm are produced. Although not an exciting film, and probably too advanced for most of them, it reinforced our small group discussions about male body changes.

On returning to groups, we got into many areas related to puberty. Wet dreams followed logically from sperm production as did masturbation. Most of the terms were new and many of the ideas as well. They were not, for instance, aware of nocturnal emissions. We were amazed by the maturity of all the students in talking about these things. Both boys and girls were keenly interested and asked intelligent questions. They brought up concerns about such things as circumcision and being unable to control erections. We also talked about the slang names associated with the male system. They enjoyed being able to openly say the slang terms, but seldom used them at other times. Ejaculation and intercourse naturally followed through questions from students such as 'What do you call that thing you do to get a baby?' Their reactions tended to be academic towards the latter topic, and many expressed a feeling of 'I'm not sure I will want to do THAT.'

In session four, Henry acquired almonds for ovaries and a dixie cup lined with plastic wrap for a uterus. We started the session once again by talking about changes that were occurring in the girls' bodies. A pelvic model, borrowed from the local Planned Parenthood office, proved helpful with the anatomy. We referred only briefly to the hormonal influences involved during menstruation. Most of the girls were aware of the fact they would menstruate but did not know many of the details. The boys appeared very vague on this subject, apparently only knowing that 'something happens to girls.' After talking about the structure and function of the female body, we had a twenty-minute movie called *Menstruation*. It effectively reviewed the process as well as talking about hygiene and feelings.

On returning to our small groups, we asked if they knew any other names for menstruation. They came up with such terms as period and curse. We then talked about some of the old ideas related to the process; for example, that one should not exercise because loss of blood makes you weak; cultural taboos; not being able to take a bath; 'bad blood.' They laughed at the myths and expressed a positive attitude towards the cycle. One athletic girl was relieved, however, to hear that swimming was possible during periods. She had been told and believed otherwise. Throughout this session questions such as 'How long does menstruation last?,' 'How often does it occur?,' and 'At what age does it start?' elicited such a variety of answers that it was evident the children had not received and/or retained adequate information.

During this session we felt the pressure of time. There was a lot to be covered, some obviously picked up ideas quicker than others, and we felt we had to keep moving on. The students were constantly sidetracking to ask questions, many of them related to birth. 'If a lady is killed in an accident, will the baby die?' 'Why take the baby out through the stomach?' 'How do you get twins?' We had decided that time did not allow for detailed talk about pregnancy and birth. This was such a strong interest, however, that we will incorporate it into our next course.

We considered it important to get the students involved as quickly as possible in the summation of the biological information, and therefore started session five with these questions:

'How big should my breasts be?'
'When you have wet dreams does it mean you could have a baby?'
'How big will my penis grow?'
'Does sperm come out when you are awake?'
'What if you don't menstruate?'
'Why do I get boners?'
'A boy I know seems to be developing in the breast; is that normal?'

Some of these questions came from our question box - a shoe box where anyone could drop in a question he or she didn't want to ask in the group. Others were ones we designed to catch points we felt we should deal with or expand. Rather than a lecture, we gave each student a question to read out and comment on if she could. This worked out very effectively in two of the groups. The other group did not get enthused about the questions so little discussion resulted.

Some of the observations we made included the following: the girls were very curious about breasts, whether they should wear bras to prevent sagging, whether it is possible to increase bust size as the magazine ads suggest, concerns about being too big, too small. In one group the girls said that their breasts would be 32" or 34" but were amazed to hear that boys worried about the size of their penis. One boy said he did not want his penis to grow too big since he could be embarrassed by 'boners.' Although many of the boys admitted to concerns about penis size, it was not related to sex with a partner. The students were surprised to realize that they would be able to reproduce within the next few years, and all said that they would not have children until they were in their twenties. They also expressed negative feelings about intercourse, and some felt they might never have children if that was how you had to get them.

In the second half of this session we shifted to the topic of masculinity and feminity. We started by dividing the kids into groups of three of the same sex. Each group was given a pile of pictures taken from magazines-mostly ads – plus scissors, glue, and a brown paper bag. We gave the following assignment: 'I want your group to create, from pictures, a collage on the bag, showing what you feel being male or female is all about and be able to talk about reasons for your choices. Use twelve to fifteen pictures, and you can write on words if you can't find a picture to express an idea you think is important.' We added the last statement since the pictures were taken from available magazines – *Good Housekeeping, Chatelaine, Sports Illustrated, Playboy* – and we realized that they were somewhat limited in scope.

After fifteen minutes of busy activity we looked at the results. Some of the bags were very broad in range; one female group had pictures representing concepts of the athletic, sexy, friendly, clean and dirty, of the housewife, mother, and fashionable woman, of feeling good about the body. A number were very interesting and gave good opportunity for discussion. One male group had nothing but pictures of athletes. Another group of boys had added the statement 'having pride in a son' with no thought for daughters. One female group consisted entirely of 'sexy' or 'seductive' pictures.

We started session six by talking about masculinity, feminity, and gender roles to finish the discussion started the previous week. Part of this summation was accomplished by a movie *Anything You Want to Be.* It is a short funny film about the dreams a young girl has for a glamorous future, and the probable reality; that is her fantasy of becoming a famous chemist turns into the reality of mixing formula. Although both boys and girls said they felt anyone could do or be anything, the paper bags and the related discussions showed that the male and female roles are strongly entrenched and that the students feel very uncomfortable about challenging them.

We felt strongly that one real need of the students was to learn how to manage not only their sexuality but also their social relationships. Since we had observed that nattering was common and often led to hurting, we put in a section dealing with 'fair fighting.' Each child was given a sheet with the following chart:

	Sticking to the topic	Not making fun	Listening to other person	Not bullying
Fighting fair				
Fighting dirty				
	Going off topic	Making fun	Not listening	Bullying (verbal or physical)

Then two of us did the following role-playing scene, taken from a classroom situation. Two girls are doing a class project. Every time Mary makes a suggestion, Barb says she knows a better way. After the giggles had subsided, everyone had to decide whether each player had been fighting fair or fighting dirty in each of the categories. We did the same situation twice, once including a lot of 'bad' fighting, once trying to be fair. We tried to draw out the idea that there was no winner or loser, but instead that the goal was to work co-operatively towards a solution. We tried to sum it up in the following way:

P – What is the real *problem* and the feeling connected with the problem?
T – Stick to the *topic* (just the facts).
A – Take some *action* that is positive (good). Did it help?

We then turned our groups loose with a sheet of role-playing situations that we had made up, or let them make up their own. They didn't hesitate to enter into both the role-playing and analysis. It was an exercise done with great enthusiasm and was a successful way of pointing out that there are constructive and destructive ways of dealing with people.

In session seven, we dealt very superficially with values. In the large group, we used the expression 'I'm OK, You're OK' to introduce the idea of the child, parent, and adult as parts of our personalities. After examples of each of these parts, we explored the possible thought process involved in making a decision whether or not to take a chocolate bar from a store: 'It would be a thrill. The storekeeper will never miss it. What if I get caught? I've got money at home so maybe I should get it.'

To give the students the chance to practice making decisions and to recognize the complexities in making choices, we had them play a game (a modification of the A B card game from *Values and Teaching* by Raths, Harmin, and Simon: Bobbs Merrill). Each person got a number from one to nine. Then the person with number one chose a card. Each card had a side A with a general statement and a side B with a specific situation. Two examples are:

'A Honesty is always the best policy.
B My best friend deliberately threw a snowball through the school window, and the principal asked me if I had done it.'
'A People are all equal no matter where they come from or what colour they are.
B The black kid gets called 'fudge face' by my friends. I feel sorry for him but don't know what to do about it.'

No one else is allowed to speak while the person is expressing his ideas, and four cards were pulled before we allowed a general discussion about any of the topics. This helped to provide a safe climate in which to express oneself. The point was not to find right or wrong answers but to consider such things as 'Is that very important to you?'; 'How do you know it is right?'; 'What are some good things about that notion?'

We had a movie break to see *Brand New Key*, a short cartoon about friendship, which provided relaxation more than stimulus for discussion, and then returned to finish the last five questions. We had used this game technique successfully with adults but were uncertain how ten- and eleven-year-olds would respond to it. Many became totally absorbed in the situations and did not want to take the movie break. They did not laugh at unusual answers, and appeared to give a lot of thought to the problems. Others had such clear-cut ideas of what was right and wrong that they produced an absolute response. Some said that 'You should never lie,' while one student made them think by suggesting that perhaps it is better to tell your grandmother the sweater she knit you is nice rather than hurt her feelings by saying it is ugly. Many of the students saw how hard it is to listen to another person when you want to add your own ideas.

Our last session was a free-wheeling review and summation begun by answering questions and adding information on topics we felt needed further work. The show box had produced more questions such as 'If I were to feel that I liked a boy how do you think I could show him?' and 'When boys go to the washroom does sperm come out?' We moved on to a movie *Up is Down*, a ten-minute cartoon. It shows a boy who was frightened by society's acceptance of hate, conformity, and competition and preferred love, individuality, and co-operation. The message seemed to be too subtle for most of them.

Next we asked each person to write a blurb, ad, message, or note to a person in another grade six class who would like to know more about the course. They were asked to tell the person their feelings about the course and whether they thought she would enjoy it and get something out of it. Our goal was primarily to get a general student reaction to the program without asking directly. The following are typical of the results:

'It's enjoyable, it's fresh and fun.'
'This course is about yourself, feelings, and sex.'
'We learned about sex and what to expect when we grow older.'
'We've got this body for the rest of our life, let's learn to live with it.'

Following this we gave a brief questionnaire. It was very subjective and was not a test of knowledge, but again helped us to judge how each individual felt about the course. The questions included: 'Did you feel comfortable working in a small group?' 'Did you feel comfortable talking about changes that are happening to your body in a mixed group?'

We have no concrete data to show whether our aims were achieved. The evaluation sheets filled out anonymously indicated a strong positive feeling in general. Only one person felt uncomfortable working in small groups and would have preferred a large group arrangement. Half of the group expressed uneasiness in talking about sexuality at the start of the program. Only one felt uncomfortable at the end. The majority also stated that they would not have preferred a group with members of the same sex only. All felt they had learned things about the opposite sex, as well as increased understanding of changes in their own bodies, and all but three felt they were now more aware of the feelings of others as well as their own.

Another indicator we used was the fact that attendance was voluntary. All the students knew this, but during the eight weeks only one child missed once.

There has been a lot of feedback from parents, all positive, ranging from 'My son now knows about menstruation' to 'My daughter seems to feel much better about herself.'

In our view we were correct in feeling that the years from ten to twelve were a good time to introduce the subject of sexuality. The students were interested in the topic, but not yet immersed in their own reactions to awakening sex drives. In this group, some of the boys and girls were at the flirting stage but none were involved in dating. They seemed to take in such facts as 'You must have intercourse if you are going to get pregnant' without any thoughts that they might do it themselves.

Finally, some random thoughts and suggestions for anyone contemplating such a program:

1 Plan to invest a lot of time in preparation of the content and previewing audio-visual material.

2 Be realistic in the number of topics you attempt to cover in your time allotment. In our enthusiasm we probably tried to include too much and felt constantly pressured by time.

3 Be comfortable with group dynamics. Be prepared to handle a disturber or people who attempt to monopolize the discussion, but to do so without destroying the atmosphere of the group.

4 Small groups are a must. You can feel confident that they work well with proper climate setting. They are the best way to generate maximum involvement and participation.

5 Anticipate parents who are willing and eager to be more heavily involved in the program. Feed them information to the level of your willingness and time. Have a policy thought out about parents 'dropping in to watch.' We felt it would be disruptive and therefore discouraged the practice. The same applied to interested outsiders who were thinking of doing a course themselves.

6 Try to have a man as one of the group leaders. Children should see that it is not just women who are able to talk about the facts and feelings related to sexuality. It is important to find ways to involve males in the program. If this is impossible, men should be clearly shown in the films and other media used.

7 We see this course as only one part of the on-going process of sexual education of the children involved.

ACKNOWLEDGMENT

We wish to express our gratitude to Peggy Jones who provided moral support and valuable suggestions, and to the Sex Information and Education Council of Canada which provided resource material, financial support, and suggestions. We also thank Gloria Torrance, Health Co-ordinator, Toronto Board of Education, for making resource material available.

The authors are all members of the Education Committee of the Sex Information and Education Council of Canada, former teachers at the high school or primary level, and themselves parents.

REFERENCES

Mayle, Peter, *Where Did I Come From?*, New Jersey: Lyle Stuart Inc., 1973.

The Daisy, Todor Dinov, Bulgaria: 1968 (in Canada: Marlin Motion Pictures), 5 minutes, colour, sound.

Burt, J. and L. Brown, *Education for Sexuality: Concepts and Programs for Teachers*, Toronto: W.B. Saunders Co.

Puberty in Boys, National Film Board of Canada, 1969, 9 minutes, colour, sound.

Menstruation, Johnson and Johnson Co. Ltd., 20 minutes, colour, sound.

Anything You Want to Be, Liane Brandon: 1971 (Marling Motion Pictures), 8 minutes, black and white.

Bach, George R. and Peter Wyden, *The Intimate Enemy*, Avon Books, 1968.

Harris, Thomas A., *I'm OK, You're OK*, New York: Harper and Row.

Raths, Harmin and Simon, *Values and Teaching*, Bobbs Merrill.

Brand New Key, John Wilson, 1973, International Telefilm, 3 minutes, colour, sound.

Up is Down, Goldsholl & Associates, 1969, International Telefilm, 10 minutes, sound, colour.

MARION G. POWELL

The role of the school counsellor in sex counselling*

Sexuality is a continuum which begins in infancy and ceases only at death. It is an integral part of our total personality. One of the critical points on the continuum is adolescence, when the child merges with the adult and conflict arises between the adolescent and his family as adult behaviour replaces childhood sexual attitudes.

Sex has always existed within the age group attending high school today. Unless a crisis arose, such as a pregnancy, it was ignored or handled discreetly by the family or school staff. Sex carried an aura of disapproval, because any open discussion begun by school staff would convey to parents an approval of intimate boy-girl relationships. However, several changes have occurred over the past decade. Studies have been published in England and the United States giving details about the attitudes and behaviour among teenagers with percentages tabulated of those engaging in intercourse.[1] An openness towards sex on college campuses finally forced university administrators to accept the reality of what had been happening for many years and led to a relaxing of rules, particularly in regard to dormitories. This was followed by a reluctant acceptance on the part of parents of the sexual behaviour of their college-age sons and daughters. This same awareness of the sexual behaviour of their younger children has come into focus as statistics on VD, illegitimacy, abortions, and the large number of sixteen-, seventeen-, and eighteen-year-old girls attending birth control clinics have been published.

*Reprinted from *The School Guidance Worker* 29 (May-June 1974), 4-8.

There are many reasons behind the change in sexual behaviour among adolescents, but the easiest explanation lies in the change in physical maturation of teenagers over the past century and the changing expectations and educational patterns of today's youth. It has been well documented that there has been a decline in the age of puberty, using the onset of menses as an indicator in girls, from 16.5 years in 1870 to 12.5 years in the 1950s.[2] This change is largely the result of improved nutrition and health during the pre-adolescent years. This earlier physical maturity, which also occurs in boys, leads boys to reach the peak of their virility before the age of twenty years. In girls, the ability to conceive and carry the pregnancy to term accounts at least in part for the increase in illegitimate births. Spontaneous abortions in teen-age girls solved many problems which must now be met by contraceptive services.

In recognition of the needs of these young people, sex education courses giving explicit information about contraception and venereal disease are being taught in many schools. Information about sexual response may be included as a topic of discussion. Despite this information pregnancies still occur with alarming frequency, prompting critics to declare that education may even encourage young people to engage in sex. One valid criticism of sex education is that many questions are left unanswered and it is these unanswered questions that lead to frustration on the part of students. Many teachers cannot give satisfying answers in response to concerns of all children reaching puberty. Where can the adult be found who can reassure the child without preaching or moralizing? Parents in many families have difficulty discussing menstruation, nocturnal emission, physical development, and masturbation – topics for which children reaching puberty want reassurance as well as information. For the child at home or in school who cannot find an adult to answer questions about physical maturation there is no one who will take on sensitive topics such as contraception and intercourse. The unanswered questions may motivate him to seek alternate sources of help. The embarrassment of asking information in class may make him write an anonymous letter to a sex information column in a newspaper or phone in to a distress centre. It is well known that the parents are usually the last source of help.

Is it realistic for guidance counsellors to become involved with students needing information and counselling on sexual matters? Are there not better qualified professionals who are already skilled in this area? There is a strong argument in favour of training the school counsellor who is already dealing with many aspects of students' lives and has skills in counselling. To move into this personal area he needs help in expanding and extending his training to enable him to understand the sexual dimension of students' lives. The role of sex counsellor is one of the more difficult positions in which a teacher may find himself. He is very vulnerable when he is taking the place of a parent and giving advice, information, and counselling in a domain which has been exclusively the responsibility of the family. There will have to be a major transition in his own attitude towards the student. Sympathy towards youth's changing values and sensitivity to the sexual needs of teenagers will force him to examine his own sexuality.

In the first place he must recognize he has grown up in an era which has been strongly influenced by the repressed attitudes of the past. He has misconceptions, misinformation, and anxieties about sexuality. There have been few opportunities for education in sexuality for any professional until very recently. Sex was discussed in the washroom often in the context of crude jokes or bragged-about performance; or it was an activity confined to the bedroom, under the covers and in the dark. In most areas in which students request counselling, the teacher's maturity, common sense, and experience give the best guidelines to follow in seeking solutions to problems. However, these three personal attributes will be of little use when he is counselling about sexuality. The taboos of the past have made it impossible to be open and frank in sexual matters because of the inseparable association of sex and reproduction with the inevitable double standard which accompanied it.

The preparation of the adult who is willing to take on the role of sexual counsellor begins with a self-examination that is aimed at increasing his own awareness of his sexuality. Before he can discuss with students their practices and preferences he must make a clear appraisal of his own attitudes. In many cases the counsellor must recognize the limitations of his own experience and not attempt to judge others by his own past performance. We usually define sex in terms of performance and competence; however, we recognize it has many other facets and dimensions. There is a wide variation of what is acceptable sexually from person to person. The counsellor, recognizing his own biases, can be sensitive to the needs of the young person on one hand and yet be careful not to impose his own attitude and behaviour on the other hand. Continuing the self-examination, he must be aware of the wide range of normal sexual practice and become familiar with the current knowledge and research about sexuality.

Sex language has developed as a colourful way of expressing and communicating about sex. The rich and diverse terms are easily and effectively used to communicate between friends and close associates yet have been unacceptable in a discussion between parent and child or student and teacher. Keeping in mind that this may be the one language in which a teenager can communicate the counsellor must become desensitized to the use of these terms. The shock of the counsellor in response to the use of slang in his office is one way of effectively letting the teenager know that sex is one topic that is unacceptable.

Sensitive areas in sexuality, such as homosexuality, premarital sex, abortion, and sexual behaviour other than intercourse, must be faced and discussed with a spouse or colleague in an attempt to sort out feelings the counsellor may have. He is not responsible for being uncomfortable in these areas but he is responsible for keeping these feelings from being transferred to the young people he is counselling. The keys to a successful interview lie in the attitude and ability of the counsellor to deal with an intimate area of behaviour with sensitivity and understanding.

Once the counsellor has worked his way through his own feelings and reached the actual session with a student seeking help his needs become practical. In this era of the published word, where among the hundreds of sex manuals does the counsellor find one or two that will give him the answers he needs? It is almost impossible to choose those that give accurate information from among the hundreds on the book shelves. These manuals, written by sex educators, paediatricians, psychologists, physicians, and sociologists are also being read by students, and it is embarrassing for the counsellor to find that the student's knowledge often surpasses his own. The requests for referral to a clinic or doctor and the questions about normal sex can be answered by simple information obtained from the local health department, the school nurse, or the medical society. Knowing where such information is available and in turn making it readily available through the guidance office can be time-consuming in a department which is short-staffed and already overburdened with requests for counselling.

There is merit in group discussions which may take place in a sex education class, in an informal 'rap session' in the counsellor's office, the school nurse's room, or in a birth control clinic. In these sessions the counsellor may act only as the catalyst and his role may be one of listener. There comes a time, however, when listening is not sufficient and he must be free to move into the role of sex counsellor.

In today's society the concerns of parents and educators are still closely related to the sexual behaviour of girls. With the consequences for the adolescent girl still uppermost in adults' anxiety about teenage sexuality, the double standard is very evident in services provided for youth. Pregnancy, with its various alternative solutions and with birth control clinics offering oral contraceptives, have made the adolescent male the forgotten partner in teenage sex. His needs are overlooked and his access to professional counselling is limited. He is rarely included in interviews in doctors' offices or birth control clinics. Staff in these clinics frequently express concern about the male partner and would welcome him if he came with his girlfriend. But he prefers to wait outside because he too has come to regard the pill as a responsibility of the girl. Frequently he is more in need of counselling than his girlfriend who has had all the attention focused on her needs. He has had an important part in the relationship as it developed. If contraception was practised it was a drugstore method that was his sole responsibility or required his co-operation. In the pattern of adolescent sexuality that is emerging, when the relationship progresses to a more permanent one, a more reliable method of contraception is chosen. The pill is the most popular method used by young people who are committed to a sexual relationship. Once the decision has been made the woman assumes sole responsibility.

In the past, society regulated sexual activity, at least among women, by taboos based on fear, emotional restraint, and silence. The taboos are being lifted by effective contraception, which provides a social control of some of the consequences. The choice being given to the adolescent is no longer being based on taboos but on the right of individual choice. Choices today are also being based on the changing role of women, changing attitudes towards marriage and parenthood, and an economic structure in our society that allows for a greater variety in life styles and an increasing acceptance of sex outside marriage based on love only. The pattern of sexual behaviour during adolescence is one of serial monogamous relationships. With less pressure to marry and have children and the acceptability of delaying childbearing, the behaviour of youth appears to be both healthy and valid. Sociologists predict a greater stability for marriage and family life in the future. Sexual patterns of behaviour will not pose a threat to either marriage or the family. However, it would be safe to assume that sexual satisfaction, which is a part of teenage sex, will continue to be important once the young people do marry. Their need for a satisfying sexual relationship and the effort they are willing to make to achieve this goal of satisfaction predicts a bright future for them within a marriage relationship. The emerging attitudes towards sexuality as not only a means of obtaining pleasure but as a way of enhancing and supporting a relationship has been one of the positive benefits of the sexual revolution of this century.

Being able to counsel students about sexuality has implied in the past an implicit approval of their behaviour. This fact has prevented many school guidance workers from opening up the discussion. The counsellor's ease with his own sexuality will enable him to meet the young people where they are, without any need to condemn or condone. As attitudes towards sexuality become more open it is well to keep in mind that many who are openly discussing sex are very traditional in their behaviour. There may be a large number of adolescents in our schools who are having intercourse but there are as many or more who hold traditional views about sex. These young people need to be helped to understand the validity of their position and to be given the same respect that is being given to those who have adopted more liberalized behaviour.

The information teenagers are looking for today in relation to their sexuality is closely related to their actual needs. They seldom seek help out of curiosity. Protecting them by denying them information about sex in an attempt to delay their emergence into the adult world of sexuality is impossible. Sexuality is a normal aspect of growing up, and interest in sexuality springs from normal life processes which are part of every human's development. Interest in sexuality cannot be avoided, nor can it be confined or sublimated by withholding information from young people. Sexuality is more than intercourse, and sex counselling is more than providing answers to technical and physical questions. Sex counselling is not providing a list of acceptable and unacceptable behaviour in accordance with parents' and teachers' standards. School counsellors may fail to take into consideration ethnic background, religious training, education, and cultural influences of the student. The counsellor uses his own values as a starting point. His values are frequently based on urban living, college education, and middle class experience.

The most commonly occurring problems among teenagers in high school will continue to be in relation to pregnancy, contraception, and VD. However, as more stress is being placed on sexual response the number of young people seeking help with sexual dysfunction will increase. Already the number of young people seeking help with premature ejaculation, impotence, and failure to reach orgasm is forcing clinic personnel, physicians, and school nurses to develop skills in dealing with their patients.

Involvement of high school boys in discussions of sex will open the way to improving personal consultations when problems arise. Expectations are still being placed on boys to achieve in the area of sex. It follows that admission of a problem is an admission of failure.

In summary, the school counsellor is finding himself in the role of sex counsellor on more occasions than in the past. The discrete solution of an adolescent's sexual problem is no longer acceptable in today's freer society. The openness with which sex is discussed is increasing the pressure on the professional to develop skills and understanding in sexuality. There is a need for teachers to examine their own sexuality in order to equip them to deal with students in this intimate area. The role of the guidance counsellor in human sexuality has been established but he is not automonically able to add this new dimension to his counselling. Time spent in re-education and the extra time required to give students the help they are seeking will be well rewarded as the young people seek answers to their problems before the crisis arises. If we are willing to be part of the counselling of the total personality of the teenager, sexuality will become an integral part of all guidance counselling in high schools.

NOTES

1 Robert C. Sorenson, *Adolescent Sexuality in Contemporary America* (New York: World Publishing, 1973). Michael Schofield, *The Sexual Behaviour of Young People* (London: Pelican Books, 1965).
2 J.M. Tanner, 'Earlier Maturation in Man,' *Scientific American* 218, no. 1 (1968).

MARION G. POWELL AND BENJAMIN SCHLESINGER

A course on human sexuality
for Canadian graduate social work students

INTRODUCTION

A few years ago, the first paper appeared in a social work journal which mentioned the necessity of introducing human sexuality content in the social work curriculum. Harvey Gochros[1] stated:

Explicit references to human sexual problems are rare in social work literature. When these references do appear, they are generally presented as one aspect of a client's behaviour which is incorporated into an overall psycho-social diagnosis, or they are regarded as 'symptoms' of a more general disease process which can not be treated as a specific entity. Sexual dysfunctioning is rarely portrayed as a discrete entity in itself, amenable to and requiring social work intervention. Social Workers have made little visible effort to undertake the epidemiological or practice research necessary to more effectively understand the nature of sexual problems and how to deal with them. (p. 47)

In 1972, Gochros and Schultz[2] published the first book of readings on human sexuality and social work. Further support in relation to this area came in a paper by Abramovitz[3] in which she reports a small study of the level of sex knowledge of a group of social work students. The findings seemed to indicate that no significant learning in the area of sexual knowledge had been acquired in the school of social work. She compared these results to studies with other professional students in medicine, law, and graduate studies. Social work students came out quite poorly in the sex knowledge area. She concluded her paper by stating: 'Basic understanding of human sexuality with a diminution of student anxiety in this area is a necessary part of the professional education of the social worker.' (p. 354)

The School of Social Work at the University of Hawaii at this time has the most complete program in Human Sexuality and Social Work.[4] There are five courses, field instruction, and research in this area offered for interested students.

THE CANADIAN SCENE

In 1971 the author offered the first course on Human Sexuality and Social Work in Canada.[5] With the support of the Family Planning Division of Health and Welfare, Canada, the Canadian Association of Schools of Social Work sponsored a symposium, 'Human Sexuality and Fertility Services,' in Hamilton in 1972.[6] Fifteen schools were represented to discuss this broad area of concern.

Following a workshop in May, 1973 in Kingston, Ontario, one of the authors surveyed Canadian schools of social work and prepared a paper to indicate the extent of human sexuality content in Canadian curricula.[7]

THE UNIVERSITY OF TORONTO COURSE

The course was jointly taught by the authors of this paper. We developed fourteen two-hour sessions for which twenty students registered (15 women and 5 men). The outline of the session and our guest lecturers were as follows:

Week 1 Introduction to Human Sexuality. Professor Michael Barrett, President of Sex Information and Education Council of Canada. A discussion of historical aspects in Canada, related to sexual attitudes about masturbation, sexuality, and the 'avoided subjects' in the early 1900s.
Reference: Michael Bliss, 'How We Used to Learn about Sex,' *Maclean's* (March 1974), 38 and 61-66.

Week 2 Human Sexual Response. Professor M. Powell and Professor B. Schlesinger. An overview of the findings of Sex Research Studies, Implications for Counselling, and Treatment.
References: (1) Fred Belleveau and Lin Richter, *Understanding Human Sexual Inadequacy* (New York: Bantam Books, 1970); (2) Ruth Brecher and Edward Brecher, eds., *An Analysis of Human Sexual Response* (New York: Signet, 1966); (3) Edward M. Brecher, *The Sex Researchers* (New York: Signet, 1970).

Week 3 Sexuality and Childhood Adolescence. Dr. Sara Isbister, University of Toronto Health Service. An examination of the major findings of studies related to the biological, physical, psychological and social aspects of sexuality in this age group. Relevance to social work intervention.

Reference: R.C. Sorenson, *Adolescent Sexual Behaviour in Contemporary America* (New York: World Publishing Co., 1973).

Week 4 Sexuality in Middle and Old Age. Professor Marion Powell. Emphasis is placed on the awareness that sexuality has been a neglected area of study and concern in this age group. Findings of research studies are presented.
References: (1) Benjamin Schlesinger and Richard Albert Mullen, 'Sexuality and the Aged,' *Medical Aspects of Human Sexuality* (Can. ed.), 3 (Nov. 1973), 46-53; (2) Isadore Rubin, *Sexual Life After Sixty* (New York: Signet, 1965); (3) Ivor Felstein, *Sex in Later Life* (London: Pelican, 1973).

Week 5 Sexuality and Reproduction. Professor Connie Swinton, School of Hygiene, University of Toronto. An overview of chemical and non-chemical methods of contraception. Ten methods are discussed, and these include sterilization. The effectiveness of each method is presented, as well as some of the negative aspects of each birth control method.
References: (1) Lionel Gendron, *Contraception* (Montreal: Harvest House, 1971); (2) Donna Cherniak and Allan Feingold, *Birth Control Handbook*, 10th edition (Handbook Collective, PO Box 1000, Station G, Montreal 130, Quebec).

Week 6 Sexual Counselling. Dr. Len Goldsmith, Psychologist, Toronto General Hospital. A discussion of sexual counselling in an interdisciplinary setting. Illustrated with case materials.
Reference: Patricia Schiller, *Creative Approach to Sex Education and Counselling* (New York: New York Association Press, 1973).

Week 7 Sexual Behaviour. Professor Benjamin Schlesinger. A review of abnormal methods of sexual functioning, choice of sexual partners, and strength of sexual drive. Case illustrations and letters to editors of sex journals are used to illustrate the various areas of this topic.
References: (1) Harold Greenwald and Ruth Greenwald, *The Sex-Life Letters* (New York: Bantam Books, 1973); (2) James Leslie McCary, *Human Sexuality* (Toronto: Van Nostrand, 1967), Chapter 14, 'Sexual Abberrations,' pp. 273-309.

Week 8 Sexual Counselling. Two films, one illustrating a case of female frigidity and the other a case of male impotence, were shown and discussed. In the first film, the patient was a woman; in the second film the couple came to see the therapist.
Reference: Ortho Pharmaceutical Co., Films on the Training of Human Sexuality in Medical Education.

Week 9 Male and Female Homosexuality. George Hislop and Nancy Walker from CHAT (Community Homophile Association of Toronto). An open and frank discussion of the position of homosexuals in Canadian Society. The male and female viewpoints were discussed.
References: (1) George Weinberg, *Society and the Healthy Homosexual* (New York: St. Martin's Press, 1972); (2) *Operation Socrates Handbook: Male and Female Homosexuality* (Waterloo: University of Waterloo, 1973).

Week 10 Touching. A seventeen-minute film showing the sexual relationship between a male paraplegic and his uninjured partner. A full discussion took place about the feelings of seminar members towards the various sexual forms of gratification illustrated in the film.
Source: Multi Media Resource Centre, San Francisco, California, USA.

Week 11 Sexuality and the Mentally Retarded. Dr. Rena Paul, Metropolitan Toronto Department of Welfare. A discussion of the problems faced by the mentally retarded, especially in the area of sexuality. Sex education and its difficulties for this group was reviewed and discussed.
Reference: Felix F. de la Cruz, and Gerald D. La Veck eds., *Human Sexuality and the Mentally Retarded* (New York: Bruner-Mazel, 1973).

Week 12 Sexuality and the Law. Alex. K. Gigeroff, lawyer, Clarke Institute of Psychiatry, Toronto. A discussion of the Criminal Code of Canada, and its sections on sex offences, including penalties. Sexual criminal statistics were also reviewed.
References: (1) Alex. K. Gigeroff, *Sexual Deviations in the Criminal Law* (Toronto: University of Toronto Press, 1968); (2) *The Criminal Code of Canada*, ed. by Cartwright (Toronto: Canada Law Book Ltd., 1970).

Week 13 Sex Education. Professor Donald H. Brundage, Ontario Institute for Studies in Education. A discussion of sex education took place, beginning with an historical review. Questions were raised as to what sex education involves; what some of its limitations are. Also covered was the development of curriculum and teacher training programs. A discussion of some programs offered in schools took place.
References: Rose M. Somerville, *Introduction to Family Life and Sex Education* (Englewood Cliffs, NJ: Prentice-Hall, 1972).

Week 14 Evaluation and Discussion of Assignments. Except for three students, the seminar members paired off in teams of two to work on their topics. We emphasized that the paper should include a review of the literature, personal research and analysis, and a discussion of the topic's application to social work practice.

The ten chosen topics were: the aged and sexuality; adolescents and sexuality; homosexuality-male; homosexuality-female; sex counselling; sexuality and the mentally retarded; sexuality and the physically handicapped; rape; masturbation; and sexual identity.

Among the interesting field experiences by the students doing this assignment were: interviews with high school students, homosexuals (male and female), and professionals working with the aged, retarded, and handicapped. Many students visited institutions to find out how the area of sexuality was dealt with by the staff. We were impressed by the amount of work undertaken for the papers, and are encouraging some of the students to publish their efforts.

EVALUATION

In our discussion about the course there were a few students who felt that the focus appeared to be on married couples and not on single people and sexuality, especially single girls. Some others felt that they would have liked to have small group discussions (groups of ten) where they would explore their own feelings, attitudes, and values about sexuality; in other words, a kind of sensitivity approach to the topic. Other students felt that they were not interested in talking about themselves but were quite satisfied at having obtained the information covered by the lectures and discussions. There was a feeling that most of them felt it easier to deal with these topics in their practice, and for many of them some misconceptions had been cleared up, especially in the research for their papers.

It is apparent that sex education of all professionals has lagged behind the education of the public through the mass media. The impact of the recent changes in sexual attitudes has been felt by everyone in society. Clients have come to expect expertise in all aspects of sexuality from the professionals they consult. The fact that formal courses in human sexuality are rarely part of the curriculum in schools of social work leads to frustration and disappointment for both client and worker.

The development of healthy sex attitudes is dependent on early childhood education. Trained professionals are no exception. The students brought into the seminar discussions their conceptions and misconceptions, information and misinformation, confidence and anxiety, regarding their own sexuality. The teaching received by the social work student provides him with no more ability to do marital and sexual counselling than the physician's study of the anatomy and physiology of the sex organs helps him to handle sexual problems in his patients.

The aim of a course in human sexuality must be to provide a bridge for the student across the gap that lies between the factual knowledge of sexuality and the understanding of the complex emotional aspects of sexual adjustment. The first need is for himself. Of secondary importance is the practical application with his clients. An accepting attitude of their sexuality, coupled with awareness of his own sexuality is an important requirement for all social workers.

We feel that a course in human sexuality should not be an elective but should be a required course for all social workers. Through courses in continuing education offered to social workers already in the field and through adequate education offered during training, a new orientation towards sexuality will be possible. Sex will cease to be bad or evil and will no longer need to be exploited and marketed, but will become a positive force in the development of deeper relationships and understanding.

It was noted that towards the end of the course the students were more willing to discuss their feelings and reactions to speakers and topics. This occasionally took the form of anger in response to a statement made during a presentation. We feel that there should be more time given for group members to express their own feelings. The course and the assignments effected a change in the students which we feel was just as important as the acquiring of knowledge and skills in the area.

COMMENTS

In offering a course on human sexuality which lasts for fourteen two-hour periods, we have to consider the following.

1 What topics do we include in this seminar? Thus the instructors have to be quite selective since this is a very broad area.

2 What emphasis should one put in a course on human sexuality? Should it be the giving of information and discussions around the various topics, or should it be a desensitizing process focussing primarily on the feelings of the seminar members about sexuality and stressing attitudes, values, standards, and misconceptions.

3 It would be difficult to combine the two approaches in such a short period and one could consider following a fourteen-week course as developed by the authors with another fifteen-week seminar which would focus primarily on feelings and attitudes and would be conducted in small groups. Thus there would be a natural sequence from the first part which allows students to explore the areas concerned and at least makes them knowledgeable, to the second part which could then focus on their own feelings.

4 A third area of concern mentioned by a few students was the desire to learn how to do sexual counselling. This part would naturally fall into the area of instruction for practice, where they are learning how to deal with individuals, families, and groups. Should this be incorporated into the existing practice courses, or should a school of social work have an optional seminar in sex counselling? This would have to be considered by the faculty concerned and be part of the total curriculum plan of a school.

5 The use of explicit films should be evaluated by faculty and students. We believe that they are useful, but that timing, planning, discussion, and follow-up are very important. It has come to our attention that some agencies providing in-service training have shown some of these films with very negative results, but in all of these cases there was no preparation, intensive discussion, and follow-up. Our limited use of the film was a very positive experience for the group.

6 It is our feeling that a seminar on human sexuality benefits from having a male and female seminar leader who can complement each other in the discussions. We also felt that the mixture of a medical and a social work teacher was beneficial in dealing with the physical, social, cultural, and psychological bases of many of the topics under discussion. Many of our students felt quite comfortable in approaching the medical practitioner for some personal advice or discussion around some of the cases in their field practice; others could discuss some of the social and psychological aspects of sexuality with the social work teacher.

7 It is also quite important that the seminar members become comfortable with each other and discuss regularly the progress of the seminar.

8 It is our hope to broaden the seminar at some stage and to make it an interdisciplinary one which would include students in social work, nursing, medicine, education, public health, and related health professions.

9 In future courses, the authors would hope to include one or more evening sessions which spouses or sexual partners would be encouraged to attend. It has been suggested that this might take the form of a weekend retreat. These sessions would lend themselves to a more informal approach and to the use of films, followed by discussion.

10 The authors met with all the students individually or in pairs and discussed the assignment. We each had read the papers separately and assigned a mark. The interview gave the students the opportunity of presenting their own evaluation of their paper and to make some comments about the course. This proved to be a valuable approach to evaluating and marking the students.

11 We feel it is important to begin with the normal physiology and psychology of sexual behaviour and relationships and then proceed to the abnormal.

NOTES

1 Harvey Gochros, 'Introducing Human Sexuality in the Graduate Social Work Curriculum,' *The Social Work Education Reporter*, XVIII (September-October 1970), 47-50.
2 Harvey Gochros and LeRoy G. Schultz, eds., *Human Sexuality and Social Work* (New York: Association Press, 1972).
3 Naomi R. Abramovits, 'Human Sexuality in the Social Work Curriculum,' *The Family Coordinator*, XX (October 1971), 349-54.
4 Harvey Gochros, 'A Concentration in Social Work Practice with Social Problems,' *Journal of Education in Social Work*, X (Spring 1974), 40-46.
5 Benjamin Schlesinger, 'Sexuality and Social Work: A Course in Human Behaviour and Social Environment: A Note and Bibliography,' *The Social Work Education Reporter*, XX (September-October 1972), 80-82.
6 Canadian Association of Schools of Social Work, *Human Sexuality and Fertility Services: Social Policy and Social Work Education* (Ottawa, 1973).
7 Benjamin Schlesinger, 'Human Sexuality and Social Work: The Canadian Scene,' *Canada's Mental Health*, XXII (June 1974), 17-20.

BIBLIOGRAPHY

Adams, Wesley J. 'The Use of Sexual Humor in Teaching Human Sexuality at the University Level,' *The Family Coordinator*, XXIII (October 1974), 365-68.
Addy, Cenovia. 'Social Work Education, Family Planning and Human Sexuality.' Ottawa: Family Planning Division, Health and Welfare Canada, May 1974, 6 pp.
– 'Family Planning Counselling.' Ottawa, November 1974, 10 pp.
– 'Philosophy of Family Planning: Implications for Social Welfare Policies and Social Work Practice.' Ottawa, November 1973, 16 pp.
Boutin, Raymond. 'The Social Worker and Family Planning.' Toronto: The Family Planning Federation of Canada, December 1973, 12 pp.
Canadian Association of Schools of Social Work. *Report of the Workshop on Family Planning and Human Sexuality*. Ottawa, 1975.
Chilman, Catherine. 'Some Knowledge Bases about Human Sexuality for Social Work Education,' *Journal of Education for Social Work*, XI (Spring 1975), 11-17.
Gochros, Harvey L. 'Introducing Human Sexuality in the Graduate Social Work Curriculum,' *Social Work Education Reporter*, XVIII (September-October 1970), 47-50.

- 'A Concentration in Social Work Practice with Sex Related Problems,' *Journal of Education for Social Work*, X (Spring 1974), 40-46.
- 'Sexual Problems in Social Work Practice,' *Social Work*, XVI (January 1971), 3-5.

Haselkorn, Florence. 'Family Planning: Implications for Social Work Education,' *Journal of Education for Social Work*, VI (Fall 1970), 13-19.
- ed. *Family Planning: Readings and Case Materials*. New York: Council on Social Work Education, 1971.

Herold, Edward, *et al*. 'Human Sexuality: A Student Taught Course,' *The Family Coordinator*, XXII (April 1973), 183-86.

Johnson, Joy, and Ord Matek. 'Critical Issues in Teaching Human Sexuality to Graduate Social Work Students,' *Journal of Education for Social Work*, X (Fall 1974), 50-55.

Schlesinger, Benjamin. 'Social Work Education and Family Planning,' *The Social Worker*, XLI (Summer 1973), 93-99.
- ed. *Family Planning in Canada: A Source Book*. Toronto: University of Toronto Press, 1974.

Tanner, Libby A. 'Teaching a Course in Human Sexuality in a Graduate School of Social Work: Strategy and Content,' *The Family Coordinator*, XXIII (July 1974), 283-89.

Ulis, David B. 'Family Living and Sex Education: A Canadian Overview.' Ottawa: Family Planning Division, Health and Welfare Canada, May 1974, 26 pp.

Valentich, Mary, and James Gripton. 'Teaching Human Sexuality to Social Work Students,' *The Family Coordinator*, XXIV (July 1975), 273-80.

CYRIL GREENLAND

Is there a future for human sexuality?*

*Some things are better than sex and some things are worse
but there is nothing exactly like it.* (W.C. Fields)

Because sex is a great amateur sport professionals in this field are suspect and distrusted. They miss the whole point of sex and spoil the show by revealing mankind's relationship to the animal kingdom rather than to angels and saints.

That is why the pioneers like Sigmund Freud, Havelock Ellis, Marie Stopes, Margaret Sanger, Alfred Kinsey and most recently William Masters and Virginia Johnson, have in turn been misinterpreted and condemned – frequently and most viciously – by their own colleagues. In the context of history this form of professional vilification has come to be a badge of merit.

In tracing the vicissitudes of human sexuality my aim will be to focus attention on religious, legal and medical practices which have tended to degrade humanity. This may also explain why sex, which takes so little time, causes so much bother. Lord Chesterfield, who did as much as anyone to make sex comfortable, said of sex: 'the enjoyment is quite temporary. The cost exorbitant and the position is simply ridiculous.'

Commenting on the vast gulf between public attitudes towards sex and private practices revealed by his pioneer studies, Alfred Kinsey said 'I believe that our culture is gradually convalescing from a sexually debilitating disease: Victorianism.' [8] The main symptom was the belief that sex was wicked, loathsome

---

*Presented to the CPHA Conference, June 9, 1972, Saskatoon, and published in abridged form in *Medical Aspects of Human Sexuality* Vol. 2 (November 1972), Canadian edition.

and likely to lead to disaster. Leading churchmen, lawyers, and especially physicians, fell easy victims to this psychosis.

However, Kinsey's diagnosis was wrong. Puritan and Victorian morality was a symptom, not the cause, of sexual repression. The disease has a much older history. Its sources can be traced to the origins of Christianity. From an objective reading of the evidence it is difficult to resist Joachim Kahl's [15] conclusion that the 'New Testament is the work of neurotic Philistines, who regarded human sexuality not as a source of joy, but a source of anxiety; not as a means of expressing love, but as a means of expressing sin.'

The misanthropical teachings of the Church follow from a literal interpretation of the gospels which leave no doubt that sexuality belongs to the sinful world. In the Kingdom of Heaven, where human life is ultimately fulfilled, sexual pleasures have no place.

St. Paul was also convinced that sexuality was a bar to ultimate human fulfilment. However, always a realist, he recognized that some devout Christians were less successful in repressing their sexuality than others – and they were allowed to marry. In this way extra-marital sex – unchastity – was made to bear the major burden of sin.

The defamation of sex lead inevitably to the degradation of women. The early Christian Church regarded women as inferior beings. St. Paul distrusted women, allowing them only the functions of serving man and bearing children. Guilt-ridden by his sexual excesses as a young man, St. Augustine was pathologically revolted by the entire process of conception. St. Jerome, who was responsible for the Latin translation of the Bible, wrote: 'Woman is the gate of the devil, the way of evil, the sting of the scorpion, in other words a dangerous thing.' He fled into the desert to avoid temptation and confessed that even while his body was half-dead from fasting, 'the fires of lust kept bubbling up before me.'

The Church continued to experience great difficulty in enforcing priestly celibacy. Pope Innocent III complained about members of the clergy who worshipped the Virgin Mary in the morning and embraced Venus at night.

The suppression of man's sexual instincts also leads to psychological repression and externalized aggression. The Church's deep hostility towards women reached a horrifying climax in the Christian witch-hunt which resulted in several million women tortured and burnt at the stake. The last witches were burnt in Switzerland in 1782 and drowned at the witches' ordeal near Danzig in 1836.

Failing to repress human sexuality Christian theologians contrived with some success to regulate its occurrence. Sexual intercourse was forbidden on Sundays, Wednesdays, and Fridays. It was also prohibited during the forty days of Lent, forty days before Christmas and for three days before receiving communion. Not satisfied with prohibiting sex for more than half of the year the Church also regulated the positions to be assumed in sexual intercourse. The missionary position - which inhibits communication by avoiding visual contact - was favoured so that intercourse could be performed as quickly and uninterestingly as possible. Long heavy night clothes with appropriate vents were worn so that the husband could impregnate his wife without it being necessary or possible to see or touch her body.

This hurried sketch of the Church's attempts to repress sexuality and demean women must serve to illustrate how the state got into the bedrooms of the nation. When the influence of the priests had run its course, lawyers and physicians took over and did what they could to proscribe sexuality.

One result of this in Canada was the Act passed in 1892 which, under the guise of prohibiting obscene literature, also outlawed 'every article or thing designed or intended for the prevention of conception or procuring of an abortion.' In moving the second reading of the Bill, speaking for the Government, a Mr. Charlton said: 'Nations enter upon their periods of decadence through effeminacy, that is the result of vice, or corruption or of crime.' [5] He continued: 'no higher functions rest upon the Government of a nation or of a people then to guard the morals and to promote the public welfare of the people in every way that it is possible to do so by legislation.' This is how the dissemination of contraceptive information was declared illegal in Canada for seventy-seven years until the ban was lifted on 18 August 1969. More will be said about sex and the law in Canada in the conclusion of this paper.

The practice of medicine from its earliest days to the present time has provided an alchemy for purveying moral judgments into forms of medical treatment. In this respect physicians were even better prepared than politicians and lawyers to assume the role of self-appointed guardians of sexual morality. Although the field is much broader than this, my comments here will be limited to medical contributions to problems of masturbation, frigidity, and impotence. First, however, a few words about birth control in the 1880s.

Leading medical men reasoned that sexual intercourse was intended for procreation. Birth control - which frustrated this end - was not only sinful but injurious to health as well. Coitus interruptus was merely conjugal masturbation. Coitus reservatus was equally harmful. Condoms inflamed the vagina and tampons caused gynaecological disease. [7]

By the end of the nineteenth century medicine was divided on the birth control issue. A few brave physicians had even joined the ranks of reformers, economists, feminists and socialists who actively campaigned for birth control clinics in England and the US. However, medicine was still united in its campaign of terror against masturbation which was regarded by the Church as an even greater sin than harlotry.

Here is an account of the grim consequences of masturbation which afflicted young men and women:

The health declines. The eyes lose their lustre. The skin becomes sallow. The muscles become flabby. There is an unnatural languor. Every little effort is followed by weariness. There is a great indifference to exertion ... [The victim] complains of pain in the back; of headache and dizziness. The hands become cold and clammy. The digestion becomes poor, the appetite fitful. The heart palpitates. He sits in a stooping posture, becomes hollow-chested, and the entire body, instead of enlarging into a strong, manly frame, becomes wasted, and many signs give promise of early decline and death ... If persisted in, masturbation will not only undermine, but completely overthrow the health. If the body is naturally strong, the mind may give way first, and in extreme cases imbecility and insanity may, and often do come as the inevitable result. Where the body is not naturally strong, a general wasting may be followed by consumption, or life may be terminated by any one of many diseases. [3]

Although this lurid statement was written by a Lutheran minister rather than a physician, the same type of information was being provided in the 1890s by 'Leading Canadian Medical Men.' [3]

Not to be outdone the new science of psychiatry invented masturbational insanity. Benjamin Rush, the founder of American psychiatry, described four cases and concluded that '... the morbid effects of intemperance with women are feeble and of transitory nature compared with the train of moral evils which this solitary vice fixes upon the mind and body.' [3]

This lead was promptly followed by eminent Canadian psychiatrists Joseph Workman [11], Daniel Clark [6] and Richard Maurice Bucke [10], who also contributed to the great masturbation scare. The rabid attitude of nineteenth century medicine towards masturbation fostered equally extreme attitudes to treatment. Since reproof, exhortation and threats were notoriously ineffective in combating the evils of masturbation, physical restraint and even surgery was tried.

Children, who were suspected of masturbation, had their hands tied or their genitals encased in a locked belt. When this failed, male genitals were cauterized or denervated. Clitoridectomy was also recommended for girls who showed symptoms of the solitary vice. Nocturnal emissions were also regarded as a health hazard. However, this condition too could be surgically treated by placing a spiked ring around the penis. Infibulation, inserting a silver wire into the prepuce, was also commonly used to prevent erections.

As time went on, less offensive but more profitable methods of preventing masturbation were also invented. Meat, spiced foods and stimulants like coffee, tea, alcohol etc. were thought to cause sexual excitation. To avoid this dreadful condition young men and women, who feared becoming victims of sexual excess, were advised vegetarian diets supplemented by frequent cold baths. Some of the legacies of the vegetarian sexologists are still enjoyed today by Canadians who consume vast quantities of peanut butter and cornflakes. These were invented by a John Harvey Kellogg to provide bland nourishment for his patients at Battle Creek Sanatorium, a health-cure establishment for victims of masturbation and nocturnal emissions. Consistent with his own theories, Kellogg remained continent throughout his life, although he was married and father to several dozen adopted children. Mrs. Kellogg also kept herself pure by working hard for the WCTU. [3]

The decline of medical interest in masturbation, as a cause of disease, is partly attributable to the advent of psychoanalysis which recognized instinctual sexual drives as a powerful fact of life. However, although psychoanalysis played a major part in the so-called sexual revolution, the result has been to exchange one set of chains for another. With psychoanalysis came a new set of myths and superstitions. This is not surprising because Freud, the founder of psychoanalysis, was himself very much a man of his time – and product of a bourgeois German, Jewish culture. From today's perspective Freud was a very prudish man. He was never really able to overcome his own sense of shame about sex and sent his sons to another doctor to inform them about the facts of life. Freud's own potency was probably diminished by his dislike of contraceptives. Having fathered six children, sexual relations with his wife came to an early end. At the age of forty-one Freud wrote to an intimate friend that: 'sexual excitation is of no more use to a person like me.' [20]

Freud's attitude towards women was also typically German and bourgeois. Like the earlier prophets, Freud thought of women as being reduced by penis envy to the level of a castrated man. Consequently, they were fated to find fulfilment only in children and a husband. Freud's followers – some of them the most gifted women of their time – agreed with this pathetic view of femininity.

Dr. Helene Deutsch [9], a distinguished psychoanalyst and a pupil of Freud, gave this as her view of the ideal woman:

... if they possess the feminine quality of intuition to a great degree, they are ideal collaborators who often inspire their men, and are themselves happiest in this role. They seem to be easily influenceable and adapt themselves to their companions and understand them. They are the loveliest and most unaggressive of helpmates and they want to remain in that role; they do not insist on their own rights – quite the contrary. They are easy to handle in every way – if one only loves them. Sexually they are easily excited and rarely frigid; but precisely in that sexual field they impose narcissistic conditions which must be fulfilled absolutely. They demand love and ardent renunciation of their own active tendencies.

In case it is thought that the psychoanalytical view of women has changed in recent times, here is a quotation from Bruno Bettelheim's paper on 'Women and the Scientific Professions,' dated 1965: '... we must start with the realization that, as much as women want to be good scientists or engineers, they want first and foremost to be womanly companions of men and to be mothers.' [2]

Freudian dogma about the essentially passive and masochistic nature of normal women was not entirely lacking in value. At least it infuriated people like Kate Millett [19] and Germaine Greer [13] and served to mobilize women all over the world. However, the negative effects of Freud's psychosexual theories must not be underestimated. The psychoanalytical view that the clitoral orgasm was inferior or less mature than orgasm per vagina probably spoiled the sexual lives of many women. The harm is not simply limited to the small group who had the time and money for psychoanalysis. Freudian dogma was also spread through vast numbers of books on sex which are read by millions of men, women and children. Here is a quotation from a very popular sex manual, called *The Power of Sexual Surrender*, published by Marie N. Robinson, MD, in 1959:

I believe that the problem of sexual frigidity in women is one of the gravest problems of our times. Over 40 per cent of married women suffer from it in one way or another of its degrees or forms.

... Those who are most closely related to the frigid woman – husband and children – suffer too. This is so because frigidity is an expression of neurosis, a disturbance of the unconscious life of the individual and destructive to personal relationships. No matter how much she may consciously wish to, the frigid woman cannot protect her loved ones from the effects of her problem. Thus, frigidity constitutes a major danger to the stability of marriage and to the health and happiness of every member of the individual family.

How is frigidity defined by Dr. Robinson? She says

we call a woman suffering from this type of frigidity a 'clitoridal' or 'masculine' type.

The clitoridal woman – that is, the woman who experiences orgasm on her clitoris alone – is very definitely suffering from a form of frigidity. Indeed, this form of frigidity is extremely widespread.

Elsewhere she says:

Remember that the woman whose orgasm is confined to the clitoris is definitely frigid. Statistics on the prevalence of this kind of sexual problem are not available, but most psychiatrists and psychoanalysts agree that it is very widespread, may even be the dominant form of frigidity in our society. [21]

Women were not alone in being humiliated by the Freudian myth of vaginal orgasm. Their male partners also suffered because the penis rarely provides an efficient means of producing a female orgasm. As a result, men – who reached a climax before their partner – were also overcome by shame and feelings of inadequacy. This gave rise to a new definition of impotence – called premature ejaculation – which medicine was equally quick to define as an illness. In many cases, however, the problem of premature ejaculation is arithmetical rather than psychological. Kinsey's research showed that 75 per cent of the American men they studied regularly ejaculated two minutes after intromission. In many cases ejaculation occurred in less than twenty seconds and only a few men lasted up to five minutes. In this respect man has much in common with his cousin, the male ape, who also ejaculates within ten to twenty seconds after intromission.

On the basis of these findings Kinsey [4] and his colleagues concluded:

The idea that the male who responds quickly in a sexual relationship is neurotic or otherwise pathologically involved is in most cases not justified scientifically.
... it would be difficult to find another situation in which an individual who was quick and intense in his responses was labelled anything but superior and that, in most instances, is exactly what the rapidly ejaculating man probably is, however inconvenient and unfortunate his qualities may be from the standpoint of the wife in the relationship.

If rapid ejaculation has such positive biological advantages why should it be so inconvenient and unfortunate for women? Kinsey found that, unlike men whose climax came in a few minutes, most women needed about fifteen to thirty minutes of coital stimulation before they reached orgasm. It is this discrepancy between the time needed by the two sexes to reach orgasm which lies at the root of the premature ejaculation problem.

For many couples, particularly in the first years of marriage, sex is not a mutually satisfying experience. Kinsey's study showed that one in four wives failed to experience orgasm during coitus. Happily, the ability to enjoy sex improves with age. After twenty years of marriage only 15 per cent of wives still failed to experience orgasm. This is not to say they were frigid. On the contrary, Kinsey found that left to their own devices 70 per cent of his female respondents were regularly able to achieve orgasm by masturbation in five minutes or less. Unlike men, many of these women were also able to enjoy multiple orgasms of increasing intensity. This finding, now confirmed by Masters and Johnson, suggests that coitus for many women is a much less effective route to orgasm than masturbation. In other words, while undoubtedly a profound source of pleasure to men, the penis, however vigorous, is not an unlimited or even a necessary instrument of sexual delight for women.

In her famous interview with *Playboy* magazine, Germaine Greer [14] makes this point in a characteristically frank way:

Playboy: Some men are perhaps reluctant to let themselves ejaculate quickly because the sex-manual culture labels this premature.
Greer: Let it be premature, then. There are times when you can *tell* that the man is doing the multiplication tables to avoid coming. He might as well not be doing anything, because it's taken the meaning out of the whole bloody thing. So many guys apologize abjectly for coming too fast. But who says it was too fast? It may have been beautiful. Then there are the guys who go on and on and on and don't come at all. They've said the multiplication tables so often that they can no longer have an ejaculation. That's not my concept of ecstasy.

Physicians, particularly psychiatrists, who claim to treat frigidity and impotence by teaching techniques for maintaining an erection and postponing ejaculation only succeed in creating a new form of iatrogenic disorder and are part of the disease rather than its cure. Excessive preoccupation with genital technique – which leads to sex with a shallow or inappropriate emotional response – is a form of sexual schizophrenia.

Enough has been said to indicate that medical attitudes towards human sexuality leave much to be desired. Although the public tends to regard them as experts, being human, physicians often have the same misconceptions, problems, and anxieties about sex as anyone else. Unfortunately, medical schools have done very little in the way of teaching students to improve their sexual knowledge and attitudes [1], [18]. In 1959 Harold Lief [16], a pioneer in this field, reported on a study carried out in five medical schools in Philadelphia. It was found that 'half of the students have a feeling that mental illness is frequently caused by masturbation. Even one faculty member in five still believes in this old, and now discredited, idea.'

This frequently quoted finding about the sexually ill-informed American medical students was reported in 1963. What is the situation in Canada today? In the absence of any comparable studies this question cannot be answered. However, a study of medico-legal problems undertaken in 1971 by Osgoode Hall Law School in co-operation with the Ontario Medical Association confirmed that practising physicians in Ontario were not particularly well informed about abortion, birth control, etc. Although this is hard to believe, only 52.4 per cent of responding physicians knew that the Criminal Code allows them to prescribe birth control pills at will. Even more incredible was the fact that 15.1 per cent of the physicians thought they could prescribe the pill for any medical reason except birth control. [23]

In regard to abortion, 53.9 per cent of the responding physicians incorrectly believed that the Canadian Criminal Code explicitly provided that a pregnant rape victim could have an abortion. Over 90 per cent of the physicians felt that such a provision should exist.

So far, this paper has been mainly concerned with the past. Now, in conclusion, some brief mention will be made to the future of human sexuality. The first point to be made is that thanks to Kinsey and to Masters and Johnson we all have access to a vast amount of scientifically valid information. Here are a few of the Masters and Johnson [17] findings which were reassuring to members of the helping professions:

1 Penis size has nothing to do with sexual effectiveness.
2 Baldness is not a sign of virility.
3 There is no physiological difference between clitoral and vaginal orgasm.
4 Humans can remain sexually active well into their ninth decade. (All they need is good health and an attractive partner.)
5 Masturbation is not harmful.

These findings reflect the growing conviction that in the practice of sex nothing is wrong or forbidden as long as it is acceptable and pleasurable to both partners. As Kinsey said the only unnatural sex act is that which you cannot perform. Under the Criminal Code in Canada, a variety of sexual expressions and relationships are still proscribed. The maximum punishment for sexual intercourse with females under fourteen is life imprisonment and whipping. For incest, fourteen years and whipping. For buggery or bestiality, fourteen years. Indecent assault, ten years and whipping, and gross indecency, five years. This tariff of punishments for sexual acts reveals that our judicial system operates on a somewhat eccentric scale of human values. Indecent assault on males by males can be punished with ten years and whipping, but the same indecent act on a woman merits only five years and whipping [12]. These sexist anomalies have been considered by the members of the Royal Commission on the Status of Women [22] who agree that the Law, as it stands, is unfair to men: 'Under the Criminal Code, no form of deception used by a woman in order to engage in sexual relations with a man is punishable. Should her persuasion become too violent, she could be convicted of common assault. In a similar situation, a man can be charged with rape, indecent assault on a female, seduction or sexual intercourse if the female is under age.'

My own view is that the Bird Commission's recommendations do not go far enough. Except for serious sexual offences against children a strong case could be made for abolishing all laws relating to sexual conduct. Crimes such as rape could be equally well dealt with as serious offences against the person. As it now stands, the Law is inequitable and ridiculous. The maximum penalty for rape is imprisonment for life and with whipping. However, if a man commits a similar sexual assault but employs a broom handle in place of his penis, he commits a lesser offence for which the maximum penalty is five years imprisonment with whipping.

Most of the provisions of the Criminal Code dealing with sexual offences were adopted at the end of the last century when attitudes towards sex and women were different from what they are today. In Law women tend to be seen as 'victims' of men's sexual assaults. A comic example of this is the sec. 146 of the Criminal Code of Canada which provides a two-year prison sentence for ship's officers who seduce female passengers.

Such paternalistic laws were probably designed by Victorian gentlemen to protect the gentler sex from what was euphemistically described as a fate worse than death. Today, however, it can be seen that the virginity cult with its inevitable double standards is nothing more than an instrument for the repression of women.

From this survey of the trials and tribulations of human sexuality it is difficult to avoid the conclusion that the equation of sex with sin and sickness has been one of the major disasters of our civilization. Since most of my generation are victims of sexual repression – and our opinions reflect this experience – to avoid mistakes of the past, our solutions must be modest. However, a great deal of harm has been done and there are many casualties to be treated before the future of human sexuality can be assured. Finally and hopefully we must not forget the extraordinary resilience of ordinary men and women against the onslaught of the Church, the state, and medicine. This is one of the most cheering aspects of the history of human sexuality.

NOTES

1 Ball, M.J. (1972), 'A Survey of Family Planning Teaching in Canadian
   Medical Colleges' (duplicated report), National Conference on Family Planning, Ottawa, February 28–March 2.
2 Bettelheim, B. (1965), quoted by Greer, G. (1971), *Female Eunuch*, p. 95.
3 Bliss, M. (1970), 'Pure Books on Avoided Subjects: Pre-Freudian Sexual Ideas in
   Canada,' The Canadian Historical Association, *Historical Papers*, 1970. I am indebted to Michael Bliss for a number of ideas and references used in this paper.
4 Brecher, E.M. (1969), *The Sex Researchers*, Little, Brown, Co., Canada.
5 Charlton, Mr. (1892), *House of Common Debates*, vol. 2, May 11, 1892.
6 Clark, D. (1895), *Mental Diseases*, Wm. Briggs, Toronto, p. 149.
7 Comfort, A. (1968), *The Anxiety Makers: Some Curious Sexual Preoccupations of the Medical Profession*, A Panther Book. I am indebted to
   Alex Comfort for a number of ideas and references used in this paper.
8 Deutch, A. (1948), ed., *Sex Habits of American Men. A Symposium on
   the Kinsey Report.* Prentice-Hall Inc., New York.
9 Deutsch, H. (1946), quoted by Greer, G. (1971), *Female Eunuch*, p. 94.
10 Greenland, C. (1964), 'R.M. Bucke, M.D., A Pioneer of Scientific Psychiatry 1837-1902,' *Canad. Med. Assn. J.* August 22.
11 – 'Three Pioneers of Canadian Psychiatry,' *J. Amer. Med. Assn.*, vol. 200,
   838-843, June 5.
12 – 'Dangerous Sexual Offenders in Canada,' *Canad. J. Crim. and Corr.*,
   vol. 14, 1, Jan.
13 Greer, G. (1970), *The Female Eunuch*, Paladin, London.
14 – (1972), *Playboy*, vol. 19, 1.
15 Kahl, J. (1971), *The Misery of Christianity: A Plea for a Humanity without
   God*. A Pelican Book, U.K. *Note:* Most of my biblical references and ideas
   are culled from this remarkable book.
16 Lief, H. (1963), 'What Medical Schools Teach about Sex,' *Tulane Med. Fac.
   Bull.*, vol. 22, 161-168, May.
17 Masters, W.H. and Johnson, V. (1966), *Human Sexual Response*, Little,
   Brown Co., Boston, U.S.
   – (1970), *Human Sexual Inadequacy*, Little, Brown Co., Boston, U.S.
   See also *Time*, 'Researchers Masters and Johnson,' May 25, 1970.
18 MacKenzie, C.J.G. (1972), 'Teaching Population Dynamics, Conception
   Control, Human Sexuality and Related Subjects in Canadian Medical
   Schools (duplicated report), n.d.
19 Millett, K. (1970), *Sexual Politics*, Doubleday and Co., New York; see also
   Cosmopolitan, November 1970.

20 Roazen, P. (1971), *Brother Animal: The Story of Freud and Tausk*, Vintage Books, v.506, New York.
21 Robinson, M.N. (1959), *The Power of Sexual Surrender*, A Signet Book, U.S.
22 *Report of the Royal Commission on the Status of Women in Canada* (1970), Ottawa, September 28, Chapter 9.
23 Sharpe, G. (1972), 'Osgoode Initiates Innovative Medical-Legal Studies Program,' *Obiter Dicta*, vol. 44, 15, 8-9, April 13.

RESOURCES

A glossary of terms used in human sexuality

Abstinence
A refraining from the use of or indulgence in certain foods, stimulants, or sexual intercourse.

Adultery
Sexual intercourse between a married person and an individual other than his or her legal spouse.

Anaphrodisiac
A drug or medicine that allays sexual desire.

Aphrodisiac
Anything, such as a drug or a perfume, that stimulates sexual desire.

Bestiality
A sexual variance in which a person engages in sexual relations with an animal.

Bisexual
Literally, having sex organs of both sexes, as in hermaphrodites; or having a sexual interest in both sexes.

Castration
Removal of the gonads (sex glands) – the testicles in the male, the ovaries in the female.

Celibacy
The state of being unmarried; abstention from sexual activity.

Chastity
Abstention from sexual intercourse.

Circumcision
Surgical removal of the foreskin or prepuce of the male penis.

Climacteric
The syndrome of physical and psychologic changes that occur at the termination of menstrual function (i.e., reproductive capability) in the female

and reduction in sex-steroid production in both sexes; menopause; change of life.

Clitoris (adj. clitoral)
A small, highly sensitive nipple of flesh in the female, located just above the urethral opening in the upper triangle of the vulva.

Coitus
Sexual intercourse between male and female, in which the male penis is inserted into the female vagina; copulation.

Coitus interruptus (or premature withdrawal)
The practice of withdrawing the penis from the vagina just before ejaculation.

Condom
A contraceptive used by men consisting of a rubber or gut sheath that is drawn over the erect penis before coitus.

Contraception
The use of devices or drugs to prevent conception in sexual intercourse.

Copulation
Sexual intercourse; coitus.

Cunnilingus
The act of using the tongue or mouth in erotic play with the external female genitalia (vulva).

Douche
A stream of water or other liquid solution directed into the female vagina

for sanitary, medical, or contraceptive reasons.

Dyspareunia
Coitus that is difficult or painful, especially for a woman.

Ejaculation
The expulsion of male semen, usually at the climax (orgasm) of the sexual act.

Erection
The stiffening and enlargement of the penis (or clitoris), usually as a result of sexual excitement.

Erogenous zone
A sexually sensitive area of the body, such as the mouth, lips, breasts, nipples, buttocks, genitals, or anus.

Erotic
Pertaining to sexual love or sensation; sexually stimulating.

Excitement phase
The initial stage in the human sexual response cycle that follows effective sexual stimulation.

Exhibitionism
A sexual variance in which the individual – usually male – suffers from a compulsion to expose his genitals publicly.

Fellatio
The act of taking the penis into the mouth for erotic purposes.

Fertility
The state of being capable of producing young; the opposite of sterility.

Fetishism
A sexual variance in which sexual gratification is achieved by means of an object, such as an article of clothing, that bears sexual symbolism for the individual.

Foreplay
The preliminary stages of sexual intercourse, in which the partners usually stimulate each other.

Fornication
Sexual intercourse between two unmarried persons (as distinguished from adultery, which involves a person who is married to someone other than his or her coital partner).

Frigidity
A common term for a form of female sexual dysfunctioning, implying coldness, indifference, or insensitivity on the part of a woman to sexual intercourse or sexual stimulation; inability to experience sexual pleasure or gratification.

Genital organs (or genitals or genitalia)
The sex or reproductive organs.

Gonad
A sex gland; a testicle (male) or ovary (female).

Gonorrhea
A veneral disease, transmitted chiefly through coitus; a contagious catarrhal inflammation of the genital mucous membrane.

Hermaphrodite
An individual possessing both male and female sex glands (ovary and testicle) or sex-gland tissue of both sexes. See also pseudohermaphrodite.

Heterosexuality
Sexual attraction to, or sexual activity with, members of the opposite sex; opposite of homosexuality.

Homosexuality
Sexual attraction to, or sexual activity with, members of one's own sex; the opposite of heterosexuality.

Hymen
The membranous fold that partly covers the external opening of the vagina in most virgin females; the maidenhead.

Hysterectomy
Surgical removal of the female uterus, either through the abdominal wall or through the vagina.

Impotence
Disturbance of sexual function in the male that precludes satisfactory coitus; more specifically, inability to achieve or maintain an erection sufficient for purposes of sexual intercourse.

Incest
Sexual relations between close rela-

tives, such as father and daughter, mother and son, or brother and sister.

Intercourse, anal
A form of sexual intercourse in which the penis is inserted into the partner's anus; sometimes termed sodomy.

Intercourse, oral
A form of sexual intercourse in which the mouth is used to receive the penis (fellatio) or the mouth and lips are used to stimulate the vulva, especially the clitoris (cunnilingus).

Intercourse, sexual
Sexual union of a male and a female in which the penis is inserted into the vagina; coitus.

Intrauterine device (IUD)
A small plastic or metal device that when fitted into the uterus prevents pregnancy. Also termed intrauterine contraceptive device (IUCD).

Labia majora
The outer and larger pair of lips of the female external genitals (vulva).

Labia minora
The inner and smaller pair of lips of the female external genitals (vulva).

Lesbian
A female homosexual.

Maidenhead
The hymen.

Masochism
A sexual variance in which an individual derives sexual gratification from having pain inflicted on him.

Masturbation
Self-stimulation of the genitals through manipulation; autoeroticism.

Mons veneris (or mons pubis)
A triangular mound of fat at the symphysis pubis of the female, just above the vulval area.

Narcissism
Excessive self-love; sexual excitement through admiration of one's own body.

Nocturnal emission
An involuntary male orgasm and ejaculation of semen during sleep; a 'wet dream.'

Nymphomania
Excessive sexual desire in a woman.

Obscene
Disgusting, repulsive, filthy, shocking – that which is abhorrent according to accepted standards of morality.

Orgasm
The peak or climax of sexual excitement in sexual activity.

Orgasmic phase
The third stage in the human sexual response cycle during which the orgasm occurs.

Pedophilia
A sexual variance in which an adult engages in or desires sexual activity with a child.

Penis
The male organ of copulation and urination.

Petting
Sexual contact that excludes coitus.

Phallus
The male penis, usually the erect penis.

Pornography
The presentation of sexually arousing material in literature, art, motion pictures, or other means of communication and expression.

Premature ejaculation
Ejaculation before, just at, or immediately after intromission; ejaculatio praecox. Ejaculation occurs before the woman can climax in at least 50 per cent of the acts of intercourse.

Promiscuous
Engaging in sexual intercourse with many persons; engaging in casual sexual relations.

Prostitute
A person who engages in sexual relationships for payment.

Pseudohermaphrodite
An individual who has both male and female external sex organs, usually in rudimentary form, but who has the sex glands (ovary or testicle) of only one sex, and is thus fundamentally male or female. See also hermaphrodite.

Rape
Forcible sexual intercourse with a person who does not give consent or who offers resistance.

Resolution phase
The last stage in the human sexual response cycle during which the sexual system retrogresses to its normal nonexcited state.

Rhythm method
A method of birth control that relies on the so-called 'safe period' or infertile days in the female menstrual cycle.

Sadism
A sexual variance in which there is the achievement of sexual gratification by inflicting physical or psychological pain upon the sexual partner.

Satyriasis
Excessive sexual desire in a man.

Secondary sex characteristics
The physical characteristics – other than the external sex organs – that distinguish male from female.

Seduction
Luring a female (sometimes a male) into sexual intercourse without the use of force.

Semen
The secretion of the male reproductive organs that is ejaculated from the penis at orgasm and contains, in the fertile man, sperm cells.

Sex drive
Desire for sexual expression.

Sex flush
The superficial vasocongestive skin response to increasing sexual tensions that begins in the plateau phase (term used by Masters and Johnson).

Sex gland
A gonad; the testicle in the male and the ovary in the female.

Sex hormone
A substance secreted by the sex glands directly into the bloodstream, e.g., androgens (male) and estrogens (female).

Sexual inadequacy
Any degree of sexual response that is not sufficient for the isolated demand of the moment or for a protracted period of time; frequent or total inability to experience orgasm.

Sexual outlet
Any of the various ways by which sexual tension is released through orgasm.

Sodomy
A form of sexual variance variously defined by law to include sexual intercourse with animals and mouth-genital or anal-genital contact between humans.

Syphilis
Probably the most serious venereal disease, it is usually acquired by sexual intercourse with a person in the infectious stage of the disease and is caused by invasion of the spirochete Treponema pallidum.

Testicle
The testis, the male sex gland.

Testis (pl. Testes)
The male sex gland or gonad, which produces spermatozoa.

Transsexualism
A compulsion or obsession to become a member of the opposite sex through surgical changes.

Tranvestism
A sexual variance characterized by a compulsive desire to wear the garments of the opposite sex; cross-dressing.

Uterus
The hollow, pear-shaped organ in females within which the fetus develops; the womb.

Vagina
The canal in the female, extending from the vulva to the cervix, that receives the penis during coitus and through which an infant passes at birth.

Vaginal lubrication
A clear fluid (like sweat) that appears on the walls of the vaginal barrel with-

in a few seconds after the onset of
sexual stimulation.

Vaginismus
Strong muscular contractions within
the vagina, preventing intromission of
the penis when intercourse is
attempted.

Vaginitis
Inflammation of the female vagina,
usually as a result of infection.

Vasectomy
A surgical procedure for sterilizing the
male involving removal of the vas defe-
rens, or a portion of it.

Venereal disease
A contagious disease such as syphilis

or gonorrhea, communicated mainly
by sexual intercourse.

Virginity
The physical condition of a person
before first intercourse.

Voyeurism
A sexual variance in which a person
achieves sexual gratification by observing others in the nude.

Vulva
The external sex organs of the female,
including the mons veneris, the labia
majora, the labia minora, the clitoris,
and the vestibule.

Womb
The uterus in the female.

A basic library in human sexuality*

ALTERNATE APPROACHES TO FAMILY LIFE

Bernard, Jessie. *The Future of Marriage.* New York: Bantam Books, 1973.
- *The Future of Motherhood.* Baltimore: Penguin Books, 1974.
Carden, Maven Lockwood. *Oneida: Utopian Community to Modern Corporation.* New York: Harper Torch Books, 1971.
Clanton, Gordon, and Chris Downing. *Face to Face: An Experiment in Intimacy.* New York: E.P. Dutton, 1975.
Constantine, Larry L., and M. Constantine. *Group Marriage.* New York: Macmillan, 1973.
Delora, Joann S., and Jack R. Delora, eds. *Intimate Life Styles: Marriage and its Alternatives*; 2nd ed. Pacific Palisades, Cal.: Goodyear Publishing, 1975.
Doberman, Lucille. *Marriage and its Alternatives.* New York: Praeger, 1974.
Fairfield, Richard. *Communes: U.S.A.* Baltimore: Penguin Books, 1972.
Feldman, Saul D., and Gerald W. Thielbar, eds. *Life Styles: Diversity in American Society.* Boston: Little, Brown, 1972.
Francoeur, Robert T. *Eve's New Rib.* New York: Delta Books, 1972.
Grierson, Denham. *Young People in Communal Living.* Philadelphia: Westminister Press, 1971.
Hart, Harold T., ed. *Marriage: For and Against.* New York: Hunt Publishing, 1972.
Holloway, Mark. *Heavens on Earth: Utopian Communities in America, 1680-1880.* New York: Dover, 1966.

*A basic selected paperbound library of 230 books, published up to January 1, 1976.

Hovriet, Robert. *Getting Back Together.* New York: Avon Books, 1972.

Howe, Louise Kapp, ed. *The Future of the Family.* New York: Simon and Schuster, 1972.

Kanter, Rosabeth Moss. *Commitment and Community: Communes and Utopias in Sociological Perspective.* Cambridge, Mass.: Harvard University Press, 1972.

- ed. *Communes.* New York: Harper and Row, 1973.

Kirkendall, Lester, and Robert N. Whitehurst, eds. *The Non Sexual Revolution.* New York: Charles Scribner's Sons, 1971.

Libby, Robert W., and Robert N. Whitehurst, eds. *Renovating Marriage.* Danville, Cal.: Consensus Publishers, 1973.

O'Neill, N., and George O'Neill. *Open Marriage.* New York: Avon Books, 1972.

Otto, Herbert A., ed. *The Family in Search of a Future.* New York: Appleton-Century-Crofts, 1970.

- *Love Today.* New York: Delta Books, 1972.

Rimmer, Robert H., ed. *Adventures in Loving.* New York: Signet, 1973.

Roberts, Ron E. *The New Communes.* New York: Spectrum Books, 1971.

Rogers, Carl R. *Becoming Partners: Marriage and its Alternatives.* New York: Delta Books, 1973.

Skinner, B.F. *Walden Two.* New York: Macmillan, 1948.

Skolnick, Arlene S., and Jerome H. Skolnick, eds. *Family in Transition.* Boston: Little, Brown, 1971.

- *Intimacy, Family and Society.* Boston: Little, Brown, 1974.

Smith, James R., and Lynn G. Smith. *Beyond Monogamy.* Baltimore: Johns Hopkins University Press, 1974.

Talmon, Yonina. *Family and Community in the Kibbutz.* Cambridge, Mass.: Harvard University Press, 1972.

Teselle, Sallie, ed. *The Family, Communes and Utopian Societies.* New York: Harper Torch Books, 1972.

Zablocki, Benjamin. *The Joyful Community: An Account of the Brudenhof.* Baltimore: Penguin Books, 1971.

ETHICS

Babbage, S.B. *Sex and Sanity.* Philadelphia: Westminster Press, 1965.

Bailey, Derrick S. *Sexual Ethics.* New York: Macmillan, 1963.

Bernard, Jessie. *The Sex Game.* Englewood Cliffs, NJ: Prentice-Hall, 1968.

Cole, William Graham. *Sex in Christianity and Psychoanalysis.* New York: Oxford University Press, 1955.

Dedek, John F. *Contemporary Sexual Morality.* New York: Sheed and Ward, 1971.

Demant, V.A. *Christian Sex Ethics.* New York: Harper and Row, 1963.

Ditzion, Sidney. *Marriage, Morals, and Sex in America: A History of Ideas.* New York: Bookman Associates, 1953.

Ellis, Havelock. *Studies in the Psychology of Sex.* New York: Random House, 1936.

Gadperille, Warren T. *The Cycles of Sex.* New York: Charles Scribner's Sons, 1975.

Grummon, Donald L., and Andrew M. Barclay. *Sexuality: A Search for Perspective.* New York: Van Nostrand, 1971.

Hart, Harold H., ed. *Sexual Latitude: For and Against.* New York: Hart Publishing Co., 1971.

Heron, Alastair, ed. *Towards a Quaker View of Sex.* London: Friends Home Service Committee, 1964.

Hiltner, Seward. *Sex Ethics and the Kinsey Reports.* New York: Association Press, 1953.

Hofmann, Hans F. *Sex Incorporated: A Positive View of the Sexual Revolution.* Boston: Beacon Press, 1967.

Kardiner, Abram. *Sex and Morality.* London: Routledge and Kegan Paul, 1955.

Kennedy, Eugene. *The New Sexuality: Myths, Fables, and Hang-ups.* New York: Doubleday, 1972.

Landau, Rom. *Sex, Life, and Faith: A Modern Philosophy of Sex.* London: Faber, 1946.

Mace, David R. *Does Sex Morality Matter?* London: Rich and Cowan, 1943.

MacKinnon, D.M., *et al., God, Sex and War.* Philadelphia: Westminster Press, 1965.

Masters, William, and Virginia Johnson. *The Pleasure Bond.* Boston: Little, Brown, 1975.

Montagu, Ashley. *Sex, Man and Society.* New York: G.P. Putnam's Sons, 1969.

Olford, Stephen F., and F.A. Lawes. *The Sanctity of Sex.* Westwood, NJ: Revell, 1963.

O'Neil, Robert P., and M.A. Donovan. *Sexuality and Moral Responsibility.* Washington, DC: Corpus, 1968.

Oraison, Marc. *The Human Mystery of Sexuality.* New York: Sheed and Ward, 1967.

Reiche, Reimut. *Sexuality and Class Struggle*; translated by S. Bennett. New York: Praeger, 1971.

Rhymes, D. *No New Morality.* Indianapolis, Ind.: Bobbs-Merrill, 1964.

Robinson, William J., *et al., Sex Morality: Past, Present, and Future.* New York: Critic Guide Co., 1912.

Rover, Constance. *Love, Morals and the Feminists.* London: Routledge and Kegan Paul, 1970.

Roy, Rustum, and Della Roy. *Honest Sex.* New York: New American Library, 1968.

Ruether, Rosemary Radford. *Religion and Sexism.* New York: Simon and Schuster, 1974.

Ruitenbeek, Hendrik M., ed. *Sexuality and Identity.* New York: Delta, 1970.

Schur, Edwin M., ed. *The Family and the Sexual Revolution.* Bloomington, Ind.: Indiana University Press, 1964.

Schwarz, Oswald. *The Psychology of Sex.* Baltimore: Penguin Books, 1949.

Shope, David F. *Interpersonal Sexuality.* Philadelphia: Saunders, 1975.

Thielicke, Helmut. *The Ethics of Sex*; translated by John Doberstein. New York: Harper and Row, 1964.

Verene, D.P., ed. *Sexual Love and Western Morality: A Philosophical Anthology.* New York: Harper and Row, 1972.

Walker, Kenneth, and P. Fletcher. *Sex and Society.* London: Penguin Books, 1955.

Whiteley, Charles H., and W.M. Whiteley. *Sex and Morals.* New York: Basic Books, 1967.

Wilson, John. *Logic and Sexual Morality.* Baltimore: Penguin Books, 1956.

Wood, Frederick C. *Sex and the New Morality.* New York: Association Press, 1968.

Wright, Helena. *Sex and Society.* Seattle: University of Washington Press, 1969.

Wynn, John C., ed. *Sexual Ethics and Christian Responsibility: Some Divergent Views.* New York: Association Press, 1970.

HUMAN SEXUALITY (OVERVIEW)

American Medical Association. *Human Sexuality.* Chicago, 1972 (hard cover).

Baker, Robert, and Frederick Elliston, eds. *Philosophy and Sex.* Buffalo: Prometheus Books, 1975.

Bell, Robert R. *Premarital Sex in a Changing Society.* Englewood Cliffs, NJ: Prentice-Hall, 1966.

Bell, Robert R., and Michael Gordon, eds. *The Social Dimension of Human Sexuality.* Boston: Little, Brown, 1972.

Browning, Mary H., and Edith P. Lewis, eds. *Human Sexuality: Nursing Implications.* New York: American Journal of Nursing Co., 1973.

Comfort, A., ed. *The Joy of Sex.* New York: Crown, 1972.

- *More Joy of Sex.* New York: Simon and Schuster, 1974.

Edwards, John N., ed. *Sex and Society.* Chicago: Markham, 1972.

Gagnon, John H., and William Simon. *Sexual Conduct.* Chicago: Aldine, 1973 (hard cover).

Gilder, George F. *Sexual Suicide.* New York: Quadrangle, 1973.

Gochros, Harvey, and LeRoy G. Schultz, eds. *Human Sexuality and Social Work.* New York: Association Press, 1972 (hard cover).

Gottesfeld, Mary L., ed. *Modern Sexuality.* New York: Behavioral Publications, 1975.

Juhasz, Anne McCreary, ed. *Sexual Development and Behavior: Selected Readings.* Homewood, Ill.: Dorsey Press, 1973.

Katchadourian, Herant A., and Donald T. Lunde. *Fundamentals of Human Sexuality*; 2nd ed. New York: Holt, Rinehart and Winston, 1975.

Lief, Harold, ed. *Medical Aspects of Human Sexuality: 750 Questions and Answers.* Baltimore: Williams and Wilkins, 1975.

Malfetti, James L., and Elizabeth M. Eidlitz, eds. *Perspectives on Sexuality: A Literary Collection.* New York: Holt, Rinehart and Winston, 1972.

McCary, James Leslie. *Human Sexuality.* New York: D. Van Nostrand, 1967 (hard cover).

Millett, Kate. *Sexual Politics.* New York: Avon Books, 1970.

Morrison, Eleanor J., and Vera Borosage, eds. *Human Sexuality: Contemporary Perspectives.* Palo Alto, Cal.: National Press, 1973.

Petrus, John W. *Sexuality in Society.* Boston: Allyn and Bacon, 1973.

Pierson, Elaine C., and William V. D'Antonio. *Female and Male: Dimensions of Human Sexuality.* New York: J.B. Lippincott, 1974.

Reiss, Ira L. *Premarital Sexual Standards in America.* New York: Free Press, 1964.

Rubin, Isadore. *Sexual Life after Sixty.* New York: Signet, 1965.

Sex Information and Education Council of the United States. *Sexuality and Man.* New York: Charles Scribner's Sons, 1970.

Shainberg, Louis W., Kenneth L. Jones, and Curtiso Byer. *Sex*; 2nd ed. New York: Harper and Row, 1973.

Young, Wayland. *Eros Denied: Sex in Western Society.* New York: Grove Press, 1964.

HISTORY OF SEX

Brusch, R. *How Did Sex Begin?* New York: Signet, 1974.

Taylor, Rattray G. *Sex in History.* New York: Vanguard Press, 1954 (hard cover).

Family planning

Bouma, Gary, and Wilma T. Bouma. *Fertility Control: Canada's Lively Social Problem.* Toronto: Longmans, 1975.

Schlesinger, Banjamin, ed. *Family Planning in Canada: A Source Book.* Toronto: University of Toronto Press, 1974.

Group sex and swapping
Bartell, Gilbert D. *Group Sex.* New York: Signet, 1971.
Lobell, John, and Mimi Lobell. *John and Mimi: A Free Marriage.* New York: Bantam, 1973.
Margolis, Herbert F., and Paul M. Rubenstein. *The Group Sex Tapes.* New York: Paperback Library, 1972.
Martin, McI. *I'm for Group Sex.* Toronto: Mystique Press, 1975.
Webber, Nancy. *The Wife Swap.* New York: Dell, 1974.
Wells, John Warren. *The Wife-Swap Report.* New York: Dell, 1970.

Homosexuality
Abbott, Sidney, and Barbara Love. *Sappho Was a Right-on Woman.* New York: Stein and Day, 1973.
Bergler, Edmund. *Homosexuality: Disease or Way of Life?* New York: Collier Books, 1962.
Caprio, Frank S. *Female Homosexuality.* New York: Grove Press, 1954.
Churchill, Wainwright. *Homosexual Behavior Among Males.* Englewood Cliffs, NJ: Prentice-Hall, 1967.
Cory, Donald Webster. *The Homosexual in America.* New York: Paperback Library, 1963.
- *The Lesbian in America.* New York: MacFadden Books, 1965.
De Becker, Raymond. *The Other Face of Love.* London: Sphere Books, 1969.
Hoffman, Martin. *The Gay World.* New York: Bantam Books, 1969.
Humphreys, Laud. *Out of the Closets: The Sociology of Homosexual Liberation.* Englewood Cliffs, NJ: Prentice-Hall, 1972.
Jones, Clinton R. *Homosexuality and Counselling.* Philadelphia: Fortress Press, 1974.
Martin, Del, and Phyllis Lyon. *Lesbian Woman.* New York: Bantam Books, 1972.
McCaffrey, Joseph A., ed. *The Homosexual Dialectic.* Englewood Cliffs, NJ: Prentice-Hall, 1972.
Morse, Benjamin. *The Lesbian.* Derby, Conn.: Monarch Books, 1961.
Peck, Ellen, and Judith Senderowitz, eds. *Pronatalism: The Myth of Man and Apple Pie.* New York: Thomas Y. Crowell, 1974.
Pleck, Joseph H., and Jack Sawyer, eds. *Men and Masculinity.* Englewood Cliffs, NJ: Prentice-Hall, 1974.
Ruitenbeek, Hendrick M., ed. *The Problem of Homosexuality in Modern Society.* New York: Dutton, 1963.
Sprague, W.D. *The Lesbian in Our Society.* New York: Tower, 1962.
Stearn, Jess. *The Grapevine* (Lesbianism). New York: MacFadden Books, 1965.

Stephenson, Marylee. *Living with Stigma: A Study of Eleven Female Homosexual Couples.* Hamilton: McMaster University, Department of Sociology, 1975.

University of Waterloo. Federation of Students. *Operation Socrates Handbook* (Homosexuality). Waterloo, 1972.

Wade, Carlson. *The Troubled Sex* (Lesbians). New York: Universal, 1961.

Weinberg, George. *Society and the Healthy Homosexual.* New York: Doubleday Anchor Books, 1973.

Weinberg, Martin J., and Colin J. Williams. *Male Homosexuals: Their Problems and Adaptation.* Toronto: Oxford University Press, 1974 (hard cover).

West, D.J. *Homosexuality.* London: Pelican, 1960.

The Wolfenden Report (Britain). New York: Lancer, 1963.

Wolff, Charlotte. *Love Between Women.* London: Duckworth, 1973.

Wyden, Peter, and Barbara Wyden. *Growing Up Straight.* New York: Signet, 1968.

Wysor, Bettie. *The Lesbian Myth.* New York: Random House, 1974 (hard cover).

Mentally retarded and sexuality

Barrett, Michael F. *Problems in Teaching the Mentally Retarded about Human Sexuality.* Toronto: University of Toronto, Department of Zoology, 1975.

De La Cruz, Felix F., and Gerald D. LaVeck, eds. *Human Sexuality and the Mentally Retarded.* New York: Brunner-Mazel, 1973 (hard cover).

Kempton, Winifred. *Guidelines for Planning a Training Course on Human Sexuality and the Retarded.* Philadelphia: Planned Parenthood Association, 1973.

Klappholz, Lowell, ed. *A Resource Guide in Sex Education for the Mentally Retarded.* New York: Siecus, 1971.

Myths and fallacies

McCary, J.L. *Sexual Myths and Fallacies*; 2nd ed. New York: Van Nostrand, 1973.

New sexual patterns

Calder, June. *Women's Sex Talk.* New York: Signet, 1974.

Friday, Nancy, ed. *Forbidden Flowers.* New York: Pocket Books, 1975.

- *My Secret Garden: Women's Sexual Fantasies.* New York: Pocket Books, 1974.

Hurwood, Bernhardt J. *The Bisexuals.* Greenwich, Conn.: Fawcett, 1974.

- *The Girls, the Massage, and Everything.* Greenwich, Conn.: Fawcett, 1973.

Kirkendall, Heston A., and Robert N. Whitehurst, eds. *The New Sexual Revolution.* New York: Charles Scribner's Sons, 1971.

Lewis, Stephen. *Sex among the Singles.* Toronto: Ace Books, 1973.
Wells, John Warren. *Total Sexuality.* New York: Warner, 1974.

Pornography
Kronhausen, Eberhard, and Phyllis Kronhausen. *Pornography and the Law.*
New York: Ballantine, 1964.
- *The Report of the Commission on Obscenity and Pornography.* New York:
Bantam Books, 1970.

Prostitution
Greenwald, Harold. *The Call Girl.* New York: Ballantine, 1958.
Hall, Swan. *Ladies of the Night.* New York: Pocket Books, 1974.
Hollander, Xaviera. *The Happy Hooker.* New York: Dell, 1972.
- *Letters to the Happy Hooker.* New York: Warner, 1973.
- *Xaviera.* New York: Warner Paperback, 1973.
- *Xaviera Goes Wild.* New York: Warner Paperback, 1974.
Jordan, Lynda, and Christopher Keane. *Lynda: The Merry Madam.* New York:
Pyramid Books, 1973.
Lane, Barbara, and Stephen Lewis. *Housewife Hookers.* New York: Ace, 1973.
- *Housewife Hookers: Part II.* New York: Ace, 1974.
Millett, Kate. *The Prostitution Papers.* New York: Avon, 1973.
Moore, Robin. *The Making of the Happy Hooker.* New York: Signet, 1973.
Tabor, Pauline. *Pauline's.* New York: Fawcett, 1971.

Rape
Amir, Menachem. *Patterns in Forcible Rape.* Chicago: University of Chicago
Press, 1971.
Brownmiller, Susan. *Against Our Will: Men, Women and Rape.* New York:
Simon and Schuster, 1975 (hard cover).
MacDonald, John M. *Rape Offenders and their Victims.* Springfield, Ill.:
Charles C. Thomas, 1971.
Medea, Andra, and Kathleen Thompson. *Against Rape.* New York: Farrar,
Straus and Giroux, 1972.

Sex counselling
Kaplan, Helen Singer. *The New Sex Therapy.* New York: Brunner-Mazel, 1974
(hard cover).
Schiller, Patricia. *Creative Approach to Sex Education and Counseling.*
New York: Association Press, 1973 (hard cover).
Vincent, Clark E., ed. *Sexual and Marital Health: The Physician as a Consultant.*
New York: McGraw-Hill, 1973 (hard cover).

Sex education

Addy, Genovia. *New Directions in Sex Education for Children in Foster Care.*
    Ottawa: Family Planning Division, Department of Health and Welfare, 1974.

Broderick, Carlfred B., and Jessie Bernard, eds. *The Individual, Sex, and Society:*
    A Siecus Handbook for Teachers and Counsellors. Baltimore: Johns Hopkins
    Press, 1969.

Burt, John J., and Linda A. Brower. *Education for Sexuality: Concepts and*
    Programs for Teaching. Philadelphia: W.B. Saunders, 1970.

Hettlinger, Richard F. *Growing up with Sex.* New York: Seabury Press, 1970.

Laycock, S.R. *Family Living and Sex Education.* Toronto: Baxter Publishing,
    1967.

Schulz, Esther D., and Sally R. Williams. *Family Life and Sex Education:*
    Curriculum and Instruction. New York: Harcourt, Bruce and World, 1968.

Sex Information and Education Council of the United States. *Siecus Study*
    Guides. (Fourteen topics). New York: Siecus (Behavioral Publications,
    72 Fifth Avenue, New York, NY 10011).

Somerville, Rose M. *Introduction to Family Life and Sex Education.* Englewood
    Cliffs, NJ: Prentice-Hall, 1972.

Sex letters

Forum. *The Best of Forum.* New York, 1973.

Greenwald, Harold, and Ruth Greenwald. *The Sex Life Letters.* New York:
    Bantam Books, 1972.

Playboy Magazine. *Sex Now.* Chicago: Playboy Press, 1971.

Sex manuals

Ellis, Albert. *The Art and Science of Love.* New York: Bantam Books, 1969.

Otto, Herbert, and Roberta Otto. *Total Sex.* New York: Signet, 1972.

Roy, Rustum, and Della Roy. *Honest Sex.* New York: Signet, 1968.

Sex research

Advisory Council on the Status of Women (63 Sparks Street, Box 1541,
    Station B, Ottawa, K1P 5R5): Selected research papers dealing with various
    aspects related to Canadian women and sexuality.

Belliveau, Fred, and Lin Richter. *Understanding Human Sexual Inadequacy.*
    New York: Bantam Books, 1970.

Brecher, Edward M. *The Sex Researchers.* New York: Signet, 1970.

Brecher, Ruth, and Edward Brecher, eds. *An Analysis of Human Sexual*
    Response. New York: Signet, 1966.

Ford, Clellan S., and Frank A. Beach. *Patterns of Sexual Behavior.* New York:
    Ace Books, 1951.

Geddes, Donald Porter, ed. *An Analysis of the Kinsey Reports* (Male and Female). New York: Mentor Books, 1954.

Hunt, Morton. *The Affair* (Extra-marital sex). New York: Signet, 1969.

K., Mr. and Mrs. *The Couple* (Masters and Johnson's sex clinic). New York: Berkley Medallion Books, 1971.

Kinsey, Alfred, *et al. Sexual Behavior in the Human Female.* New York: Pocket Books, 1965.

Lehrman, Nat. *Masters and Johnson Explained.* Chicago: Playboy Press Book, 1970.

Money, John, ed. *Sex Research: New Developments.* New York: Holt, Rinehart and Winston, 1965.

Robbins, J., and June Robbins. *An Analysis of Human Sexual Inadequacy.* New York: Signet, 1970.

Scott, Valerie X. *Surrogate Wife* (Masters and Johnson). New York: Dell, 1971.

Von Krafft-Ebing, Richard. *Psychopathia Sexualis.* New York: Bantam Books, 1969.

Wyden, Peter, and Barbara Wyden. *Inside the Sex Clinic.* New York: Signet, 1971.

Sexuality and the adolescent

Gordon, Sol. *The Sexual Adolescent.* Belmont, Cal.: Duxbury Press, 1973.

Osofsky, Howard. *The Pregnant Teenager.* Springfield, Ill.: Charles C. Thomas, 1972.

Sorenson, Robert C. *Adolescent Sexuality in Contemporary America.* New York: World Publishing, 1974 (hard cover).

Sexuality and the aged

Felstein, Ivor. *Sex in Later Life.* London: Pelican, 1973.

Rubin, Isidor. *Sexual Life after Sixty.* New York: Signet, 1965.

Sexual problems

Gagnon, John H., and William Simon, eds. *Sexual Deviance.* New York: Harper and Row, 1967.

– *The Sexual Scene.* Chicago: Trans Action Books, 1970.

Gigeroff, A.K. *Sexual Deviations in the Criminal Law.* Toronto: University of Toronto Press, 1968.

Maish, Herbert. *Incest.* London: André Deutsch, 1973 (hard cover).

Masters, R.E.L. *Patterns of Incest.* New York: Ace Books, 1963.

Mohr, J.W., R.E. Turner, and M.B. Gerry. *Pedophilia and Exhibitionism: A Handbook.* Toronto: University of Toronto Press, 1964.

Neubeck, Gerhard, ed. *Extra-Marital Relations.* Englewood Cliffs, NJ: Prentice-Hall, 1969.

Packard, Vance. *The Sexual Wilderness.* New York: Pocket Books, 1970.
Sagarin, Edward, and Donal MacNamara, eds. *Problems of Sex Behavior.*
  New York: Thomas Y. Crowell, 1968.
Weinberg, Kirson S. *Incest Behavior.* New York: Citadel Press, 1955.

Vocabulary of sex
Sagaris, Edward. *The Anatomy of Dirty Words.* New York: Paperback, 1962.
Wilson, Robert A., ed. *Forbidden Words.* Chicago: Playboy Press, 1974.

REFERENCES AND BIBLIOGRAPHIES

Ellis, A., and A. Abarbanel, eds. *Encyclopedia of Sexual Behavior.* New York:
  Hawthorne, 1967.
Indiana University, Institute for Sex Research. *Selected Bibliographies on
  Human Sexuality Topics.* Bloomington, Indiana, 47401, USA.
Minnesota Council on Family Relations. *Family Life: Literature and Films.*
  Minneapolis, 1972, 1974. (1219 University Avenue S.E., Minneapolis,
  55414, USA).
Multi-Media Resource Center. *Human Sexuality: A Current Bibliography.*
  San Francisco, 1974 (540 Powell St., San Francisco, Cal. 94102).

ADDENDUM

Anicar. Tom. *Secret Sex: Male Erotic Fantasies.* New York: Signet, 1976.
Brownmiller, Susan. *Against Our Will: Men, Women, and Rape.* New York:
  Simon and Schuster, 1975.
Davis, Murray S. *Intimate Relaions.* New York: Free Press, 1973.
Duberman, Lucile. *Gender and Sex in Society.* New York: Praeger, 1975.
Green, Richard, ed. *Human Sexuality: A Health Practitioner's Text.* Baltimore:
  The Williams and Wilkins Co., 1975.
Gross, Leonard, ed. *Sexual Issues in Marriage.* Toronto: John Wiley and Sons,
  1975.
Heiman, Julia, Leslie Lo Piccolo, and Joseph Lo Piccolo. *Becoming Orgasmic:
  A Sexual Growth Program for Women.* Englewood Cliffs, NJ: Prentice-Hall,
  1976.
Hettlinger, Richard F. *Human Sexuality: A Psychosocial Perspective.* Belmont,
  Cal.: Wadsworth Publishing, 1975.
Hite, Shere. *The Hite Report.* New York: Macmillan, 1976.
Hunt, Morton. *Sexual Behavior in the 1970s.* New York: Dell, 1975.
Kaplan, Alexandra G., and Joan P. Bean. *Beyond Sex-Role Stereotypes.*
  Toronto: Little, Brown & Co., 1976.

Kronhausen, Phyllis and Eberhard Kronhausen. *Erotic Fantasies.* New York: Grove Press, 1970.

Mailer, Norman. *Prisoner of Sex.* New York: Signet, 1971.

McCarthy, B.W., Marg Ryan, and Fred A. Johnson. *Sexual Awareness.* San Francisco: The Scrimshaw Press, 1975.

McCary, James Leslie, and Donna R. Copeland, eds. *Modern Views of Human Sexual Behavior.* Toronto: Science Research Associates, 1976.

Morrison, Eleanor S., and Rita Underhill Price. *Values in Sexuality: A New Approach in Sex Education.* New York: Hart Publishing, 1974.

Pengelley, Eric T. *Sex and Human Life.* Toronto: Addison-Wesley, 1974.

Pleck, Joseph H., and Jack Sawyer, eds. *Men and Masculinity.* Englewood Cliffs, NJ: 1974.

Ruebsaat, Helmut J., and Raymond Hull. *The Male Climacteric.* New York: Hawthorn Books, 1975.

Scanzoni, John H. *Sex Roles, Life Styles, and Childbearing.* New York: Free Press, 1975.

Shope, David E. *Interpersonal Sexuality.* Toronto: W.B. Saunders, 1975.

Wagner, Nathaniel W., ed. *Perspectives on Human Sexuality.* New York: Behavioral Publications, 1974.

Wiseman, Jacqueline P., ed. *The Social Psychology of Sex.* New York: Harper and Row, 1976.

Woods, Nancy Fugate. *Human Sexuality in Health and Illness.* Saint Louis: C.V. Mosby, 1975.

Yorburg, Betty. *Sexual Identity.* John Wiley and Sons, 1975.

CANADIAN REFERENCES

Bouma, Gary D., and Wilma J. Bouma. *Fertility Control: Canada's Lively Problem.* Toronto: Longman, 1975.

Esprit Magazine. (A Gay magazine) – Esprit Publishing, Fourth Floor, 105 Carlton Street, Toronto, Ontario, M5B 1M2.

Greenglass, Esther. *After Abortion.* Toronto: Longman, 1977.

Health and Welfare Canada. *Sex Education: A Teacher's Guide.* Ottawa: Family Planning Division, 1976 (6 booklets).

Herold, Edward S. *Sex Education in Ontario Schools.* Guelph: Dept. of Family Studies, University of Guelph, 1975.

Marsden, Lorna R. *Population Probe: Canada.* Toronto: Copp Clark, 1972.

Schlesinger, Benjamin. *Family Planning in Canada: A Source Book.* Toronto: University of Toronto Press, 1974.

Stevenson, Marylee. 'Living with a Stigma: A Study of Eleven Female Homosexual Couples,' unpublished paper, available from the author, Dept. of Sociology, McMaster University, Hamilton, Ontario.

Young, Connie. *Sex, Sexuality and our Changing Society.* Toronto: University of Toronto, Guidance Centre, 1975 – booklet (1000 Yonge Street, Suite 304, Toronto, Ontario, M4W 2K8).

Canadian periodical articles*

Acres, S.E., and J.W. Davies, 'Venereal Disease Problem in Canada,' *Canadian Nurse* 67 (July 1971), 24-27.

Barr, Donald, 'The Morning After Pill,' *Canadian Family Physician* 18 (March 1972), 67-68.

Bliss, Michael, 'Pure Books on Avoided Subjects: Pre-Freudian Sexual Ideas in Canada,' *Historical Papers 1970*, 80-108. (Published by the Canadian Historical Association.)

Bond, I.K., and D.R. Evans, 'Sex Deviations, Avoidance Therapy: Its Use in Two Cases of Underwear Fetishism,' *C.M.A. Journal* 96 (April 22, 1967), 1160-1163.

Brennan, Michael, 'The Patient with Homosexual Problems,' *Canadian Family Physician* 18 (March 1972), 58-61.

Canadian Review of Sociology and Anthropology, 'Women in the Canadian Social Structure,' Special issue 12 (November-December 1975), Part I.

Chernenkoff, William, 'The Premarital Examination,' *Canadian Family Physician* 19 (April 1973), 64.

- 'Regressive Hypnosis in Treatment of Temporary Anorgasm,' *Canadian Family Physician* 18 (March 1972), 56-57.

Collins, Larry D., 'The Legal Aspect of Abortion,' *Canadian Journal of Public Health* 66 (May-June 1971), 234-236.

Cormier, B., and S.P. Simons, 'The Problem of the Dangerous Sex Offender,' *Canadian Psychiatric Association Journal* 14 (August 1969), 329-336.

*65 articles published up to November 1, 1976.

Dunbar, John, Marvin Brown, and Donald M. Amoroso, 'Some Correlates of Attitudes toward Homosexuality,' *Journal of Social Psychology* 89 (1973), 271-279.

Eaid, C.R.M., 'Sex Counselling for Geriatric Patients,' *Canadian Family Physician* 18 (December 1972), 58-60.

Family Coordinator, 'Special Issues: New Life Styles,' 21 (October 1972).

Ferrari, Harriet E., 'The Nurse and V.D. Control,' *Canadian Nurse* 67 (July 1971), 28-31.

Glick, Daniel, 'Hypnotherapy and Female Sexual Inadequacy,' *Canadian Family Physician* 18 (March 1972), 53-55.

Grauer, H., 'A Study of Contraception as Related to Multiple Unwanted Pregnancies,' *C.M.A. Journal* 111 (November 16, 1974), 1083-1087.

Greenglass, E.R., 'Therapeutic Abortion and the Psychological Implications: A Canadian Experience,' *C.M.A. Journal* 113 (October 18, 1975).

Greenland, Cyril, 'Dangerous Sexual Offenders in Canada,' *Canadian Journal of Criminology and Corrections* 14 (January 1972), 1-11.

- 'What Every Young Doctor Should Know About Sex,' *Medical Aspects of Human Sexuality* (Canadian edition) 4 (November-December 1974), 5-29.

Hammill, Sister Noreen, 'Changing Services for Unwed Mothers,' *Canadian Welfare* 49 (March-April 1973), 18-20.

Henderson, D.J., 'Incest: A Synthesis of Data,' *Canadian Psychiatric Association Journal* 17 (August 1972), 299-314.

Herold, E.S., Kathryn E. Kopt, and Maria De Carlo, 'Family Life Education: Student Perspectives,' *Canadian Journal of Public Health* 65 (September-October 1974), 365-368.

Kintner, Elgin P., 'Sex Education in Schools: Doctor's Role,' *C.M.A. Journal* 96 (January 7, 1967), 56.

Lamont, John A., 'The Role of the Family Physician in Human Sexuality,' *Medical Aspects of Human Sexuality* 4 (March 1974), 4-15.

- 'Sexuality and Pregnancy: A Review,' *Canadian Family Physician* 19 (April 1973), 58-60.

Lowy, F.H., and Thomas L. Kolibakis, 'Autocastration by a Male Transsexual,' *Canadian Psychiatric Association Journal* 16 (October 1971), 399-406.

Marshall, W.L., and R.O. McKnight, 'An Integrated Treatment Program for Sexual Offenders,' *Canadian Psychiatric Association Journal* 20 (March 1975), 133-138.

Maurice, W.I., Freida Stuart, and George Szasz, 'Sex Therapy: Consideration in the Selection of Patients,' *Canadian Medical Association Journal* 115 (August 21, 1975), 317-320.

Miller, Raymond, 'Sex Education in Schools: Doctor's Role,' *C.M.A. Journal* 96 (March 11, 1967), 615.

Molnar, G., and P. Cameron, 'Incest Syndromes: Observations in a General Hospital Psychiatric Unit,' *Canadian Psychiatric Association Journal* 20 (August 1975), 373-377.

Moore, K.L., 'Sex Determination, Sexual Differentiation and Intersex Development,' *C.M.A. Journal* 97 (August 5, 1967), 292-296.

Neiger, Stephen, 'Short Term Treatment Methods for Delaying Ejaculation,' *Canadian Family Physician* 18 (March 1972), 62-66.

– 'Some New Approaches in Treating the Anorgasmic Woman,' *Canadian Family Physician* 17 (May 1971), 52-56.

O'Neil, Agnes E., 'Illegitimacy in Canada: Bridging the Communications Gap,' *Canadian Journal of Public Health* 62 (March-April 1971), 156-158.

Orton, Maureen J., 'Parenthood and Social Work,' *in* Ontario Association of Professional Social Workers. *Fertility and Sexuality*. Toronto, 1975, 1-25.

Pappert, Ann, 'Male Menopause: New Urges near 50,' *Canadian Doctor* 39 (May 1973), 46-48.

Price, Verne, 'Rape Victims: The Invisible Patients,' *Canadian Nurse* 71 (April 1974), 29-34.

Quinsey, Vernon L., Sidney L. Bergersen, and Cury M. Steinman. 'Changes in Physiological and Verbal responses of Child Molesters during Aversion Therapy,' *Canadian Journal of Behavioural Science* 8 (April 1976), 202-212.

Rancourt, H., and T. Limoges, 'Homosexuality among Women,' *Canadian Nurse* 63 (December 1967), 42-45.

Rhea, David L., 'Sex Counselling – Unlocked,' *Canadian Doctor* 39 (March 1973), 55-60.

Roper, Peter, 'Effects of Hypnotherapy on Homosexuality,' *C.M.A. Journal* 96 (February 11, 1967), 319-328.

Salutin, Marilyn, 'Stripper Morality,' *Transaction* 9 (June 1971), 12-22.

School Guidance Worker, 'Human Sexuality in the School,' Special issue (May-June 1974). (Published by the Guidance Centre, Faculty of Education, University of Toronto.)

Seeman, Mary V., 'The Search for Cupid or the Phantom-Lover Syndrome,' *Canadian Psychiatric Association Journal* 16 (April 1971), 183-185.

Shedden, D.A., 'Sex and Venereal Disease Education in Central Newfoundland Schools,' *Canadian Journal of Public Health* 58 (June 1967), 265-269.

Smith, M., 'A Young Pregnant Girl Tells her Story,' *Canadian Nurse* 71 (October 1975), 30-35.

Spano, Linda, and John A. Lamont, 'Dyspareunia: A Symptom of Female Sexual Dysfunction,' *Canadian Nurse* 71 (August 1975), 22-25.

Standage, K.F., J.A. Moore, and M.G. Cole, 'Self Mutilation of the Genitalia by a Female Schizophrenic,' *Canadian Psychiatric Association Journal* 19 (February 1974), 17-20.

Steiner, B.W., A.S. Zajac, and J.W. Mohr, 'A Gender Identity Project,'
    Canadian Psychiatric Association Journal 19 (February 1974), 7-12.
Stennett, R.G., and T.D. Bounds, 'Premarital Pregnancy and Marital Stability,'
    Social Worker 34 (July 1966), 142-148.
Stone, S.H., and K.E. Stott, 'The Unwanted Pregnancy,' *C.M.A. Journal* 111
    (November 16, 1974), 1093-1099.
Sullivan, Gail, and Susan Watt, 'Legalized Abortion: Myths and Misconcep-
    tions,' *Social Worker* 43 (Summer 1975), 78-86.
Swartz, David, 'Panel Discussion: Sexual Difficulties after 50,' *C.M.A. Journal*
    9 (January 29, 1966), 207-217.
Szasz, George, 'Sex Education and the Public Health Nurse,' *Canadian Journal of
    Public Health* 60 (November 1969), 429-434.
- 'Adolescent Sexual Activity,' *Canadian Nurse* 67 (October 1971), 39-44.
- 'Sex Education of the Family Physician,' *Canadian Family Physician* 18
    (March 1972), 48-50.
- 'An Exercise in Sex Education: What is "Normal" in Sexual Behaviour?,'
    Canadian Family Physician 19 (March 1973), 93-95.
- 'An Approach to Discussing Sexuality in the Classroom,' *School Guidance
    Worker* 30 (May-June 1975), 13-18.
Ulis, David B., 'Family Living and Sex Education: A Canadian Overview,'
    Canadian Journal of Public Health 66 (March-April 1975), 107-113.
Veevers, J.E., 'The Life Style of Voluntarily Childless Couples,' *in* Lyle E.
    Larson, ed., *The Canadian Family in Comparative Perspective.* Toronto:
    Prentice-Hall, 1975, 395-411.
- 'The Moral Careers of Voluntary Childless Wives: Notes on the Defense of a
    Variant World View,' *Family Coordinator* 24 (October 1975), 473-487.
Walker, J.L., and N.F. White, 'The Varieties of Therapeutic Experience: Con-
    joint Therapy in a Homosexual Marriage,' *Canada's Mental Health* 23
    (June 1975), 3-5.
Waring, E.M., and J.J. Jeffries, 'The Conscience of a Pornographer,' *Journal of
    Sex Research* 10 (February 1974), 40-46.

Bibliographic sources

CANADA

Sex Information and Education Council of Canada, 423 Castlefield Avenue,
Toronto, M5W 1L4.
Family Planning Division, Health and Welfare Canada, General Purpose
Building, Tunney's Pasture, Ottawa, K1A 1B5.
Resource Catalogue: Family Planning Federation of Canada, 1226A
Wellington Street, Ottawa, K1T 3A1.

UNITED STATES

Multi-media Resource Center, 1523 Franklin Street, San Francisco,
California 94109. Resource Guide.
Sex Information and Education Council of the United States, 137 – 155
N. Franklin, Hempstead, L.I., New York 11550.
Indiana University: Institute for Sex Research, Morrison Hall 416,
Bloomington, Indiana 47401.
Flora C. Seruya, Susan Losher, and Albert Ellis. *Sex and Sex Education:
A Bibliography.* New York: R.R. Bowker Co., 1972.

FILMS

SOUND FEELINGS LTD. PO Box 7040, Postal Station E, London, Ontario,
N5Y 4J9

Titles *Sexual Communication in Marriage; As Sexuality Matures, The Taming of the Screw, The Role of Ignorance in Sexual Dysfunction, Marital Communication in Chronic Illness, Sex in the Seventies,* and *The Business of Marriage Counselling.* Developed by Drs. Beryl and Avinoam Chernick.

NATIONAL FILM BOARD OF CANADA PO Box 6100, Montreal, Quebec, H3C 3H5
Titles *About Puberty and Reproduction, About Conception and Contraception,* and *About V.D.* All silent films for teaching use. Other films dealing with sexual themes are listed in *National Film Board of Canada: Film Catalogue – 1974-1976.*

ORTHO PHARMACEUTICAL – CANADA LTD. 19 Green Belt Drive, Don Mills, Ontario, M3C 1L9
Sexuality in the Medical School Curriculum Series
Titles *An Introductory Film for Medical Educators, The Frigid Wife,* and *The Impotent Husband.* Produced by the Center for the Study of Sex Education in Medicine, University of Pennsylvania School of Medicine.

MORELAND-LATCHFORD FILMS 299 Queen Street West, Toronto, Ontario, M5V 2S6
A film series on family living and sex education. Sixty films are listed in their catalogue.

MULTI-MEDIA RESOURCE FILMS – CALIFORNIA International Tele-Film Enterprises, 47 Densley Avenue, Toronto, Ontario, M6M 5A8
An extensive film collection dealing with all aspects of human sexuality. Catalogue on request.

JOHN WILEY AND SONS 22 Worcester Road, Rexdale, Ontario, M9W 1L1
Titles *Achieving Sexual Maturity, The Sexually Mature Adult, Venereal Diseases,* and *Contraception.*

AMERICAN SOURCES

Minnesota Council on Family Relations. *Family Life: Literature and Films, An Annotated Bibliography.* 1219 University Avenue Southeast, Minneapolis, Minnesota. 1972; 1974 Supplement.

Singer, Laura J., and Judith Buskin. *Sex Education on Film: A Guide to Visual Aids and Programs.* New York: Teachers College Press. 1971 (children and adolescents)

SIECUS. *Film Resources for Sex Education.* (Annotated guide to materials for pre-school to adult.) Distributed by Human Sciences Press, 72 Fifth Avenue, New York, NY 10011.

A-V Distributors

Many standard publishers and film producers also distribute A-V materials; check their catalogs.

EDCOA Productions, 520 South Dean Street, Englewood, NJ 17631

Focus International, 505 West End Avenue, New York, NY 10024

Multi Media Resource Center, Inc., 1523 Franklin, San Francisco, CA 94109

Perennial Films, 1825 Willow Road, Northfield, IL 60093

Texture Films, Inc., 1600 Broadway, New York, NY 10019

Washington University School of Medicine, Department of Illustration,
    4950 Audubon Avenue, St. Louis, Missouri 63110 (slide set of female
    sexual response)

American sources and references

NATIONAL ORGANIZATIONS

These organizations publish journals, newsletters, and reading lists of immediate interest to sex educators.

American Association for Health, Physical Education and Recreation, National Education Association. 1201 Sixteenth Street, Washington, D.C. 20036

American Association of Marriage and Family Counselors. 225 Yale Avenue, Claremont, Calif. 91711

American Association of Sex Educators and Counselors. 3422 N Street, N.W., Washington, D.C. 20007

The American Institute of Family Relations. 5287 Sunset Blvd., Los Angeles, Calif. 90027

American Medical Association, Department of Community Health and Health Education. 535 North Dearborn Street, Chicago, Ill. 60610

American Psychological Association. Task Force on Psychology, Family Planning and Population Policy. 1200 Seventeenth Street, N.W., Washington, D.C. 20036

American Public Health Association. 1015 Eighteenth Street, N.W., Washington, D.C. 20036

American School Health Association. 107 South Depeyster Street, Kent, Ohio 44240

American Social Health Association. 1740 Broadway, New York, N.Y. 10019

Association for Creative Change. Route 1, Box 35A, Chelsea, Ala. 35043

Association for the Study of Abortion, Inc. 120 West 57th Street, New York, N.Y. 10019

Association for Voluntary Sterilization. 14 West 40th Street, New York, N.Y. 10019

Bureau of Community Health Services. Health Services Administration, Department of Health, Education and Welfare. 5600 Fishers Lane, Room 12A-33, Rockville, Md. 20852

California Institute for Human Sexuality. P.O. Box 77671, Los Angeles, Calif. 90007

Carolina Population Center. University of North Carolina. University Square, Chapel Hill, N.C. 27514

Center for Family Planning Program Development. Division of Planned Parent-hood – World Population. 1666 K Street, N.W., Washington, D.C. 20006

Center for the Study of Sex Education in Medicine. 4025 Chestnut Street, Philadelphia, Pa. 19104

Child Study Association of America. 9 East 89th Street, New York, N.Y. 10028

Center for Population Research. National Institute for Child Health and Human Development, National Institute of Health. Room A-721, Landow Building, Bethesda, Md. 20014

Community Sex Information, Inc. 888 7th Avenue, New York, N.Y. 10019

Consortium on Early Childbearing and Childrearing. Research Utilization and Information Sharing Project. Suite, 1145 Nineteenth Street, N.W. Washington, D.C. 20036

East-West Center. 1777 East West Road, Honolulu, Hawaii 96822

E.C. Brown Center for Family Studies. 1802 Moss Street, Eugene, Oregon 97463

Educational Foundation for Human Sexuality. Montclair State College, Upper Montclair, N.J. 07043

Erickson Education Foundation. 1627 Moreland Avenue, Baton Rouge, La. 70808

Family Planning Program. Emory University School of Medicine. 80 Butler Street, Atlanta, Ga. 30303

Family Service Association of America. 44 East 23rd Street, New York, N.Y. 10010

Health Services and Mental Health Administration. Center for Disease Control, Atlanta, Ga. 30333

Homosexual Community Counseling Center. 921 Madison Avenue, New York, N.Y. 10021

Institute for Family Research and Education. 760 Ostrom Avenue, Syracuse, N.Y. 13210

Institute for Rational Living. 45 East 65th Street, New York, N.Y. 10021

Institute for Sex Education. 162 N. State Street, Suite 1018, Chicago, Ill. 60601

Institute for Sex Research, Inc. Indiana University. Room 416, Morrison Hall, Bloomington, Ind. 47401

International Academy of Sex Research. State University of New York Medical School, Health Sciences, Department of Psychiatry, Stony Brook, N.Y. 11790

International Family Planning Research Associates, Inc. 2960 West 8th Street, Los Angeles, Calif. 90005

International Planned Parenthood Federation. 18-20 Lower Regent Street, London, S.W. 1, England

Joint Strategy and Action Committee. 475 Riverside Drive, Room 1700A, New York, N.Y. 10027

Koba Associates, Inc. 1133 15th Street, N.W., Suite 508, Washington, D.C. 20005

Midwest Association for the Study of Human Sexuality. 100 East Ohio Street, Chicago, Ill. 60611

National Alliance Concerned with School-age Parents (NACSAP). 3746 Cumberland Street, N.W., Washington, D.C. 20016

National Abortion Rights of Action League. 250 West 57th Street, Room 2428, New York, N.Y. 10019

National Council of Churches. Commission on Marriage and the Family, 475 Riverside Drive, New York, N.Y. 10027

National Council on Family Relations. 1219 University Avenue, S.E., Minneapolis, Minn. 55414

National Gay Task Force. Room 903, 80 Fifth Avenue, New York, N.Y. 10011

National Institute for Human Relations. 180 North Michigan Avenue, Chicago, Ill. 60601

National Operation Venus Program. 1620 Summer Street, Philadelphia, Pa. 19103

National Organization for Non-parents. Box 10495, Baltimore, Md. 21209

National Sex Forum (Multi-media Resource Center). 1523 Franklin Street, San Francisco, Calif. 94109

Negative Population Growth. 103 Park Avenue, Suite 414, New York, N.Y. 10017

Planned Parenthood Federation of America, Inc. 810 7th Avenue, New York, N.Y. 10019

Planned Parenthood – World Population. 810 Seventh Avenue, New York, N.Y. 10019

Population Association of America, Inc. Box 14182, Benjamin Franklin Station, Washington, D.C. 20044

Population Council. 245 Park Avenue, New York, N.Y. 10017

Population Institute. 110 Maryland Avenue, N.E., Washington, D.C. 20002

Population Services International. 105 North Columbia Street, Chapel Hill, N.C. 27514

Program in Human Sexuality. University of Minnesota Medical School, Mayo Building 842, Minneapolis, Minn. 55455

Reproductive Biology Research Foundation. (Masters and Johnson), 4910 Forest
Park Blvd., St. Louis, Mo. 63108

Religious Coalition for Abortion Rights. 100 Maryland Avenue, N.E.,
Washington, D.C. 20002

Resource Center on Sex Roles in Education. National Foundation for the
Improvement of Education. 1156 15th Street, N.W., Washington, D.C.
20005

Sex Information and Education Council of the U.S. (SIECUS). 1855 Broadway,
New York, N.Y. 10028

Society for the Scientific Study of Sex, Inc. 12 East 41st Street, New York, N.Y.
10017

Synagogue Council of America. Committee on the Family. 234 Fifth Avenue,
New York, N.Y. 10016

Transnational Research in Family Planning Behavior. 8555 Sixteenth Street,
Silver Spring, Md. 20910

United States Catholic Conference. Family Life Bureau. 1312 Massachusetts
Avenue, N.W., Washington, D.C. 20005

Zero Population Growth. 1346 Connecticut Avenue, N.W., Washington, D.C.
20036

JOURNALS AND NEWSLETTERS

AASEC Newsletter. American Association of Sex Education and Counselors.
3422 N. Street, N.W., Washington, D.C. 20007

Abortion Research Notes. International Reference Center for Abortion
Research Transnational Family Research Institute. 8555 Sixteenth Street,
Silver Spring, Md. 20910

Archives of Sexual Behavior: An Interdisciplinary Research Journal. Plenum
Publishing Corp. 227 West 17th Street, New York, N.Y. 10011

Emko Newsletter. 7912 Manchester Avenue, St. Louis, Mo. 63143. A monthly
digest of sex information available free.

Equilibrium (a quarterly publication of Zero Population Growth, Inc.).

Erickson Educational Foundation Newsletter (available from Erickson
Educational Foundation)

Family Planning Perspectives. Center for Family Planning Program Development.
515 Madison Avenue, New York, N.Y. 10022 (free)

Homosexual Counseling Journal (a quarterly journal of the Homosexual
Community Counseling Center)

Information, Education, Communication in Population. East-West Center,
1777 East-West Road, Honolulu, Hawaii 96822 (free)

Intercom: The International Newsletter on Population and Family Planning. Population Services International. 1050 Potomac Street, N.W., Washington, D.C. 20007

Institute for Sex Education Newsletter (available from the Institute for Sex Education)

Journal of Homosexuality. Hawarth Press. 130 West 72nd Street, New York, N.Y. 10023

Journal of Marriage and the Family. The National Council on Family Relations. 1219 University Avenue, S.E., Minneapolis, Minn. 55414

Journal of Sex and Marital Therapy. Behavioral Publications. 72 Fifth Avenue, New York, N.Y. 10011

Journal of Sex Role Research. Available from Dr. Phyllis A. Katz, Graduate Center, CUNY. 33 West 42nd Street, New York, N.Y. 10036

Medical Aspects of Human Sexuality. Clinical Communications, Inc. 18 East 48th Street, New York, N.Y. 10017

Ms Magazine. 370 Lexington Avenue, New York, N.Y. 10017

Newsletter of Division 34. American Psychological Association. 1200 17th Street, N.W., Washington, D.C. 20036

Perspectives in Material and Child Health. Dept. of Hygiene and Public Health, Johns Hopkins University, Room 1511. 615 N. Wolfe Street, Baltimore, Md. 21205

Public Affairs Pamphlets. 381 Park Avenue, New York, N.Y. 10016

School Health Review. The American Association for Health, Physical Education and Recreation. 1201 Sixteenth Street, N.W., Washington, D.C. 20036

Sex News. Available from P.K. Houdek. 7140 Oak, Kansas City, Mo. 64114 (a monthly digest of resources)

Sexology. 200 Park Avenue, New York, N.Y. 10003

SIECUS Report. Publication of Sex Information and Education Council of the U.S. This, and all other SIECUS publications are now available from Behavioral Publications, 72 Fifth Avenue, New York, N.Y. 10011

The Journal of Sex Research (published by The Society for the Scientific Study of Sex, Inc.)

Contributors

Bonnie Bean, Education Committee SIECCAN, Toronto

F. Michael Barrett, Assistant Professor, Dept. of Zoology, University of Toronto, Chairperson SIECCAN (Sex Information and Education Council of Canada)

Ann Barrett, Education Committee SIECCAN, Toronto

Kathleen Belanger, formerly Research Associate, Family Service Centres of Greater Vancouver, deceased, in memoriam

Avinoam B. Chernick, Physician, Private Practice, London

Beryl A. Chernick, Physician, Private Practice, London

Lorenne M.G. Clark, Associate Professor, Dept. of Philosophy and Centre of Criminology, University of Toronto

Renée Cloutier, Professor, Dept. of Administration and Educational Politics, Science of Education, Université de Laval, Québec

Jocelyn Dingman, Freelance Writer, deceased

Federation of Students, University of Waterloo, Waterloo

Jules-H. Gourgues, Professor, School of Social Work, University of Laval, Quebec, Director, Family Planning Policies, Dept. of Social Affairs, Province of Quebec

Bernard Green, Professor, Faculty of Law, University of Toronto

Cyril Greenland, Professor, School of Social Work, McMaster University, Hamilton

Carl F. Grindstaff, Associate Professor, Dept. of Sociology, University of Western Ontario, London

Susan Hanley, Social Worker, Vancouver

J. Hoenig, Professor and Chairman, Dept. of Psychiatry, Memorial University of Newfoundland

Law Reform Commission of Canada, Ottawa

Andrew I. Malcolm, Psychiatrist, Private Practice, Toronto

Johann W. Mohr, Professor, Osgoode Hall Law School, and Dept. of Sociology, York University

Richard Albert Mullen, Social Worker, Children's Aid Society, Newmarket, Ontario

Stephen Neiger, Director, Behaviour Therapy Clinic, Lakeshore Psychiatric Hospital, Toronto

James Oldham, Psychiatrist, Private Practice

Rena Paul, Administrator, Training and Communications, Metropolitan Toronto, Department of Social Services

Marion G. Powell, Head, Population Unit, Dept. of Health Administration, Faculty of Medicine, Division of Community Health, University of Toronto

Liz Roberts, Social Worker, Medical Health Clinic, North York General Hospital, Toronto

G. Erlick Robinson, Director of Ambulatory Care, Dept. of Psychiatry, Toronto General Hospital, Assistant Professor, Faculty of Medicine, University of Toronto

Marilynn Ryan, Education Committee, SIECCAN, Toronto

Benjamin Schlesinger, Professor, Faculty of Social Work, University of Toronto

Dolores L. Shymko, Assistant Professor, Macdonald College, McGill University, Montreal

Marlaina Sniderman, Social Work Coordinator, Dept. of Psychiatry, Toronto General Hospital

Paul Steinberg, Social Worker, Dept. of Psychiatry and Community Service, St. Joseph's Hospital, Hamilton

Johanna Stuckey, Associate Professor, English and Humanities, Chairman, Division of Humanities, York University, Toronto

Connie Young, Counsellor in Private Practice, Toronto